New Testament
GREEK PRIMER

New Testament
GREEK PRIMER

From Morphology to Grammar

Third Edition

GERALD L. STEVENS

CASCADE *Books* • Eugene, Oregon

NEW TESTAMENT GREEK PRIMER, 3rd ed.

Copyright © 2010 Gerald L. Stevens. All rights reserved. Except for brief quotations in critical publications or reviews, no part of this book may be reproduced in any manner without prior written permission from the publisher. Write: Permissions, Wipf & Stock, 199 W. 8th Ave., Eugene, OR 97401.

ISBN 13: 978-1-60899-467-0

Cascade Books
An imprint of Wipf and Stock Publishers
199 W. 8th Ave., Suite 3
Eugene, OR 97401

Cataloging-in-Publication data:

Stevens, Gerald L.
New Testament Greek primer / Gerald L. Stevens.
3rd edition

xxiv + 594 p.; 23 cm.

Includes photographs and index.
ISBN 13: 978-1-60899-467-0

1. Bible. N.T.—Language, style. 2. Greek language, Biblical—Grammar. I. Title.

PA258 .S73 2010

Manufactured in the U.S.A.

Dedicated to my students past, present, and future

Contents

Preliminaries

LIST OF FIGURES ix
LIST OF TABLES xi
PREFACE: First Edition Reception xvii
ACKNOWLEDGMENTS xxi
INTRODUCTION: Getting Started xxiii

Greek Primer

CHAPTER 1:   Alpha, Beta, Gamma 3
Language Lesson 1: Words and Meaning 17
CHAPTER 2:   Greek Verbs 21
CHAPTER 3:   Middle/Passive Voice 29
Language Lesson 2: Translation Is Interpretation 39
CHAPTER 4:   Greek Nouns 43
CHAPTER 5:   First Declension 53
CHAPTER 6:   The Article 63
Vocabulary Review 1: Vocabularies 1-6 73
CHAPTER 7:   Third Declension 75
CHAPTER 8:   Adjectives 89
CHAPTER 9:   Pronouns 109
CHAPTER 10: Prepositions 131
CHAPTER 11: Adverbs and More 153

Vocabulary Review 2: Vocabularies 7-11 173
CHAPTER 12: Contract Verbs 175
Language Lesson 3: Verb Morphology 187
CHAPTER 13: Imperfect Tense 191
CHAPTER 14: Conditional Sentences 207
Language Lesson 4: Tense Stems 223
CHAPTER 15: Future Tense........................... 227
CHAPTER 16: First Aorist 243
CHAPTER 17: Second Aorist, Liquids 255
CHAPTER 18: The Passive System 267
Vocabulary Review 3: Vocabularies 12-18 283
CHAPTER 19: The Perfect System 285
Language Lesson 5: Indicative Verb Summary 311
CHAPTER 20: Subjunctive & Optative 315
CHAPTER 21: Imperative 333
CHAPTER 22: Infinitives 343
CHAPTER 23: Adverbial Infinitives 365
Vocabulary Review 4: Vocabularies 19-23 375
CHAPTER 24: Participles 377
CHAPTER 25: Adjectival Participles 391
CHAPTER 26: Adverbial Participles 405
CHAPTER 27: MI Verbs 1 423
CHAPTER 28: MI Verbs 2 433

English Appendix

ENGLISH 1: Words 445
ENGLISH 2: Word Groups 455
ENGLISH 3: Sentences 465
ENGLISH 4: Sentence Sense 477
ENGLISH 5: Sentence Diagramming 497

 **Answer Key and Indexes**

ANSWER KEY	515
VOCABULARY	547
PRINCIPAL PARTS	553
PARADIGMS	561
SUBJECT INDEX	583

Fig. 1. Façade, Library of Celsus. Of the remains in Ephesus, Turkey, one of the most outstanding is the Library of Celsus. The front wall has been reconstructed.

Figures

List of Figures

FIGURE 1:	Façade, Library of Celsus	viii
FIGURE 2:	Gold Stater of Alexander the Great	x
FIGURE 3:	Bust of Augustus (31 B.C.-A.D. 14)	xx
FIGURE 4:	Bust of Tiberius (A.D. 14-37)	xxii
FIGURE 5:	Greek Key	20
FIGURE 6:	Athenian Warrior	42
FIGURE 7:	Chariot Races	74
FIGURE 8:	Gladiator Stele	88
FIGURE 9:	Gladiator Helmut	108
FIGURE 10:	Ephesus Theater	174
FIGURE 11:	Hierapolis Theater	190
FIGURE 12:	Laodicea Inscription	206
FIGURE 13:	Thessaloniki Inscription	254
FIGURE 14:	Commander Token	282
FIGURE 15:	The Via Egnatia	284
FIGURE 16:	Asklepios Inscription	310
FIGURE 17:	Cuirass of Hadrian	342
FIGURE 18:	Hadrian Inscription	376
FIGURE 19:	Codex Vaticanus	390
FIGURE 20:	Manuscript 𝔓46	404
FIGURE 21:	Temple of Apollo at Corinth	442

FIGURE 22: Herod Atticus Arches 464
FIGURE 23: Sardis Bathhouse 546
FIGURE 24: Curetes Street 552
FIGURE 25: Timotheos Inscription 553
FIGURE 26: Temple of Hephaestus 582

Photo © Gerald L. Stevens

Fig. 2. Gold Stater of Alexander the Great. This coin dates before 281 B.C. The obverse has the Head of Athena with a Corinthian helmet. Archaeological Museum Thessaloniki, Thessalonica, Macedonia, Greece.

Tables

Greek Primer

TABLE 1.1:	History of Greek Language	3
TABLE 1.2:	Greek Marks	5
TABLE 1.3:	Greek Diphthongs	5
TABLE 1.4:	Gamma Combinations	7
TABLE 1.5:	Table of Stops	8
TABLE 1.6:	Syllable Positions	9
TABLE 1.7:	Accent Positions	10
TABLE 2.1:	Present Active Indicative	23
TABLE 3.1:	Present (Durative) Passive Indicative	29
TABLE 3.2:	Present Middle Indicative	31
TABLE 3.3:	Primary Endings	33
TABLE 3.4:	Preposition Lighthouse	38
TABLE 3.5:	Preposition Line	38
TABLE 4.1:	Second Declension Endings—Set 1	45
TABLE 4.2:	Second Declension: Set 1 Paradigm	45
TABLE 4.3:	Second Declension Endings—Set 2	46
TABLE 4.4:	Second Declension: Set 2 Paradigm	47
TABLE 5.1:	First Declension Endings—Set 1 (α-pure)	54
TABLE 5.2:	First Declension: α-Pure Paradigm	54
TABLE 5.3:	First Declension Endings—Set 2 (η-pure)	54
TABLE 5.4:	First Declension: η-Pure Paradigm	55

TABLE 5.5:	First Declension Endings—Set 3 (mixed)	55
TABLE 5.6:	First Declension: Mixed Paradigm	56
TABLE 5.7:	First Declension Endings—Set 4 (-ης Nom.)	56
TABLE 5.8:	First Declension: -ης Nom. Paradigm	56
TABLE 5.9:	First Declension Endings—Set 5 (α pure Con.)	57
TABLE 6.1:	The Greek Article	63
TABLE 7.1:	Third Declension Endings	75
TABLE 7.2:	Sigma Stop Interactions	76
TABLE 7.3:	3D Inflection Shortcuts	77
TABLE 7.4:	3D Inflection: Always	78
TABLE 7.5:	3D Inflection: Almost Always	79
TABLE 7.6:	3D Inflection: Rare Birds	79
TABLE 7.7:	Typical: σάρξ, σαρκός, ἡ	80
TABLE 7.8:	Significant: ἄρχων, -οντος, ὁ	81
TABLE 7.9:	Neuter: σῶμα, -τος, τό	82
TABLE 7.10:	Distinctive: πίστις, -εως, ἡ	82
TABLE 7.11:	Odd: ἔθνος, ἔθνους, τό	83
TABLE 8.1:	Articular Constructions	93
TABLE 8.2:	The Copulative Verb Εἰμί	95
TABLE 8.3:	Subject vs. Predicate Nominatives	96
TABLE 9.1:	Personal, Relative Systems	109
TABLE 9.2:	First Person	110
TABLE 9.3:	Second Person	110
TABLE 9.4:	Third Person Masculine	111
TABLE 9.5:	Third Person Neuter	111
TABLE 9.6:	Third Person Feminine	112
TABLE 9.7:	Possessive Pronoun Summary	114
TABLE 9.8:	Possessive Pronoun Plural Concord	115
TABLE 9.9:	Reflexive Pronoun Summary	116
TABLE 9.10:	Indefinite Pronoun Summary	117
TABLE 9.11:	Negative Pronoun Summary	118

TABLE 9.12:	Demonstrative Pronoun Summary	118
TABLE 9.13:	Relative Pronoun Summary	119
TABLE 9.14:	Indefinite Relative Pronoun Summary	120
TABLE 9.15:	Correlative Pronoun Summary	122
TABLE 9.16:	Interrogative Pronoun Summary	123
TABLE 9.17:	Pronouns: A Summary	124
TABLE 10.1:	Prepositions	132
TABLE 10.2:	Word Group Functions	135
TABLE 10.3:	Preposition Spelling Variations	137
TABLE 11.1:	Degrees of Comparison	154
TABLE 11.2:	Cardinals 1-4	157
TABLE 12.1:	Present Active Contract Verbs	176
TABLE 12.2:	Present Middle Contract Verbs	176
TABLE 12.3:	Contraction Results	176
TABLE LL3.1:	*Verb Morphology*	188
TABLE LL3.2:	*Morphology—Present Active Indicative*	189
TABLE 13.1:	Imperfect Tense Morphology	192
TABLE 13.2:	Secondary Endings	195
TABLE 13.3:	Primary and Secondary Endings	196
TABLE 13.4:	Imperfect Active Indicative	197
TABLE 13.5:	Imperfect Midd/Pass Indicative	197
TABLE 13.6:	Imperfect Active Contract Verbs	197
TABLE 13.7:	Imperfect Midd/Pass Contract Verbs	198
TABLE 13.8:	Imperfect Indicative of Εἰμί	198
TABLE 14.1:	Conditional Sentences: Grammar, etc.	210
TABLE LL4.1:	*Greek Tense Stems*	224
TABLE 15.1:	Future Tense Morphology	228
TABLE 15.2:	Future Stems	229
TABLE 15.3:	Irregular Futures	230
TABLE 15.4:	Sigma Stop Interactions	230
TABLE 15.5:	Future Active Indicative	233

TABLE 15.6:	Future Middle Indicative	233
TABLE 15.7:	Future Active Contract Verbs	234
TABLE 15.8:	Future Middle Contract Verbs	234
TABLE 15.9:	Future Consonant Examples	234
TABLE 15.10:	Future Indicative of Εἰμί	235
TABLE 15.11:	So-Called "Deponent Future"	236
TABLE 16.1:	First Aorist Tense Morphology	243
TABLE 16.2:	First Aorist Stem Formative	244
TABLE 16.3:	First Aorist Active Indicative	247
TABLE 16.4:	First Aorist Middle Indicative	247
TABLE 17.1:	Second Aorist Morphology	255
TABLE 17.2:	Second Aorist Stems	256
TABLE 17.3:	Second Aorist Active Indicative	258
TABLE 17.4:	Second Aorist Middle Indicative	258
TABLE 17.5:	Liquid Verbs	259
TABLE 18.1:	Aorist First Passive Morphology	267
TABLE 18.2:	Theta Stop Interactions	269
TABLE 18.3:	Theta Liquid Interactions	269
TABLE 18.4:	Aorist First Passive Indicative	271
TABLE 18.5:	Future First Passive Morphology	272
TABLE 18.6:	Future First Passive Indicative	274
TABLE 18.7:	Aorist Second Passive Indicative	275
TABLE 18.8:	Future Second Passive Indicative	277
TABLE 19.1:	Perfect First Active Morphology	285
TABLE 19.2:	Perfect First Active Indicative	291
TABLE 19.3:	Perfect Second Active Indicative	292
TABLE 19.4:	Perfect Second Active Verbs	292
TABLE 19.5:	Perfect Middle/Passive Morphology	293
TABLE 19.6:	Perfect (Middle) Passive Indicative	296
TABLE 19.7:	Pluperfect First Active Morphology	296
TABLE 19.8:	Pluperfect First Active Indicative	299

TABLE 19.9:	Pluperfect Second Active Indicative	299
TABLE 19.10:	Pluperfect Middle/Passive Morphology	300
TABLE 19.11:	Pluperfect (Middle) Passive Indicative	301
TABLE LL5.1:	*Greek Indicative Verb System*	*312*
TABLE LL5.2:	*Tense (Kind, Time)*	*313*
TABLE 20.1:	Active Subjunctive	317
TABLE 20.2:	Middle Subjunctive	317
TABLE 20.3:	Passive Subjunctive	318
TABLE 20.4:	Present Active Contracts	319
TABLE 20.5:	Present Subjunctive of Εἰμί	320
TABLE 20.6:	Active Optative	321
TABLE 20.7:	Middle Optative	322
TABLE 20.8:	Passive Optative	322
TABLE 20.9:	Conditional Sentence Diagram	326
TABLE 21.1:	Imperative Endings	333
TABLE 21.2:	Active Imperative	335
TABLE 21.3:	Middle Imperative	335
TABLE 21.4:	Passive Imperative	335
TABLE 21.5:	Present Imperative of Εἰμί	336
TABLE 22.1:	Word Group Functions	344
TABLE 22.2:	Infinitive Endings	344
TABLE 22.3:	Infinitive Paradigms	344
TABLE 22.4:	Paradigm of Δύναμαι	351
TABLE 23.1:	Word Group Functions	365
TABLE 24.1:	Word Group Functions	377
TABLE 24.2:	Present Active Participle	378
TABLE 24.3:	First Aorist Active Participle	379
TABLE 24.4:	Second Aorist Active Participle	380
TABLE 24.5:	Perfect First Active Participle	381
TABLE 24.6:	Aorist First Passive Participle	382
TABLE 25.1:	Word Group Functions	391

TABLE 26.1:	Word Group Functions	405
TABLE 27.1:	Present Active MI Verb Morphology	424
TABLE 27.2:	Primary MI Endings	426
TABLE 27.3:	Imperfect Active MI Verb Morphology	427
TABLE 27.4:	Present, Imperfect of Δίδωμι	428
TABLE 27.5:	Subjunctive, Imperative of Δίδωμι	428
TABLE 28.1:	Future Indicative of Δίδωμι	435
TABLE 28.2:	Aorist Indicative of Δίδωμι	435
TABLE 28.3:	Aorist Subjunctive of Δίδωμι	436
TABLE 28.4:	Aorist Imperative of Δίδωμι	436
TABLE 28.5:	Perfect Indicative of Δίδωμι	436
TABLE 28.6:	Present Active Participle of Δίδωμι	437
TABLE 28.7:	Synopsis of Other Participle Forms	437

English Appendix

TABLE E1.1:	The Eight Parts of Speech	445
TABLE E1.2:	Prepositions	451
TABLE E1.3:	Conjunctions	452
TABLE E2.1:	Word Group Functions	456
TABLE E2.2:	Clause Connectors	459
TABLE E3.1:	Subject Person Configurations	466
TABLE E3.2:	Common Auxiliary Verbs	472
TABLE E3.3:	Tense (Kind, Time)	473
TABLE E4.1:	Verb Principle Parts: Examples	484
TABLE E4.2:	Indicative Verb Formation Patterns	486

Preface
Third Edition

 ### *Improving and Consolidating*

The opportunity to produce a third edition of this text is a chance to reflect on its reception in schools and colleges representing a broad spectrum of educational settings. I still remain amazed that what started out as class handouts so many years ago has evolved and matured to this present form. From the many communications over time with both instructors and their students, I realized that the basic content of this grammar was solid and its format, layout, and copious tables and examples helpful to the process of learning and studying. Such defining elements were not to be trifled with too much without changing the character of the text or disappointing expectations. To all who have used this text productively, let me say straightaway you can breathe a sigh of relief. We are of no mind to mess with a successful formula.

Improving

Improvements, however, always can be made. What amazes me is how a volume so combed over still can have various errors discovered only after the publisher has the proofs. Such errors are the bane of my existence, as I am solely responsible for them. I only can console myself that a foreign language grammar, after all, is quite a technical production in the first place. On top of its technicality one adds multiple fonts, rich graphics, numerous tables, and complex layout issues. I am ever reminded in the midst of a busy teaching schedule that my best is less than perfect. Another edition allows for needed corrections.

Another edition also allows for clarification of certain points of discussion that do not read in the student's head like they do in one's own. You only learn this when going over exercises and a hand pops up with a question that no one ever has asked before, but, once asked, seems immediately obvious. Then you are jotting yourself a note in the margin of the book for a point of clarification in the chapter's discussion in the next edition of the text. Such marginal notations I have tried to implement for this edition of the text.

Other areas of improvement have been in examples and exercises. Ever on the prowl for illustrations, sometimes I stumble on a better example of a particular grammatical feature. I have incorporated these new examples here and there. Sometimes I also discover a phrase or verse that reinforces a grammatical principle an exercise intends to address even better. Instructors will want to take note that a few exercises have been changed for this purpose.

Consolidating

My publisher has encouraged this project from the beginning and has provided invaluable support and suggestions. With the favorable reception of the *Primer* throughout both its first and second editions, the possibility of extending the effort into a set of books presented itself. The idea began to grow for a three-volume set providing a rounded study of New Testament Greek in all its rich and beautiful complexity and expression. The first volume of the set is the present text, *New Testament Greek Primer: From Morphology to Grammar*. The *Primer* takes a student from the formation of the alphabet to the logic of sentences. The concept for the second volume evolved into the publication of *New Testament Greek Intermediate: From Grammar to Translation*. The *Intermediate* text reinforces the gains of the *Primer* but expands vocabulary acquisition and takes the student from the logic of sentences to the full context of paragraphs and their authors. The third and final volume on the drawing board is *New Testament Greek Syntax: From Translation to Exegesis*. This text will be an in-depth study of syntactical elements of New Testament Greek pragmatically focused on their contribution to translation and exegesis of a given New Testament text in its context. Hints of syntactical elements have been dropped along the way in the previous two volumes. The goal of the three-volume corpus would be to train students in the way of Greek for teaching and preaching such that when they are old, graduate, and move into ministry positions in the local church they will not depart from genuine exegesis.[1]

Communicating

The author maintains a personal website on the Internet to afford his students, as well as those who use these language texts, an opportunity to get to know him more personally. The website also provides his students information and resources related to particular classes he teaches in his seminary setting. The website is reached easily at: *www.drkoine.com*.

---

[1]My first publication, *New Testament Greek* (University Press of America, 2d ed., 1997), has been taken out of print. The basic content of this older text is preserved in the first two volumes of the present set (that is, the *Primer* and *Intermediate* texts). The original work is still accessible as a module in the Accordance software; *Accordance*, OakTree Software Specialists, Altamonte Springs, Florida.

Fig. 3. Bust of Augustus (31 B.C.-A.D. 14). Augustus was emperor when Jesus was born (Lk. 2:1). Istanbul Archaeology Museum, Istanbul, Turkey.

Acknowledgments

 ### Gratitude to All

As always, I owe an enormous debt to many individuals for this third edition. Current and former colleagues, friends in the halls of academia, and my own students have helped as I have traveled this road. I never will be able to repay the huge debt I owe my wife, Jean, for her unwaivering support. After the Lord Jesus, she is God's greatest act of grace in my life. Special acknowledgements are given below for kind permission to use copyrighted material.

Bibliotheca Apostolica Vaticana, 00120 Città del Vaticano, for the image of MS. Vat. gr. 1209 ("Codex Vaticanus") on p. 390. Used by permission. All rights reserved.

The Chester Beatty Library, Dublin, Ireland, for the image of $\mathfrak{P}^{46}$ on p. 404, © The Trustees of the Chester Beatty Library, Dublin. By permission of the Trustees of the Chester Beatty Library. All rights reserved.

Gerald L. Stevens, 3777 Mimosa Court, New Orleans, La. 70131 for use of the images pp. viii, x, xx, xxii, 20, 42, 74, 88, 108, 174, 190, 206, 254, 282, 284, 310, 342, 376, 390, 404, 442, 464, 546, 552, 553, 582, © 2002 Gerald L. Stevens. Used by permission. All rights reserved.

Linguist's Software, P.O. Box 580, Edmonds, Wash. 98020 for the use of the SymbolGreekU font. Used by permission. All rights reserved.

United Bible Societies, 1865 Broadway, New York, N.Y. 10023 for selections from *The Greek New Testament*, Fourth Revised Edition, edited by Barbara Aland, Kurt Aland, Johannes Karavidopoulos, Carlo M. Martini, and Bruce M. Metzger in cooperation with the Institute for New Testament Textual Research, Münster/Westphalia, © 1993 Deutsche Bibelgesellschaft, Stuttgart. Used by permission. All rights reserved.

Fig. 4. Bust of Tiberius (A.D. 14-37). Tiberius was emperor during the ministry of Jesus (cf. Lk. 3:1). Tiberius appointed Pontius Pilate procurator of Judea (26-36 A.D.). Herod Antipas, Tiberius's client king in Galilee, founded and named the city of Tiberius on the coast of the Sea of Galilee in behalf of his patron emperor. Ephesus Museum, Selçuk, Turkey.

Introduction ΑΩ

Getting Started

Greek instructors will know what they need to do with the material in this text to accomplish their classroom objectives. Some will choose to begin immediately with the Greek grammar material. Others will choose to work through the English Appendix material first to review the basics of English grammar before proceeding to introduce elements of Greek grammar.

Instructors can use the English Appendix flexibly. They might choose to study the English material in whole at one time or only in part, that is, in targeted selections. Applicable English material also could be referenced at various points along the way through the Greek grammar.

Students studying independently will have to evaluate their own needs. I could suggest that if you jump right into the Greek but constantly are getting an "I just don't get it" reaction, you might want to see if working through the English review helps. Students who have studied some Greek, but a long time ago, also might want to start with the English review first. Getting warmed back up to Greek might really need getting warmed back up to English.

Providing you, the student, an answer key is a help and a hindrance. The help is positive feedback, the reassurance that you are getting the material. The hindrance is a crutch, the illusion that you are learning when you are missing most of the questions that do not have an answer given. That problem, of course, boils down to each individual student's own motives and agenda. Use the answer key, but be sure you truly are learning the material.

This text may fulfill all your purposes for studying New Testament Greek. On the other hand, an inquiring mind probably will want to know more than is presented in this text. Your next step would be to buy a copy of the next volume in the series, *New Testament Greek Intermediate* (Wipf and Stock, 2008) as a desk reference. The material in that text is presented similarly, but in greater depth. From there you could move on to study issues of syntax, which would be covered in a future third volume planned for this series. In addition to the two volumes already published, the student also can consult an abundant number of recent works and electronic resources for further study.

I am asked often about Greek software for the computer. You simply cannot best Accordance, the Cadillac of concording software, hands down. Accordance forges into a perfect temper accuracy, power, elegance, and usability in a *tour de force* of programming wizardry exploiting all the genius of the Macintosh platform. Not even Harry Potter could conjure this much magic against Lord Voldemort.

Greek Primer

ΑΩ

Chapter 1

Alpha, Beta, Gamma

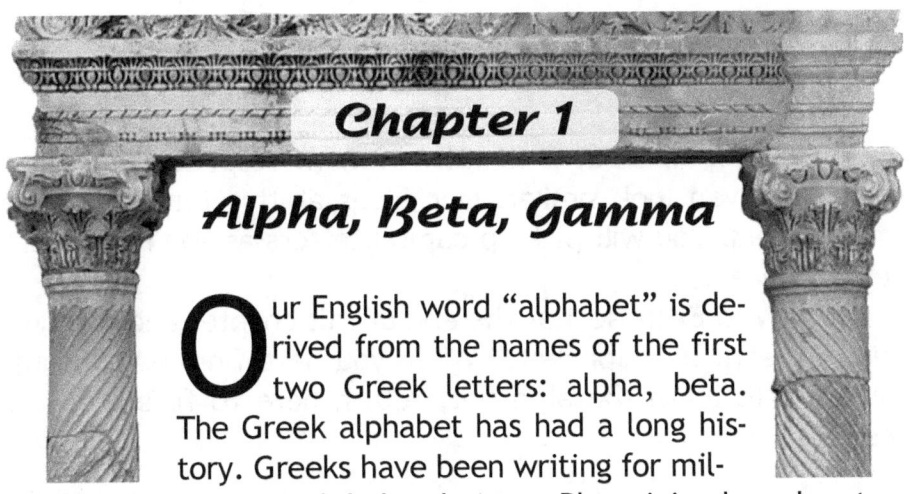

Our English word "alphabet" is derived from the names of the first two Greek letters: alpha, beta. The Greek alphabet has had a long history. Greeks have been writing for millennia, their lasting alphabet being a Phoenician-based system (as was Hebrew). This history usually is broken down into five stages, as in the table below.

Table 1.1—History of Greek Language

Stage	Time Frame
(1) Linear B	13th-8th cent. B.C.
(2) Classical	8th-4th cent. B.C.
(3) Hellenistic	4th cent. B.C.-4th cent. A.D.
(4) Byzantine	4th cent.-1453
(5) Modern	1453-present

Stages 1-3 help to explain various features you encounter in New Testament Greek. Stages 3-4 provide the backdrop for the origin and preservation of the New Testament. Stage 5 covers that time period of the movement of our copies of the Greek New Testament from Constantinople into Europe and then the Reformation movement that spawned a renewed interest in "the original language" of the Bible. Perhaps one day you might investigate further into this fascinating story.

New Testament Greek is called *koine* Greek. Koine means "common." This Greek is the everyday spoken language one would hear on the street and in the marketplace of that day.

Greek Alphabet

The Greek alphabet is familiar in many respects. A number of letters even look similar. Our focus at this time is on the small letters. You will pick up capital letters as you need them along the way.

Go now to Exercise 1 at the end of this chapter and do number 1, "Learn the Alphabet." When you have finished your initial work to learn the alphabet, return here to finish reading the chapter.

Greek Marks

Greek is accented. The *acute* accent is a right-leaning stroke like a syllable stress mark in English. The *grave* accent is just an acute leaning backwards. The *circumflex* is a slight upside down curve above a vowel (in some Greek fonts a squiggly stroke).

Greek has various other marks. A breathing mark is used to distinguish rough or smooth breathing when pronouncing a beginning vowel (equivalent to our English letter "h"). *Diaeresis* consists of two parallel dots above the second vowel of a two-vowel unit normally pronounced as one sound but in some cases pronounced as two separate vowels. Greek represents a letter dropped in the middle of a word with a mark called a *coronis*.[1]

Greek punctuation is similar to English. Both the semicolon and the colon are a raised dot. The main difference in punctuation is the Greek question mark, which looks like an English

---

[1] Dropping of a letter for pronunciation technically is called *elision*, such as making "do not" into "don't." Notice how we represent the dropped letter with an apostrophe mark.

Chapter 1: Alpha, Beta, Gamma

semicolon. These various Greek marks are detailed in the table below.

Table 1.2—Greek Marks

acute = ά	diaeresis = αϊ
grave = ὰ	coronis = τ'
circumflex = ᾶ	question = α;
rough breathing = ἁ	semicolon = α·
smooth breathing = ἀ	colon = α·

Classifying the Alphabet

The letters of the alphabet can be classified for analysis. The two basic groups are vowels and consonants.

Vowels

(1) Vowel Combinations
    Diphthongs are vowel combinations ended by either iota (ι) or upsilon (υ) and pronounced together as one sound. On rare occasions a standard diphthong combination is pronounced as two distinct vowels, not as a diphthong unit. The mark to indicate this exception is diaeresis. The Greek diphthongs and their approximate sounds in English are given below.

Table 1.3—Greek Diphthongs

αι = **aisle**	αυ = **out**
ει = **eight**	ευ = "ehoou" (also "you" or "ehwe")
οι = **oil**	ου = **group**
υι = **suite**	ηυ = "aoou"
	ωυ = **soul**

(2) Vowel Quantity

Vowels are classified by length (the relative time taken for pronunciation). Knowing vowel quantities helps us with pronunciation and accents. The two short vowels are epsilon (ε) and omicron (ο). These two short vowels have their long vowel counter parts in eta (η) and omega (ω). Three vowels can be either short or long: alpha (α), iota (ι), and upsilon (υ). Diphthongs almost always are long.

(3) Iota Subscript

Iota subscript is the iota (ι) written underneath alpha (α), eta (η), and omega (ω) rather than following them, as follows: ᾳ, ῃ, and ῳ. This iota (ι) subscript is not pronounced. Since this vowel is not pronounced, the two-vowel combination is called an *improper diphthong*. Thus, iota subscript is not important for pronunciation; however, observing any iota subscript can be important in forms that give words meaning in a sentence. Therefore, *always be aware of iota subscript*.

Consonants

(1) Double Consonants

Four Greek consonants combine two consonants to get their equivalent pronunciation in English: θ = th, φ = ph, χ = ch, and ψ = ps. Sometimes a fifth consonant is added to the list when internal to a word: ζ = dz.

(2) Gamma Combinations

Sometimes gamma is pronounced with an "n" sound when combined with certain other consonants. You already know this from the word "angel." "Angel" in English is borrowed straight from the Greek word ἄγγελος (aggelos). Minus the -ος inflection on the end, the word stem is ἀγγελ- (aggel-). However, the Greek double gamma is *pronounced* like an English "ng." Thus, the double gamma Greek word comes across into English as "angel." The table below shows four gamma combinations in Greek in which the *first* gamma actually is *pronounced* with an "n" sound in English (but still transliterated with a "g").

Table 1.4—Gamma Combinations

γγ = sing   γξ = larynx
γκ = ink   γχ = anchor

(3) Breathing Marks

Our English "h" is the equivalent of breathing roughly just before pronouncing a vowel. A vowel preceded by "h" would be "rough" in sound; without an "h" would be "smooth" in sound. *Rough breathing* is making the "h" sound before pronouncing a vowel.[2] *Smooth breathing* is not making this "h" sound, the difference between saying "as" and "has."

Greek uses a *breathing mark* for this breathing pattern instead of a letter. This breathing mark occurs over any initial vowel, as well as the letter rho (ρ). While an initial vowel may be rough or smooth, an initial rho (ρ) or upsilon (υ) *always* receives rough breathing. In Greek composition (that is, in an actual sentence), the breathing mark is written:

- above the initial vowel or rho: ἀ, ἁ, ῥ
- above the second diphthong vowel: αὐ, αὑ
- before an acute or grave accent mark: ἄ, ἅ, ἂ, ἃ
- underneath the circumflex accent mark: ἆ, ἇ
- in front of the vowel when capitalized: Ἀ, Ἁ

(4) Consonant Classes

Divide and conquer. Dividing consonants into consonant classes helps conquer word formation issues. The three classes are liquids, stops, and sibilants. Each class has distinct patterns for

---

[2]Technically called *aspiration*.

how the letter is vocalized. Memorize the consonants that belong to each class. These groups will be helpful later.

(1) Sibilants

The sibilants are four: sigma (σ), zeta (ζ), xi (ξ), and the psi (ψ). They derive their class due to a hissing "s" sound as air expelled from the lungs flows over the teeth during pronunciation.

(2) Liquids

The liquids are four: lambda (λ), mu (μ), nu (ν), and the rho (ρ). They derive their class due to a continuous breathing pattern through the mouth cavity during pronunciation.

(3) Stops

The stops are nine: pi (π), beta (β), phi (φ), kappa (κ), gamma (γ), chi (χ), tau (τ), delta (δ), theta (θ). They derive their class due to controlling air flow during pronunciation. The stops have three physical patterns on how the air flow is controlled: (1) *labials* using lips, (2) *palatals* using tongue and palate, and (3) *dentals* using tongue and teeth. Arranging the stops like one side of a Rubik's cube in rows of their formation patterns helps in analyzing their reactions in word formation. So, you do well for future study to memorize this "Table of Stops" by rows.

Table 1.5—Table of Stops

	smooth		rough
labials	π	β	φ
palatals	κ	γ	χ
dentals	τ	δ	θ

Greek Syllables

Syllable Divisions

Understanding Greek word formation, patterns of inflection, and Greek accents depends upon dividing a Greek word into syllables. The basic principle is simple: *a Greek word has as many syllables as vowels and/or diphthongs.* You divide after each vowel or diphthong, and a single vowel can be a syllable. Divide between two consonants, and for three or more, after the first. Some consonant pairs, however, never divide, but these exceptions are learned by observation.[3] Thus:

- after vowels and diphthongs: ἑαυτοῦ = ἑ-αυ-τοῦ
- between two consonants: ἑορτή = ἑ-ορ-τή
- after the first consonant in a group: ἄνθρωπος = ἄν-θρω-πος
- consonants never dividing: ἀστήρ = ἀ-στήρ

Syllable Names

The last three syllables of a word are named by position. The *ultima* is the very last syllable. The *penult* is next to last. The *antepenult* is third from last. A one-syllable word has an ultima; a two-syllable word has a penult and ultima.

Table 1.6—Syllable Positions

Antepenult	Penult	Ultima
ἄν-	θρω-	πος

---

[3] Here's a neat trick: notice how any consonant pair that can begin a word never will divide in a word. Check vocabulary lists.

Accent Positions

The three Greek accents are restricted to the last three syllables of a Greek word. The acute accent can be over any of the last three, the circumflex accent only the last two (penult, ultima), and the grave accent only on the last (ultima). These restrictions of position are illustrated in the table.

Table 1.7—Accent Positions

	Antepenult	Penult	Ultima
acute	´	´	´
circumflex		῀	῀
grave			`

A syllable's quantity is the vowel quantity in that syllable. Using syllable quantity, combine and apply these rules of accents:

- Acute
  -- *Antepenult possibility.* The acute is the only accent that can stand over the antepenult: ἄνθρωπος.
  -- *Antepenult restriction.* The acute can be on the antepenult only if the ultima is short: ἄν-θρω-πος, but ἀν-θρώ-που.
- Circumflex
  -- *Long syllables only.* The circumflex stands over long syllables only: ἐκεῖνον.
  -- *Long ultima restriction.* The circumflex is restricted to the ultima if the ultima is long: ἑαυτοῦ.
- Grave
  -- *Modified acute.* The grave is simply an ultima acute modified to less stress because other words with accent follow in composition: καὶ πάλιν.
  -- *Ultima only.* The grave is restricted to the ultima syllable only: θεὸς ὅτι.

Chapter 1: Alpha, Beta, Gamma

 **Exercise 1**

1. *Learn the Alphabet*. Practice writing and pronouncing the Greek letters. Memorize them. Be able to say them in order. Not every English letter with which you are familiar has a Greek counterpart (f, j, q, v, w). Neither does every Greek letter have an English counterpart (η, θ, φ, ζ, ψ, ω). Still, you will observe easily that numerous letters in both alphabets are similar in look and/or sound.

    Using an English "a" is allowed for alpha (α). The English letter used to transliterate the Greek letter is given in parentheses, along with the name of the Greek letter. Notice some Greek letters are the equivalent of two English letters in pronunciation. Also, two Greek letters, eta (η) and omega (ω), are just long vowel forms of their short vowel cousins, epsilon (ε) and omicron (o). Carefully distinguish letters that have strokes that go *below* the line (β, γ, ζ, η, μ, ξ, ρ, φ, χ, ψ, ς). Do not confuse letters whose form is similar: nu (ν) has a pointed bottom, but upsilon (υ) has a rounded bottom. When final (i.e., last letter in a word), sigma (σ) is written in the form of ς.

α (a = alpha): _____

β (b = beta): _____

γ (g = gamma): _____

δ (d = delta): _____

ε (e = epsilon): _____

ζ (z = zeta): _____

η (long e = eta): _____

θ (th = theta): _____

ι (i = iota): _____

κ (k = kappa): _____

λ (l = lambda): _____

μ (m = mu): _____

ν (n = nu): _____

ξ (x = xi): _____

ο (o = omicron): _____

π (p = pi): _____

ρ (r = rho): _____

σ (s = sigma): _____ ς (final): _____

τ (t = tau): _____

υ (y = upsilon; diphthong = u): _____

φ (ph = phi): _____

χ (ch = chi): _____

ψ (ps = psi): _____

ω (long o = omega): _____

2. Transliterate the following Greek lines. Use "i" following a vowel for iota subscript. Ignore smooth breathing; use "h" for rough breathing. Put a straight line over "e" for eta, and over "o" for omega. Use "y" when υ occurs as a single vowel by itself, but "u" when the υ is part of a diphthong.

(1) ἀκροβυστίᾳ τῆς σαρκὸς ὑμῶν;

_____

(2) συνεζωοποίησεν ὑμᾶς σὺν αὐτῷ,

_____

(3) χαρισάμενος ἡμῖν πάντα τὰ

_____

(4) παραπτώματα. ἐξαλείψας τὸ καθ'

_____

(5) ἡμῶν χειρόγραφον τοῖς δόγμασιν·

_____

3. Answer the following questions about marks and consonants related to the five lines of Greek above.

3.1 How many total acute accents are there in the lines above? How many grave? How many circumflex?

_____ acute, _____ grave, _____ circumflex

3.2 How many total smooth breathing marks are there? How many rough? Iota subscripts?

_____ smooth, _____ rough, _____ iota subscript

3.3 _____ Which line has a Greek semicolon?

3.4 _____ Which line has a Greek question mark?

3.5 _____ What is the name of the mark at the end of the word κατ᾽ in line 4? What does this mark indicate?

3.6 _____ Does any word in the lines above have an "ng" pronunciation?

3.7 a. _____ (line _____) Which word in what line has three of the four sibilant consonants?

   b. _____ Which of the four sibilants does *not* occur in this word?

   c. _____ (line _____) Which word in what line has this missing sibilant letter?

3.8 a. _____ Which lines have examples of only two of the four liquids?

   b. _____ (line _____) What liquid has only one example? Which line has this only example?

3.9 a. _____ Circle all the stop consonants in each line. Which line has the fewest total number of stops?

   b. _____ Is every stop consonant represented?

Chapter 1: Alpha, Beta, Gamma

c. _____ Which stop consonants occur only once each?

4. Divide the following Greek words into syllables:

   4.1 ὑμῶν = _____

   4.2 αὐτῷ = _____

   4.3 σαρκός = _____

   4.4 συνεζωοποίησεν = _____
   (note: συν is a preposition; divide after preposition)

   4.5 ἀκροβυστία = _____ (hint: κρ and στ are non-divisible)

5. Answer the following questions on vowel quantities and accents:

   5.1 πάντα = Why is this accent not grave?

   _____

   5.2 ὑμῶν = Why is the circumflex not over the υ?

   _____

   5.3 ὑμᾶς = Is the α long or short? How do you know?

   _____

   5.4 ἡμῖν = Is the ι long or short? How do you know?

   _____

5.5 παραπτώματα = Is the final α long or short? How do you know? Why is this accent not circumflex?

_____

5.6 δόγμασιν = Is the final ι long or short? How do you know?

_____

5.7 κατέβη = Why is the accent not on the antepenult?

_____

 **Vocabulary 1**

καί, *and*
δέ, *but*
οὐ, *not*
εἷς, *one*

ἐν, *in* (endemic)
διά, *through* (diameter)
θεός, *God* (monotheism, theocracy, theology)

Vocabulary notes:

(1) Make vocabulary cards about the size of a business card with a Greek word on one side and the definition on the other. Review these cards several times each day.

(2) See the discussion following Vocabulary 3 at the end of Chapter 3 for suggestions on learning prepositions.

(3) The negative οὐ is spelled οὐκ before a word beginning with a vowel and οὐχ before rough breathing.

Words and Meaning

Vocabulary lists provide "definitions" to words. Such definitions, however, really are only approximations of word meanings. These short, one or two word phrases given as "definitions" are meant to be descriptive more than prescriptive (suggestive more than sacrosanct). They actually are called "glosses" because they explain a typical usage, but the one explanation given is not exhaustive of the word's full range of meaning. A gloss gets you oriented to a word, but is no substitute for studying the use of a word in context. Words in context brings us to an important principle of language study.

Meaning vs. Usage

Here is a real showstopper when you've never thought much about how language actually works: *"meaning" is not an inherent property of a word.* "Of course it is," you react instinctively. "Providing the meaning to a word is what the dictionary does, isn't it?" No, not really. A word does not "have" meaning. "So what does a word have?" you demand. Glad you asked.

Usage in Context

A word has "usage in context." Quite simply, words often do change "meaning" over time. As usage in context changes over time, words change in meaning.

Take the verb "prevent." In seventeenth-century England, you might be surprised to learn that this verb was used for the idea of *sequence*: "prevent" meant "go before." Now check out the difference between the King James Version of 1 Th. 4:15 and any modern translation. Today our verb "prevent" is used as the idea of *hindrance*. Since hindrance is not at all what the ancient Greek author meant in 1 Th. 4:15, modern translations struggle to find a better verb than the old seventeenth-century "prevent" to convey the actual thought of the writer.

So what is a dictionary definition in the first place? The concise "definition" that you look up in an English dictionary is only a *suggestion of customary usage* in *contemporary speech*. People in a particular language group assign meaning by customary usage. Word meaning is a social construct evolving over time. Sometimes the movement is quite slow, like one of our meandering bayous down here in south Louisiana. Sometimes movement is quite rapid, like the mighty Mississippi rushing down to the Gulf of Mexico swollen with spring rains. Some words still "mean" what they did centuries ago. Other words can change radically over just a few decades. We also invent new words for new experiences, such as technology ("Did you Google that?" "I texted you, but you never responded.")

Why isn't the act of language pure chaos? How do we communicate at all? *Customary* usage is the key word. "Customary" means we already have agreed beforehand in general about the usage of most words. We work with a *common understanding* of the words we use. Beyond this customary usage, though, you still have to be aware of the immediate context and a speaker's intent to decipher what a word "means" each and every time any word is used.

Language Lesson 1: Words and Meaning

Greek Vocabulary

Bottom line? That words have usage, not meaning, means a Greek dictionary is not enough to understand Greek! You have to develop a sense not only of the common understanding of the first-century use of words in the New Testament, but also a speaker's culture, society, and immediate context. How do you do that? Well, let's see—there's history, sociology, archaeology, literature, rhetoric, etc. In other words, learning a language is more than learning just grammar and vocabulary; language also requires careful historical research. The more you research, the better you will understand a language. To these skills you then add a careful study of the surrounding and immediate context of your document, keeping a keen eye on the speaker's intent. Then you translate. Put simply, the more you know, the better you translate.

Application

And now, a word from our sponsors. Please do not be too glib in sermons or Bible lessons about "what the Greek means." More work is involved than a three-second Google search for online Greek dictionaries. Greek instructors have to walk a fine line: wanting to facilitate an exhilarating insight, the blessing of discovering New Testament truth born of original language labor versus fearing to spawn an authoritative ignorance, the curse of idiosyncratic interpretations born of original language laziness. Working on vocabulary is more than memorizing glosses.

Fig. 5. Greek Key. Famous in Greek art and architecture, the "Greek key" is a symbol comprised of interlocking rectangular lines that evoke the idea of waves in motion on the sea. This inscribed decoration is part of the remains next to the famous theater of Ephesus, Turkey.

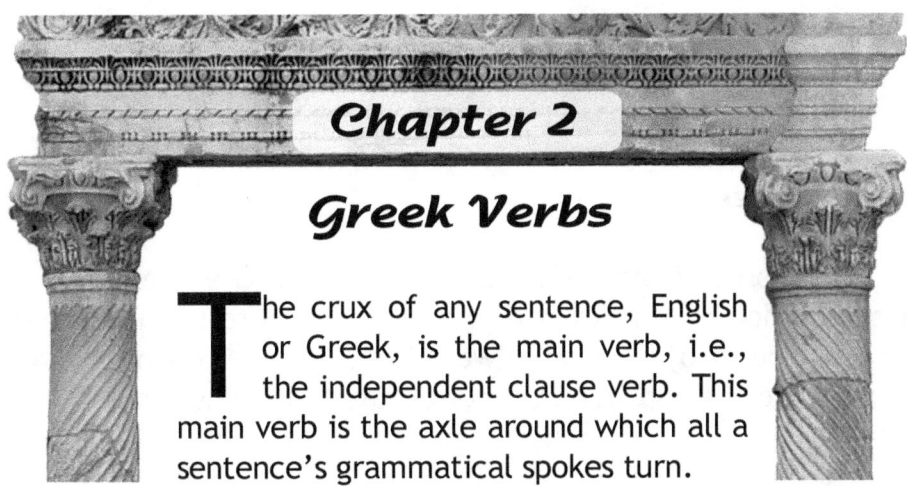

Chapter 2

Greek Verbs

The crux of any sentence, English or Greek, is the main verb, i.e., the independent clause verb. This main verb is the axle around which all a sentence's grammatical spokes turn. Verbs are crucial to sentence sense. For this reason, we look at Greek verb structure first to get you up and running on Greek sentence sense.

Basics of Greek Verbs

Inflection

Verbs must convey six action parameters: performer, receiver, interest, kind, time, and mood (see English 3 of the appendix). How an English verb expresses these parameters must be converted into Greek.

First, and foremost, remember that English is not highly inflected. As a result, English must depend on personal pronouns, auxiliary verbs, and position for conveying a verb's action parameters. The illustration we used in the English appendix was our story of the magic card barker in the mall.

In contrast, Greek *is* highly inflected. Greek does not depend as much on pronouns, auxiliary verbs, or position to express action parameters. Greek verbs express action parameters more by the internal structure of inflection than by the external structure of word order. This structuring by inflection requires concentration to get used to, as this method is not how you have been trained to seek sentence structure from verbs in the English language.

Word Order

Word order is not as crucial to inflected Greek as to uninflected English. You will struggle to get used to this feature of Greek. Your subject is not always first. Your verb is not always second. Your direct object is not always third. You'll really miss that!

♦ *You must focus on a Greek word's spelling, not its word order, for sentence sense!*

The quicker you pay attention to Greek spelling, the quicker you'll be making sense of a Greek sentence. Just like "go" and "gone" may look similar to the uninitiated English speaker but, in fact, convey quite different verb parameters, you have to pay even more attention to spelling in Greek.

Principal Parts

(1) English System

You will recall that English has only *three* principal parts (present, past, past participle). At first this small number seems to make life in the tense lane easier. Yet, in reality, as a result of this system, English incorporates a cumbersome system of auxiliary verbs to create various tenses and show different kinds of action. As a result, the tense traffic in English is bumper-to-bumper.

(2) Greek System

In contrast, Greek has *six* principal parts (present, future, aorist, perfect active, perfect middle, aorist passive). Double the number of principal parts as English seems more complex.

In reality, Greek is easier, because Greek does not need any cumbersome system of auxiliary verbs like English does to create various tenses and kinds of action! For now, all we want you to remember is this connection:

♦ *The Greek present tense is the first principal part.*

Present Active Indicative

Paradigm

With so much weight on inflection, which usually happens at the end of a word (e.g., "box," "boxes," "love," "loved"), then learning organized systems of word endings is essential to learning Greek. *Paradigms* are organized systems of inflection using example words. A *conjugation* is a verb paradigm organized by the three action parameters of tense (action kind and time), voice (action performer), and mood (action potential). Let's lay out a conjugation of the:
- *present* (durative action in present time)
- *active* (subject performing the action)
- *indicative* (action reality assumed or asserted)

We use as our example the paradigm verb λύω, "I loose."

Table 2.1—Present Active Indicative

λύω	I am loosing
λύεις	you are loosing
λύει	he (she, it) is loosing
λύομεν	we are loosing
λύετε	you are loosing
λύουσι(ν)	they are loosing

Notice two key differences from English:

(1) The subject parameter is in an *ending*, not a pronoun. A Greek sentence's subject is in the verb's spelling on the end. Note these: -ω, -εις, -ει, -ομεν, -ετε, -ουσι(ν).[1] Memorize these endings!
(2) The tense parameter (kind and time) is in a verb's *stem*, such as λυ-, not an auxiliary verb, as in English.

Formation

We can use the λύω paradigm to form any other similar verb as present, active, indicative. Recognizing that the -ω on the end is a part of inflection, not stem, we can drop the -ω off any such verb in the dictionary to identify the stem and then create the six forms of singular and plural for that verb. For example, ἔχω means "I have." Drop the -ω on the end and we have the stem εχ-. Adding the six endings for singular and plural personal subjects, we have: ἔχω, ἔχεις, ἔχει, ἔχομεν, ἔχετε, ἔχουσι(ν). Simple enough!

Translation

Present tense usually is durative action. The English auxiliary construction, *I am loosing*, conveys this durative idea. Still, *I loose* could be a legitimate translation of λύω as well. The durative nature of the action is just not as explicit in this form.

An independent clause is a subject-verb word group that makes a complete thought. A single word in Greek can be an independent clause if that word is an inflected verb. Translations provided above show that one word in Greek can be a complete sentence, since the subject is built into the verb! An example is τετέλεσται in John 19:30: "It is finished!"

---

[1]The third plural form has what is called a "movable ν," given in parentheses, which shows up before punctuation, opening vowels, and so forth.

Location

Location is locating what slot in a paradigm any given inflected form fits. To locate a verb is to identify the following parameters of a particular verb form: tense, voice, mood, person, number, and lexical (dictionary) form. Thus, if asked to "locate" the verb form λύομεν, one would respond: "present, active, indicative, first person plural, from λύω." That location is the "slot" in the λύω paradigm that λύομεν would fit. Likewise, if asked to locate ἔχεις, one would say: "present, active, indicative, second person singular, from ἔχω." That location is the "slot" in the λύω paradigm that ἔχεις would fit.

Diagramming

The verb in the paradigm is translated as intransitive (i.e., no object). Intransitives diagram as two slots instead of three:

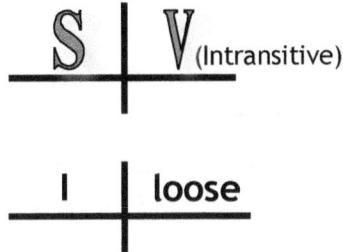

Our problem in Greek is representing the subject when the subject is buried in the verb itself by inflection. We have to substitute the English pronoun in brackets:

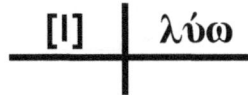

 **Exercise 2**

1. Identify the six principal parts of the Greek verb:

   _____ = First Principal Part

   _____ = Second Principal Part

   _____ = Third Principal Part

   _____ = Fourth Principal Part

   _____ = Fifth Principal Part

   _____ = Sixth Principal Part

2. Complete the following paradigms:

   γράφ -_____ = _____
   γράφ -_____ = _____
   γράφ -_____ = _____
   γράφ -_____ = _____
   γράφ -_____ = _____
   γράφ -_____ = _____

   λέγ -_____ = _____
   λέγ -_____ = _____
   λέγ -_____ = _____
   λέγ -_____ = _____
   λέγ -_____ = _____
   λέγ -_____ = _____

Chapter 2: Greek Verbs

3. Translate the following verb forms and locate (refer to vocabulary 2 at the end of this chapter):

   3.1 λύεις = _____

   Location = _____

   3.2 λαμβάνομεν = _____

   Location = _____

   3.3 πιστεύω = _____

   Location = _____

   3.4 θέλετε = _____

   Location = _____

   3.5 ἐσθίουσιν = _____

   Location = _____

   3.6 γινώσκετε = _____

   Location = _____

   3.7 γράφεις = _____

   Location = _____

   3.8 εὑρίσκομεν = _____

   Location = _____

   3.9 ἔχει = _____

   Location = _____

3.10 ἀκούουσιν = _____

Location = _____

3.11 λέγω = _____

Location = _____

4. Diagram 3.9 and 3.10 from above:

    4.1 ἔχει =

    4.2 ἀκούουσιν =

Vocabulary 2

ἀκούω, *I hear* (acoustic)

γινώσκω, *I know* (diagnosis)

γράφω, *I write* (graphic)

δύο, *two* (duo)

εἰς, *into* (eisegesis)

ἐκ, ἐξ, *out of* (exegesis)

ἐπί, *upon* (epicenter)

ἐσθίω, *I eat*

εὑρίσκω, *I find* (heuristic)

ἔχω, *I have*

θέλω, *I wish, want*

λαμβάνω, *I take, receive*

λέγω, *I say* (legend)

λύω, *I loose*

πιστεύω, *I believe*

Vocabulary notes: See Vocabulary 3 for suggestions on learning prepositions. The prepositional form ἐξ is simply a spelling variation before vowels.

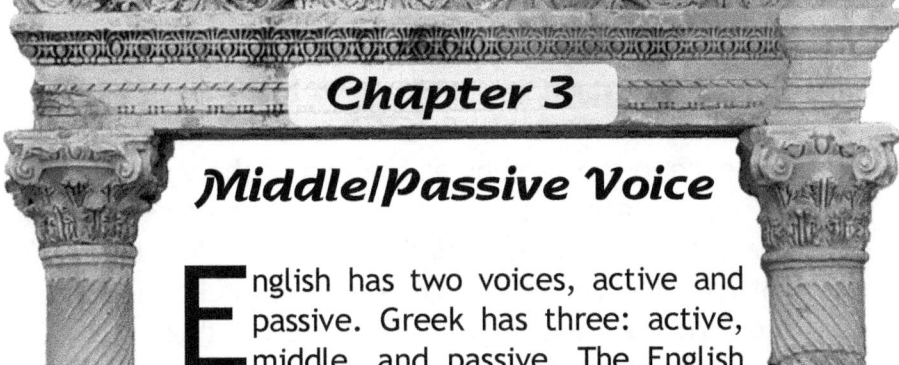

Chapter 3

Middle/Passive Voice

English has two voices, active and passive. Greek has three: active, middle, and passive. The English formation of the durative passive is a real twister of forms: the auxiliary verb "be," plus the durative auxiliary form "being," and the past participle of the verb in question ("am being loosed").

Compared to that convoluted contortion, Greek seems to be a breeze! We first present the Greek passive voice, because passive voice already is familiar to you.

Greek Passive Voice

Voice is the verb parameter indicating the role of the subject in the verbal action. The subject is actively participating or passively receiving. Passive voice presents the subject as being acted upon, passively receiving the action of the verb.

Table 3.1—Present (Durative) Passive Indicative

λύομαι	I am (being) loosed
λύῃ	you are (being) loosed
λύεται	he (she, it) is (being) loosed
λυόμεθα	we are (being) loosed
λύεσθε	you are (being) loosed
λύονται	they are (being) loosed

Notice in the forms two key differences from English:
(1) The subject voice parameter is in the *ending*, not in an auxiliary verb. You will find the passive voice of a Greek sentence in the spelling at the end of the verb as: -μαι, -η, -ται, -μεθα, -σθε, -νται. Memorize these endings!
(2) The tense parameter (kind/time) is in the *stem*, λυ-, not an auxiliary verb. So the durative kind of action is in the verb's present tense stem, not an auxiliary verb.

Thematic Vowel

Did you notice a letter has inserted itself right before the ending that you did not see in most active voice endings? The person and number pattern is ο, ε, ε, ο, ε, ο. The *thematic vowel* is a vowel used to join verb endings to tense stems in the present, imperfect, and future tenses. Why did you often *not* see this vowel in active voice endings? Well, the vowel really is there but already has gone through interactions with vowels of the (original) personal endings. We just did not bother you with that. You're welcome. The vowels show up in all passive forms except for the second person singular. In this form, in a manner similar to the active voice forms, a change has taken place.[1]

Translation

Present tense is usually durative action. Such action is most clear in English translation by using an auxiliary verb construction: *I am being loosed*. Still, *I am loosed* could be a legitimate translation of λύομαι as well. The durative nature of the action is just not as explicit in this form of translation.

---

[1]The real ending is -σαι. When this -σαι combines with the thematic vowel for that slot, -ε, the sigma slides out (-εσαι → -εαι). The left over vowels (-εαι) combine in a normal pattern: ε + α = η. The remaining iota following the eta (-ηι) then becomes iota subscript (-η). Remember: *always* pay attention to iota subscript!

Agency

Passive voice invokes the question of agency (who did it?). Agency can be personal, intermediate, or impersonal. Specific prepositions are used for each of these agencies:

- ὑπό = personal agency ("by John")
- διά = intermediate agency ("through your prayers")
- ἐν = impersonal agency ("by fire")

Greek Middle Voice

Table 3.2—Present Middle Indicative

λύομαι	I am loosing (for myself)
λύῃ	you are loosing (for yourself)
λύεται	he is loosing (for himself)
λυόμεθα	we are loosing (for ourselves)
λύεσθε	you are loosing (for yourselves)
λύονται	they are loosing (for themselves)

Middle Endings

Here's good news: middle voice endings are the same as the passive voice. So how will you tell whether a middle or passive voice is meant? Context tells you; however, learn this dictum:

♦ *Assume a middle/passive form is passive unless context dictates middle.*

You will be right about three out of four times. This generalization, however, has to contend with the issue of the (so-called) "deponent" verb (see below).

Active versus Middle Definitions

Oddly enough, a few verbs do not have the same meaning in the middle voice as in the active voice. For example, αἴρω, active voice, means "I take," but αἱρέομαι, the same verb in the middle voice, means "I choose." Again, ἄρχω as active means "I rule," but ἄρχομαι as middle means "I begin."

Not too many verbs show such distinctions in meaning between active and middle forms. However, you will want to try to remember the few that do; otherwise your translation simply will not "work" for you and you will not have a clue why.

"Deponents"

Deponents traditionally have been described as verbs with only middle/passive voice endings because they lost their active voice. Greek grammarians, however, are shifting away from this category used to describe a feature of Latin verbs. In fact, so-called "deponent" Greek verbs *never had active voice forms*. English translation simply fails to convey their middle force. So, ἔρχομαι, "I go, come," never appearing in active voice, is a so-called "deponent." Yet, the active voice is not lost in history as with Latin verbs; rather, this verb *never* had an active form. Further complicating the picture, the Greek middle sense is lost in English translation; your translation has to default to active voice because you have no choice. Such "middle-only" Greek verbs have dictionary forms ending in -μαι, not -ω.

Translation

In Greek middle voice, the subject has "self-interest" in the action. English does not have a middle voice verb form. English reflexive pronouns ("myself," "yourself," etc.) are used as a work-a-round, but this style reflects the direct middle, which is rare in Greek. Since English has no middle voice, you simply have no actual grammatical slot into which to put this feature of Greek grammar.[2]

Primary Tenses

Primary tenses are tenses of the indicative mood in present and future time. A fundamental rule of the indicative mood is that:

♦ *Primary tenses take primary endings.*

The sets of endings you have learned for both present active and middle, then, are the primary endings. These endings are used on several other Greek tenses. For this reason, you want to learn them well. For your convenience, they are summarized below.

Table 3.3—Primary Endings

Active	Middle/Passive
-ω	-μαι
-εις	-η (σαι)
-ει	-ται
-μεν	-μεθα
-τε	-σθε
-ουσι	-νται

---

[2]Translation is *never* a one-to-one correspondence of every grammatical feature of one language with an exact grammatical counterpart in another language. Thus, interlinears are misleading at best and dangerously disguise the complexity of translation issues. Avoid them like the plague. That's my two-cents worth. For a review of sentence-level functions, see the discussion in the chapter "English 3" in the English appendix.

Exercise 3

1. Fill in the blank:

   _____ = The verb parameter indicating action performer.
   _____ = The voice indicating that the subject is being acted upon.
   _____ = The two vowels ε/ο used to join verb endings onto tense stems.
   _____ = The preposition indicating personal agency.
   _____ = Verbs with only mid./pass. forms but "active" voice translation.
   _____ = Those indicative tenses expressing present and future time.

2. Complete the following paradigm as passive voice and translate using the lexical "call" rather than "say":

   λέγ-_____ = _____
   λέγ-_____ = _____
   λέγ-_____ = _____
   λεγ-_____ = _____
   λέγ-_____ = _____
   λέγ-_____ = _____

3. Complete the following paradigms as middle voice. This time use the idea of "say" for the stem λέγ-. Remember that the verb ἔρχομαι is a "middle only" verb (used to be called a "deponent") before you translate (i.e., middle in voice, but defaults to an *active* sound in translation):

Chapter 3: Middle/Passive Voice 35

λέγ-_____ = _____

λέγ-_____ = _____

λέγ-_____ = _____

λεγ-_____ = _____

λέγ-_____ = _____

λέγ-_____ = _____

ἔρχ-_____ = _____

ἔρχ-_____ = _____

ἔρχ-_____ = _____

ἐρχ-_____ = _____

ἔρχ-_____ = _____

ἔρχ-_____ = _____

4. Translate the following verb forms and locate (refer to Vocabulary 3 at the end of this chapter for some words). Assume they are passive, but treat the underlined verbs as middle:

   4.1 ἀποκρίνῃ = _____

   Location = _____

   4.2 γινόμεθα = _____

   Location = _____

   4.3 <u>πιστεύομαι</u> = _____

   Location = _____

   4.4 γινώσκεται = _____

   Location = _____

4.5 ἔρχεσθε = _____

Location = _____

4.6 εἰσέρχονται = _____

Location = _____

4.7 γινώσκεσθε = _____

Location = _____

4.8 κάθηται = _____

Location = _____

4.9 εὑρισκόμεθα = _____

Location = _____

4.10 πορεύεσθε = _____

Location = _____

4.11 <u>ἀκούονται</u> = _____

Location = _____

4.12 <u>λέγομαι</u> = _____

Location = _____

5. Diagram 4.10 and 4.11 from above:

    5.1 πορεύεσθε =

    5.2 ἀκούονται =

Chapter 3: Middle/Passive Voice

 **Vocabulary 3**

ἀνά, *up* (analogy)

ἀπό, *away from* (apostle)

ἀποκρίνομαι, *I answer*

γίνομαι, *I am, become*

ἔρχομαι, *I go, come*
   ἀπέρχομαι, *I go away, depart*
   εἰσέρχομαι, *I go, come into*

ἐξέρχομαι, *I go, come out*

προσέρχομαι, *I go to, approach*

κάθημαι, *I sit, sit down*

κατά, *down* (cataclysm)

πορεύομαι, *I go, proceed, travel* (pore)

πρός, *to, toward* (proselyte)

τρεῖς, *three* (trio)

Vocabulary notes:

(1) Verbs often are compounded with prepositions in order to strengthen the sense, change the meaning, or direct the motion. English does the same: "downsize," "outrun," etc. Greek prepositions often drop their final vowel when compounded onto verb stems; an exposed consonant then might suffer further change; note both of these changes with κατά in καθοράω.

(2) The verb γίνομαι is intransitive. Its predicate can have a noun or adjective complement (always *after* the verb in English). *The predicate complement will be nominative case.*

(3) The verb κάθημαι comes from another conjugation, but you can recognize the middle endings if you just think of the η of the stem acting like a thematic vowel for now.

(4) Prepositions can be arranged in various logical groups to make learning them easier. One category is spatial:

- interior space: *in*
- exterior space: *upon, beside, around, over, under*

- horizontal motion: *toward, into, through, out of, away from*
- vertical motion: *up, down*
- positional: *before, after; with, against*

Another concept is to think of opposite pairs, as in: *over, under; toward, away from; into, out of; up, down; before, after; with, against*. Tables 3.4 and 3.5 below might help to illustrate prepositional use. Be aware that other meanings for these prepositions besides directional will be added later.

Table 3.4—Preposition Lighthouse

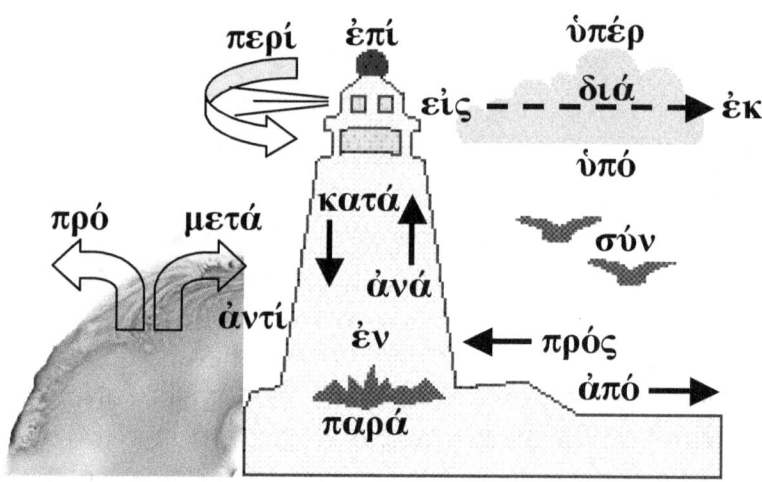

Table 3.5—Preposition Line

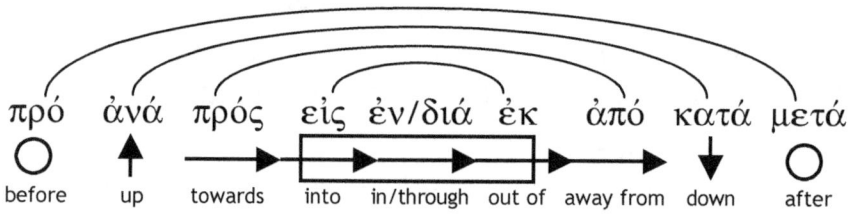

Translation Is Interpretation

Being introduced to the Greek middle voice and finding that no real equivalent for this grammatical structure exists in the English language might be somewhat disconcerting. How is any translation supposed to work in the first place?

Interlinear Illusions

Perhaps you even thought naively that interlinears were a student's best friend. They are not. Interlinears only give the illusion of translation. For learning to translate, they are addictive and crippling, a crutch that cuts off oxygen to the brain. In trying to pass this class, please avoid using an interlinear. You are only hurting yourself.

What's wrong with an interlinear? Oh, please. Don't get me started. I will say this much here: inasmuch as an interlinear suggests some wooden, one-to-one correspondence between every grammatical feature in Greek with its exact grammatical counterpart in English, interlinears are misleading and unhelpful in training for translation. You already have encountered the very heart of the problem with an interlinear in studying the Greek middle voice.

Translation Reality

Encountering the Greek middle voice has taught you an important language lesson, a datum of translation:

♦ *Every translation is, by definition, an interpretation.*

Translation is interpretation. This reality will become even more apparent as we proceed through Greek grammar. You might have different reactions to this thought—that translation is interpretation.

You might be discouraged. How can any divine truth at all be determined, if this is so? Does this reality create a pit of despair,[1] a quicksand trap of subjectivity, or, worse, even total arbitrariness? No, absolutely not. Such fear of complete subjectivity is unfounded. This concern ignores the many historical controls that set parameters on historical meaning. Such concern also ignores that many elements of language are universals of human experience grasped immediately and intuitively by the reader without any need for a literary degree from college.

You might be intimidated. You might be overwhelmed by a sense of grave responsibility as you attempt to translate. You might worry as though God's Word coming through your pen will be corrupted and become less than "perfect." Again, that is just not so. Remember, God always has worked *through* human beings, not in spite of them. Sometimes the translation effort is less a matter of trying to hit a bull's eye than trying not to miss

---

[1] Yes, of course, "The Princess Bride."

the target completely. So, you should give the translation effort your best shot, utilizing all the knowledge, skills, and tools you have available to you at this time, which is all you can be held accountable for, and trust God to bless the result. And while you are translating, never forget this fundamental datum that balances out the first datum:

♦ *No word is God's Word without the quickening of the Holy Spirit, no matter how perfectly translated.*

Photo © Gerald L. Stevens

Fig. 6. Athenian Warrior. This image shows an Athenian warrior with spear and shield. The bowl upon which the scene is depicted is the earliest known calyx krater, or bowl, dating to 530 B.C. This example also is the only one known of this shape to have been fashioned by the famous craftsman Exekias. Attalus Stoa Museum, Ancient Agora, Athens, Greece.

Chapter 4

Greek Nouns

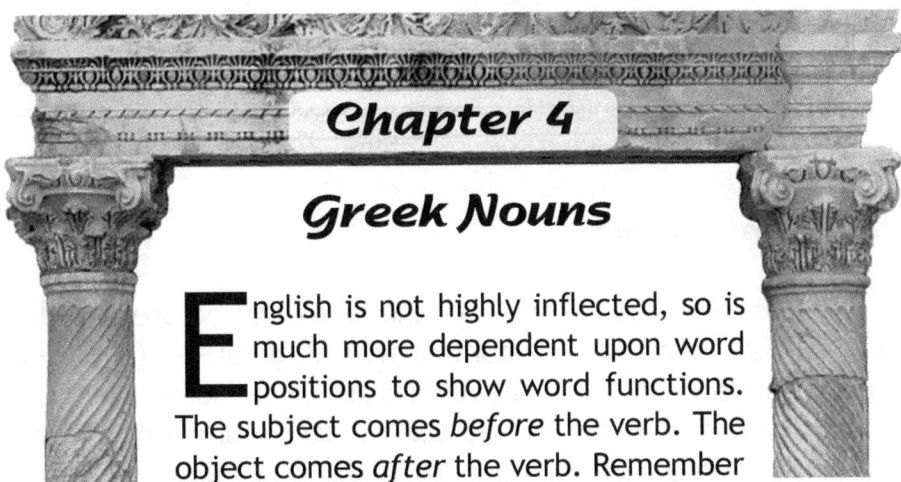

English is not highly inflected, so is much more dependent upon word positions to show word functions. The subject comes *before* the verb. The object comes *after* the verb. Remember the mall barker and mail truck analogies (in the English appendix)? We now have to refocus how we show function.[1]

Greek is highly inflected. Greek, then, is much less dependent on position to show word function. Greek spelling indicates sentence function. A Greek word that is subject could be after the verb. The Greek direct object could be before the verb. The verb could be first. The verb could be last. A highly inflected language leaves you no choice: you are going to have to wander through the wilderness of paradigms before you can see the promised land of translation.

Greek Cases

Noun Junction

Case is named noun function in word relationships. English has three cases: nominative, accusative, and genitive. Nominative names; accusative extends the verb; genitive shows possession. In sentences, these cases show sentence roles: subject, direct object, etc. Greek splits the object function into two distinct cases, accusative for direct object, but dative for indirect

---

[1] Not completely new; English does have some inflection for function.

object. Greek also adds a distinct case for the vocative function. (Remember the English appendix story, the little girl who bested the mall barker?) Thus, Greek has five cases.

Case Arrangement

The Greek cases in the order that they will be presented as rows in paradigms are: (1) nominative, (2) genitive, (3) dative, (4) accusative, and (5) vocative. Three quick notes are given about this arrangement. First, the vocative form often is not distinct from the nominative. A four-row noun paradigm means the vocative form repeats the nominative.

Second, for convenience, we refer to the genitive and dative as the "interior cases" in the paradigm order. This is no official term, just descriptive. These are the two inside rows of any paradigm, the genitive and dative cases.

Third, both English and Greek have an accusative objective case. Greek, however, also adds a dative objective case that covers special functions such as the indirect object.

Second Declension Inflection

Greek substantives have three *declensions*, or patterns of inflection: first, second, and third. We start with second first because second has the least variations. Second declension has two sets of inflection patterns. Set 1 is for masculine and feminine nouns. Set 2 is for neuter nouns.

Second Declension Inflection—Set 1 (Mas./Fem.)

(1) Set 1 Formation
This declension is called a "vowel" declension because the noun stems end in vowels. However, just as with the primary active voice endings for verbs, learning the already-changed

endings after vowels have combined into resultant forms is easier to do. For this purpose, simply drop the -ος ending of the nominative form in the dictionary entry, and you have the base form you need for the rest of the paradigm.

Table 4.1—Second Declension Endings—Set 1

	Singular	Plural
Nominative:	-ος	-οι
Genitive:	-ου	-ων
Dative:	-ῳ	-οις
Accusative:	-ον	-ους

Table 4.2—Second Declension: Set 1 Paradigm

	Singular	Plural	Gloss
Nominative:	λόγος	λόγοι	word(s)
Genitive:	λόγου	λόγων	of, from a word(s)
Dative:	λόγῳ	λόγοις	to, in, by a word(s)
Accusative:	λόγον	λόγους	word(s)
Vocative:	λόγε	λόγοι	Word(s)

Notice that the Greek interior cases (genitive, dative) create prepositional phrases in English. Exactly how to translate a particular interior form when multiple options exist is decided often by other signals in the context.

(2) Noun Location

Noun "location" (or, "parsing") means identifying the three noun properties discussed in the English 4 lesson (case, gender, number), plus lexical form. To "locate" ("parse") a given form, you specify the particular slot that form would fit in its paradigm. For example, the form λόγοι would be located as: "nominative, masculine, plural, from λόγος." The form υἱούς would be located as: "accusative, masculine, plural, from υἱός."

(3) Feminine Second Declension

Most nouns of the second declension set 1 inflection you will discover are masculine in gender. However, a few are feminine. Three feminine nouns that take set 1 endings are: παρθένος (*virgin*), ὁδός (*way, road*), and ἔρημος (*wilderness*). You can remember these feminine nouns using this mock sentence: "a *virgin* will find a *way* in the *wilderness*."

Noun gender must be learned as part of vocabulary work. A Greek dictionary will indicate a noun's gender.

Second Declension Inflection—Set 2 (Neuter)

(1) Set 2 Formation

This inflection is exclusively neuter gender. Study the second declension set 2 inflection pattern provided in the table below.

Table 4.3—Second Declension Endings—Set 2

	Singular	Plural
Nominative:	-ον	-α
Genitive:	-ου	-ων
Dative:	-ῳ	-οις
Accusative:	-ον	-α

Good news. You already know the endings of the neuter interior cases—they repeat set 1! Did you notice? More good news. The neuter accusative form repeats the neuter nominative, both in singular and plural. These two basic observations formulate two principles that can be applied to neuter Greek inflection across all declension patterns, which are:

♦ *Neuter interior cases replicate masculine interiors.*

♦ *Neuter accusative replicates neuter nominative.*

Table 4.4—Second Declension: Set 2 Paradigm

	Singular	Plural	Gloss
Nominative:	ἔργον	ἔργα	work(s) (voc. sg. = ἔργε)
Genitive:	ἔργου	ἔργων	of, from a work(s)
Dative:	ἔργῳ	ἔργοις	to, in, by a work(s)
Accusative:	ἔργον	ἔργα	work(s)

Greek interior cases create prepositional phrases in English. How to translate a particular interior form when multiple options exist is decided often by other signals in context.

Diagramming

The subject, regularly in nominative case, goes in the first position. The direct object, regularly accusative case, goes in the third position. The interior cases (genitive, dative) create modifying phrases that go under the word modified.

τὴν ἀγάπην τοῦ θεοῦ οὐκ ἔχετε ἐν ἑαυτοῖς
"You do not have the love of God in you." (Jn. 5:42)

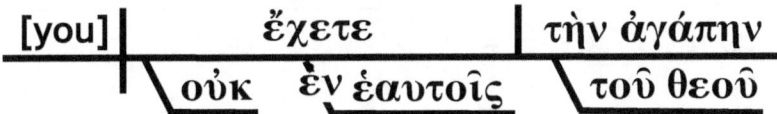

 **Exercise 4**

1. True or False:

    _____ = Inflection is a sure sign of a noun's gender.

    _____ = Any noun whose lexical (dictionary) ending is -ον is feminine gender.

    _____ = English has only three cases, but Greek has five.

    _____ = The case of the Greek indirect object is the dative.

    _____ = The Greek vocative case always is distinct from the nominative.

2. Complete the following paradigm as a second declension masculine *singular* and provide a gloss:

    θε-_____ = _____
    θε-_____ = _____
    θε-_____ = _____
    θε-_____ = _____

3. Complete the following paradigm as a second declension masculine *plural* and provide a gloss:

    κύρι-_____ = _____
    κυρί-_____ = _____
    κυρί-_____ = _____
    κυρί-_____ = _____

4. Complete the following paradigm as a second declension neuter *singular* and provide a gloss:

εὐαγγέλι-_____ = _____
εὐαγγελί-_____ = _____
εὐαγγελί-_____ = _____
εὐαγγέλι-_____ = _____

5. Complete the following paradigm as second declension neuter *plural* and provide a gloss:

τέκν-_____ = _____
τέκν-_____ = _____
τέκν-_____ = _____
τέκν-_____ = _____

6. Give a gloss for the following forms from vocabulary 4, and locate. If a form has more than one possible location, indicate options. For prepositional phrases, use the indefinite article ("a," "an"). Pay close attention to gender. (Some endings look the same but represent different cases depending on gender.)

   6.1 ἄνθρωπος = _____

   Location = _____

   6.2 Χριστόν = _____

   Location = _____

   6.3 ἀδελφοῦς = _____

   Location = _____

6.4 υἱῶν = _____
Location = _____

6.5 ἀγγέλῳ = _____
Location = _____

6.6 τέκνα = _____
Location = _____

6.7 ἔργον = _____
Location = _____

6.8 σημείοις = _____
Location = _____

6.9 εὐαγγελίου = _____
Location = _____

6.10 οὐρανοί = _____
Location = _____

6.11 Ἰησοῦς = _____
Location = _____

6.12 κόσμῳ = _____
Location = _____

7. Translate. (Warning: be careful *not* to depend on word order!) These notes should help with the exercises:

   (1) The τά in 7.1 is the neuter article modifying τέκνα (either nom. or acc. plu.; take this form as nom.)

(2) Similarly, the ὁ in 7.4 is the masculine article (nom., sing.) modifying ἄγγελος.

(3) *The Greek subject and verb will agree in number*, as in English. *One exception is the neuter plural*. Neuter plurals can be taken as a collective unit, that is, as singular. Thus, you may encounter a *neuter plural* subject used with a *singular* verb, a Greek idiom, not a mistake (note this Greek idiom in exercise 7.1).

7.1 ἔρχεται τὰ τέκνα.

7.2 ἐν σημείῳ οὐ πιστεύομεν.

7.3 Ἰησοῦν[2] εὑρίσκεις καὶ πιστεύεις.

7.4 λόγους ἀνθρώποις λέγει ὁ ἄγγελος ἐκ οὐράνου.

8. Diagram 7.4 (put article in front of the noun modified):

---

[2]See vocabulary note 1.

 **Vocabulary 4**

ἄγγελος, ὁ, *messenger, angel* (angel)

ἀδελφός, ὁ, *brother* (Philadelphia)

ἄνθρωπος, ὁ, *man, mankind* (anthropology)

ἔργον, τό, *work* (energy)

εὐαγγέλιον, τό, *good news, gospel* (evangelism)

Ἰησοῦς, ὁ, *Jesus*

κόσμος, ὁ, *world, universe* (cosmos)

κύριος, ὁ, *master, lord, sir*

λόγος, ὁ, *word, message* (logic, analogy, dialogue, trilogy)

μετά, *after, with* (metaphor)

οὐρανός, ὁ, *heaven, sky* (Uranus)

πρό, *before* (prologue, prognosis)

σημεῖον, τό, *sign, mark, wonder, miracle* (semantics, semaphore)

τέκνον, τό, *child*

τέσσαρες, *four* (tetrarch)

υἱός, ὁ, *son*

ὑπέρ, *over* (hyper-, hyperbole)

ὑπό, *under* (hypodermic, hypothesis)

Χριστός, ὁ, *Christ, Messiah*

Vocabulary notes:

(1) Proper nouns have unpredictable inflexion, sometimes not inflected at all (like English proper nouns). Only singular forms show up in an inflection. The proper name "Jesus" is frequent. Its inflection is irregular, but only three forms. All other cases are Ἰησοῦ, except the accusative is Ἰησοῦν.

(2) The ὁ following a noun is the masculine article, used in a gloss to indicate masculine gender.

(3) The τό following a noun is the neuter article, used in a gloss to indicate neuter gender.

(4) For the prepositions, consult the discussion with Vocabulary 3 and the following tables at the end of Chapter 3.

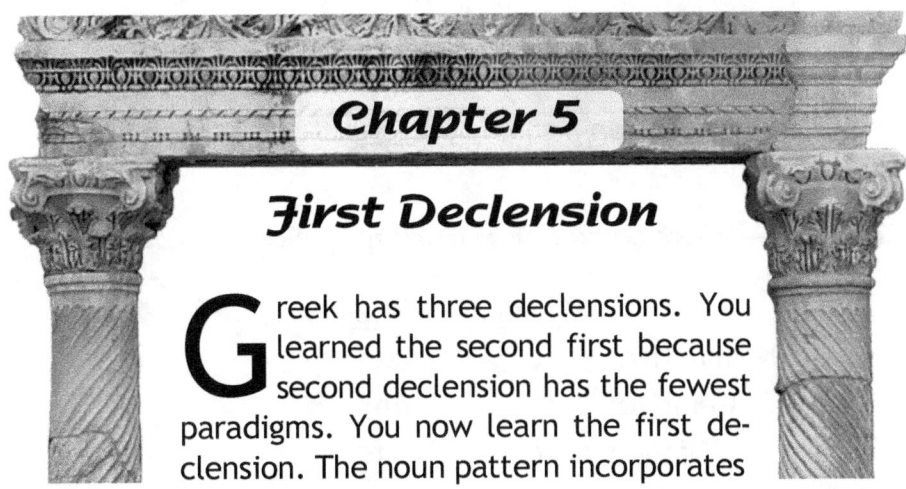

Chapter 5

First Declension

Greek has three declensions. You learned the second first because second declension has the fewest paradigms. You now learn the first declension. The noun pattern incorporates either an -α or -η. Five paradigms cover the variations on using these vowels.

Major Patterns

First declension, like the second, also is called a "vowel" declension because the noun stems end in vowels, either α or η. However, like with second declension, learning the already-changed endings after vowels have combined into resultant forms is easier. For this purpose, simply drop the -α or -η ending of the nominative form in the dictionary entry, and you have the inflectional base for the rest of the paradigm.

First Declension Inflection—Set 1 ("α pure")

(1) Set 1 Formation

First declension has five sets of inflection patterns. Set 1 is for "α-pure" nouns; an α vowel shows up throughout the singular. Set 2 is for "η pure" nouns; an η vowel shows up throughout the singular. Set 3 in effect combines sets 1 and 2, mixing α and η vowels in singular forms. Sets 4 and 5 are minor variations of the η pure paradigm. These singular patterns are all similar. Plus, we have this plural dictum:

♦ *First declension has only one plural pattern.*

Table 5.1—First Declension Endings—Set 1 (α-pure)

	Singular	Plural
Nominative:	-α	-αι
Genitive:	-ας	-ων
Dative:	-ᾳ	-αις
Accusative:	-αν	-ας

As in second declension, accusatives end in -ν and -ς. Datives have iota either as a *subscript* or as *non-final*. Genitive plural always is -ων. Nominative plural has non-subscript *final* iota. Warning: *genitive singular is the same as accusative plural*! Only context distinguishes. Nouns that have this type inflection have stems that end in either ε, ι, or ρ.

Table 5.2—First Declension: α-Pure Paradigm

	Singular	Plural	Gloss
Nom.:	καρδία	καρδίαι	heart(s)
Gen.:	καρδίας	καρδιῶν	of, from a heart(s)
Dat.:	καρδίᾳ	καρδίαις	to, in, by a heart(s)
Acc.:	καρδίαν	καρδίας	heart(s)

Table 5.3—First Declension Endings—Set 2 (η-pure)

	Singular	Plural
Nominative:	-η	-αι
Genitive:	-ης	-ων
Dative:	-ῃ	-αις
Accusative:	-ην	-ας

Notice close similarities in look to the second declension, as with α-pure. Hint: unlike the α-pure paradigm, the *genitive singular is distinct from accusative plural*. Nouns that have this type inflection have nominative singulars that end in η.

Table 5.4—First Declension: η-Pure Paradigm

	Singular	Plural	Gloss
Nom.:	ἀγάπη	ἀγάπαι	love(s)
Gen.:	ἀγάπης	ἀγαπῶν	of, from a love(s)
Dat.:	ἀγάπῃ	ἀγάπαις	to, in, by a love(s)
Acc.:	ἀγάπην	ἀγάπας	love(s)

Table 5.5—First Declension Endings—Set 3 (mixed)

	Singular	Plural
Nominative:	-α	-αι
Genitive:	-ης	-ων
Dative:	-ῃ	-αις
Accusative:	-αν	-ας

Nouns that have this type inflection have stems that end in one of the sibilants σ, ξ, or ζ. The singular starts in α like an α-pure, but slips to η like an η-pure in the interiors, then goes back to α for the accusative. Notice close similarities in look to the second declension, as with both α- and η-pure. Hint: like η-pure, *genitive singular is distinct from accusative plural*. When one observes that both set 2 and set 3 endings distinguish the genitive singular from the accusative plural, then the only time one has confusion about the case of the specific -ας ending in first declension is for set 1, that is, the α-pure pattern (also true for set 4 and set 5 endings as well).

Table 5.6—First Declension: Mixed Paradigm

	Singular	Plural	Gloss
Nom.:	δόξα	δόξαι	glory(ies)
Gen.:	δόξης	δοξῶν	of, from a glory(ies)
Dat.:	δόξῃ	δόξαις	to, in, by a glory(ies)
Acc.:	δόξαν	δόξας	glory(ies)

Minor Variations

Table 5.7—First Declension—Set 4 (-ης Nom.)

	Singular	Plural
Nominative:	-ης	-αι
Genitive:	-ου	-ων
Dative:	-ῃ	-αις
Accusative:	-ην	-ας

Table 5.8—First Declension: -ης Nom. Paradigm

	Singular	Plural	Gloss
Nom.:	μαθητής	μαθηταί	disciple(s) (voc. sg. = -α)
Gen.:	μαθητοῦ	μαθητῶν	of, from a disciple(s)
Dat.:	μαθητῇ	μαθηταῖς	to, in, by a disciple(s)
Acc.:	μαθητήν	μαθητάς	disciple(s)

Any noun whose lexical form ends in -ης is first declension masculine. Note how the nominative singular ends in -ς and the genitive singular in -ου, like a second declension masculine.

Otherwise, however, the form is η-pure, except accent.[1] A variation of this pattern is a nominative in -ας. These forms, however, are rare in the New Testament; two examples would be μεσσίας ("messiah") and Ἠσαΐας ("Isaiah"). Another well-known word, σατανᾶς ("Satan"), has a genitive in -ᾶ.

Table 5.9—First Declension—Set 5 (α-pure Contract)

	Singular	Paradigm	Gloss
Nom.:	-ῆ	γῆ	earth
Gen.:	-ῆς	γῆς	of, from earth
Dat.:	-ῇ	γῇ	to, in, by earth
Acc.:	-ῆν	γῆν	earth

Contraction is the process of vowels combining to form long vowels or diphthongs. The noun γῆ ("earth," "land") contracts the ε of its stem with the α of the first declension α-pure singular endings. Contraction of ε + α gives η. The noun then has a resultant η-pure look in the singular. A circumflex accent gives away the contraction process.

Exercise 5

1. Fill in the blank:

First declension singular has either the vowel _____ or the vowel _____. First declension has only _____ plural pattern. Nominative singular forms end in a vowel, except for masculine nouns, whose nominatives end in _____. For these masculine

---

[1] Accent is oxytone (last syllable), so interior cases are circumflex.

nouns, the genitive singular has the _____ ending like the second declension. Although rare in the New Testament, another masculine first declension form has a nominative that ends in _____. Two New Testament examples of this rare form are the words _____ and _____. One problem in recognizing case for the α-pure inflection is the ending _____ for both the _____ (case) singular and the _____ (case) plural. This ending is not a problem in the η-pure inflection, because the _____ (case) singular form has the inflection _____. A first declension noun that contracts its ε stem vowel with the α-pure endings to create an η-pure look in the singular is the noun _____. This contraction is easy to spot because of the _____ accent.

2. Complete the following paradigm as the first declension feminine singular and provide a gloss:

ἡμέρ-_____ = _____
ἡμέρ-_____ = _____
ἡμέρ-_____ = _____
ἡμέρ-_____ = _____

3. Complete the following paradigm as the first declension feminine singular and provide a gloss:

ψυχ-_____ = _____
ψυχ-_____ = _____
ψυχ-_____ = _____
ψυχ-_____ = _____

Chapter 5: First Declension

4. Complete the following paradigm as the first declension feminine singular and provide a gloss:

   θάλασσ-_____ = _____
   θαλάσσ-_____ = _____
   θαλάσσ-_____ = _____
   θάλασσ-_____ = _____

5. Complete the following paradigm as the first declension *masculine* singular and provide a gloss:

   προφήτ-_____ = _____
   προφήτ-_____ = _____
   προφήτ-_____ = _____
   προφήτ-_____ = _____

6. Complete the following paradigm as the first declension feminine *plural* and provide a gloss:

   ἁμαρτί-_____ = _____
   ἁμαρτι-_____ = _____
   ἁμαρτί-_____ = _____
   ἁμαρτί-_____ = _____

7. Give a gloss for the following forms using Vocabulary 5, and locate. If a form has more than one possible location, indicate options. For prepositional phrases, use the indefinite article ("a," "an"). Pay close attention to the stems. (Some endings are the same but represent different cases depending on stem.)

7.1 βασιλείας = _____

Location = _____

7.2 φωνάς = _____

Location = _____

7.3 ζωῆς = _____

Location = _____

7.4 ἀγάπην = _____

Location = _____

7.5 ψυχαί = _____

Location = _____

7.6 δόξαν = _____

Location = _____

7.7 Ἰωάννου = _____

Location = _____

7.8 μαθηταῖς = _____

Location = _____

7.9 γῇ = _____

Location = _____

8. Translate. (Warning: do *not* depend on word order!)

   8.1 μαθητὴς γίνομαι.²

   8.2 κάθηται καὶ πορευόμεθα.

   8.3 ἐσθίουσιν παρὰ θάλασσῃ.

   8.4 βασιλείαν δόξης ἔχω.

   8.5 ἐκ Ἰησοῦ λαμβάνομεν ζωήν.

   8.6 Ἰησοῦν ἀκούουσιν μαθηταί Ἰωαννοῦ καὶ γράφουσιν λόγους ζωῆς.

9. Diagram 8.6:

---

²For the word γίνομαι, review vocabulary note 2, p. 37.

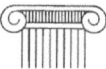 **Vocabulary 5**

ἀγάπη, ἡ, *love*
ἁμαρτία, ἡ, *sin, mistake*
βασιλεία, ἡ, *kingdom* (basilica)
γῆ, ἡ, *earth, land* (geography, apogee)
δόξα, -ης, ἡ, *glory* (doxology, paradox)
ζωή, ἡ, *life* (zoo, protozoa)
ἡμέρα, ἡ, *day* (ephemeral)
θάλασσα, -ης, ἡ, *sea*
Ἰωάννης, ὁ, *John*
καρδία, ἡ, *heart* (cardiac)

μαθητής, -οῦ, ὁ, *disciple, learner* (mathematics)
παρά, *beside* (parallel)
πέντε, *five* (pentagon)
περί, *around* (perimeter)
προφήτης, -ου, ὁ, *prophet* (prophet)
φωνή, ἡ, *sound, voice* (phonetics, telephone)
ψυχή, ἡ, *life, soul, person* (psyche, psychology)

Vocabulary notes:
   (1) The proper name "John" is frequent. Inflection follows the first declension nominative in -ης (masculine).
   (2) The ἡ following a noun in the vocabulary entry is the feminine article, used in a gloss to indicate feminine gender.
   (3) Noun inflection in vocabulary above is by stem ending:
   • ε, ι, or ρ stems (α-pure)
   • nominatives in -η (η-pure)
   • the sibilants σ, ξ, and ζ (mixed α/η)
   • nominatives in -ης (masculine)
   • contract stem (ε + α = ῆ)
   (4) Genitive endings are given for non-pure forms, such as sibilants (δόξα, -ης) or nominatives in -ης (μαθητής, -οῦ).
   (5) For the prepositions, consult the discussion with Vocabulary 3 and following tables at the end of Chapter 3.

Chapter 6

The Article

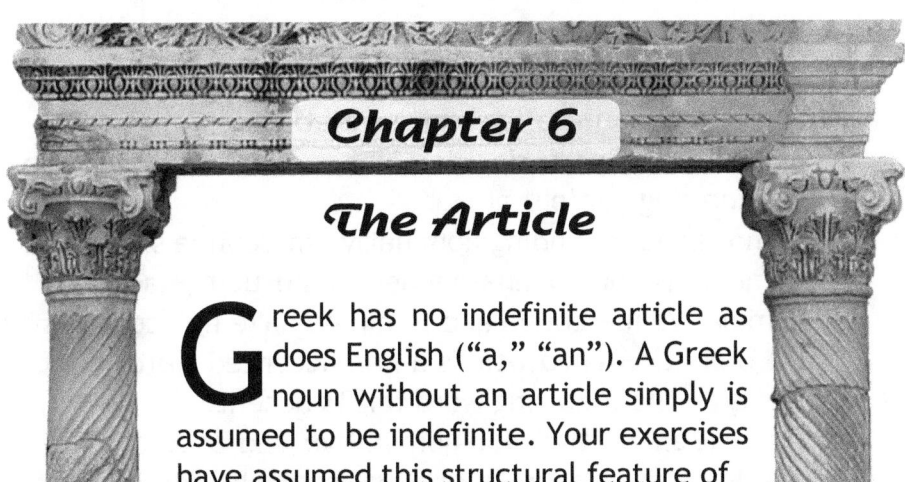

Greek has no indefinite article as does English ("a," "an"). A Greek noun without an article simply is assumed to be indefinite. Your exercises have assumed this structural feature of Greek to this point. The Greek article, which corresponds to the English definite article, transcends English article use. First, we overview the formation of the Greek article. Then, we investigate the article's sentence structure and function.

Formation

Good news: nothing new to learn, almost. Study the following paradigms arranged by gender. Notice the close similarities to second and first declension patterns.

Table 6.1—The Greek Article

	Masculine		Neuter		Feminine	
	Sing.	Plur.	Sing.	Plur.	Sing.	Plur.
Nom.:	ὁ	οἱ	τό	τά	ἡ	αἱ
Gen.:	τοῦ	τῶν	τοῦ	τῶν	τῆς	τῶν
Dat.:	τῷ	τοῖς	τῷ	τοῖς	τῇ	ταῖς
Acc.:	τόν	τούς	τό	τά	τήν	τάς

We can make a few observations:

(1) Inflection is second/first declension, with tau (τ).
(2) Nominative forms offer minor variations:
   - no tau (τ) prefacing nominative masculine and feminine singular/plural
   - no sigma (ς) ending nominative masculine singular
   - no nu (ν) on nominative neuter singular (+ acc.)
(3) Nominative masculine and feminine have no accent; they are proclitic. A *proclitic* is a non-accented word that depends on the following word for its accent.
(4) Translation is "the" for nominative and accusative. The interior cases generate prepositional phrases ("of the," "from the," "in the," "to the," "in the," "by the," etc.)

Structure

Anarthrous

An *anarthrous* noun is a noun without the article. The anarthrous Greek noun is translated with the indefinite article ("a," "an") or simply no article at all. For example:

ἀπὸ δόξης εἰς δόξαν
"from *glory* unto *glory*" (2 Cor. 3:18)

Articular

An *articular* noun has the article. The articular Greek noun is translated with the definite article ("the"). For example:

τὰς βασιλείας τοῦ κόσμου
"*the* kingdoms *of the* world" (Matt. 4:8)

Concord

Concord is grammatical agreement. For nouns, this agreement is in case, gender, and number. An article is "in concord" with its associated noun, that is, the article agrees in case, gender, and number with its associated noun. The noun βασιλείας in the example above is accusative feminine plural. Notice that the article τάς with the noun also is accusative feminine plural. Again, the noun κόσμου in the same example is genitive masculine singular. Notice the article τοῦ also is genitive masculine singular.

Warning: *do not confuse spelling with concord.* The article's inflection will not always be *spelled* exactly the same as the noun's inflection, but that does not mean lack of concord.

ἐκ τῆς καρδίας
"out *of the* heart" (Matt. 15:88)

Here, καρδίας is genitive feminine singular, following the "α-pure" first declension pattern. The article's inflection is τῆς, following the "η-pure" first declension pattern. The article, however, is the same case, gender, and number as the noun.

Concord of an article always will locate its associated noun. Therefore, locate the article, and you've located the noun! The following will save precious time:

♦ *Article location declares noun location.*

In other words, the article is your best friend in Greek. When you deal with third declension nouns in the next chapter (and later, participles), article concord will save the day on location. When lost in location, the article, if present, can be a life saver. Therefore, nail the article paradigms!

Position

An article not always will be positioned right in front of its associated noun. Even in English the article can be separated from its noun, as when using an adjective: "the righteous man." Greek too will sometimes have an adjective or another word between the article and its noun. A postpositive is a good example. A *postpositive* is a word that never occurs first in its clause, such as the conjunction γάρ ("for"):

τὸ <u>γὰρ</u> ἔργον κυρίου
"*for* the work of the Lord" (1 Cor. 16:10)

The conjunction γὰρ by Greek convention never is first in its clause. Thus, the conjunction comes *between* the article τὸ and its associated noun, ἔργον.

Junction

Specificity

In English, a definite article points out a noun to make that noun specific. The phrase "a tree" is non-specific; you could be referring to any tree. The phrase "the tree," in contrast, is specific; you are referring to a particular tree.

Greek articles function similarly. The word βασιλεία with no article is non-specific, so means simply "a kingdom," or just "kingdom"; you could be referring to any kingdom. The articular construction ἡ βασιλεία, in contrast, is specific; you now are referring to a particular kingdom.

(1) Non-translated specificity

Greek has a few conventions on specificity and use of the article. One convention is use of the article when English would not. The Greek article is used:

- <u>with proper names</u>: ὁ Ἰησους translated into English is simply "Jesus," not "the Jesus."
- <u>in reference to God</u>: τοῦ θεοῦ translated into English is "of God," not "of the God."
- <u>with abstract nouns</u>: ἡ ἀγάπη translated into English is simply "love," not "the love" (cf. 1 Cor. 13:13).

(2) Anarthrous specificity

Another convention on specificity is *non-use* of the article when English would. Nouns that have a distinctive character or are a unique representative of an entire class are inherently specific in the Greek mind, so do not need added specificity grammatically with the Greek article. This means a word may be anarthrous in Greek (without the article) but, properly translated from the context, will have the English definite article. Such an anarthrous noun is labeled "inherently articular," which is just a descriptive term.

Astronomical terms, such as "sun" (ἥλιος), "moon" (σελήνη), and "star" (ἀστήρ), often fit this category due to different cosmologies. The sun is unique in its class to ancient Greeks. So are the moon and stars. Other terms that often qualify for this use are "God" (θεός), "Spirit" (πνεῦμα), "world" (κόσμος), and "law" (νόμος). Context is the final arbiter on whether to translate certain anarthrous nouns using the definite article.

Grouping

The Greek article also pulls together grammatically associated words and word groups. You almost could say the article "ropes in" associated modifiers like a cowboy culling an animal from the herd. Items so "roped in" could be adjectives, prepositional phrases, or entire infinitive and participial phrases.

(1) Article Repetition

English has no equivalent to this Greek idiom. An article can be repeated in front of another phrase. Article repetition makes clear the grammatical relationship of that phrase as a modifier of the article's associated noun. For example:

ὁ ναὸς τοῦ θεοῦ ὁ ἐν τῷ οὐρανῷ
"*the* temple of God *which is* in heaven" (Rev. 11:19)

Notice the first article ὁ, used with ναός to make that noun specific, later is repeated in front of a prepositional phrase, ὁ ἐν τῷ οὐρανῷ. The repeated article "ropes in" ἐν τῷ οὐρανῷ to make clear that this phrase is a modifier of the noun ναός. We have used a relative clause to translate this adjectival function that the second article has generated.

(2) Article Pairs
English has no equivalent to this Greek idiom. Two Greek articles can occur immediately together, making a pair of articles. The first article will be associated with a later substantive; the second article is associated with an immediate substantive being pulled in as a modifier of the later substantive. For example:

ὑπὲρ τῆς τοῦ κόσμου ζωῆς
"for *the life* of the world" (Jn. 6:51)

Notice the concord. The first article, τῆς, goes with the *later* noun, ζωῆς. The second article, τοῦ, goes with the *immediately following* noun, κόσμου. This construction means the first article, τῆς, is being used to "rope in" the prepositional phrase τοῦ κόσμου as modifying the first article's associated noun of concord, ζωῆς.

Antecedent Reference

In English, an item introduced for the first time in a story will use an indefinite article. Later reference to that item, once introduced, will have a definite article: "Bob went to the kitchen and got *a* plate. He then took *the* plate and . . ." Greek is similar. While Greek does not have an indefinite article, Greek writers often will introduce an item the first time in a story in anarthrous construction; later reference to that item then will be articular.[1] For example, in Matthew's nativity story, the wise men are introduced first in 2:1; after describing Herod's reaction, Matthew's next reference to the wise men, when Herod calls for them, is articular. Thus:

... μάγοι ...
"wise men from the east came to Jerusalem" (Matt. 2:1)

... τοὺς μάγους ...
"Herod secretly called for *the* wise men" (Matt. 2:7)

Substantive Substitution

English has no equivalent to this Greek idiom. The article can take the place of a noun or pronoun (personal, demonstrative, alternative, possessive, or relative). Study the two examples below.

(1) Personal Pronoun
The article can stand for a personal pronoun. For example:

ὁ δὲ λέγει αὐτοῖς
"And *he* said to them" (Matt. 17:20)[2]

The disciples had asked Jesus about their difficulty casting out a demon. The article ὁ stands for the subject of the verb λέγει ("he") and ties back to the explicit reference, τῷ Ἰησοῦ ("to Jesus"), in verse 19. The verb's subject is masculine singular, so the article ὁ substituting as subject also is masculine singular.

(2) Demonstrative Pronoun
Another example of substitution is when the article is taking the place of a demonstrative pronoun ("this," "that," "these," "those"). A good illustration is the following composition:

---

[1] The technical term for this use is the *anaphoric* article.
[2] Here λέγει, though present tense, is translated past as part of a narrative; this use of the present tense is called the "historic present."

ὁ δὲ Πέτρος καὶ οἱ σὺν αὐτῷ
"Now Peter and *those* with him" (Lk. 9:32)

The article οἱ takes the place of the demonstrative pronoun (ἐκεῖνοι, "those"). The gender and number of οἱ (masculine plural) matches what would have been the gender and number of the pronoun had the demonstrative been used instead.

Exercise 6

1. Translate. Be ready to answer questions about article constructions.

    1.1 ἐσθίουσιν τοὺς ἄρτους. (Mk. 7:2)

    _____

    1.2 πορεύεσθε ἐν εἰρήνῃ. (Acts 16:36)

    _____

    1.3 ὀλίγον (short) καιρὸν ἔχει. (Rev. 12:12)

    _____

    1.4 πορεύεται εἰς ἔρημον (wilderness) τόπον. (Lk. 4:42*)[3]

    _____

    1.5 ἐξουσίαν ἔχει ὁ υἱὸς τοῦ ἀνθρώπου ἐπὶ τῆς γῆς. (Matt. 9:6)

    _____

---

[3] An asterisk indicates text adapted.

Chapter 6: The Article

1.6 καὶ εἰσέρχεται εἰς τὸν οἶκον τοῦ Φαρισαίου. (Lk. 7:36*)

1.7 ἔρχεται γὰρ Ἰωάννης πρὸς ὑμᾶς (you) ἐν ὁδῷ δικαιοσύνης. (Matt. 21:32*)

1.8 τί (why?) δὲ βλέπεις τὸ κάρφος (splinter) τὸ ἐν τῷ ὀφθαλμῷ τοῦ ἀδελφοῦ σου (of you = your); (Matt. 7:3)

2. Diagram 1.8. Put articles immediately before their word of concord or the word group to which they point:

 *Vocabulary 6*

ἀντί, *against* (anti-, antonym, antithesis)

ἄρτος, ὁ, *bread, loaf, food*

βλέπω, *I see*

δικαιοσύνη, ἡ, *justice, righteousness*

εἰρήνη, ἡ, *peace* (irenic)

ἕξ, *six* (hexagon)

ἐξουσία, ἡ, *authority*

καιρός, ὁ, *time, season*

ὁ, ἡ, τό, *the*

ὁδός, ἡ, *road, way* (odometer, Exodus)

οἰκία, ἡ, *house, family* (economy)

ὀφθαλμός, ὁ, *eye, sight* (ophthalmology)

σύν, *with* (synonym, synthesis)

τόπος, ὁ, *place* (topic, topography)

Φαρισαῖος, ὁ, *Pharisee*

Vocabulary notes:

(1) The article is listed in the traditional pattern of masculine, feminine, and neuter forms of the nominative singular.

(2) The ἡ following ὁδός is correct. The noun has *second* declension inflection but is *feminine* gender. Thus, article concord would be, for example, τῆς ὁδοῦ ("of the way"). This ὁδός is one of three second declension nouns that have feminine gender. Review page 46, "Feminine Second Declension."

(3) For the prepositions, consult the discussion with Vocabulary 3 and following tables at the end of Chapter 3.

Vocabulary Review 1

The following list summarizes words introduced up to this point in the grammar, generally by frequency of occurrence. The number is the chapter.

Vocabularies 1–6

ἀγάπη 5
ἄγγελος 4
ἀδελφός 4
ἀκούω 2
ἁμαρτία 5
ἀνά 3
ἄνθρωπος 4
ἀντί 6
ἀπέρχομαι 3
ἀπό 3
ἀποκρίνομαι 3
ἄρτος 6
βασιλεία 5
βλέπω 6
γῆ 5
γίνομαι 3
γινώσκω 2
γράφω 2
δέ 1
διά 1
δικαιοσύνη 6
δόξα 5

δύο 2
εἰρήνη 6
εἷς 1
εἰς 2
εἰσέρχομαι 3
ἐκ, ἐξ 2
ἐν 1
ἕξ 6
ἐξέρχομαι 3
ἐξουσία 6
ἐπί 2
ἔργον 4
ἔρχομαι 3
ἐσθίω 2
εὐαγγέλιον 4
εὑρίσκω 2
ἔχω 2
ζωή 5
ἡμέρα 5
θάλασσα 5
θέλω 2
θεός 1

Ἰησοῦς 4
Ἰωάννης 5
κάθημαι 3
καί 1
καιρός 6
καρδία 5
κατά 3
κόσμος 4
κύριος 4
λαμβάνω 2
λέγω 2
λόγος 4
λύω 2
μαθητής 5
μετά 4
ὁ, ἡ, τό 6
ὁδός 6
οἰκία 6
οὐ 1
οὐρανός 4
ὀφθαλμός 6
παρά 5

πέντε 5
περί 5
πιστεύω 2
πορεύομαι 3
πρό 4
πρός 3
προσέρχομαι 3
προφήτης 5
σημεῖον 4
σύν 6
τέκνον 4
τέσσαρες 4
τόπος 6
τρεῖς 3
υἱός 4
ὑπέρ 4
ὑπό 4
Φαρισαῖος 6
φωνή 5
Χριστός 4
ψυχή 5

Photo © Gerald L. Stevens

Fig. 7. Chariot Races. Chariot races often were a part of ancient festivals in both Greek and Roman society. Pictured in this stone relief is a Greek hoplite soldier dismounting a speeding chariot and remounting immediately as the chariot driver continues to guide the horses. This required part of the chariot race was called the *anabaton*.

Chapter 7

Third Declension

Second declension noun stems end in an omicron. Most first declension stems end in an alpha. As a result, these two declensions are called "vowel" declensions. Their stem vowels act like a verb's thematic vowels by joining endings to word stems. Sometimes these vowels interact with vowels of endings. For example, the -ου of the second declension genitive singular is really an ο stem vowel that has combined with an ο vowel ending, creating the diphthong result, -ου.

In contrast to first and second declension, third declension has no theme vowel. Further, most third declension stems end in consonants. These third declension stem consonants can interact with third declension endings in predictable ways that create the resultant forms you actually see on the end of a third declension word. First, we learn the third declension endings.

Formation

Table 7.1—Third Declension Endings

	Mas./Fem.		Neuter	
	Sing.	Plur.	Sing.	Plu.
Nom.:	-ς, --	-ες	--	-α
Gen.:	-ος	-ων	-ος	-ων
Dat.:	-ι	-σι	-ι	-σι
Acc.:	-α, -ν	-ας	--	-α

Dashes in the table mean no ending is used—the noun stem alone occurs. Note well the following:

♦ *In third declension, the -ος ending usually is genitive!*

Consonants can interact. For example, try to say a pi (π) and a sigma (σ) together. You cannot help but wind up making the sound of psi (ψ). Thus, if a third declension noun opts for the nominative singular sigma or uses the -σι of the dative plural, certain reactions could be expected.

Remember the table of stops?[1] We use that table and add a sigma to the rows. Either a complex sibilant results, or a stop drops, leaving only the sigma. Learn these interactions!

Table 7.2—Sigma Stop Interactions

labials: π, β, φ	+σ	=ψ
palatals: κ, γ, χ	+σ	=ξ
dentals: τ, δ, θ	+σ	=σ

Third declension shows other reactions. These reaction patterns plus the sigma stop interactions above yield twenty or more paradigms for third declension. That could be intimidating! Good news: we will not learn all these paradigms. Why?

Well, as we cut through this dense undergrowth we see a clearing where we can set camp. The clearing is in summary statements about paradigm patterns. A number of these statements are "always" or "almost always" true. If you nail these, you are on your way to conquering third declension. These third declension patterns are not as difficult as first appears.[2]

---

[1] Table 1.5, p. 8.
[2] Realize, though, that a few third declension inflections look like certain second and first declension inflections. Such third declension inflec-

Table 7.3—3D Inflection Shortcuts

Nominative Case:
  (1) Singular is memorized (vocabulary).
    -ς frequently is nominative singular
    -ις, -υς, -ης always are nominative singular:
      • ἐλπίς (dental stem, -α accusative)
      • χάρις (dental stem, -ν accusative)
      • ἰχθύς (υ stem, -υ throughout)
      • ἱερεύς (ευ stem)
      • πραΰτης (-ητος stem)
  (2) -ους can be nominative singular.
      • ὀδούς (ντ stem with ς nominative)
  (3) -ες always is nominative plural.
  (4) -εις is nominative or accusative plural.
      • πίστεις (-ι stem, ε before vowels)
      • ἱερεῖς (-ευ stem)
  (5) -α is either nominative or accusative.[3]

Genitive Case:
  (1) -ος almost always is genitive singular.
    Exception:
      • ἔθνος (εσ stem with ος nominative)
  (2) -ους can be genitive singular.
      • ὀδούς (ντ stem with ς nominative)
  (3) -εως always is genitive singular.
  (4) -ων almost always is genitive plural.
    Exceptions:
      • ἄρχων (ντ stem with no ending)
      • αἰών (ν stem with long vowel)
      • εἰκών (ν stem with short vowel)

---

tions represent different case and number than their second or first declension counterpart. That is, you still have to be aware of a noun's declension to parse the case of an inflectional ending correctly.

[3]Nominative singular is represented in neuter -μα, -ματ nouns.

Dative Case:
   (1) Final -ι always is dative.[4]

Accusative Case:
   (1) -α is either accusative or nominative.[5]
   (2) -ν always is accusative singular.[6]
   (3) -ας always is accusative plural.
   (4) -εις is nominative or accusative plural.
      - πίστις (-ι stem, ε before vowels)
      - ἱερεύς (-ευ stem)

We provide tables divided into three types: (1) "always" = inflectional forms distinct to case and number; (2) "almost always" = almost distinct forms; (3) "rare birds" = unusual.

Table 7.4—3D Inflection: Always

	Mas./Fem. Sing.	Mas./Fem. Plur.	Neuter Sing.	Neuter Plu.
Nom.:	-ις, -υς, -ης	-ες	--	--
Gen.:	-εως	--	--	--
Dat.:	-ι	-σι	-ι	-σι
Acc.:	-ν	-ας	--	--

---

[4]Usually with a consonant: -βι, -δι, -κι, -νι, -ξι, -ρι, -σι, -τι, -ψι. Sibilants -ξι, -σι, -ψι may add a movable nu: -ξιν, -σιν, -ψιν. On rare occasion, the final iota is part of a diphthong, either -ει or -υι. This final iota formulation, then, is completely distinct and can never be confused with the *nominative* plural οι or αι of the vowel declensions.

[5]Nominative singular is represented in neuter -μα, -ματ nouns.

[6]When not genitive plural -ων or sibilant dative plurals with movable ν (-ξιν, -σιν, -ψιν).

Table 7.5—3D Inflection: Almost Always

	Mas./Fem.		Neuter	
	Sing.	Plur.	Sing.	Plu.
Nom.:	(-μα)	--	--	-α
Gen.:	-ος	-ων	-ος	-ων
Dat.:	--	--	--	--
Acc.:	-α	--	--	-α

Table 7.6—3D Inflection: Rare Birds

	Mas./Fem.		Neuter	
	Sing.	Plur.	Sing.	Plu.
Nom.:	-ος, -ους, -ων	-εις	--	-η
Gen.:	-ους	--	--	--
Dat.:	--	--	--	--
Acc.:	-ος	-εις	--	-η

Paradigms

Dictionary Format

The dictionary will give a second entry after the nominative singular, as we have done in the table title below, which will be either the entire genitive singular form or just the genitive singular stem ending. This entry format is because the genitive singular form provides the actual stem for the rest of the inflection. Providing this genitive form is necessary because nominative forms in third declension often have changed the look of the noun stem due to nominative ending interactions.

Typical Paradigm

Table 7.7—Typical: σάρξ, σαρκός, ἡ

	Singular	Plural	Gloss
Nom.:	σάρξ	σάρκες	flesh
Gen.:	σαρκός	σαρκῶν	of, from flesh
Dat.:	σαρκί	σαρξί(ν)	to, in, by flesh
Acc.:	σάρκα	σάρκας	flesh

Many third declension nouns show a similar pattern to the inflection of σάρξ, once you realize that the nominative singular form has gone through a stop reaction that hides the sigma ending in a complex sibilant. The word ἐλπίς is nearly exactly the same. The nominative singular sigma ending that is hidden in σάρξ, shows up in ἐλπίς, even though the dental stop, δ, of the ἐλπίς stem has dropped (ἐλπίδς→ ἐλπίς; ἐλπίδσι→ ἐλπίσι). The word χάρις has a similar dental reaction as does ἐλπίς in the nominative singular and dative plural (χάρις, χάρισι), only opting for a nu rather than an alpha in the accusative singular (χάριν).

A good number of third declension nouns, then, are quite similar to σάρξ. Once you memorize the vocabulary word, you have the nominative singular form and genitive stem and often can guess the look of the rest of the inflection just on the basis of the σάρξ paradigm.

Nom. Sing., Dat. Plu. Pattern

The noun σάρξ also illustrates another pattern you will see regularly in third declension to which we have referred already:

frequent nominative singular and dative plural reactions. Why do they change their look in nominative singular and dative plural? Because these inflections involve a sigma. Sigma is one of the most reactive consonants. The volatility of sigma is why for third declension you need to be aware of sigma stop consonant interactions. With σάρξ, for example, the kappa of the noun stem has combined with the sigma of the nominative and dative inflections (ς and σι) in the standard sigma stop interaction (σάρκς→σάρξ; σαρκσί→σαρξί).

Significant Paradigm

Table 7.8—Significant: ἄρχων, -οντος, ὁ

	Singular	Plural	Gloss
Nom.:	ἄρχων	ἄρχοντες	ruler(s)
Gen.:	ἄρχοντος	ἀρχόντων	of, from a ruler(s)
Dat.:	ἄρχοντι	ἄρχουσι(ν)	to, in, by a ruler(s)
Acc.:	ἄρχοντα	ἄρχοντας	ruler(s)

We label the paradigm ἄρχων "significant" not as a third declension noun paradigm. In truth, *nouns* following the pattern of ἄρχων are not frequent in the New Testament. However, the present active *participle* has *exactly* these endings, and the participle form you do see often enough in the New Testament. You might as well learn the ἄρχων pattern now for less work later. Nominative singular and dative plural show reactions, as with numerous third declension nouns.[7]

---

[7]Unfortunately, this -ουσι *noun* ending can be confused easily with the -ουσι *verb* ending. Often, though, noun stems are distinct from verb stems.

Neuter Paradigm

Table 7.9—Neuter: σῶμα, -τος, τό

	Singular	Plural	Gloss
Nom.:	σῶμα	σώματα	body(ies)
Gen.:	σώματος	σωμάτων	of, from a body(ies)
Dat.:	σώματι	σώμασι(ν)	to, in, by a body(ies)
Acc.:	σῶμα	σώματα	body(ies)

The word σῶμα represents a special group of New Testament words, always neuter gender. These neuter nouns always have this typical "-μα, -ματ" pattern in their inflection.

Distinctive Paradigm

Table 7.10—Distinctive: πίστις, -εως, ἡ

	Singular	Plural	Gloss
Nom.:	πίστις	πίστεις	faith(s)
Gen.:	πίστεως	πίστεων	of, from a faith(s)
Dat.:	πίστει	πίστεσι(ν)	to, in, by a faith(s)
Acc.:	πίστιν	πίστεις	faith(s)

The word πίστις has distinctive inflection characteristics. Several New Testament words follow this pattern. Unique is the -εως of the genitive singular.[8] Unusual is the -εις of the nominative and accusative plural. You will see this -εις inflection in some pronouns and some numbers, so don't let this one fly by too fast.

---

[8] A genitive form coming from Attic Greek dialect, so sometimes called the "Attic genitive."

Odd Paradigm

Table 7.11—Odd: ἔθνος, ἔθνους, τό

	Singular	Plural	Gloss
Nom.:	ἔθνος	ἔθνη	nation(s)
Gen.:	ἔθνους	ἐθνῶν	of, from a nation(s)
Dat.:	ἔθνει	ἔθνεσι(ν)	to, in, by a nation(s)
Acc.:	ἔθνος	ἔθνη	nation(s)

A few words follow this peculiar ἔθνος pattern. Genitive, accusative singular and the nominative, accusative plural are odd. You will locate the nominative singular correctly simply because this -ος form is exactly like the second declension nominative singular -ος, and violates the observation that third declension -ος endings most often are not nominative.

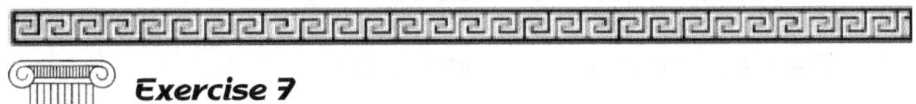

Exercise 7

1. Complete the following chart of sigma stop reactions:

   labials: ____, ____, ____ + σ = ____
   palatals: ____, ____, ____ + σ = ____
   dentals: ____, ____, ____ + σ = ____

2. The "always" third declension endings are dependably distinct:

   2.1 ____, ____, and ____ always are nominative singular.

   2.2 ____ always is nominative plural.

2.3 _____ always is genitive singular.

2.4 _____ (not movable) always is accusative singular.

2.5 _____ always is accusative plural.

2.6 _____ always is nominative or accusative plural.

2.7 _____ always is dative when final.

3. The interior cases of the third declension are pretty easy to identify, since they are fairly dependably distinct, because:

   _____ (sg.) and _____ (pl.) almost always are genitive.

4. Finally, the inflection -α only has to be distinguished as to whether:

   4.1 _____ singular for masculine or feminine.

   4.2 _____ singular for -μα, -ματ neuter nouns.

   4.3 _____ or _____ plural for neuter.

5. Translate. Be ready to locate nouns.

   5.1 αἱ πόλεις τῶν ἐθνῶν ἔπεσαν (fell). (Rev. 16:19)

   _____

   5.2 ἢ εἰς τὸ ὄνομα Παύλου ἐβαπτίσθητε; (were you baptized) (1 Cor. 1:13)

   _____

   5.3 εὑρίσκει τὴν πίστιν ἐπὶ τῆς γῆς; (Lk. 18:8*)

   _____

Chapter 7: Third Declension

5.4 χάρις ἔλεος (mercy) εἰρήνη ἀπὸ θεοῦ πατρὸς (1 Tim. 1:2)

5.5 ἐν τῇ σαρκί μου (my) ὑπὲρ (for the sake of) τοῦ σώματος αὐτοῦ (his) (Col. 1:24)

5.6 οὖν πορεύεται ὁ Πετρός ἀπὸ πόλεως εἰς πόλιν.

5.7 Τότε ὁ Ἰησοῦς λέγει τοῖς ὄχλοις καὶ τοῖς μαθηταῖς. (Mt. 23:1*)

5.8 οὐ γάρ ἐστιν (is) ἀνὴρ ἐκ γυναικὸς ἀλλὰ γυνὴ ἐξ ἀνδρός· (1 Cor. 11:8)

5.9 τότε πορεύεται καὶ λαμβάνει ἕτερα (other) πνεύματα ἑπτὰ (Lk. 11:26*)

5.10 Καὶ λαμβάνει τὸ βιβλαρίδιον (scroll) ἐκ τῆς χειρὸς τοῦ ἀγγέλου. (Rev. 10:10*)

___

 **Vocabulary 7**

ἀλλά, *but*

ἀνήρ, ἀνδρός, ὁ, *man, husband* (android)

γάρ, *for*

γυνή, -αικός, ἡ, *woman, wife* (gynecology)

ἔθνος, -ους, τό, *nation, people, Gentile* (ethnic)

ἑπτά, *seven* (heptagon)

ἤ, *or, either, nor, than*

ἰδού, *behold!*

καθώς, *as, just as*

μέν, *on the one hand, indeed*

ὄνομα, -ατος, τό, *name* (pseudonym)

οὖν, *therefore*

ὄχλος, ὁ, *crowd, multitude*

πατήρ, πατρός, ὁ, *father* (patriarch)

Παῦλος, ὁ, *Paul*

Πέτρος, ὁ, *Peter*

πίστις, -εως, ἡ, *faith*

πνεῦμα, -ατος, τό, *spirit* (pneumatic)

πόλις, -εως, ἡ, *city, town* (metropolis)

σάρξ, σαρκός, ἡ, *flesh, body* (sarcophagus)

σῶμα, -ματος, τό, *body* (psychosomatic)

τέ, *and*

τότε, *then*

χάρις, -ιτος, ἡ, *grace, favor* (Eucharist)

χείρ, χειρός, ἡ, *hand* (chiropractic)

Vocabulary notes:

(1) Review the use of conjunctions, pp. 451-52.

(2) The second entry in third declension forms indicates either the genitive singular form (ἀνήρ, ἀνδρός) or the genitive singular ending (γυνή, -αικός).

(3) The third declension nominative form of γυνή is simply called "irregular." Other γυνή forms follow typical patterns.

(4) Both ἀνήρ and πατήρ "syncopate" (drop stem vowels to bring consonants together), making a "trill," which is a common Mediterranean speech pattern (see the genitive form ἀνδρός above; compare Spanish "r").

(5) The conjunction γάρ is a postpositive. A *postpositive* is a word that never occurs first in its clause—a Greek idiom. In English, conjunctions always are first in their clause. In Greek, some words are never first in their clause, even if they are conjunctions, such as γάρ and δέ. So one might see οὐ γάρ ἐστιν, as in Exercise 5.8, not the English order with the conjunction first in the clause (never γὰρ οὐ ἐστιν). The conjunction still is translated into normal English idiom as first in its clause.

Photo © Gerald L. Stevens

Fig. 8. Gladiator Stele. This stele memorializing gladiator fights with wild beasts alludes to the raw violence of these wildly popular public displays. Herod the Great condemned criminals to wild beasts in the amphitheater in Jerusalem (Josephus *Antiquities* 15.8.1). After the tragic fall of Jerusalem to the Romans in A.D. 70, Jewish captives were consigned to death by wild beasts (Josephus *Wars* 7.3.1).

The gladiatorial burial ground at Ephesus was discovered in 1993, about 300 yards from the ancient theater/stadium complex. (On the theater at Ephesus, see p. 174.) These bones date to about A.D. 200-300, the height of gladiatorial combat. This discovery has allowed the first mass autopsy ever performed on gladiator remains. A wealth of new information has surfaced, especially on diet, training, and combat, that defies traditional depictions. For example, gladiators were heavily built, bulking up on a rich carbohydrate diet to help absorb cutting blows in the arena. They fought barefoot on floors covered in sand to absorb their blood. Gladiators had excellent medical care, even rivaling that of today. They often employed their own personal physicians. The famous doctor, Galen, personal physician to the emperor Marcus Aurelius (161–180), treated gladiators at Ephesus. Even with such medical care, most Ephesian gladiators died their first year of combat.

Paul often used strong images in his letters, one of the strongest being his enigmatic comment evoking the gladiatorial violence of the Roman world: "But even if with human hope only I fought with wild beasts at Ephesus" (1 Cor. 15:32). Due to a similar reference by the martyred church father, Ignatius, referring to his Roman captors (*To the Romans* 5.1), most interpreters have understood Paul's remark as metaphorical. Others, however, have taken Paul's words as literal in order to argue for an Ephesian imprisonment of Paul.

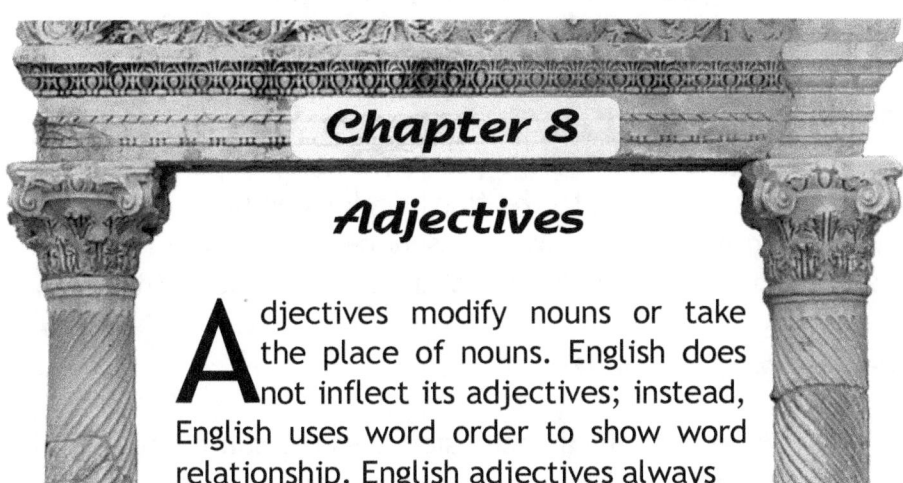

Chapter 8

Adjectives

Adjectives modify nouns or take the place of nouns. English does not inflect its adjectives; instead, English uses word order to show word relationship. English adjectives always are placed immediately *before* the noun they modify. Notice how you always say *"good* food," not "food *good."* Poetic style catches our attention by changing expected word functions or order: "Star light, star *bright* . . ." The second phrase is the hook in that opening line of poetry, because the adjective has had its order "misplaced" *after* the noun.

Inflection

Greek uses inflection to show word relationship more than word order. To show which noun the adjective is modifying, Greek inflects the adjective like the noun modified. You have seen this process at work already with the Greek article (and in the next chapter for possessive, demonstrative pronouns).

Good news! The bulk of adjectives follow second and first declension patterns; a minority follows third declension. So, for adjective inflection, you have nothing new to learn.

Mixed Inflection

Certain adjectives *mix inflection per gender,* but if you already know the three declension patterns in general, mixing patterns per gender will not present a problem for recognizing location. For example, the little adjective πᾶς ("all") is third declension in masculine (πᾶς) and neuter forms (πᾶν), but first declension in feminine forms (πᾶσα). Again, ταχύς ("quick") is similar in its inflection to the third declension noun πίστις, with that distinctive -εως genitive masculine singular form (ταχέως) and the -εις of the nominative and accusative plural (ταχεῖς).

Gender and Concord

Remember that third declension uses the same inflection for both masculine and feminine nouns (as well as a few *second* declension adjectives; e.g., ἔρημος, "wilderness," and αἰώνιος, "forever"). These are called "two-termination" adjectives since they have only two sets of endings for the three genders. So, the two-termination adjective "eternal" (αἰώνιος) when modifying the feminine noun "life" (ζωή) would be ζωὴ αἰώνιος. A frequent form of this phrase in the New Testament is the accusative singular: ζωὴν αἰώνιον.

Concord Issues

The adjective αἰώνιος raises concord issues. We treat these briefly, but translation experience is the best teacher.

First, some feminine adjectives follow an "α-pure" pattern, but others follow "η-pure." For example, ἀγαθός ("good") is "η-pure" as feminine singular (ἀγαθή), but ἅγιος ("holy") is "α-pure" (ἁγία). Remember that the "α-pure" pattern has the same ending for genitive singular and accusative plural (-ας), which can create a minor problem for location.[1]

Second, gender may confuse you. Thus, ὁδός ("road") while neuter to you is feminine in Greek. Also, ὁδός is one of those rare *second* declension feminine nouns. That is, though feminine, ὁδός is inflected *second* declension, not first.[2] Observe:

---

[1] Table 5.2, p. 54.
[2] See discussion p. 46.

τῆς ἁγίας ὁδοῦ
"the *holy* path"

The article τῆς is first declension "η-pure" in feminine singular, but the adjective ἅγιος is first declension "α-pure." The noun ὁδός is feminine *second* declension. So, article, adjective, and noun are all in concord, though each spelled differently!

Again, some words are *first* declension in their inflection but *masculine* in their gender, such as προφήτης.[3] Observe:

τοὺς ἀγαθοὺς προφήτας
"the *good* prophets"

Here, the *masculine* accusative plural, προφήτας, requires a *masculine* form of the adjective ἀγαθός, which has second declension inflection for its masculine forms.

Function

Attributive

More significant than an adjective's inflection is its function. We originally said an adjective modifies.[4] This statement is true but oversimplifies. Adjectives actually have three functions.

The *attributive* function is attributing a characteristic or a quality to substantives. Attributive is the "modifying" role. This function is the adjective's main job description, the role you find most adjectives playing: "She is a *good* student."

Substantival

The *substantival* function is substituting for a noun. Substantival is the "surrogate" role. This function is the adjective's job

---
[3]Table 5.8, p. 56.
[4]English 1, "Words," p. 447.

as subject or some other noun role. Note, as subject: "*Good* is achieved"; as direct object: "We want *the good* of all."

Predicative

The *predicative* function is as a predicate adjective. Predicative is just a special category of substantival function. This function is the adjective's job when placed in the predicate of copulative verbs (the intransitives "be" and "become"): "She is *good*."

Attributive, substantival, and predicative are the three adjective functions. To conquer these functions in Greek, note:

♦ *The key to adjective function is article construction.*

Construction

Articular Construction

(1) Attributive Function
Attributive function is use of the adjective to attribute a quality to a noun. In common parlance we would say the adjective "modifies" the noun. A modifying (attributive) function can be made clear in Greek by using the article. An articular construction of the adjective is  the "roping in" function we discussed in the previous chapter.[5]

The table below illustrates attributive use of articular adjectives. Notice that these articular adjectives are attributive, regardless whether the adjective comes before or after the noun, or whether the noun itself is articular.

---

[5]See the section on "Grouping," p. 67.

Table 8.1—Articular Construction

ὁ ἀγαθὸς ἄνθρωπος
"the *good* person" (Lk. 6:45)

τὸ πνεῦμα τὸ ἅγιον
"the *Holy* Spirit" (Mk. 13:11)

From this construction we can state a dictum that is nice to hang your hat on. For Greek adjectives:

♦ *Articular adjectives always are attributive.*

That is, if a noun in concord is cruising the neighborhood.

(2) Substantival Function

Our caveat above covers substantival use. As a substantive, the adjective substitutes in a noun role (subject/object). An adjective by itself (no noun in concord in the neighborhood) is a dead give-a-way to the substantival use. Note:

ὅτι δὲ ἐγείρονται οἱ νεκροί, καὶ Μωϋσῆς . . .
"and that *the dead* are raised, even Moses . . ." (Lk. 20:37)

The οἱ νεκροί adjective is articular, but no noun in concord is in the neighborhood. Here, οἱ νεκροί is used as subject of the verb in a substantival role. For substantival adjectives, gender could be included in the translation for clarity:

καὶ αἱ λοιπαὶ σὺν αὐταῖς
"and *the rest of the women* with them" (Lk. 24:10)

Anarthrous Construction

The articular dictum given above is pleasant relief against the ambiguity of anarthrous adjectives. A negative corollary related to adjective construction is:

♦ *Anarthrous adjectives are ambiguous.*

What do we mean? We mean deciding whether an adjective is to be understood as attributive, substantival, or predicative. An *anarthrous* adjective could be *any* of these three.

(1) Attributive Function
Adjectives do not *have* to be articular to be attributive. An anarthrous adjective *could* be attributive. Such attributive use is likely if *both* adjective *and* noun are anarthrous. Thus:

πᾶν δένδρον ἀγαθὸν
"every *good* tree" (Mt. 7:17)

The adjective ἀγαθός is anarthrous and is used attributively.

(2) Substantival Function
An anarthrous adjective also *could* be substantival. Such a substantival use is likely if no noun in concord is nearby. That is, an anarthrous adjective by itself likely is substantival (similar to articular construction). Thus:

πολλοὶ γάρ εἰσιν κλητοί, ὀλίγοι δὲ ἐκλεκτοί.
"For *many* are *called* but *few* are *chosen*." (Mt. 22:14)

This parallel construction uses four substantival adjectives! Both πολλοί and ὀλίγοι are functioning as subjects, and the κλητοί and ἐκλεκτοί are functioning as predicate adjectives (for the copulative verb εἰσιν, from εἰμί, "I am").

(3) Predicative Function
A copulative is an intransitive verb that may take a complement that completes its meaning.[6] The *predicate adjective* is the complement of a copulative verb. This adjective further de-

---

[6]You may want to review the section on intransitive verbs, pp. 469-70.

scribes or limits the subject of the copulative verb. The copulative verb γίνομαι already has been met in Chapter 3.

a.) The Verb Εἰμί

We now present the king of the Greek copulatives, εἰμί. Its inflection is different than what you have learned. This verb comes from the second of the two Greek verb conjugations.[7]

Table 8.2—The Copulative Verb Εἰμί

εἰμί	I am
εἶ	you are (sg.)
ἐστί(ν)	he (she, it) is
ἐσμέν	we are
ἐστέ	you are (pl.)
εἰσί(ν)	they are

i.) Conjugation of Εἰμί. Your best approach for learning these forms of εἰμί is simply to treat each of the six inflections as six vocabulary words. A few notes are in order.

First, all forms of εἰμί are enclitic except the one form that is a monosyllable, εἶ. This means in composition you will not see any accent on forms of εἰμί as you do in the table, and you may see more than one accent on the word coming before εἰμί to compensate (e.g., κύριός ἐστιν or δοῦλοί εἰσιν).

Second, εἰμί does not have voice. The location of any form of εἰμί would leave off the voice component. Thus, ἐσμέν is present indicative, first person plural, *not* present *active* indicative, first person plural.

---

[7] Called "μι verbs" because their first person singular form uses the inflection -μι. The conjugation you have learned is called the "omega verb" conjugation for an obviously similar reason.

ii.) Copulative Function of Εἰμί. Εἰμί is a copulative verb linking predicate with subject. Thus, a predicate expressed with εἰμί is complementing the subject. To show that the predicate complements the subject and is not the object of a transitive verb, the copulative predicate is *nominative* case, *not* accusative. A nominative noun in the predicate is called a *predicate noun* to indicate its copulative function. Similarly, a nominative adjective in the predicate is called a *predicate adjective* to indicate its copulative function. Both adjective and noun could be classed together as *predicate nominatives*.

You need to know this, because when you hit a form of εἰμί or γίνομαι you often encounter *two nominatives*. One nominative will be the subject; the other will be part of the predicate. The question is, which? Since order *is* important in English, how do you decide which Greek nominative to put as subject before the verb and which to put as predicate after the verb?

iii.) Levels of Precedence for Εἰμί. We can sort this out by noting a hierarchy for Greek predicate grammar. Three levels of precedence make this decision straightforward. We first give a graphic summary, then offer New Testament examples. In our examples of levels of precedence we will underline the <u>subject nominative</u> and double underline the <u>predicate nominative</u>.

Table 8.3—Subject vs. Predicate Nominatives

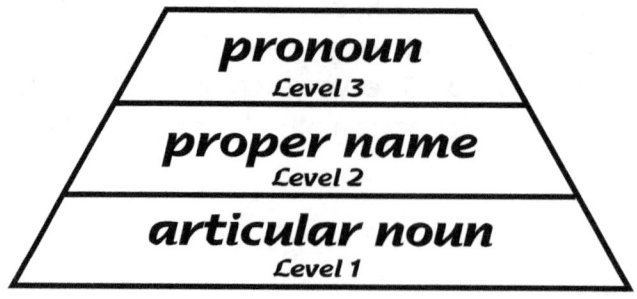

Level 1—Articular Noun. Level one is the substantive versus substantive. *An articular substantive is subject.* With two nouns as the nominative substantives:

κύριος γάρ ἐστιν τοῦ σαββάτου ὁ υἱὸς τοῦ ἀνθρώπου.
"For the Son of Man is Lord of the sabbath." (Mt. 12:8)

With adjective and noun as the two nominative substantives:

Πιστὸς δέ ἐστιν ὁ κύριος
"But the Lord is faithful" (2 Thess. 3:3)

An obvious but rare exception is within poetic phrasing. The predicate nominative is expressed first for poetic emphasis:

μακάριοί ἐστε
"Blessed are you" (Lk. 6:22)

What about when both nominatives are symmetrical in their construction, that is, both nominatives are articular, or both anarthrous? That decision is a coin toss—simply best judgment based on context. Compare the two different translations of Mt. 6:22 below:

Ὁ λύχνος τοῦ σώματός ἐστιν ὁ ὀφθαλμός.
"The lamp of the body is the eye." (Mt. 6:22, ASV)
"The eye is the lamp of the body." (Mt. 6:22, NRSV)

Level 2—Proper Name. Level two is the proper name versus substantive. *The proper name is subject.* Thus:

Ἰωάννης ἐστὶν ὄνομα αὐτοῦ.
"'John' is his name." (Lk. 1:63)

Level 3—Pronoun. Level three is a pronoun versus anything. *The pronoun is subject* (your Rocky Balboa). Thus:

ἐγώ εἰμι ἡ ὁδὸς
"I am the way" (Jn. 14:6)

οὗτός ἐστιν ὁ ἀντίχριστος
"This one is the antichrist" (1 Jn. 2:22)

ἥτις ἐστὶν Ἁγάρ
"Which is Hagar" (Gal. 4:24)

Τοῦτο γάρ ἐστιν θέλημα τοῦ θεοῦ
"For this is the will of God" (1 Thess. 4:3)

b.) Verbless Predicative Function

i.) General Rule. English requires an explicit form of the verb "to be" for expressing predicative function. Greek does not. Greek can use a specific anarthrous construction to create a *predicate adjective* that is *without* explicit use of the verb εἰμί. Here is the construction dictum that guides recognizing this "verbless" predicative idiom in Greek:

♦ *Anarthrous adjectives with articular nouns are predicative if both are nominative.*

The articular noun is the key. If the nominative noun is articular, an anarthrous nominative adjective nearby is predicative. For such a construction, you would insert a form of the verb "to be" in English translation, even though this verb does not "show up" in Greek. Thus:

πιστὸς ὁ θεός
"God *is* faithful" (1 Cor. 1:9)

Here, the anarthrous nominative adjective πιστός is used as a predicate adjective, specifically because the nominative noun θεός is articular. English has to supply the correct form of the copulative verb "to be" for an appropriate translation. Reverse the order (articular noun, adjective) and the translation is still predicative if the noun is articular:

ἡ ἐντολὴ ἁγία
"The commandment *is* holy" (Rom. 7:12)

In poetic speech, you intentionally can reverse the subject noun and predicate adjective position in English for emphasis:

μακάριοι οἱ εἰρηνοποιοί
"Blessed are the peacemakers" (Mt. 5:19)

ii.) Adjective Exceptions (always attributive). Exceptions to this predicative construction are a few adjectives regularly used as attributive regardless the construction of a nominative noun. Examples would include ὅλος ("entire," "whole"), πᾶς ("all," "every"), μόμος ("alone," "only"), πολύς ("much," "many"), as well as both possessive (ἐμός, ἡμετερος, etc.) and demonstrative pronouns (οὗτος, εκεῖνος). Note the following examples:

ὅλος ὁ νόμος
"the *whole* law" (Mt. 22:40)

πάντες οἱ ἄγγελοι
"*all* the angels" (Mt. 25:31)

μόνος ὁ ἀρχιερεύς
"*only* the high priest" (Heb. 9:11)

You generally will not miss translating these adjectives, since they occur so much in the New Testament that you will get used to them in a hurry. Also, a copulative verb translation often does not "work" in these cases anyway.

Diagramming

Attributive adjectives diagram underneath the element they modify. Substantival adjectives are put in the slot for which they function, usually subject. Predicate adjectives are part of a copulative construction. Their slot after the copulative verb has a slanted line instead of the direct object's vertical line. The following examples illustrate these forms.

Attributive

ἡ τελεία ἀγάπη ἔξω βάλλει τὸν φόβον
"*Perfect* love casts out fear." (1 Jn. 4:18)

Substantival and Predicative

πολλοὶ γάρ εἰσιν κλητοί
"For *many* are *called*" (Mt. 22:14)

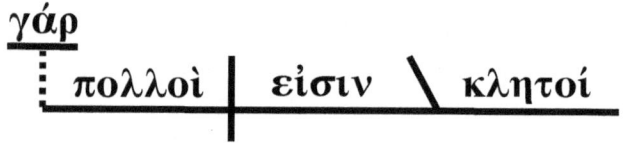

Verbless Predicative

πιστὸς ὁ θεός
"God *is* faithful" (1 Cor. 1:9)

ὁ θεός | (ἐστιν) \ πιστὸς

Chapter 8: Adjectives

 **Exercise 8**

1. Let's review declension endings.

    1.1 Second Declension

    Mas./Fem.   *Neuter*

Sing.	Plu.	Sing.	Plu.
___	___	___	___
___	___	___	___
___	___	___	___
___	___	___	___

    1.2 First Declension

    Feminine   *Mas.*

α-Sng.	η-Sng.	Mix S.	-ης Nom.	Plurals
___	___	___	___	___
___	___	___	___	___
___	___	___	___	___
___	___	___	___	___

    1.3 Third Declension

    Mas./Fem.   *Neuter*

Sing.	Plu.	Sing.	Plu.
___	___	___	___
___	___	___	___
___	___	___	___
___	___	___	___

2. Explain the three adjective functions:

   2.1 Attributive: _____

   _____

   2.2 Substantival: _____

   _____

   2.3 Predicative: _____

   _____

3. Identify the adjective, adjective function, and sentence role in the following sentences:

   3.1 *The poor man had no help.*

   adj.: _____ function: _____

   sentence role: _____

   3.2 *You have the poor with you always.*

   adj.: _____ function: _____

   sentence role: _____

   3.3 *The poor need our help.*

   adj.: _____ function: _____

   sentence role: _____

   3.4 *The poor are helpless.*

   a. adj.: _____ function: _____

   sentence role: _____

   b. adj.: _____ function: _____

   sentence role: _____

4. Working with Greek adjectives:

Chapter 8: Adjectives

4.1 The key to adjective function in Greek is _____ _____.

4.2 Articular adjectives always are _____.

4.3 Anarthrous adjectives are _____.

4.4 Anarthrous adjectives with _____ nouns are predicative if both are _____.

5. Complete the following paradigm for εἰμί:

Inflection		Gloss
_____	=	_____
_____	=	_____
_____	=	_____
_____	=	_____
_____	=	_____
_____	=	_____

6. Define a copulative verb:

   _____

   _____

7. Deciding between two nominatives as subject or predicate in copulative constructions:

   7.1 Level 1 _____ vs. _____.
   The one with the _____ is subject.

   7.2 Level 2 _____ vs. _____.
   The _____ is subject.

   7.3 Level 3 _____ vs. _____.

The _____ is subject.

7.4 Circle the subject nominative; double underline the predicate nominative; explain the precedence:

7.4a ἐγώ εἰμι ὁ ἄρτος τῆς ζωῆς.

7.4b Ἰησοῦς ἐστιν ὁ χριστός.

7.4c τὸ φῶς τὸ ἐν σοὶ σκότος ἐστίν.

8. Translate. Be ready to identify adjectives and their use. (You should look up unknown words in a Greek dictionary; you have a dictionary in the back of your UBS text.)[8]

8.1 μόνος οὐκ εἰμί. (Jn. 8:16)

8.2 καλὸν τὸ ἅλας. (Mk. 9:50) (Hint: verbless predicative)

8.3 ἔχει ζωὴν αἰώνιον. (Jn. 3:36)

8.4 δέκα καὶ ὀκτὼ ἔτη (ἔτος). (Lk. 13:16)

---

[8]*The Greek New Testament, Fourth Edition,* Kurt Aland et al. eds., in cooperation with the Institute for New Testament Textual Research, Münster/Westphalia (New York: United Bible Societies, 1966, 1968, 1975, 1983, 1993), an "edited" Greek text produced by scholars. Many manuscripts available today were not even known to the King James translators; e.g., 𝔓46, a Pauline epistles collection including Hebrews but not the Pastorals (about A.D. 200), was not published until the 1930s. This early manuscript is an important witness to the text of the New Testament. (For an image of 𝔓46, see p. 404.)

Chapter 8: Adjectives

8.5 οὐδενὶ οὐδὲν λέγουσιν. (Mk. 16:8*)

8.6 καὶ ὅλης τῆς ἐκκλησίας (Rm. 16:23)

8.7 βλέπει ἄλλους δύο ἀδελφούς. (Mt. 4:21*)

8.8 Τότε παραλαμβάνει (παραλαμβάνω) αὐτὸν (him) ὁ διάβολος εἰς τὴν ἁγίαν πόλιν. (Mt. 4:5)

8.9 καὶ ὁράω τοὺς νεκρούς, τοὺς μεγάλους καὶ τοὺς μικρούς (μικρός). (Rev. 20:12*)

8.10 μετὰ (after) δὲ πολὺν χρόνον (χρόνος) ἔρχεται ὁ κύριος τῶν δούλων ἐκείνων (those). (Mt. 25:19)

8.11 ἐκπορεύονται (ἐκπορεύομαι) πρὸς αὐτὸν (him) πᾶσα ἡ Ἰουδαία χώρα καὶ οἱ Ἱεροσολυμῖται (Ἱεροσολυμίτης) πάντες. (Mk. 1:5*)

8.12 καὶ λέγει αὐτῷ· (to him) πᾶς ἄνθρωπος πρῶτον τὸν καλὸν οἶνον (οἶνος) τίθησιν (he serves). (Jn. 2:10)

_____

_____

8.13 ὁ ἀγαθὸς ἄνθρωπος ἐκ τοῦ ἀγαθοῦ θησαυροῦ (θησαυρός) τῆς καρδίας προφέρει (προφέρω) τὸ ἀγαθόν. (Lk. 6:45)

_____

_____

9. Diagram 8.1 and 8.13

   9.1 [8.1]

   μόνος οὐκ εἰμί.

   9.2 [8.13]

   ὁ ἀγαθὸς ἄνθρωπος ἐκ τοῦ ἀγαθοῦ θησαυροῦ τῆς καρδίας προφέρει τὸ ἀγαθόν.

Chapter 8: Adjectives

 **Vocabulary 8**

ἀγαθός, ἀγαθή, ἀγαθόν, *good, useful*

ἅγιος, ἁγία, ἅγιον, *holy* (hagiographa)

αἰώνιος, αἰώνιον, *eternal* (eon)

ἄλλος, ἄλλη, ἄλλον, *other, another* (allegory)

εἰμί, *I am* (takes predicate nom.)

Ἰουδαῖος, Ἰουδαία, Ἰουδαῖον, *Jew, Jewish*

καλός, καλή, καλόν, *beautiful, good* (calligraphy)

μέγας, μεγάλη, μέγα, *great, large, loud* (megahertz, megaphone, omega)

μόνος, μόνη, μόνον, *only, alone, deserted* (monarch, monograph, monologue, monotheism)

νεκρός, νεκρά, νεκρόν, *dead* (necrosis)

ὀκτώ, *eight* (octopus)

ὅλος, ὅλη, ὅλον, *whole, entire, complete* (holistic)

οὐδείς, οὐδεμία, οὐδέν, *no, no one, nothing*

πᾶς, πᾶσα, πᾶν, *every, all* (panorama, pantheism)

πολύς, πολλή, πολύ, *much, many, great, large* (polygon, polytheism, polygamy)

πρῶτος, πρώτη, πρῶτον, *first, foremost* (proton, prototype, protagonist, protoplasm)

Vocabulary notes:

(1) Entry order of adjectives is the traditional masculine, feminine, neuter. Remember that neuter interior forms repeat masculine. Later, only endings are given (ἀγαθός, -ή, -όν). Not adjectives are δέκα and pronoun οὐδείς (see p. 103).

(2) Αἰώνιος has the same second declension inflection for both masculine *and* feminine.

(3) The four adjectives μόνος, ὅλος, πᾶς, and πολύς are always attributive.

Photo © Gerald L. Stevens

Fig. 9. Gladiator Helmet. "Gladiator" in Latin means "swordsman," taken from *gladius*, "sword." Etruscan funeral rites were the original context out of which the professional class of gladiators arose in Roman society. The games were a popular blood sport. Hundreds of gladiator pairs fought at a time, with the games extending for days. From Julius Caesar's (d. 44) 300 pairs of gladiators to Trajan's (d. 117) 5,000 pairs, these gladiatorial contests became an integral part of the Roman world. The helmet above may represent the *mirmillones* class of gladiator, who wore Gallic style armor, comprised of a helmet, sword, and shield. The *mirmillones* helmet had a fish crest, which gave the name to this class of gladiator.

The Greek word ἀγών, meaning "contest," was used to advertise gladiator events in widely distributed flyers (as seen in the movie "Gladiator"). Luke is the only New Testament writer to describe the Gethsemane experience of Jesus with this term (Lk. 22:44). Luke might have been alluding to Jesus' impending contest to the death, a struggle such a term might conjure in his Greco-Roman world. Royal Ontario Museum, Toronto, Canada.

Chapter 9

Pronouns

Pronouns take the place of nouns. The substituted noun is called the antecedent. Pronouns agree with their antecedents in gender and number, but case is determined by the pronoun's function in its own clause. English and Greek usage basically is similar. Greek has more pronouns, though, and also has a few idiomatic uses that need to be mastered. Some pro-nouns are adjectives, and some can be used as adjectives.

This chapter's material is to be divided over several lessons. Pronouns are meant to be covered when introduced in vocabulary. Students are to refer back to this chapter for the relevant reading material as pronouns are encountered in later chapters.

Table 9.1—Personal, Relative Systems

Personal: "I"	Relative: "who"
• Intensive: "myself"	• Indefinite Rel.: "whoever"
• Possessive: "my"	• Correlative: "such"
• Reflexive: "myself"	
• Reciprocal: "ourselves"	
• Indefinite: "someone"	
• Negative: "no one"	

Twelve pronoun categories are organized into four systems: *personal, demonstrative, relative,* and *interrogative*. Of the twelve pronoun categories, seven relate to the personal system, and three to the relative system.

(1) Personal System

Personal Pronouns

(1) Formation

Table 9.2—First Person

	Singular	Plural	Gloss
Nom.:	ἐγώ	ἡμεῖς	I, we
Gen.:	ἐμοῦ (μου)	ἡμῶν	of, from me, us
Dat.:	ἐμοί (μοι)	ἡμῖν	to, in, by me, us
Acc.:	ἐμέ (με)	ἡμᾶς	me, us

Table 9.3—Second Person

	Singular	Plural	Gloss
Nom.:	σύ	ὑμεῖς	you
Gen.:	σοῦ (σου)	ὑμῶν	of, from you
Dat.:	σοί (σοι)	ὑμῖν	to, in, by you
Acc.:	σέ (σε)	ὑμᾶς	you

The μου, μοι, με and σου, σοι, σε are alternate enclitic forms encountered in composition.[1] Their meaning is the same. Both the ἡμεῖς and ὑμεῖς forms looks like πίστις (p. 82). On distinguishing *first* and *second* person *plural* forms, note that the first person plural long "e" vowel reminds one of the "e" vowel in the English first person "we," and the plural "υ" vowel reminds one of the "u" in "you." For second person "you," note that English does not distinguish number as does Greek.

---

[1] Enclitics have no accent. Proclitics lean forward on the next word for accent; enclitics lean backward to the previous word for accent.

Table 9.4—Third Person Masculine

	Singular	Plural	Gloss
Nom.:	αὐτός	αὐτοί	he, they
Gen.:	αὐτοῦ	αὐτῶν	of, from him, them
Dat.:	αὐτῷ	αὐτοῖς	to, in, by him, them
Acc.:	αὐτόν	αὐτούς	him, them

The inflection is second declension masculine. English does not distinguish plural gender as does Greek.

Table 9.5—Third Person Neuter

	Singular	Plural	Gloss
Nom.:	αὐτό	αὐτά	it, they
Gen.:	αὐτοῦ	αὐτῶν	of, from it, them
Dat.:	αὐτῷ	αὐτοῖς	to, in, by it, them
Acc.:	αὐτό	αὐτά	it, them

English does not distinguish plural gender as does Greek. Neuter inflection is second declension, but with what is called the "pronoun pattern." That is:

♦ *Neuter nominative and accusative singular pronouns may omit the final -ν, leaving only -ο.*

This observation is conditional. That is, some pronouns will express the final -ν. In such cases, the pronoun simply looks "normal" to you (has the expected -ον ending of second declension neuter) and easily can be identified.

Table 9.6—Third Person Feminine

	Singular	Plural	Gloss
Nom.:	αὐτή	αὐταί	she, they
Gen.:	αὐτῆς	αὐτῶν	of, from her, them
Dat.:	αὐτῇ	αὐταῖς	to, in, by her, them
Acc.:	αὐτήν	αὐτάς	her, them

The feminine inflection is first declension "η-pure." English does not distinguish plural gender as does Greek.

(2) Special Functions

Subject Emphasis

The Greek verb already includes the pronoun subject in its inflection. Using a personal pronoun for subject is unnecessary. Including the personal pronoun, then, can show emphasis on the subject. Koine, however, increasingly expressed the pronoun for subject redundantly, especially the third personal pronoun. The use of first and second person pronouns, though, probably still retains this subject emphasis most of the time (and third person on occasion). Context always is the final arbiter on any question of emphasis. Since the *subject* is being emphasized, the grammar of this personal pronoun is *anarthrous* and *nominative*. This use also is called an *emphatic pronoun*. Note the following:

ἐγὼ δὲ λέγω ὑμῖν
"but *I* say to you" (Mt. 5:22)

Genitive of Possession

While Greek has a possessive pronoun (ἐμός, ἡμέτερος; σός, ὑμέτερος; ἴδιος), Koine began using the third *personal* pronoun in the genitive case. The expression was similar to, for example, "the son *of her*," which in essence means "*her* son."

This koine idiom eliminated having to maintain another entire set of pronouns. This use is called the "genitive of possession." English translation uses a personal pronoun in the possessive case (i.e., "my," "our"; "your"; "his," "her" "its," "their"). For example:

Ἰωάννην τὸν ἀδελφὸν <u>αὐτοῦ</u>
"John *his* brother" (Mk. 1:19)

Intensive Pronouns

While the *emphatic* personal pronoun above emphasizes the *subject*, the *intensive* personal pronoun emphasizes *any noun*. In English one can intensify any substantive in two ways: (1) by using a reflexive pronoun (= "-self"): "he *himself* did that," or (2) by using the adjective "the same": "*the same* word." Greek intensifies nouns by *recycling the third personal pronoun*. This usage is idiomatic, so requires careful attention to spot. In distinction from the emphatic use above, the intensive pronoun shows *case concord* with the intensified noun.

(1) Reflexive Intensification (= "-self")
An *anarthrous third personal pronoun* showing case and number concord with a noun nearby is intensifying that noun, becoming the equivalent of a reflexive pronoun. For example:

ὅτι καὶ <u>αὐτὴ</u> ἡ κτίσις
"that even creation *itself*" (Jn. 6:35)

(2) Adjectival Intensification (= "the same")
English intensifies a noun by using the adjective "same," often including the article, "the same." Greek also intensifies adjectivally, but not with an adjective, as in English. Instead, Greek *recycles* the third personal pronoun (again!), this time including the article, all in concord with the modified noun:

<u>τῷ αὐτῷ</u> λόγῳ
"by *the same* word" (2 Pet. 3:7)

Possessive Pronouns

All masculine and neuter forms follow second declension.[2] All feminine forms follow either "η-pure" or "α-pure" patterns; feminine plurals are first declension plural.

The third person possessive often is the koine habit of *third personal* pronoun in *genitive* case, the "genitive of possession." A second method for expressing third person possession is to use the *reflexive* pronoun with possessive force, as in "his own," "her own," "their own" (note ἴδιος in the table below).

Table 9.7—Possessive Pronoun Summary

	Masculine		Neuter		Feminine	
	Singular	Plural	Singular	Plural	Singular	Plural
1st s.	ἐμός	ἐμοί	ἐμόν	ἐμά	ἐμή	ἐμαί
p.	ἡμέτερος	ἡμέτεροι	ἡμέτερον	ἡμέτερα	ἡμέτερα	ἡμέτεραι
2nd s.	σός	σοί	σόν	σά	σή	σαί
p.	ὑμέτερος	ὑμέτεροι	ὑμέτερον	ὑμέτερα	ὑμέτερα	ὑμέτεραι
3rd	ἴδιος	ἴδιοι	ἴδιον	ἴδια	ἰδία	ἴδιαι

Translation is:

- first person: "my," "our"
- second person: "your"
- third person: "his," "her," "its," "their"

Possessive pronouns function as adjectives. Adjectives must show concord with the modified noun (substantive). Even plural possessive pronouns in Greek, then, are inflected to show the

---

[2]In remaining tables, we give nominative forms only, since inflections follow the three noun declensions. For full paradigms, see pp. 564-69.

case, gender, *and number* of the noun. English does not inflect possessives for number. Thus, "my" or "our," for example, are spelled the same whether house is singular or plural as "my/our house" or "my/our houses.") The table below illustrates.

Table 9.8—Possessive Pronoun Plural Concord

"my house"
ὁ ἐμός οἶκος
"our house"
ὁ ἡμέτερος οἶκος

"my houses"
οἱ ἐμοί οἶκοι
"our houses"
οἱ ἡμέτεροι οἶκοι

So, as adjectives, Greek possessive pronouns have an entire set of plural inflections for plural number. This plural inflection allows Greek possessive pronouns to express concord with plural nouns they modify.

The possessive pronoun can be used as a substantive. When used this way in English, the pronoun is inflected, most often with an "s" suffix ("mine," "ours," "yours," "his," hers," "its," "theirs"). Thus, "This house is *ours*." Note plural concord in the first example below, and the substantival use in the last:

ἡ κοινωνία δὲ ἡ ἡμετέρα μετὰ τοῦ πατρὸς
"and *our* fellowship is with the Father" (1 Jn. 1:3)

οἱ δὲ σοὶ μαθηταὶ
"but *your* disciples" (Mk. 2:18)

καὶ πάντα τὰ ἐμὰ σά ἐστιν
"and all that is *mine* is *yours*" (Lk. 15:31)

Reflexive Pronouns

Reflexive pronouns do not have nominative forms, and first and second do not have neuter gender. Masculine and neuter forms follow second declension. Feminine follows the "η-pure" first declension singular patterns and all feminine plurals are first declension. First person is translated as "myself," "ourselves"; second person, "yourself," "yourselves"; third person, "himself," "herself," "itself," and all plurals "themselves."

Table 9.9—Reflexive Pronoun Summary

	Masculine		Neuter		Feminine	
	Singular	Plural	Singular	Plural	Singular	Plural
1st	ἐμαυτοῦ	ἑαυτῶν	----	----	ἐμαυτῆς	ἑαυτῶν
2nd	σεαυτοῦ	ἑαυτῶν	----	----	σεαυτῆς	ἑαυτῶν
3rd	ἑαυτοῦ	ἑαυτῶν	ἑαυτοῦ	ἑαυτῶν	ἑαυτῆς	ἑαυτῶν

For example:

ἀγαπήσεις τὸν πλησίον σου ὡς <u>σεαυτόν</u>
"you will love your neighbor as *yourself*" (Mk. 12:31)

Reciprocal Pronouns

Only masculine and plural, the only three reciprocal pronoun forms in the New Testament are: ἀλλήλων, "of one another"; ἀλλήλοις, "to one another"; ἀλλήλους, "one another." Note:

ἔλεγον οὖν οἱ μαθηταὶ πρὸς <u>ἀλλήλους</u>
"So, the disciples were saying to *one another*" (Jn. 4:33)

⟹ (Note: for Chapter 9, now go to the homework.)

Indefinite Pronouns

Indefinite pronouns make inexact reference, as "someone," "something," "a certain ___." Forms repeat exactly those of the interrogative pronoun with its third declension inflection, but *with no accent*; that is, indefinite pronouns are enclitic.

Table 9.10—Indefinite Pronoun Summary

Masculine/Fem.		Neuter	
Singular	Plural	Singular	Plural
τις	τινές	τι	τίνα

Examples include:

εἴ τινός τι ἐσυκοφάντησα
"if *anyone anything* I have defrauded" (Lk. 19:8)

οὖν ἐκ τῶν Φαρισαίων τινές
"therefore *certain ones* from the Pharisees" (Jn. 9:16)

Negative Pronouns

Negative pronouns ("no one," "nothing") by definition are singular. Inflection follows that of the number one, so third declension for masculine and neuter, but first declension for the feminine. When you break down the vocabulary word, you can see that the forms literally are a composite of three words:

- οὐ = "not"
- δέ = "and" or "even"
- εἷς, μία, ἕν = the numeral "one," inflected for masculine, feminine, and neuter gender.

The literal result would be something along the order of "not even one." This literal idea translates as "no one," etc.

Table 9.11—Negative Pronoun Summary

Masculine		Neuter		Feminine	
Singular	Plural	Singular	Plural	Singular	Plural
οὐδείς	---	οὐδέν	---	οὐδεμία	---

Examples include:

σκοτία ἐν αὐτῷ οὐκ ἔστιν <u>οὐδεμία</u>
"*no* darkness is in him *at all*" (Mt. 7:15)

<u>οὐδεὶς</u> γὰρ ἡμῶν ἑαυτῷ ζῇ
"for *no one* of us lives to himself" (Rom. 14:7)

(2) Demonstrative System

Demonstrative pronouns point like the Greek article. They can point out nearby (proximate: "this, these") or at a distance (remote: "that, those"). Demonstratives, like possessives, are used as adjectives; however, they are always anarthrous.

Demonstratives have second declension masculine and neuter endings and first declension ("η-pure") feminine endings. Note that all proximate forms are prefaced with the letter tau (e.g., τούτου) except for *nominative* masculine and feminine, which have rough breathing instead (e.g., οὗτος). All forms of the remote have the stem ἐκειν-.

Table 9.12—Demonstrative Pronoun Summary

	Masculine		Neuter		Feminine	
	Singular	Plural	Singular	Plural	Singular	Plural
Pr.	οὗτος	οὗτοι	τοῦτο	ταῦτα	αὕτη	αὗται
Re.	ἐκεῖνος	ἐκεῖνοι	ἐκεῖνο	ἐκεῖνα	ἐκείνη	ἐκεῖναι

Examples include:

Ἔχομεν δὲ τὸν θησαυρὸν <u>τοῦτον</u>
"But we have *this* treasure" (2 Cor. 4:7)

οὐαὶ δὲ τῷ ἀνθρώπῳ <u>ἐκείνῳ</u>
"But woe to *that* man" (Mt. 26:24)

(3) Relative System

Relative Pronouns

Relative pronouns function as a special class of conjunctions introducing dependent clauses acting as adjectives.[3] They will be either subject or object in their own clause, which determines case inflection. Relatives look like inflectional endings with rough breathing and accent. That *rough breathing with accent* distinguishes relative pronouns from almost identical forms of the article and the verb εἰμί ("I am"). Remember:

◆ *Relatives are rough.*

Table 9.13—Relative Pronoun Summary

Masculine		Neuter		Feminine	
Singular	Plural	Singular	Plural	Singular	Plural
ὅς	οἵ	ὅ	ἅ	ἥ	αἵ

A relative pronoun's reference can be generalized in English translation by adding the suffix "-ever" to the relative pronoun:

---

[3]*Who, whom, whose, which, that, what*; review pp. 508-9.

"whoever," "whomever," "whichever," etc. Context can infer that a relative pronoun should be generalized in this way. This generalizing method is illustrated in the first example below.

Examples include:

ὃς οὐ λαμβάνει τὸν σταυρὸν αὐτοῦ
"*whoever* does not take up his cross" (Mt. 10:38)

νῦν ὃν ἔχεις οὐκ ἔστιν σου ἀνήρ
"*he whom* you now have is not your husband" (Jn. 4:18)

ὁ λόγος ὃν ἀκούετε οὐκ ἔστιν ἐμὸς
"the word *that* you hear is not mine" (Jn. 14:24)

ἔρχονται ἡμέραι ἐν αἷς ἐροῦσιν
"the days are coming in *which* they will say" (Lk. 23:29)

Indefinite Relative Pronouns

Indefinite relative pronouns ("who," "whoever") combine two forms. They make inexact reference, thus use the indefinite pronoun. They connect relative dependent clauses, hence add the relative pronoun. Forms in the New Testament almost exclusively are nominative, since the pronoun almost always is subject in its clause.[4]

Table 9.14—Indefinite Relative Pronoun Summary

Masculine		Neuter		Feminine	
Singular	Plural	Singular	Plural	Singular	Plural
ὅστις	οἵτινες	ὅτι	ἅτινα	ἥτις	αἵτινες

Examples include:

---

[4] The genitive ὅτου occurs five times; accusative ὅτι once.

<u>ὅστις</u> γὰρ ἔχει
"for *whoever* has" (Jn. 9:16)

<u>οἵτινες</u> ἔρχονται πρὸς ὑμᾶς
"*who* come to you" (Mt. 7:15)

<u>ἅτινά</u> ἐστιν ἀλληγορούμενα
"*which things* are an allegory" (Gal. 4:24)

<u>ἥτις</u> λέγεται Ἅγια
"*which* is called 'the Holy Place'" (Heb. 9:2)

Correlative Pronouns

Correlative pronouns express relative comparative ideas: "such," "as," "so much (great, many)," "as much as." Greek correlatives have second declension masculine and neuter endings and first declension ("η-pure") feminine endings. Correlatives, like possessives, function as adjectives. When you study their formation patterns, you discover that what is significant for distinguishing them is the opening syllable, as follows:

- <u>"such" (τοι-)</u>: The correlative "such" looks like a proximate demonstrative pronoun prefaced with a τοι- pattern instead of τ- (τοιοῦτος).
- <u>"so much" (τοσ-)</u>: The correlative "so much" (also "so great," "so many") looks like a proximate demonstrative pronoun prefaced with τοσ- instead of τ- (τοσοῦτος).
- <u>"as" (οἱ-)</u>: The correlative "as" opens with οἱ- and adds endings. The only forms in the New Testament are masculine singular inflections of οἷος, the two neuter inflections οἷον and οἷα, and the one feminine inflection οἷα.
- <u>"as much as" (ὅσ-)</u>: The correlative "as much as" opens with ὅσ- and adds endings.

Table 9.15—Correlative Pronouns Summary

Masculine		Neuter		Feminine	
Singular	Plural	Singular	Plural	Singular	Plural
τοιοῦτος	τοιοῦτοι	τοιοῦτο	τοιοῦτα	τοιαύτη	τοιαῦται
τοσοῦτος	τοσοῦτοι	τοσοῦτο	τοσοῦτα	τοσαύτη	τοσαῦται
οἷος	οἷοι	οἷον	οἷα	οἷα	οἷαι
ὅσος	ὅσοι	ὅσον	ὅσα	ὅσα	ὅσαι

Examples include:

<u>τοιοῦτον</u> ἔχομεν ἀρχιερέα
"we have *such* a high priest" (Heb. 8:1)

<u>τοσούτῳ</u> χρόνῳ μεθ᾽ ὑμῶν εἰμι;
"Have I been with you for *so great* a time?" (Jn. 14:9)

οὐχ <u>οἵους</u> θέλω
"not *as* I wish" (2 Cor. 12:20)

<u>ὅσον</u> χρόνον ἔχουσιν τὸν νυμφίον μετ᾽ αὐτῶν
"*as long as* they have the bridegroom with them" (Mk. 2:19)

(4) Interrogative System

The *referential* interrogative ("who?" "which?" "what?") is τίς inflected as pure *third* declension with acute accent all the way. The neuter form τί placed at the head of a clause is used adverbially to ask "why?" or "what?" (See first example below.) The *qualitative* interrogative ("what kind?" "which?" "what?") is ποῖος inflected as second and first declension, but occurs almost exclusively as singular (31 of 33 times). The *quantitative* interrogative ("how many?" "how much?") is πόσος inflected as second and first declension.

Table 9.16—Interrogative Pronoun Summary

Masculine/Fem.		Neuter	
Singular	Plural	Singular	Plural
τίς	τίνες	τί	τίνα

Masculine		Neuter		Feminine	
Singular	Plural	Singular	Plural	Singular	Plural
ποῖος	ποῖοι	ποῖον	ποῖα	ποία	ποῖαι
πόσος	πόσοι	πόσον	πόσα	πόσα	πόσαι

Examples include:

<u>τί</u> οὖν οἱ γραμματεῖς λέγουσιν;
"*why* therefore do the scribes say?" (Mt. 17:10)

ἀπὸ <u>τίνων</u> λαμβάνουσιν;
"*from whom* do they receive?" (Mt. 17:25)

<u>τίσιν</u> δὲ ὤμοσεν;
"and *to whom* did he swear?" (Heb. 3:18)

<u>τίς</u> ἐστιν ἡ μήτηρ μου καὶ <u>τίνες</u> εἰσὶν οἱ ἀδελφοί μου;
"*who* is my mother and *who* are my brothers?" (Mt. 12:48)

λέγει αὐτῷ· <u>ποίας</u>;
"he says to him: '*which ones?*'" (Mt. 19:18)

<u>πόσους</u> ἄρτους ἔχετε;
"*how many* loaves do you have?" (Mt. 15:34)

Pronoun Summary

The table below summarizes Greek pronouns. Italics means no distinct English counterparts. Most adjective inflections are second and first declension. Less frequent third declension inflections have the same forms for both masculine and feminine. Adjectival pronouns (possessive, demonstrative, correlative) show full concord; these also can be used substantivally.

Table 9.17—Pronouns: A Summary

Type	English	Greek
Personal	I	ἐγώ
	we	ἡμεῖς
	you (s)	σύ
	you (p)	ὑμεῖς
	he, it, she	αὐτός, -ή, -ό
	they	αὐτοί, -αί, -ά
• *Intensive*	-self	αὐτός, -ή, -ό
	the same	ὁ (αὐτός, -ή, -ό)
• *Possessive*	my	ἐμός, ἐμή, ἐμόν
	our	ἡμέτερος, -α, -ον
	your (s)	σός, σή, σόν
	your (p)	ὑμέτερος, -α, -ον
	his, her, its	ἴδιος, -α, -ον
	their	ἴδιοι, -αι, -α
• *Reflexive*	myself	ἐμαυτοῦ, -ῆς, --
	ourselves	ἑαυτῶν, -ῶν, --
	yourself	σεαυτοῦ, -ῆς, --
	yourselves	ἑαυτῶν, -ῶν, --
	himself (etc.)	ἑαυτοῦ, -ῆς, -οῦ
	themselves	ἑαυτῶν, -ῶν, --
• *Reciprocal*	one another	ἀλλήλων, -οις, -ους
• *Indefinite*	someone (s)	τις, τις, τι
	someone (p)	τινές, τινές, τινά
• *Negative*	no one	οὐδείς, οὐδεμία, οὐδέν

Table 9.17—Pronouns: A Summary (cont.)

Type	English	Greek
Demonstrative (Proximate/Remote)	this/these that/those	οὗτος, αὕτη, τοῦτο ἐκεῖνος, -η, -ο
Relative	who	ὅς, ἥ, ὅ
• Indef. Rel.	who/ever (s) who/ever (p)	ὅστις, ἥτις, ὅτι οἵτινες, αἵτινες, ἅτινα
• Correlative	such so much as as much as	τοιοῦτος, -αύτη, -ο τοσοῦτος, -αύτη, -ο οἷος, οἵα, οἷον ὅσος, ὅσα, ὅσον
Interrogative (Referential, Qualitative, Quantitative)	who? what kind? how many?	τίς, τίς, τί (τίνες, τίνα) ποῖος, ποία, ποῖον πόσος, πόσα, πόσον

We can summarize the four main pronoun systems in terms of their functions: personal *refers*; demonstrative *points*; relative *relates*; interrogative *asks*.

Exercise 9

1. Complete the following chart of personal pronouns:

	1st Per. sg.	Gloss	1st Per. pl.	Gloss
N	_____	= _____	_____	= _____
G	_____	= _____	_____	= _____
D	_____	= _____	_____	= _____
A	_____	= _____	_____	= _____

	2ⁿᵈ Per. sg.	Gloss	2ⁿᵈ Per. pl.	Gloss
N	_____ =	_____	_____ =	_____
G	_____ =	_____	_____ =	_____
D	_____ =	_____	_____ =	_____
A	_____ =	_____	_____ =	_____

	3ʳᵈ Neu. sg.	Gloss	3ʳᵈ Neu. pl.	Gloss
N	_____ =	_____	_____ =	_____
G	_____ =	_____	_____ =	_____
D	_____ =	_____	_____ =	_____
A	_____ =	_____	_____ =	_____

2. _____ For masculine and neuter genders, most pronoun inflection patterns follow what declension? (1ˢᵗ, 2ⁿᵈ, or 3ʳᵈ?)

3. _____ For feminine gender, most pronoun inflection patterns follow what declension? (1ˢᵗ, 2ⁿᵈ, or 3ʳᵈ?)

4. Explain what is called the "pronoun exception" related to second declension neuter inflection:

_____

5. 5.1 _____ ; _____ When the personal pronoun is used to emphasize the verb's subject, what case is used? What construction is this emphatic pronoun related to the Greek article (i.e., articular or anarthrous?)

5.2 Make the following verb subjects emphatic using the personal pronoun. The pronoun has to be the same person (1ˢᵗ, 2ⁿᵈ, 3ʳᵈ) and number (sg., pl.) as the subject of the verb, and the case and construction you indicated above:

Chapter 9: Pronouns

	Pronoun		Translation
a.	_____	ἀπέρχεται =	_____
b.	_____	γινόμεθα =	_____
c.	_____	γινώσκεις =	_____
d.	_____	πιστεύουσιν =	_____

6. ___; _____ Greek intensifies any noun by making special use of what personal pronoun (1st, 2nd, 3rd)? What construction is this pronoun (articular or anarthrous?)

7. The four pronoun systems can be summarized in terms of their basic functions (see page 125):

   7.1 Personal _____.

   7.2 Demonstrative _____.

   7.3 Relative _____.

   7.4 Interrogative _____.

8. Translate. Be ready to locate assigned pronouns and their use. Some words you may need to look up in a dictionary.

   8.1 ἐν (by) τῷ αὐτῷ πνεύματι (1 Cor. 12:9)

   _____

   8.2 ἡμεῖς νόμον (a law) ἔχομεν (Jn. 19:7)

   _____

   8.3 (insert "what is" after verb) ἔχεις τὸ σόν. (Mt. 25:25)

   _____

8.4 οὐ πιστεύουσιν εἰς ἐμέ (Jn. 16:9)

8.5 σὺ πιστεύεις εἰς τὸν υἱὸν τοῦ ἀνθρώπου; (Jn. 9:35)

8.6 λέγουσιν οὖν οἱ μαθηταὶ πρὸς ἀλλήλους· (Jn. 4:33*)

8.7 ἀκούομεν . . . (them speaking in) ταῖς ἡμετέραις γλώσσαις (γλῶσσα) (Acts 2:11)

8.8 Τότε προσέρχεται αὐτῷ ἡ μήτηρ (mother) τῶν υἱῶν Ζεβεδαίου (Zebedee) μετὰ τῶν υἱῶν αὐτῆς (Mt. 20:20*)

8.9 ὀφείλουσιν (ought) οἱ ἄνδρες ἀγαπᾶν (to love) τὰς ἑαυτῶν γυναῖκας (γυνή) ὡς (as) τὰ ἑαυτῶν σώματα. (Eph. 5:28)

Vocabulary 9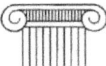

ἐγώ, ἡμεῖς, *I, we* (egotism)
σύ, ὑμεῖς, *you* (s/p)
αὐτός, -ή, -ό, *he, she, it*
  (automatic, automobile)
αὐτοί, -αί, -ά, *they*
ἐμός, ἐμή, ἐμόν, *my*
ἡμέτερος, -α, -ον, *our*
σός, σή, σόν, *your* (s)
ὑμέτερος, -α, -ον, *your* (p)
ἴδιος, -α, -ον, *his, her, its*
  (idiom)

ἐμαυτοῦ, -ῆς, --, *myself*
σεαυτοῦ, -ῆς, --, *yourself*
ἑαυτοῦ, -ῆς, -οῦ, *himself, herself, itself*
ἑαυτῶν, -ῶν, --, *ourselves (yourselves, themselves)*
ἀλλήλων, *of one another*
  (parallel)
ἀλλήλοις, *to one another*
ἀλλήλους, *one another*
ἐννέα, *nine* (ennead)

Vocabulary notes:

1st Person		
Pers.	Poss.	
ἐγώ	ἐμός	**ἐμοί**
ἐμοῦ	ἐμοῦ	ἐμῶν
ἐμοί	ἐμῷ	ἐμοῖς
ἐμέ	**ἐμόν**	ἐμούς

2nd Person		
Pers.	Poss.	
σύ	σός	**σοί**
σοῦ	σοῦ	σῶν
σοί	σῷ	σοῖς
σέ	**σόν**	σούς

(1) Do not confuse 1st person inflections:
  • ἐμοί, *personal dat. sg.*; ἐμοί, *possessive nom. pl.*
  • ἐμέ, *personal* acc. sg.; ἐμόν, *possessive* acc. sg.
(2) Do not confuse 2nd person inflections:
  • σοί, *personal dat. sg.*; σοί, *possessive nom. pl.*
  • σέ, *personal* acc. sg.; σόν, *possessive* acc. sg.

(3) Common in John is the verb πιστεύω followed by εἰς (meaning simply "in") and the accusative ἐμέ.

(4) Reciprocal pronouns often occur in fixed prepositional phrases. Three frequent examples would be: μετ᾽ ἀλλήλων ("with one another"); ἐν ἀλλήλοις ("with one another"); and πρὸς ἀλλήλους ("to one another").

(5) The following is a brief synopsis of the introduction of pronoun categories into vocabulary by chapter:

Chapter 8	Negative	no one	οὐδείς
Chapter 9	Personal	I	ἐγώ
	Intensive	-self, same	αὐτός
	Possessive	my	ἐμός
	Reflexive	myself	ἐμαυτοῦ
	Reciprocal	one another	ἀλλήλων
Chapter 10	Demonstrative	this	οὗτος
	Demonstrative	that	ἐκεῖνος
	Correlative	such	τοιοῦτος
	Correlative	so much	τοσοῦτος
	Correlative	as	οἷος
	Correlative	as much	ὅσος
Chapter 11	Relative	who	ὅς
Chapter 12	Interrogative	who?	τίς
	Interrogative	what kind?	ποῖος
	Interrogative	how many?	πόσος
	Indefinite	someone	τις
	Indefinite Rel.	whoever	ὅστις

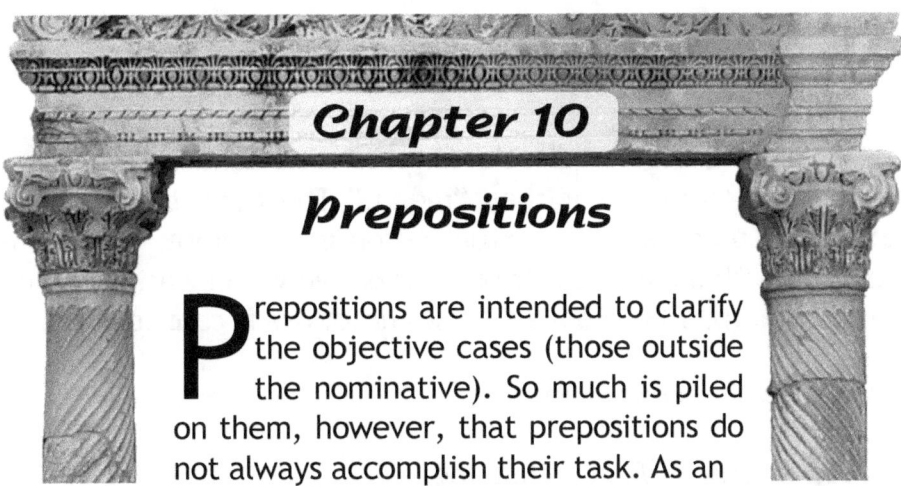

Chapter 10

Prepositions

Prepositions are intended to clarify the objective cases (those outside the nominative). So much is piled on them, however, that prepositions do not always accomplish their task. As an example, ἐπί is so over used that you can find this preposition showing up in *every* objective case. Since a preposition's meaning is determined by its case in its context, contextualization is key to translating Greek prepositions.

Contextualization

Contextualization of prepositions is imperative in English as well. For example, what do you tell someone "by" means? You might suggest a meaning that has to do with "location": "He was *by* the seashore." Another might suggest a meaning that has to do with "means": "You will know me *by* my works." Still another might suggest something along the lines of "personal agency": "I was helped *by* John." A person wanting to learn English could be thoroughly confused and exasperated: "Could someone please just tell me what 'by' means?" When you insist "by" means all of the above, another question immediately follows: "Well, how am I supposed to know *which* one is meant?" The answer is not easy, if you ever have tried to explain English to a learner. You would be dealing with *customary usage* (What is the typical range of meaning for this preposition?), *grammar* (Is agency indicated, e.g., passive voice? Is the agency personal or impersonal?), and *context* (verb, clause, sense).

Translation

Whether English or Greek, all prepositions have to be contextualized to say what they "mean." The table below shows customary usage and contextualization issues. Here, genitive is nuanced with ablative function, and dative with locative and instrumental (p. 138). Above all else, note: *use is case specific.*

Table 10.1—Prepositions

Prep	Case	Fnc.	Meaning
ἀνά	Acc.		*up* (direction) *through, in* (position) *each* (distributive)
ἀντί	Gen.	Abl.	*against* (direction) *because of* (cause) *for, instead of* (relation)
ἀπό	Gen.	Abl.	*away from* (direction) *from* (source) *by* (agency) *because of* (cause)
διά	Gen. Acc.	Abl. Abl.	*through* (adv. of place) *through* (agency) *through* (means) *because of* (cause)
εἰς	Acc.		*into* (adv. of measure) *in* (adv. of manner) *with respect to* (adv. of reference) *resulting in* (result)
ἐκ	Gen.	Abl.	*out of* (separation) *from* (source) *by* (personal agency) *by* (means) *because of* (cause)

Table 10.1—Prepositions (cont.)

Prep	Case	Fnc.	Meaning
ἐν	Dat.		*to* (indirect object)
			with respect to (adv. of reference)
		Loc.	*among* (place)
			in (place)
			in (sphere)
			at (time)
		Ins.	*by, with* (means)
			in, with (manner)
			by (personal agency)
			because of (cause)
ἐπί	Gen.		*upon* (adv. of place)
			during (adv. of time)
	Dat.		*to, for* (indirect object)
			with respect to (reference)
		Loc.	*on, at* (place)
			in (sphere)
		Ins.	*because of* (cause)
			by (means)
	Acc.		*upon* (adv. of measure)
κατά	Gen.		*down* (directional)
			by (oath)
		Abl.	*against* (opposition)
	Acc.		*by* (distributive)
			as (adv. of reference)
			according to (adv. of reference)
μετά	Gen.		*with* (association)
			with (attendant circumstances)
	Acc.		*after* (adv. of measure)

Table 10.1—Prepositions (cont.)

Prep	Case	Fnc.	Meaning
παρά	Gen.	Abl.	*from* (source)
			by (agency)
	Dat.	Loc.	*with* (place)
			beside (place)
			with (sphere)
		Ins.	*with* (association)
	Acc.		*beside* (adv. of measure)
			than (comparison)
περί	Gen.		*for, concerning* (adv. of reference)
			for (advantage)
	Acc.		*around* (adv. of measure)
			in regard to (adv. of reference)
πρό	Gen.	Abl.	*from, before* (separation)
			above (rank)
πρός	Dat.	Loc.	*at, on* (place)
	Acc.		*beside* (place)
			with, to (adv. of measure)
			with respect to (adv. of reference)
			for (purpose)
σύν	Dat.	Ins.	*with, together* (association)
ὑπέρ	Gen.		*for* (advantage)
			in behalf of (adv. of reference)
			concerning (adv. of reference)
	Acc.		*over* (place)
			than (comparison)
ὑπό	Gen.	Abl.	*by* (personal agency)
			by (impersonal agency = means)
	Acc.		*under* (adv. of measure)

The table above illustrates possible options for translating a preposition. In trying to learn these uses over time, remember:

♦ *Always note the case of the noun constructed with a preposition to narrow your options for translation.*

Review the table below from the material on "Word Groups" in the English appendix. A preposition creates a phrase that has a noun, adjective, or adverb role in the sentence.

Table 10.2—Word Group Functions

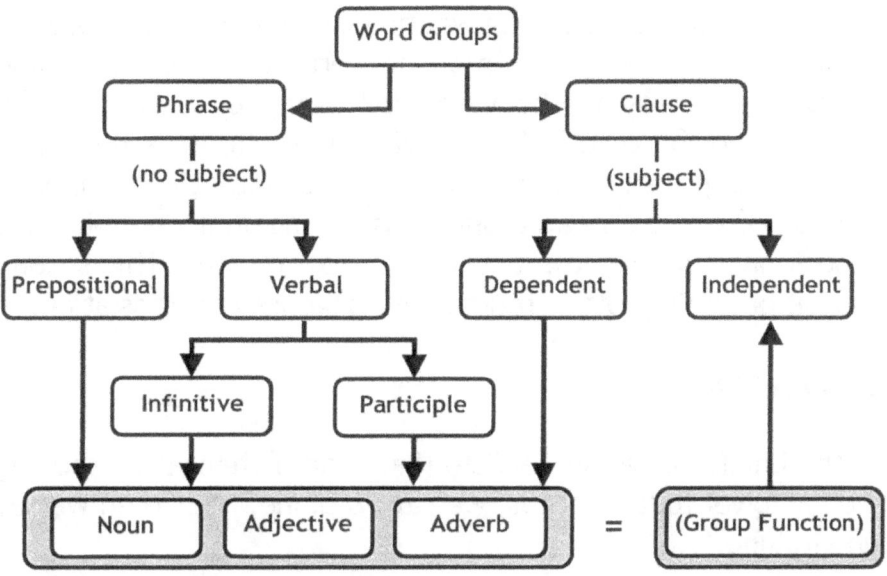

Compound Verbs

Compound verbs are verbs modified by prepositions. Prepositions strengthen, direct, or completely change the nature of the verb action. In English we "outlive," "downsize," "underwrite," overcharge," "uphold," "withstand," etc. Greek also compounds verbs with prepositions that impact verb action to:

- <u>strengthen</u>: γινώσκω, "I know"; ἐπιγινώσκω, "I know fully"
- <u>direct</u>: βάλλω, "I throw"; ἐκβάλλω, "I throw out"
- <u>change</u>: γινώσκω, "I know"; ἀναγινώσκω as "I read" (makes sense: "I know up" = the words go from down on the page up to your eyes)

Koine Greek so overused some compound verbs that original meaning often washed out. One cannot, therefore, woodenly say every occurrence of ἐπιγινώσκω means "I know fully." The verb in context could just mean, "I know."

Evidence of verb meaning wearing thin by overuse is seen in the habit of following a compound verb with the very same preposition already in the verb. For example, ἐκβάλλει ἐκ τοῦ θησαυροῦ αὐτοῦ, "he brings out of his treasure" (Mt. 13:52). The preposition ἐκ already built into the compound verb ἐκβάλλει is repeated unnecessarily again in the following prepositional phrase, ἐκ τοῦ θησαυροῦ αὐτοῦ. This second preposition, being totally redundant, is ignored in translation.

Spelling Variations

The English indefinite article ("a," "an") changes its spelling when a vowel follows. Thus, we say "*a* plane," but then we say "*an* airplane."

Greek prepositions also show spelling variations depending on what letter follows. A preposition's final vowel is dropped before vowels. Before rough breathing a smooth stop changes to a rough stop (Table 1.5, p. 8, left and right columns). The preposition's meaning does not change, just its spelling. The issue is recognizing a preposition you already know as vocabulary. The table below summarizes these spelling variations.

Table 10.3—Preposition Spelling Variations

	Vowel	Rough
ἀνά	ἀν'	ἀν'
ἀντί	ἀντ'	ἀνθ'
ἀπό	ἀπ'	ἀφ'
διά	δι'	δι'
ἐπί	ἐπ'	ἐφ'
κατά	κατ'	καθ'
μετά	μετ'	μεθ'
παρά	παρ'	παρ'
ὑπό	ὑπ'	ὑφ'

Similar changes occur in compound verbs. Here are some examples:

$$\text{ἀπό} + \text{ἄγω} \rightarrow \text{ἀπάγω}$$
$$\text{διά} + \text{ἔρχομαι} \rightarrow \text{διέρχομαι}$$
$$\text{ἐκ} + \text{ἔρχομαι} \rightarrow \text{ἐξέρχομαι}$$

Diagramming

Prepositional phrases diagram on slanted lines underneath the modified sentence element.[1] Matthew 2:1 will serve to illustrate both modifying a noun and modifying a verb:

μάγοι ἀπὸ ἀνατολῶν παρεγένοντο εἰς Ἰεροσόλυμα
"wise men from the east came to Jerusalem"

---

[1]See p. 506.

μάγοι | παρεγένοντο
ἀπὸ ἀνατολῶν | εἰς Ἱεροσόλυμα

Illustrative Examples

Beyond the Basics

You may choose to skip the following illustrations and go straight to the exercises for this chapter. Those who want to dig deeper for a firmer grasp of the material should read on.

The glosses provided with preposition vocabulary are only trainer wheels. (Think about our example of trying to educate someone about the uses of the English preposition "by.") In vocabulary work, we start with the idea of direction for prepositions because direction is an easy concept to grasp and invites graphic visualization, as in our lighthouse analogy.

Here is an example of what the following material is trying to communicate. The preposition κατά you learned as meaning "down." However, κατά means "down" only when used with the genitive case. Even within genitive case κατά might mean "by," as in oath swearing, or "against." Further, κατά with the accusative could mean "by" in a distributive sense, as in "house *by* house, or "as," or even "according to."

Interior Case Junctions

Note in Table 10.1 that we subdivided the interior cases as ablative, locative, and instrumental. This subdivision is more a question of syntax (how words work together) than of grammar (what words look like and do). A preposition used as ablative, in other words, looks no different in inflection than one used as genitive. The difference is contextual, that is, depends on other words in the neighborhood. Likewise, prepositions used as locative and instrumental look no different in inflection than dative. If the spelling is not different, what is the sense of these uses?

The basic genitive function is description or possession. The ablative, however, centers on separation, origin, or source. The dative basically expresses personal interest, so is used for items such as the indirect object. Locative, however, centers on location, and instrumental centers on means or agency.

One-Hit Wonders

Seven of seventeen prepositions are used in only one case or function (ἀνά, ἀντί, ἀπό, εἰς, ἐκ, πρό, σύν). Memorize these seven prepositions with their case/function. They will save time in locating substantives within prepositional phrases. For example, σύν always is instrumental function. Any noun or substantive connected to σύν is going to be dative case with instrumental function. Our one-hit wonders reduce what you have to memorize about prepositional usage. Know them!

Helpful Hints

Hint 1: any preposition starting with an alpha is a one-hit wonder (ἀνά, ἀντί, ἀπό). Further, these alpha prepositions also are used in the only two categories that start with "a" (accusative or ablative).

Hint 2: any "e" is high frequency. Any preposition starting with an epsilon is high frequency. You will meet these often.[2]

We now summarize prepositional use with examples. Study these examples to learn more about their use.

---

[2]King of the hill is ἐν, occurring over 2,000 times. Then, εἰς occurs over 1,700 times. A distant third are ἐκ and ἐπί, each used about 900 times. (Of others: πρός, 700 times; διά and ἀπό, each over 600 times.)

Use of ἀνά (accusative, 13)[3]

1. *Compound*: ἀναβαίνομεν, "we are going *up*" (Mt. 20:18)
2. *Position (in)*: ἀνὰ μέσον τῶν ὁρίων Δεκαπόλεως, "*in the midst* of the regions of the Decapolis" (Mk. 7:31)
3. *Distributive (by)*: καὶ ἀπέστειλεν αὐτοὺς ἀνὰ δύο, "and he sent them *by pairs*" (Mt. 20:18)

Use of ἀντί (ablative, 22)

1. *Compound*: ἀντιλέγει, "he speaks *against*" (Jn. 19:12)
2. *Cause (because)*: ἀνθ' ὧν οὐκ ἐπίστευσας τοῖς λόγοις μου, "*because* you did not believe my words" (Lk. 1:20)
3. *Relation (for, instead of)*: δὸς αὐτοῖς ἀντὶ ἐμοῦ καὶ σοῦ, "give (it) to them *for me and you*" (Mt. 17:27)

Use of ἀπό (ablative, 646)

1. *Compound*: ἀποχωρεῖ, "it will depart *from*" (Lk. 9:39)
2. *Separation (from)*: ῥῦσαι ἡμᾶς ἀπὸ τοῦ πονηροῦ, "deliver us *from the evil one*" (Mt. 6:13)
3. *Source (from)*: ἰδοὺ μάγοι ἀπὸ ἀνατολῶν, "behold, wise men *from the east*" (Mt. 2:1)
4. *Agency (by)*: ἀπὸ τῶν καρπῶν αὐτῶν ἐπιγνώσεσθε αὐτούς, "*by their fruits* you will know them" (Mt. 7:16)
5. *Cause (because)*: Οἱ μὲν οὖν διασπαρέντες ἀπὸ τῆς θλίψεως, "Therefore, those who were scattered *because of the persecution*" (Acts 11:19)

Use of διά (667)

1. *Compound*: διέρχεται, "it passes *through*" (Mt. 12:43)

---

[3] The number is frequency in the New Testament. Note that all proper prepositions in this chapter have been acquired by Vocabulary 6.

Genitive
2. *Adverbial of place (through)*: ὁ μὴ εἰσερχόμενος διὰ τῆς θύρας, "the one who does not enter *through the door*" (Jn. 10:1)

Ablative
3. *Agency (through)*: ὧν ἐποίησεν ὁ θεὸς ἐν τοῖς ἔθνεσιν διὰ τῆς διακονίας αὐτοῦ, "what God did among the Gentiles *through his ministry*" (Acts 21:19)
4. *Means (through, by)*: ἡμᾶς ἐξεγερεῖ διὰ τῆς δυνάμεως αὐτοῦ, "he will raise us *by his power*" (1 Cor. 6:14)

Accusative
5. *Cause (because)*: ἐπίστευσαν διὰ τὸν λόγον αὐτοῦ, "they believed *because of his word*" (Jn. 4:41)

Use of εἰς (accusative, 1,767)

1. *Compound*: οὐκ εἰσέρχεσθε, "you do not enter *in*" (Mt. 23:13)
2. *Adverbial of measure (to, unto)*: ἀναβαίνομεν εἰς Ἱεροσόλυμα, "we are going up *to Jerusalem*" (Mt. 20:18)
3. *Adverbial of manner (in)*: οὗ γάρ εἰσιν δύο ἢ τρεῖς συνηγμένοι εἰς τὸ ἐμὸν ὄνομα, "for where two or three are gathered *in my name*" (Mt. 18:20)
4. *Adverbial of reference (for, with respect to)*: ἀγόρασον ὧν χρείαν ἔχομεν εἰς τὴν ἑορτήν, "buy what we have need *for the feast*" (Jn. 13:29)
5. *Result (resulting in)*: εἰς δικαίωσιν ζωῆς, "*resulting in* the righteousness of life" (Rm. 5:18)

Use of ἐκ (ablative, 914)

1. *Compound*: ἐκβάλλει, "he is casting *out*" (Mt. 12:24)

2. *Separation (out, out of)*: ἔκβαλε πρῶτον ἐκ τοῦ ὀφθαλμοῦ σοῦ τὴν δοκόν, "first take the log *out of your own eye*" (Mt. 7:5)
3. *Source (from)*: ἰδοὺ φωνὴ ἐκ τῶν οὐρανῶν, "behold, a voice *from heaven*" (Mt. 3:17)
4. *Personal Agency (by)*: ἐκ τοῦ στόματός σου κρινῶ σε, "*by your own mouth* I will judge you" (Lk. 19:22)
5. *Means (by)*: ἐκ γὰρ τοῦ καρποῦ τὸ δένδρον, "for a tree is known *by its fruit*" (Mt. 12:33)
6. *Cause (because of)*: Ἐκ τούτου πολλοὶ τῶν μαθητῶν αὐτοῦ ἀπῆλθον, "*because of this* many of his disciples left" (Jn. 6:66)

Use of ἐν (2,752)

1. *Compound*: ἐνετύλιξεν, "he wrapped it *in*" (Lk. 23:53)

Dative
2. *Indirect Object (to)*: εἶπον ἐν ἑαυτοῖς, "they said *to themselves*" (Mt. 21:38)
3. *Adverbial of Reference (with respect to)*: οὐδὲν κακὸν εὑρίσκομεν ἐν τῷ ἀνθρώπῳ τούτῳ, "we find nothing wrong *with respect to this man*" (Acts 23:9)

Locative
4. *Place (among)*: πόσαι μυριάδες εἰσὶν ἐν τοῖς Ἰουδαίοις, "how many thousands there are *among the Jews*" (Acts 21:20)
5. *Place (in)*: αὐτὸς γὰρ Δαυὶδ λέγει ἐν βίβλῳ ψαλμῶν, "for David himself says *in the book of Psalms*" (Lk. 20:42)
6. *Time (in, at, on, when)*: ἐν ἡμέραις Ἡρῴδου τοῦ βασιλέως, "*in the days* of Herod the king" (Mt. 2:1)
7. *Sphere (in)*: ὅσα ὁ νόμος λέγει τοῖς ἐν τῷ νόμῳ λαλεῖ, "whatsoever the law says it speaks to those who are *in the law*" (Rom. 3:19)

Instrumental
8. *Means (by, with)*: Τοῦτο γὰρ ὑμῖν λέγομεν ἐν λόγῳ κυρίου, "For this we say to you *by the word of the Lord*" (1 Thess. 4:15)
9. *Cause (because of)*: πάντες ὑμεῖς σκανδαλισθήσεσθε ἐν ἐμοὶ ἐν τῇ νυκτὶ ταύτῃ, "all of you will be offended *because of me* on this night" (Mt. 26:31)
10. *Manner (in, with)*: καρποφοροῦσιν ἐν ὑπομονῇ, "they bear fruit *with patience*" (Lk. 8:15)
11. *Personal Agency (by)*: ἔλεγον· ἐν τῷ ἄρχοντι τῶν δαιμονίων ἐκβάλλει τὰ δαιμόνια, "they were saying *by the ruler of the demons* he casts out the demons" (Mt. 9:34)

Use of ἐπί (890)

1. *Compound*: ἐπιβάλλουσιν, "they put *on*" (Mk. 11:7)

Genitive
2. *Adverbial of Time (during)*: πολλοὶ λεπροὶ ἦσαν ἐν τῷ Ἰσραὴλ ἐπὶ Ἐλισαίου τοῦ προφήτου, "many lepers were in Israel *during the time of Elijah the prophet*" (Lk. 4:27)
3. *Adverbial of Place (at, on, upon)*: τοὺς φύλακας ἑστῶτας ἐπὶ τῶν θυρῶν, "the guards who were standing *at the doors*" (Acts 5:23)

Dative
4. *Indirect Object (to, for)*: προσέχετε ἑαυτοῖς ἐπὶ τοῖς ἀνθρώποις τούτοις τί μέλλετε πράσσειν, "take heed to yourselves what you are about to do *to these men*" (Acts 5:35)
5. *Reference (concerning, with respect to)*: οὐ γὰρ συνῆκαν ἐπὶ τοῖς ἄρτοις, "for they did not understand *concerning the loaves*" (Mk. 6:52)

Locative
6. *Place (on, at)*: ἐγγύς ἐστιν ἐπὶ θύραις, "he is near, *at the gates*" (Mk. 13:29)
7. *Sphere (in)*: ἐπ' ἐλπίδι ζωῆς αἰωνίου, "*in* hope of eternal life" (Tit. 1:2)

Instrumental
8. *Means (by)*: οὐκ ἐπ' ἄρτῳ μόνῳ ζήσεται ὁ ἄνθρωπος, "a person will not live *by bread alone*" (Mt. 4:4)
9. *Cause (because of)*: εἰ ἡμεῖς σήμερον ἀνακρινόμεθα ἐπὶ εὐεργεσίᾳ, "if we are being questioned today *because of the good deed*" (Acts 4:9)

Accusative
10. *Adverbial of Measure (on, upon)*: οὐκ ἀφήσουσιν λίθον ἐπὶ λίθον, "they will not leave one stone *upon another*" (Lk. 19:44)

Use of κατά (473)

1. *Compound*: καταβαίνει, "he goes *down*" (Jn. 5:7)

Genitive
2. *Oath (by)*: ἐξορκίζω σε κατὰ τοῦ θεοῦ τοῦ ζῶντος, "I adjure you *by the living God*" (Mt. 26:63)

Ablative
3. *Opposition (against)*: ἐζήτουν ψευδομαρτυρίαν κατὰ τοῦ Ἰησοῦ, "they were seeking false testimony *against Jesus*" (Mt. 26:59)

Accusative
4. *Adverbial of Measure: distributive (by, in)*: ἔσονται λιμοὶ καὶ σεισμοὶ κατὰ τόπους, "there will be famines and earthquakes *in various places*" (Mt. 24:7)
5. *Adverbial of Reference (as)*: Οὐ κατ' ἐπιταγὴν λέγω, "Not *as a command* am I speaking" (2 Cor. 8:8)

6. *Adverbial of Reference (according to)*: γένοιτό μοι κατὰ τὸ ῥῆμά σου, "may it be to me *according to your word*" (Lk. 1:30)

Use of *μετά* (469)

1. *Compound*: μεταλαμβάνει, "he shares in" (Heb. 6:7; literally: "receives with")

Genitive
2. *Association (with)*: ἐβασίλευσαν μετὰ τοῦ Χριστοῦ χίλια ἔτη, "they reigned *with Christ* a thousand years" (Rev. 20:4)
3. *Attendant circumstances (with)*: μετὰ φόβου καὶ τρόμου τὴν ἑαυτῶν σωτηρίαν κατεργάζεσθε, "*with fear and trembling* work out your own salvation" (Phil. 2:12)

Accusative
4. *Adverbial of Measure: (after)*: μετὰ τρεῖς ἡμέρας ἐγείρομαι, "*after three days*, I will rise again" (Mt. 27:63)

Use of *παρά* (194)

1. *Compound*: παράγει, "he is (was) passing *by*" (Mt. 20:30)

Ablative
2. *Source (from)*: κατὰ τὸν χρόνον ὃν ἠκρίβωσεν παρὰ τῶν μάγων, "according to the time which he had learned *from the wise men*" (Mt. 2:16)
3. *Agency (by)*: γενήσεται αὐτοῖς παρὰ τοῦ πατρός μου, "it will be done for you *by my Father*" (Mt. 18:19)

Locative
4. *Place (with)*: παρεκλήθημεν παρ' αὐτοῖς ἐπιμεῖναι, "we were invited to stay *with them*" (Acts 28:14)

5. *Place (beside)*: Εἱστήκεισαν δὲ <u>παρὰ τῷ σταυρῷ</u> τοῦ Ἰησοῦ, "Now, they were standing *beside the cross* of Jesus" (Jn. 19:25)
6. *Sphere (with)*: <u>παρὰ δὲ θεῷ</u> πάντα δυνατά, "but *with God* all things are possible" (Mt. 19:26)

Instrumental
7. *Association (with)*: <u>παρὰ ἁμαρτωλῷ ἀνδρὶ</u> εἰσῆλθεν καταλῦσαι, "he has gone to be a guest *with a sinful man*" (Lk. 19:7)

Accusative
8. *Adverbial of Measure (beside)*: ᾧ ἐστιν οἰκία <u>παρὰ θάλασσαν</u>, "whose house is *beside the sea*" (Acts 10:6)
9. *Comparison (than)*: πλείονος γὰρ οὗτος δόξης <u>παρὰ Μωϋσῆν</u> ἠξίωται, "for this one is worthy of more glory *than Moses*" (Heb. 3:3)

Use of περί (333)

1. *Compound*: <u>περιάγετε</u>, "you travel *around*" (Mt. 23:15)

Genitive
2. *Adverbial of Reference (for, concerning)*: <u>περὶ καλοῦ ἔργου</u> οὐ λιθάζομέν σε ἀλλὰ <u>περὶ βλασφημίας</u>, "we are not going to stone you *for a good* work but *for blasphemy*" (Jn. 10:33)
3. *Advantage (for)*: Ἐγὼ <u>περὶ αὐτῶν</u> ἐρωτῶ, "I am asking *for them*" (Jn. 17:9)

Accusative
4. *Adverbial of Measure (around)*: εἶδον ὄχλον πολὺν <u>περὶ αὐτούς</u>, "they saw a great crowd *around them*" (Mk. 9:14)
5. *Adverbial of Reference (in regard to)*: ἡ δὲ Μάρθα περιεσπᾶτο <u>περὶ πολλὴν διακονίαν</u>, "but Martha was distracted <u>in regard to her many tasks</u>" (Lk. 10:40)

Use of πρό (ablative, 47)

1. *Compound*: προλέγω, "I warned *beforehand*" (2 Cor. 13:2)
2. *Separation (before, from)*: Σπούδασον πρὸ χειμῶνος ἐλθεῖν, "Do your best to come *before winter*" (2 Tim. 4:21)
3. *Rank (above)*: πρὸ πάντων τὴν εἰς ἑαυτοὺς ἀγάπην ἐκτενῆ ἔχοντες, "*Above all*, maintain constant love for one another" (1 Pet. 4:8)

Use of πρός (700)

1. *Compound*: προσέρχονται, "they come to" (Mt. 9:14)

Locative
2. *Place (at, on)*: ἦν δὲ ἐκεῖ πρὸς τῷ ὄρει, "Now there was there *on the hillside*" (Mk. 5:11)

Accusative
3. *Place (beside)*: πᾶς ὁ ὄχλος πρὸς τὴν θάλασσαν ἐπὶ τῆς γῆς ἦσαν, "the whole crowd was *beside the sea* on the land" (1 Pet. 4:8)
4. *Adverbial of Measure (with, to)*: ἔρχεται πρὸς τοὺς μαθητάς, "he came *to the disciples*" (Mt. 26:40)
5. *Adverbial of Reference (with respect to)*: πρεσβείαν ἀποστείλας ἐρωτᾷ τὰ πρὸς εἰρήνην, "he sends a delegation to ask the terms *with respect to peace*" (Lk. 14:32)
6. *Purpose (for)*: θεάσασθε τὰς χώρας ὅτι λευκαί εἰσιν πρὸς θερισμόν, "observe the fields, that they are white *for harvesting*" (Jn. 4:35)

Use of σύν (instrumental, 128)

1. *Compound*: συνεσθίει, "he eats *with*" (Lk. 15:2)

2. *Association (with)*: καὶ οὕτως πάντοτε <u>σὺν κυρίῳ</u> ἐσόμεθα, "and thus we shall forever be *with the Lord*" (1 Thess. 4:17)

Use of ὑπέρ (150)

1. *Compound*: <u>ὑπερ</u>αυξάνει, "it overgrows" (2 Thess. 1:3)

Genitive
2. *Advantage (for)*: ὁ ποιμὴν ὁ καλὸς τὴν ψυχὴν αὐτοῦ τίθησιν <u>ὑπὲρ τῶν προβάτων</u>, "The good shepherd lays down his life *for the sheep*" (Jn. 10:11)
3. *Adverbial of Reference (in behalf of)*: τὸν μὴ γνόντα ἁμαρτίαν <u>ὑπὲρ ἡμῶν</u> ἁμαρτίαν ἐποίησεν, "the one who did not know sin he made to be sin *on our behalf*" (2 Cor. 5:21)
4. *Adverbial of Reference (concerning)*: Ἐρωτῶμεν δὲ ὑμᾶς, ἀδελφοί, <u>ὑπὲρ τῆς παρουσίας</u> τοῦ κυρίου ἡμῶν Ἰησοῦ Χριστοῦ, "Now we beg you, brothers, *concerning the appearing* of our Lord Jesus Christ" (2 Thess. 2:1)

Accusative
5. *Comparison (than)*: οὐκέτι ὡς δοῦλον ἀλλ' <u>ὑπὲρ δοῦλον</u>, ἀδελφὸν ἀγαπητόν, "no longer as a slave but *more than a slave*, a beloved brother" (Philem. 1:16)

Use of ὑπό (220)

1. *Compound*: <u>ὑπο</u>μένω, "I endure (abide *under*)" (2 Tim. 2:10)

Ablative
2. *Personal Agency (by)*: Τότε Ἡρῴδης ἰδὼν ὅτι ἐνεπαίχθη <u>ὑπὸ τῶν μάγων</u>, "When Herod saw that he had been tricked *by the wise men*" (Mt. 2:16)

3. *Impersonal Agency = means (by)*: καὶ ὑπὸ τῶν ὄφεων ἀπώλλυντο, "and they were destroyed *by the serpents*" (1 Cor. 10:9)

Accusative
4. *Adverbial of Measure (under)*: οὐ γάρ ἐστε ὑπὸ νόμον ἀλλὰ ὑπὸ χάριν, "for you are not *under law* but *under grace*" (Rom. 6:14)

Exercise 10

1. Prepositions change spelling under certain conditions.

   1.1 _____ What do they do to their final vowel when the next word begins with a vowel?

   1.2 _____ A smooth stop is converted to what type of stop when the next word begins with rough breathing?

   Explain the following spelling changes:

   1.3 καθ' ὑμῶν = _____

   1.4 ἀπ' ἐμοῦ = _____

   1.5 μεθ' ἡμέρας = _____

   1.6 ἐπ' αὐτόν = _____

   1.7 ὑφ' ὑμῶν = _____

   1.8 δι' ὑμᾶς = _____

   1.9 ἀνάγω = _____

   1.10 διέρχομαι = _____

2. Translate. Be ready to locate prepositions and their use. Look up unknown words in your UBS text dictionary.

2.1 μετὰ τρεῖς ἡμέρας ἐγείρομαι. (Mt. 27:63)

2.2 ἰδοὺ ἐγὼ ἀποστέλλω τὸν ἄγγελόν μου. (Mt. 11:10)

2.3 ἔρχεται ὁ κύριος τῶν δούλων ἐκείνων. (Mt. 25:19)

2.4 ἀμὴν λέγω ὑμῖν, ἀπέχουσιν (ἀπέχω) τὸν μισθὸν (μισθός) αὐτῶν. (Mt. 6:5)

2.5 οἱ γὰρ τοιοῦτοι τῷ κυρίῳ ἡμῶν Χριστῷ οὐ δουλεύουσιν (δουλεύω, takes a dative dir. obj.). (Rom. 16:18)

2.6 ἡμεῖς νόμον ἔχομεν καὶ κατὰ τὸν νόμον ὀφείλει (ὀφείλω) ἀποθανεῖν (to die). (Jn. 19:7)

2.7 οὐ σπείρουσιν (σπείρω) οὐδὲ θερίζουσιν (θερίζω) οὐδὲ συνάγουσιν (συνάγω) εἰς ἀποθήκας (ἀποθήκη). (Mt. 6:26)

2.8 δόξα ἐν ὑψίστοις (ὕψιστος) θεῷ καὶ ἐπὶ γῆς εἰρήνη ἐν ἀνθρώποις εὐδοκίας (εὐδοκία). (Lk. 2:14)

2.9 καὶ τοσούτῳ μᾶλλον ὅσῳ (ὅσος) βλέπετε ἐγγίζουσαν (coming near) τὴν ἡμέραν. (Heb. 10:25)

2.10 εἰρήνην ἔχομεν πρὸς τὸν θεὸν διὰ τοῦ κυρίου ἡμῶν Ἰησοῦ Χριστοῦ. (Rom. 5:1)

2.11 Καὶ εἰς τὴν οἰκίαν πάλιν οἱ μαθηταὶ περὶ τούτου ἐπηρώτων (were asking) αὐτόν. (Mk. 10:10)

2.12 ἀπὸ δὲ τῶν ἡμερῶν Ἰωάννου τοῦ βαπτιστοῦ ἕως ἄρτι ἡ βασιλεία τῶν οὐρανῶν βιάζεται (βιάζω). (Mt. 11:12)

 **Vocabulary 10**

ἀμήν, *truly*

ἀποστέλλω, *I send* (apostle)

δέκα, *ten* (decade, Decalogue, decathlon)

δοῦλος, ὁ, *slave, servant*

ἐγείρω, *I raise up*

ἕως, *until*

λαός, ὁ, *people* (laity)

νόμος, ὁ, *law* (autonomous)

οὐδέ, *neither*

πάλιν, *again* (palindrome)

οὗτος, αὕτη, τοῦτο, *this, these* (tautology)

ἐκεῖνος, ἐκείνη, ἐκεῖνο, *that, those*

τοιοῦτος, τοιαύτη, τοιοῦτο, *such*

τοσοῦτος, τοσαύτη, τοσοῦτο, *so much*

οἷος, οἷα, οἷον, *as*

ὅσος, ὅσα, ὅσον, *as much as*

Vocabulary notes:

(1) The conjunction οὐδέ in sequence, οὐδέ . . . οὐδέ, is the equivalent of our own expression, "neither . . . nor."

(2) The words ἀμήν, ἕως, and πάλιν are adverbs.

(3) Review the appropriate sections in Chapter 9 for the pronouns: two demonstratives, οὗτος and ἐκεῖνος, and the similar correlatives, τοιοῦτος, τοσοῦτος, οἷος, and ὅσος.

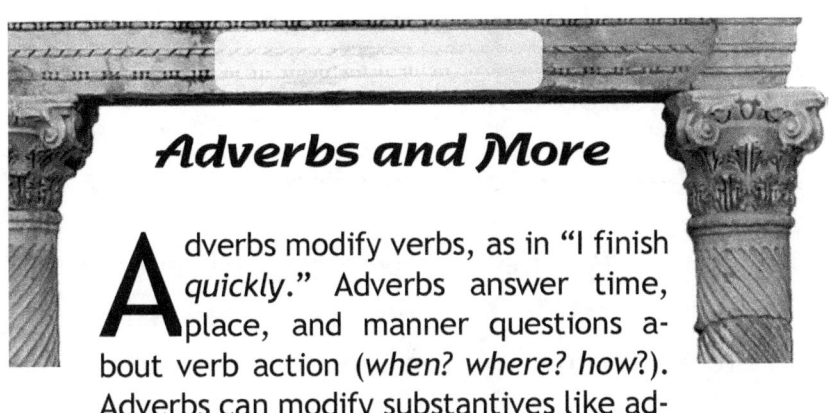

Adverbs and More

Adverbs modify verbs, as in "I finish *quickly*." Adverbs answer time, place, and manner questions about verb action (*when? where? how?*). Adverbs can modify substantives like adjectives: "The man *outside* is my father." Adverbs can act like prepositions, taking noun objects: "The man *outside the house* is my father." Adverbs can act like substantives as the *object* of a preposition in Greek, even taking an article in construction: ἀπὸ τοῦ νῦν, "from the *present*" (literally, "from the *now*"). So, adverbs just about can do anything. Good news! Adverbs are not inflected! Often, adverbs have an -ως ending. The following examples illustrate these diverse adverb uses:

<u>νῦν</u> κρίσις ἐστὶν τοῦ κόσμου τούτου
"*now* is the judgment of this world" (Jn. 12:31)

<u>πάλιν</u> δὲ λέγω ὑμῖν
"*again* I say to you" (Mt. 19:24)

καὶ <u>οὕτως</u> πᾶς Ἰσραὴλ σωθήσεται
"and *in this way* all Israel will be saved" (Rm. 11:26)

ἀπ' ἀρχῆς κόσμου ἕως τοῦ <u>νῦν</u>
"from the beginning of the world until *now*" (Mt. 24:21)

καὶ ἦν <u>ἐκεῖ</u> <u>ἕως</u> τῆς τελευτῆς Ἡρῴδου
"and he was *there* *until* the death of Herod" (Mt. 2:15)

ἡ δὲ <u>ἄνω</u> Ἰερουσαλὴμ ἐλευθέρα ἐστίν
"now the Jerusalem *above* is free" (Gal. 4:26)

Comparisons

Adjective Comparisons

Table 11.1—Degrees of Comparison

	Positive	Comparative	Superlative
English:	new	new-er	new-est
Greek:	νεός	νεώ-τερος	νεώ-τατος

(1) English Formation

Adjectives have three degrees of comparison: positive, comparative, and superlative. Positive degree is the simple adjective. Comparative is *more*. Superlative is *most*. English degrees can be formed regularly or irregularly. Regular formation is by: (1) suffixes: *high, high-er, high-est*, or (2) auxiliary words: *high, more high, most high*. Irregular formation uses alternate words: *good, better, best*.

(2) Greek Formation

Greek degrees also are formed regularly or irregularly. Regular suffixes are: comparative -τερ-; superlative either a -τατ- or -ιστ-. Inflection is added for case, gender, and number according to adjective declensions. Irregular formation represents vocabulary words to be learned (as in English). Common irregular forms are: πλείων ("more," "greater," 57 times; πολύς); μείζων ("greater," "larger," 48 times; μέγας); and κρείττων (or κρείσσων, "better," 19 times; ἀγαθός).

(3) Substantival Use

As with any adjective, an adjective degree form also can be made into a substantive when constructed with the article. So, ὁ ἐλάχιστος means "the least," and could be the subject, or predicate complement, or some other nominative case role.

(4) Koine Changes

As with other grammatical items, koine Greek was changing the rules for the comparative degree. Adjectives in comparative form were used with superlative meaning. That is, the *form* you see may be comparative (e.g. *smaller*), but the *meaning* in context is superlative (e.g., *smallest*). Context is your only guide.

Examples of adjective degrees follow. (Mt. 13:32 illustrates comparative form but superlative meaning.)

- *Regular adjectives:*

ὅτε ἦς <u>νεώτερος</u>
"when you were *younger*" (Jn. 21:18)

τῇ <u>ἁγιωτάτῃ</u> ὑμῶν πίστει
"on your *most holy* faith" (Jude 1:20)

Ἐγὼ γάρ εἰμι <u>ὁ ἐλάχιστος</u> τῶν ἀποστόλων
"For I am *the least* of the apostles" (1 Cor. 15:9)

ὃ <u>μικρότερον</u> μέν ἐστιν πάντων τῶν σπερμάτων
"which is *the smallest* of all the seeds" (Mt. 13:32)

- *Irregular adjectives:*

οὐχὶ ἡ ψυχὴ <u>πλεῖόν</u> ἐστιν τῆς τροφῆς;
"Is not your life *more* than food?" (Mt. 9:16)

καὶ <u>χεῖρον</u> σχίσμα γίνεται
"and a *worse* tear happens" (Mt. 9:16)

Adverb Comparisons

Greek adverbs have degrees too; unlike adjectives, adverb degrees are not inflected (as adverbs are not). Adverb degrees are uncommon in the New Testament. Of the *comparative* adverbs, most occurrences are the word μᾶλλον ("more," 81 of 144). Of the *superlative* adverbs, most occurrences are the one word μάλιστα ("most," 12 of 19). Thus, if you know "more" (μάλλον) and "most" (μάλιστα), you know more than most. ☺ Observe the following examples:

φίλε, προσανάβηθι <u>ἀνώτερον</u>
"Friend, move up *higher*" (Lk 14:10)

μακάριόν ἐστιν <u>μᾶλλον</u> διδόναι ἢ λαμβάνειν
"to give is *more* blessed than to receive" (Acts 20:35)

καὶ <u>μάλιστα</u> ἐπὶ σοῦ, βασιλεῦ Ἀγρίππα
"and *especially* before you, O King Agrippa" (Acts 25:26)

Constructions for Comparison

(1) Ablative of Comparison
Three basic constructions occur for comparisons. The first is putting the substantive after the comparative adjective in genitive case with ablative function without a preposition. English translation inserts "than":

οὐκ ἔστιν δοῦλος μείζων <u>τοῦ κυρίου αὐτοῦ</u>
"a servant is not greater *than his master*" (Jn. 13:16)

(2) Accusative of Comparison
A second method uses prepositions, either παρά or ὑπέρ, with the substantive in accusative case after the comparative adjective:

τομώτερος <u>ὑπὲρ πᾶσαν μάχαιραν δίστομον</u>
"sharper *than any two-edged sword*" (Heb. 4:12)

(3) Conjunction ἤ ("than")
A third method uses the conjunction ἤ, which means "or," but used in comparisons means "than." The words, phrases, or clauses compared will be the same case. Often, this comparison is of expanded clauses:

εὐκοπώτερον δέ ἐστιν τὸν οὐρανὸν καὶ τὴν γῆν παρελθεῖν <u>ἢ</u> τοῦ νόμου μίαν κεραίαν πεσεῖν.

"For heaven and earth to pass away is easier *than* one small stroke of a letter of the law to fall." (Lk. 16:17)

Genitive of Relationship

The genitive can be used to express assumed family relationship. That is, the author does not spell out a relationship. Rather, a personal name is given in the genitive case and the reader supplies the relationship. Observe:

Ἰάκωβον τὸν τοῦ Ζεβεδαίου
"James the *son of* Zebedee" (Mt. 4:21)

Μαρία ἡ Ἰακώβου
"Mary the *mother of* James" (Lk. 24:10)

Numerals

Cardinal Numbers

Cardinal numbers are counting numbers: *one, two,* etc. In Greek, the numbers *one* through *four* are inflected, a mixture of the three declensions. *One* is only singular; *two, three,* and *four* are only plural. *Five* to *nine* are not inflected.

Table 11.2—Cardinals 1–4

One			Two	Three		Four	
Mas.	Neu.	Fem.	M/N/F	M/F	N	M/F	N
εἷς	ἕν	μία	δύο	τρεῖς	τρία	τέσσαρες	-α
ἑνός	ἑνός	μιᾶς	δύο	τριῶν	τριῶν	τεσσάρων	-ων
ἑνί	ἑνί	μιᾷ	δυσί	τρισί	τρισί	τέσσαρσι	-σι
ἕνα	ἕν	μίαν	δύο	τρεῖς	τρία	τέσσαρας	-α

Teens are numbers added to the base of *ten*. Single-digit additions can be:

- prefixed: ἕνδεκα ("eleven")
- suffixed: δεκατρεῖς ("thirteen")
- with καί: ἕπτά καὶ δέκα ("seventeen")

Between *twenty* and a *hundred*, numbers are added to the appropriate ten-interval base. All ten-intervals use a -κοντα suffix, except *twenty* (εἴκοσι). Single-digit additions can be:

- before καί: τρεῖς καὶ εἴκοσι ("twenty-three")
- after καί: τριάκοντα καὶ τρεῖς ("thirty-three")
- without καί: τεσσεράκοντα τρεῖς ("forty-three")

One hundred is ἑκατόν. All other hundred intervals use a -κόσιοι suffix (διακόσιοι, τριακόσιοι, etc.), always plural, with second and first declension inflection for gender.

One thousand is χίλιοι. All other thousand intervals then use this χίλιοι as a suffix (δισχίλιοι, τρισχίλιοι, etc.), always plural, with second and first declension inflection for gender.

Ten thousand is μύριοι, always plural (Mt. 18:24). Greeks had no cardinal intervals past the ten thousand unit. After that, you just had the noun "myriads" (μυριάς, μυριάδες). A few times one sees χιλιάδες with a number (cf. Lk. 14:31).

Numbers are written out exactly as spoken. "One hundred fifty three" is ἑκατὸν πεντήκοντα τριῶν (Jn. 21:11). "Six hundred sixty six" is ἑξακόσιοι ἑξήκοντα ἕξ (Rev. 13:18).

What to know for cardinals? Know vocabulary for *one* to *ten*, *twenty*, *one hundred*, *one thousand*, *ten thousand*. Then, know the interval suffixes: -κοντα (ten), -κοσιοι (hundred), -χιλιοι (thousand), and that μυριάδες is "myriads," and you've got it!

Ordinal Numbers

Ordinals are ordering numbers: *first*, *second*, etc. The only ordinals that occur with significant frequency in the New Testament are *first*, *second*, and *third* (πρῶτος, δεύτερος, and τρῖτος). These ordinal numbers function as adjectives and are inflected like adjectives. Observe:

λέγει αὐτῷ πάλιν <u>δεύτερον</u>
"he says to him again *a second time*" (Jn. 21:16)

When articular, ordinals become substantives, just as with any adjective. Observe:

ὁμοίως καὶ <u>ὁ δεύτερος</u> καὶ <u>ὁ τρίτος</u> ἕως <u>τῶν ἑπτά</u>.
"likewise also *the second* and *the third* until *the seventh*"
(Mt. 22:26)

Adverbials

Adverbials are a few cardinal numbers transformed into adverbs: *once, twice*, etc. The difference between cardinals and adverbials is that cardinals are adjectives; they modify substantives and are inflected. Adverbials are adverbs; they modify verbs and are not inflected.

Only two adverbials are in common use in English: *once* and *twice*. The now archaic word *thrice* used to be a part of this adverbial group, but its use has fallen out completely in contemporary English. Above *twice*, English idiom reverts to counting the number of times (a cardinal number modifying the word "times": *three times, four times*, etc.).

Three adverbials occurring with some frequency in the New Testament are *once, twice*, and *thrice* (ἅπαξ, δίς, τρίς). The expression "once and twice" (ἅπαξ καὶ δίς) is proverbial for "more than once," "many times," or "often." Observe:

Χριστὸς <u>ἅπαξ</u> περὶ ἁμαρτιῶν ἔπαθεν
"Christ suffered for sins *once*" (1 Pet. 3:18)

<u>ἅπαξ καὶ δίς</u> εἰς τὴν χρείαν μοι ἐπέμψατε
"*more than once* you sent (help) for my need" (Phil. 4:16)

Clause Connectors

Independent Clauses

Coordinate conjunctions typically join items of equal grammatical rank.[1] Only coordinate conjunctions can connect independent clauses. The four coordinate conjunctions, *and*, *but*, *therefore*, and *for*, connect clauses expressing copulative, adversative, inferential, and causal logic respectively. In addition to their main job joining equal grammatical items, coordinate conjunctions also can join unequal grammatical items.

(1) Copulative
The workhorse coordinate *copulative* in Greek is καί. This copulative regularly joins independent clauses. This use is common and obvious. However, "and" is not the only translation for καί. When not dealing with clauses, you should look for other nuances for καί, such as "also," "even," or even an adversative idea, such as "and yet" or "but." For example:

ὡς <u>καὶ</u> ἡμεῖς ἀφήκαμεν τοῖς ὀφειλέταις ἡμῶν
"as we *also* have forgiven our debtors" (Mt. 6:12)

Another feature about καί is its double construction in the form καί . . . καί, equivalent to our *both . . . and*. Note:

<u>καὶ</u> ἐμὲ <u>καὶ</u> τὸν πατέρα μου
"*both* me *and* my Father" (Jn. 15:24)

(2) Adversative
The workhorse coordinate *adversatives* in Greek are δέ and ἀλλά. We translate these regularly as "but." The two independent clauses are placed in contrast. The stronger term is ἀλλά and can also be translated by "yet" or "rather." The weaker term is δέ and can be translated by "now" or "and," or even

---

[1]See p. 451-52.

just a connecting particle without translation. (A close variant of δέ is the Classical form τέ). Note:

οὐχί, <u>ἀλλὰ</u> κληθήσεται Ἰωάννης
"No! *Rather*, he will be called John" (Lk. 1:60)

Ἐγένετο <u>δὲ</u> ἐν ταῖς ἡμέραις ἐκείναις
"*Now*, it came about in those days" (Lk. 2:1)

(3) Inferential

The workhorse coordinate *inferential* in Greek is οὖν. We translate this regularly as "therefore." The clause after οὖν is inferred from the clause before. We also could use "so" or "consequently." Note:

οὕτως <u>οὖν</u> προσεύχεσθε ὑμεῖς
"*Consequently*, you pray in this way" (Mt. 6:9)

(4) Causal

The workhorse coordinate *causal* in Greek is γάρ, normally translated "for." This conjunction joins logical clauses that can go on for verses. For example, notice how Paul began Rom. 1:8 with a γάρ series that literally goes on through the rest of the chapter! This long γάρ series includes the famous theme statement beginning in 1:16:

Οὐ <u>γὰρ</u> ἐπαισχύνομαι τὸ εὐαγγέλιον
"*For* I am not ashamed of the gospel" (Rom. 1:16)

Dependent Clauses

Dependent clauses function as nouns, adjectives, or adverbs within independent clauses. Dependent clauses always are introduced by one of three connectors: subordinate conjunctions, relative pronouns, or conjunctive adverbs.[2]

---

[2]See pp. 459-61. *Study relative pronouns (vocabulary)!* Cf. pp. 119-20.

(1) Dependent Noun Clauses

A workhorse noun clause connector is the subordinate conjunction ὅτι, meaning "that." For example, verbs of perception (e.g., *see, hear, think, know, read*) require an object clause that a following ὅτι usually introduces. For example:

γινώσκομεν <u>ὅτι</u> ἐν αὐτῷ ἐσμεν
"we know *that* we are in Him" (1 Jn. 2:5)

Reported speech always is a direct object of a verb of saying, in Greek regularly introduced by ὅτι. Direct discourse is a report of what a person directly says, put in quotation marks. Indirect discourse is a second-hand report of what a person said. When introducing a *direct discourse* clause, the ὅτι is the equivalent of our quotation marks and simply is not translated:

λέγει αὐτοῖς <u>ὅτι</u> ἦραν τὸν κύριόν μου
"She said to them, 'They have taken my Lord.'" (Jn. 20:13)

When introducing *indirect discourse*, the ὅτι *is* translated:

οὐ καλῶς λέγομεν ἡμεῖς <u>ὅτι</u> Σαμαρίτης εἶ σύ;
"do we not say well *that* you are a Samaritan?" (Jn. 8:48)

English idiom is to convert indirect discourse tenses one step backward in time in reported speech. Note, direct discourse: "I *am* going"; but reported as indirect discourse: "He said that he *was going*" (*present* versus *past*). Again, "I *went*"; but "He said that he *had gone*" (*past* versus *past perfect*). Greek idiom simply maintains the original direct discourse tense in the indirect discourse report. You *may* have to convert Greek tenses in discourse translation to represent the proper English idiom.

(2) Dependent Adjective Clauses

The workhorse connector to introduce adjective clauses is the relative pronoun (ὅς, ὅ, ἥ). Review pages 119-20 on the relative pronoun now. Carefully study the examples. Relative pronouns are used heavily in both English and Greek.

Conjunctive adverbs also introduce adjective clauses. So:

ἴδετε τὸν τόπον <u>ὅπου</u> ἔκειτο
"see the place *where* he lay" (Mt. 28:6)

ἐν ἡμέρᾳ <u>ὅτε</u> κρίνει ὁ θεός
"on the day *when* God judges" (Rom. 2:16)

Less often, ὅτι can introduce an adjective clause. Thus:

ὁ λόγος . . . <u>ὅτι</u> ὁ μαθητὴς ἐκεῖνος οὐκ ἀποθνῄσκει
"the rumor . . . *that* that disciple would not die" (Jn. 21:23)

(3) Dependent Adverb Clauses

The workhorse connector to introduce adverb clauses is the conjunctive adverb (the adverb used as a conjunction). Note:

τὸ πνεῦμα <u>ὅπου</u> θέλει πνεῖ
"the wind blows *where* it wishes" (Jn. 3:8)

<u>ὅτε</u> ἤμην νήπιος, ἐλάλουν ὡς νήπιος
"*when* we were infants, we spoke as infants" (1 Cor. 13:11)

ἴσθι <u>ἐκεῖ</u> <u>ἕως</u> ἂν εἴπω σοι
"stay *there* <u>until</u> I tell you" (Mt. 2:13)

<u>τότε</u> λέγει αὐτῷ ὁ Ἰησοῦς
"*then* Jesus says (said) to him" (Mt. 4:10)

περιπατεῖτε <u>ὡς</u> τὸ φῶς ἔχετε
"walk *while* you have the light" (Jn. 12:35)

The subordinate conjunction ὅτι not only can introduce noun clauses with the translation "that" but also adverb clauses with the translation "because" (causal). For example:

ὑμεῖς γινώσκετε αὐτό, <u>ὅτι</u> παρ᾽ ὑμῖν μένει
"You know him *because* he abides with you" (Jn. 14:17)

ὁ ὀφθαλμός σου πονηρός ἐστιν <u>ὅτι</u> ἐγὼ ἀγαθός εἰμι;
"Is your eye evil *because* I am good?" (Mt. 20:15)
Idiomatic: "Are you envious because I am good?"

Diagramming

Adverbs and comparatives go under the element modified. If substantival, a comparative acts as subject or predicate adjective, so takes the appropriate slot for its function.

Numerals are adjectives. They go under the element modified or in a substantival slot (subject, object) when so used.

Copulative or adversative conjunctions join separate verb lines. Inferentials and causals can be placed at the beginning of their clause in front of the subject on a support.

Dependent clauses act as nouns, adjectives, or adverbs. Noun function requires a standard in subject or object slots. Adjective and adverb clauses go under the element modified.

Relative pronouns require a separate verb line. The pronoun is connected by a dotted line from its function in its own clause back to its antecedent in the independent clause.

Adverbs

καὶ <u>οὕτως</u> πᾶς Ἰσραὴλ σωθήσεται
"and *in this way* all Israel will be saved" (Rm. 11:26)

Comparisons (substantival use)

οὐχὶ ἡ ψυχὴ <u>πλεῖόν</u> ἐστιν τῆς τροφῆς;
"Is not your life *more* than food?" (Mt. 9:16)

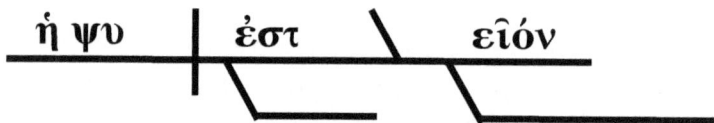

Chapter 11: Adverbs and More

Numerals

ἐν τρισὶν ἡμέραις ἐγερῶ αὐτόν
"in *three* days I will raise it" (Jn. 2:19)

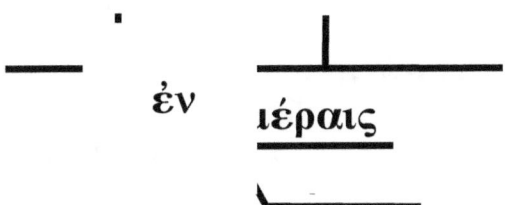

Coordinating Conjunctions

ὁ οἶνος ἐκχεῖται καὶ οἱ ἀσκοὶ ἀπόλλυνται.
"The wine is poured out *and* the skins are destroyed." (Mt. 9:17)

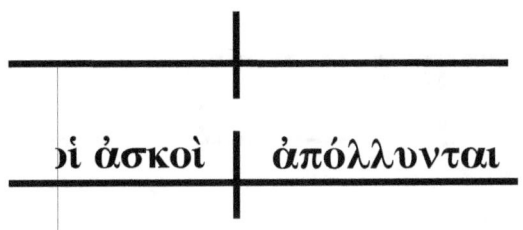

Dependent Noun Clause

λέγω δὲ ὑμῖν ὅτι τοῦ ἱεροῦ μεῖζόν ἐστιν ὧδε.
"But I tell you *that* greater than the temple is here." (Mt. 12:6)

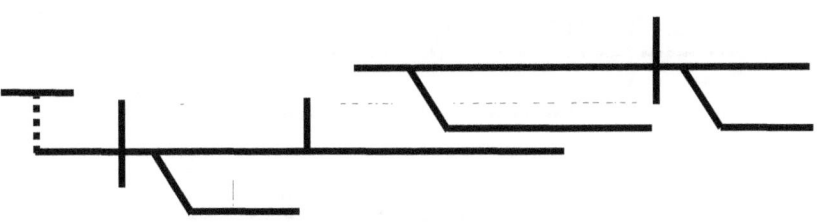

Dependent Adjective Clause

ἴδετε τὸν τόπον ὅπου ἔκειτο
"see the place *where* he lay" (Mt. 28:6)

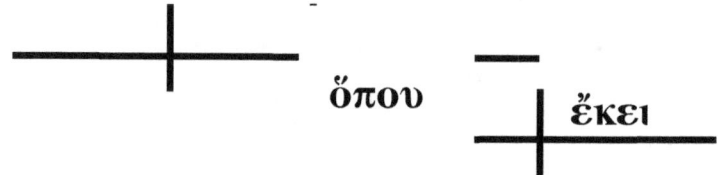

Dependent Adverb Clause

περιπατεῖτε ὡς τὸ φῶς ἔχετε.
"Walk *while* you have the light." (Jn. 12:35)

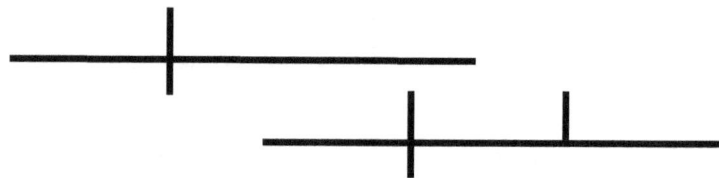

Relative Pronoun

νῦν ὃν ἔχεις οὐκ ἔστιν σου ἀνήρ.
"*Whom* you now have is not your husband." (Jn. 4:18)

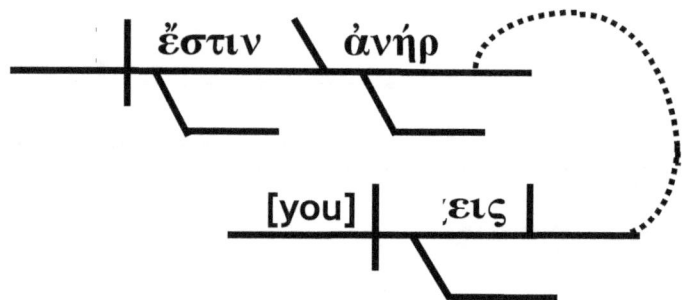

Chapter 11: Adverbs and More

Exercise 11

1. **Degrees of Comparison**

    1.1 *Formation:* Complete the following. For the last example, supply the Greek word for the English adjective in the previous example; the comparative is in this chapter's vocabulary; the superlative stem is supplied, but use the *alternate* superlative ending.

	Positive	Comparative	Superlative
Eng.:	strong	_____	_____
Grk.:	ἰσχυρός	ἰσχυρο-_____	ἰσχυρο-_____
Eng.:	good	_____	_____
Grk.:	_____	_____	κράτ-_____

    1.2 *Construction—three methods:*

    1.2a <u>No preposition</u>: after the comparative adjective the noun is constructed in _____ case with _____ function. English translation supplies the word _____.

    1.2b <u>Prepositions</u>: after the comparative adjective, either of the two prepositions _____ or _____ is used with the _____ case for the noun.

    1.2c <u>Conjunction</u>: the conjunction _____ is used.

2. In family relationships, sometimes the author will put a name in the _____ case and expect the reader to supply the relationship.

3. Numerals

   3.1 *Cardinals*

   _____ one   _____ six
   _____ two   _____ seven
   _____ three   _____ eight
   _____ four   _____ nine
   _____ five   _____ ten

   _____ twenty   _____ one thousand
   _____ one hundred _____ ten thousand
   _____ ten intervals (suffix)
   _____ hundred intervals (suffix)
   _____ thousand intervals (suffix)

   3.2 *Ordinals*

   _____ first, _____ second, _____ third

   3.3 *Adverbials*

   _____ once, _____ twice, _____ thrice

4. Translate. Analyze adverbs. Identify the dependent clause functions. Use your UBS dictionary for unknown words.

   4.1 ὃ δὲ ὑμῖν λέγω πᾶσιν λέγω. (Mk. 13:37)
   _____

Chapter 11: Adverbs and More

4.2 νῦν δὲ λέγετε ὅτι βλέπομεν. (Jn. 9:41)

4.3 ἀλλὰ ἔρχεται ὥρα καὶ νῦν ἐστιν. (Jn. 4:23)

4.4 λέγει ὅτι ἐγὼ οὐκ εἰμὶ ὁ χριστός. (Jn. 1:20*)

4.5 ὅς ἐστιν εὐλογητὸς εἰς τοὺς αἰῶνας, ἀμήν. (Rom. 1:25)

4.6 ἰσχυρότερός (ἰσχυρός) μού ἐστιν, οὗ οὐκ εἰμὶ ἱκανὸς. (Mt. 3:11)

4.7 καὶ ἐκ (from) τῶν ἐθνῶν εἰς οὓς ἐγὼ ἀποστέλλω σε. (Acts 26:17)

4.8 Ἐγὼ δὲ ἔχω τὴν μαρτυρίαν (μαρτυρία) μείζω τοῦ Ἰωάννου. (Jn. 5:36)

4.9 καὶ αὐτή ἐστιν χήρα ἕως ἐτῶν ὀγδοήκοντα τεσσάρων. (Lk. 2:37*)

4.10 ἀλλὰ ὑμεῖς οὐ πιστεύετε, ὅτι οὐκ ἐστὲ ἐκ τῶν προβάτων (πρόβατον) τῶν ἐμῶν. (Jn. 10:26)

4.11 οἶδά (I know) σου τὰ ἔργα ὅτι ὄνομα ἔχεις ὅτι ζῇς (ζάω, 2ps), καὶ νεκρὸς εἶ. (Rev. 3:1)

4.12 ἀκούω τὴν πίστιν ὑμῶν ἐν Χριστῷ Ἰησοῦ καὶ τὴν ἀγάπην ἣν ἔχετε εἰς πάντας τοὺς ἁγίους. (Col. 1:4*)

4.13 ἔσονται (they will be) γὰρ ἀπὸ τοῦ νῦν πέντε ἐν ἑνὶ οἴκῳ διαμεμερισμένοι (will be divided), τρεῖς ἐπὶ (against) δυσὶν καὶ δύο ἐπὶ τρισίν. (Lk. 12:52)

5. Diagram the following from above.

   5.1 [4.1]

   ὃ δὲ ὑμῖν λέγω πᾶσιν λέγω.

5.2 [4.4]

λέγει ὅτι ἐγὼ οὐκ εἰμὶ ὁ χριστός.

5.3 [4.8]

Ἐγὼ δὲ ἔχω τὴν μαρτυρίαν μείζω τοῦ Ἰωάννου.

5.4 [4.10]

ἀλλὰ ὑμεῖς οὐ πιστεύετε, ὅτι οὐκ ἐστὲ ἐκ τῶν προβάτων τῶν ἐμῶν.

5.5 [4.11]

οἶδά (I know) σου τὰ ἔργα ὅτι ὄνομα ἔχεις ὅτι ζῇς (ζάω, 2ps), καὶ νεκρὸς εἶ.

 **Vocabulary 11**

αἰών, -ος, ὁ, *age, eternity* (eon)

ἀρχιερεύς, -εως, ὁ, *high priest*

βάλλω, *I throw* (ballistics)

δύναμις, -εως, ἡ, *power, strength* (dynamic, dynasty, aerodynamic)

ἕν, *one* (neuter)

θάνατος, ὁ, *death* (euthanasia)

κρείττων, *better*

μάλιστα, *most*

μᾶλλον, *more*

μείζων, *greater, larger*

μία, *one* (feminine)

πλείων, *more, greater* (pleonastic)

εἷς, μία, ἕν, *one* (inflected)

εἴκοσι, *twenty*

ἑκατόν, *one hundred*

χίλιοι, *one thousand* (kilogram)

μύριοι, *ten thousand*

μυριάδες, *myriads*

-κοντα, *(ten interval)*

-κοσιοι, *(hundred interval)*

-χιλιοι, *(thousand interval)*

δεύτερος, *second* (Deuteronomy)

τρίτος, *third*

ἅπαξ, *once*

δίς, *twice*

τρίς, *three times*

ἐκεῖ, *there*

νῦν, *now*

ὅπου, *where*

ὅς, ἥ, ὅ, *who, whom, whose, which, that, what*

ὅτε, *when*

ὅτι, *that, because*

οὕτως, *thus, so, in this way*

πῶς, *how?*

ὡς, *as, while*

Vocabulary notes:

   (1) Words are grouped to facilitate recognition and include the three suffixes -κοντα, -κοσιοι, and -χιλιοι.

   (2) The relative pronoun (ὅς) is crucial. Review pp. 119-20.

Vocabulary Review 2

The following list summarizes words introduced since Review 1, generally by frequency of occurrence. The number is the chapter. (Check the next page too.)

Vocabularies 7–11

ἀγαθός 8
ἅγιος 8
αἰών 11
αἰώνιος 8
ἀλλά 7
ἀλλήλοις 9
ἀλλήλους 9
ἀλλήλων 9
ἄλλος 8
ἀμήν 10
ἀνήρ 7
ἅπαξ, 11
ἀποστέλλω 10
ἀρχιερεύς 11
αὐτός 9
βάλλω 11
γάρ 7
γυνή 7
δέκα 10
δεύτερος 11
δίς 11
δοῦλος 10

δύναμις 11
ἑαυτοῦ 9
ἑαυτῶν 9
ἐγείρω 10
ἐγώ 9
ἔθνος 7
εἴκοσι 11
εἰμί 8
ἑκατόν 11
ἐκεῖ 11
ἐκεῖνος 10
ἐμαυτοῦ 9
ἐμός 9
ἕν 11
ἐννέα 9
ἑπτά 7
ἕως 10
ἤ 7
ἥ 11
ἡμεῖς 9
ἡμέτερος 9
θάνατος 11

ἴδιος 9
ἰδού 7
Ἰουδαῖος 8
καθώς 7
καλός 8
κρείττων 11
λαός 10
μάλιστα 11
μᾶλλον 11
μέγας 8
μείζων 11
μέν 7
μία 11
μόνος 8
μυριάδες 11
μύριοι 11
νεκρός 8
νόμος 10
νῦν 11
ὅ 11
οἷος 10
ὀκτώ 8

ὅλος 8
ὄνομα 7
ὅπου 11
ὅς 11
ὅσος 10
ὅτε 11
ὅτι 11
οὐδέ 10
οὐδείς 8
οὖν 7
οὗτος 10
οὕτως 11
ὄχλος 7
πάλιν 10
πᾶς 8
πατήρ 7
Παῦλος 7
Πέτρος 7
πίστις 7
πλείων 11
πνεῦμα 7
πόλις 7

πολύς 8	σός 9	τοσοῦτος 10	ὑμέτερος 9
πρῶτος 8	σύ 9	τότε 7	χάρις 7
πῶς 11	σῶμα 7	τρίς 11	χείρ 7
σάρξ 7	τέ 7	τρίτος 11	χίλιοι 11
σεαυτοῦ 9	τοιοῦτος 10	ὑμεῖς 9	ὡς 11

Photo © Gerald L. Stevens

Fig. 10. Ephesus Theater. The famous Ephesian Theater could hold as many as 25,000 people. The beautiful Marble Way avenue ran in front. Across the street is the lower agora (market). At the top right runs the Acadian Way, the harbor road bringing commerce in and out of this beautiful, bustling metropolis of the ancient world. The Greek theater complex was modified for gladiatorial contests by the Romans. (See Gladiator Stele, p. 88.)

Paul's Third Missionary Journey came to an abrupt end in the public riot led by Demetrius, a silversmith whose trade in Artemis figurines adversely had been affected by Paul's preaching. The agora mob moved across the street into the Ephesian theater, most in confusion even about the reason for the disturbance. In this state of unreasoned uproar, they still chanted, "Great is Artemis of the Ephesians," for about two hours (Acts 19:34).

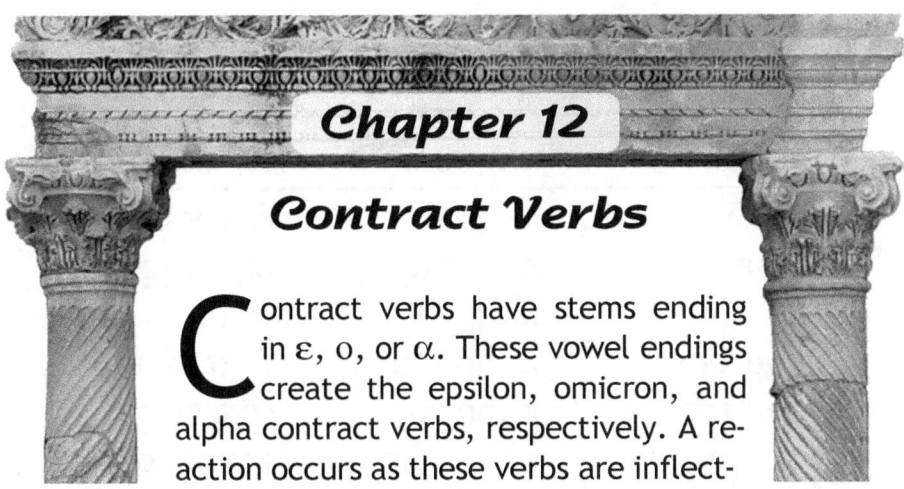

Chapter 12

Contract Verbs

Contract verbs have stems ending in ε, ο, or α. These vowel endings create the epsilon, omicron, and alpha contract verbs, respectively. A reaction occurs as these verbs are inflected. The ε, ο, or α short stem vowels of contract verbs combine with the ε and ο thematic vowels to create diphthongs or long vowels marked by circumflex accent. You need to recognize the results of contraction in order to find the correct contract verb in the dictionary. The question is, which contract vowel was on the verb stem before hidden in the contraction process?

Contraction Changes

First, verbs normally have acute accent only. (Did you notice?) If you see a circumflex accent over a verb, you likely have had contraction. Contraction occasionally can leave an acute accent, but even in this case the vowel has morphed.

Second, you no longer have the ε or ο thematic vowel. The verb's spelling in the text is with a *resultant* diphthong or long vowel. The resultant forms are easily identified. By consulting the tables below, you will discover that:

- Any α form—is alpha contract only.
- Any diphthong ι—is originally the other vowel.
- Diphthong ῇ—is epsilon contract.
- Diphthong οῦ—is either ε or ο contract.
- First singular ῶ—can be any of the three contracts.
- Any other ῶ—is alpha contract only.

175

Table 12.1—Present Active Contract Verbs

ποιέω	πληρόω	ἀγαπάω
ποιῶ	πληρῶ	ἀγαπῶ
ποιεῖς	πληροῖς	ἀγαπᾷς
ποιεῖ	πληροῖ	ἀγαπᾷ
ποιοῦμεν	πληροῦμεν	ἀγαπῶμεν
ποιεῖτε	πληροῦτε	ἀγαπᾶτε
ποιοῦσι(ν)	πληροῦσι(ν)	ἀγαπῶσι(ν)

Table 12.2—Present Middle Contract Verbs

ποιέω	πληρόω	ἀγαπάω
ποιοῦμαι	πληροῦμαι	ἀγαπῶμαι
ποιῇ	πληροῖ	ἀγαπᾷ
ποιεῖται	πληροῦται	ἀγαπᾶται
ποιούμεθα	πληρούμεθα	ἀγαπώμεθα
ποιεῖσθε	πληροῦσθε	ἀγαπᾶσθε
ποιοῦνται	πληροῦνται	ἀγαπῶνται

Table 12.3—Contraction Results

all	ε/ο	ε only		ο only	α only	
ῶ	οῦ	ῇ	εῖ	οῖ	ᾶ	ᾷ

In other words, only the final -ῶ and the -οῦ- are ambiguous about the original contract vowel! That's good news. We give three paradigms, one for each of the three contract verb types. Note: in the New Testament you never will see the verb in the uncontracted form at the top of the table (ποιέω, πληρόω, ἀγαπάω). That form is only the dictionary entry, which lets you know the stem vowel. (Originally, forms were uncontracted in earlier Greek dialects.)

Middle voice adds only one ending beyond what you see in active voice, the -ῇ of the epsilon contract. The second person singular -σαι changed as expected, but note circumflex accent!

Active and middle voice for both omicron and alpha contracts have two slots with the same result, which might confuse location. Compare *third* person singular *active* with *second* person singular *middle* for both (-οῖ, -ᾷ). However, context usually will indicate whether second person (*you*) or third person (*he, she, it*) is the subject. Practically speaking, you now will have to be able to recognize -οῖ and -ᾷ as verb endings.

One last word. Contracts affect form only. The meaning of the verb does not change. Thus, contract verbs are a recognition issue only.

Cases for Direct Object

Ever notice how some verbs just seem to scream to be followed by certain prepositions? Take "believe." The verb "believe" just screams for the preposition "in," as in, "Do you *believe in* capitalism?" Or take the verb "hear." The verb "hear" just screams for the preposition "of," as in, "I never *heard of* that"; also note the verb "afraid" in "What are you *afraid of?*"

Recall that "in" typically is dative case in English and "of" is genitive case. That is, certain verbs seem to demand certain prepositions—think of cases—to follow them to express the object. The verb's object is more like the object of the preposition expected to follow. This effect could be due to the nature of the action inherent in particular verb stems.

Greek is similar. Certain Greek verbs just screamed for certain cases to follow them to express the verb's direct object other than just accusative.

Object Cases—Ἀκολουθέω (Dative)

ἀκολουθοῦσιν αὐτῷ οἱ μαθηταὶ αὐτοῦ
"his disciples follow (followed) him" (Mk. 6:1)

Object Cases—Ἀκούω (Genitive, Accusative)

(1) Genitive Case

ἀκούει μου τῆς φωνῆς
"he hears my voice" (Jn. 18:37)

(2) Accusative

ἀκούεις τί οὗτοι λέγουσιν;
"do you hear what these are saying?" (Mt. 21:16)

Object Cases—Πιστεύω (Dative, Accusative)

(1) Dative Case

οὐ πιστεύετέ μοι
"you do not believe me" (Jn. 8:45)

ὁ πιστεύων ἐπ' αὐτῷ
"the one who believes in him" (Rom. 9:33)

(2) Accusative Case (ἐπί, εἰς)

πιστεύσομεν ἐπ' αὐτόν
"we will believe in him" (Mt. 27:42)

οὐ πιστεύουσιν εἰς ἐμέ
"they do not believe in me" (Jn. 16:9)

Take note of the three verbs you encounter regularly that have other cases for direct object given above. Otherwise, you will miss your direct object and be completely stumped. Your sentence will make no sense, and you will get a "return to sender" on your sentence truck (pp. 494-95).

Copulative Verbs

Already you have met the two copulative verbs γίνομαι and εἰμί. These verbs are intransitive, so do not take an object. However, they *can* take a predicate complement in the nominative case, either a predicate noun or a predicate adjective.

One other verb used as a copulative is ὑπάρχω. This verb often was used as a participle to refer to one's possessions, in the literal sense of "that which exists to me." Use of ὑπάρχω represents a more refined Greek. Neither Mark nor John use this verb, and Matthew clocks in only three times. A full two-thirds of all New Testament occurrences are in Luke and Acts. Paul has the lion's share of the rest.

ἡμῶν γὰρ τὸ πολίτευμα ἐν οὐρανοῖς <u>ὑπάρχει</u>
"for our citizenship *is* in heaven" (Phil. 3:20)

Historical Present

Sometimes we have included with a present tense translation a past tense form in parentheses. Notice this format in our illustration of ἀκολουθέω earlier, repeated below:

ἀκολουθοῦσιν αὐτῷ οἱ μαθηταὶ αὐτοῦ
"his disciples follow (followed) him" (Mk. 6:1)

Using present tense in a past tense narrative was a feature of colloquial Greek to add vividness to story telling (a "we were there" approach). Even today we switch to present tense in telling a story: "So, after he *had witnessed* the accident, he *calls* for an ambulance and *rushes off* to the hospital." In a story, such as gospel material, when you are in a series of past tense verbs and suddenly hit a present tense, you probably have the "historical present," properly translated with past tense. So, whenever you see a present tense verb translated as past tense, probably that verb has been understood as an historical present. This Greek idiom happens only in *indicative* mood, with *past* time narrative, and only *third* person. Present tense forms of copulatives (especially εἰμί) are not historical presents. Note that some grammarians now are arguing to leave these present tenses as present tense for the sake of vividness, especially, for example, in the (highly koine) Gospel of Mark.

Uses of the Negative

We have learned one negative, οὐ (οὐκ, οὐχ). Greek has a second negative, μή. This second negative mainly is used in the non-indicative moods, which we have not studied. Yet, μή does have some special uses in the indicative. We cover two of these uses now. A third use is with conditional sentences (chap. 14).

(1) Rhetorical Questions—Expected Answers
When you ask a rhetorical question, you have a particular answer you expect, either yes or no. For example, you could ask, "You *will* study tonight, *won't* you?" Notice use of the future tense auxiliary "will," followed by its immediate negation (in contracted form), "won't." That grammatical framing signals that a "yes" answer is expected.

On the other hand, you could say, "You *would not* go to the movie, *would* you?" Notice here the use of a negated subjunctive mood auxiliary, "would *not*," followed by its immediate affirmation, "would." That grammatical framing expects a "no" answer.

Greek signals are much more simple—either οὐ or μή with the indicative mood! Use of οὐ expects a "yes" answer. Use of μή expects a "no" answer. Notice:

<u>οὐκ</u> εἰμὶ ἀπόστολος;
"Am I *not* an apostle?" (1 Cor. 9:1)
(answer expected: οὐ = "yes")

μὴ ἰσχυρότεροι αὐτοῦ ἐσμεν;
"Are we stronger than he?" (1 Cor. 10:22)
(answer expected: μή = "no")

Notice English would repeat the verb as a question at the end of the translation ("are we?") if the basic assertion were framed in the negative: "We are *not* stronger than he, *are we?*"

(2) Emphatic Negation (οὐ μή)

English considers a double negative improper. "Don't *never* do that again!" a guy shouts in the hallway. The English teacher on hall duty rushes into the melee: "You mean, 'Don't *ever*,' right?" she corrects. The student, assuming the teacher simply has affirmed his remonstrance and is backing him up, turns back to the offender, pushes him in the chest, and says with a newly presumed authority, "Right. That's exactly what I said!"

Greek allows a double negative. Using οὐ and μή together as οὐ μή (notice the order) is equivalent to strong emphasis; the οὐ μή can be translated variously as "not," "never," "in no way." For example, Jesus' opponents at one point demand that he confess that he is the Messiah. Jesus, however, responds emphatically:

ἐὰν ὑμῖν εἴπω, οὐ μὴ πιστεύσητε
"If I told you, you would *never* believe!" (Lk. 22:67)

Genitive: "Of" = ?

The little preposition "of" is more ambiguous than first appears. For example, "the love of God" means what? My love of God, or God's love for me? Those options are two different realities altogether! When we meet a genitive in Greek that is to be translated as "of," we need to be prepared to decide which of these two options we intend to convey in translation. When specifically does this ambiguity for "of" crop up?

The problem with "of" occurs when the noun involved with our "of" construction is one that could be made into a verb. A noun that could be made into a verb is called a "noun of action." The noun "love" can be made into the verb "love," so the noun "love" is a "noun of action." Such "noun of action" constructions with "of" have to clarify whether option one or option two above is meant.

Notice that the very construction grammatically of the first option, "my love of God," makes the genitive God the *object* of the preposition connected to the noun of action, "love." This option is called the *objective genitive*.

Notice in the grammatical construction of the other option, "God's love for me," that the genitive God is transformed into a subject performing the action of the noun of action (love). This option is called the *subjective genitive*.

The problem described above traditionally is called the issue of the "subjective or objective genitive." To summarize, this issue: (1) involves a noun of action and asks whether the following genitive noun is a (2) subjective genitive: the genitive noun *performs* the implied verbal action, or an (3) objective genitive: the genitive noun *receives* the implied verbal action.

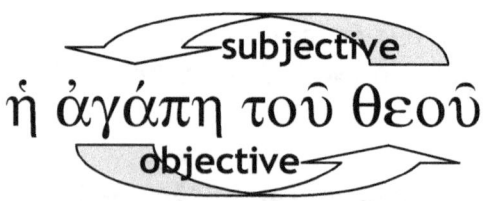

Note the following:

> But whoever keeps his word,
> indeed in this person ἡ ἀγάπη τοῦ θεοῦ
> has been perfected. (1 Jn. 2:5)

Is this a subjective or an objective genitive? Be ready to defend your choice, but your arguments must be contextual.

Chapter 12: Contract Verbs

Exercise 12

1. Translate. Be ready to locate contract verbs. Look up unknown words in your UBS dictionary.

   1.1 γεννῶσιν μάχας (μάχη). (2 Tim. 2:23)

   1.2 φοβῇ σὺ τὸν θεόν; (Lk. 23:40*)

   1.3 ἐν αὐτῷ γὰρ ζῶμεν. (Acts 17:28)

   1.4 πάντες ζητοῦσίν σε. (Mk. 1:37)

   1.5 ἧσσον (less) ἀγαπῶμαι; (2 Cor. 12:15)

   1.6 σὺ δὲ πόσον ὀφείλεις (ὀφείλω); (Lk. 16:7)

   1.7 ὁ πατὴρ ἀγαπᾷ τὸν υἱόν. (John 3:35)

   1.8 οὐκ κατὰ ἀγάπην περιπατεῖς. (Rom. 14:15*)

1.9 ἐν ποίᾳ ἐξουσίᾳ ταῦτα ποιεῖς; (Mt. 21:23)

_____

1.10 παρακαλούμεθα αὐτοὶ ὑπὸ τοῦ θεοῦ. (2 Cor. 1:4)

_____

1.11 οὐ τὸ ἔργον μου ὑμεῖς ἐστε ἐν κυρίῳ; (1 Cor 9:1)

_____

_____ Does Paul expect a *yes* or a *no* answer?

1.12 λέγει δέ· ὁ Ἰησοῦς· ἄνθρωπός τις ἔχει δύο υἱούς. (Lk. 15:11*)

_____

_____

1.13 καὶ λέγει αὐτοῖς ὁ Ἰησοῦς· πόσους ἄρτους ἔχετε; (Mt. 15:34)

_____

_____

1.14 πιστεύεις, βασιλεῦ (vocative) Ἀγρίππα, τοῖς προφήταις; (Acts 26:27)

_____

_____

1.15 Τί δέ με καλεῖτε· κύριε κύριε (vocative), καὶ οὐ ποιεῖτε ἃ λέγω; (Lk. 6:46)

Chapter 12: Contract Verbs

1.16 οἱ βασιλεῖς τῆς γῆς ἀπὸ τίνων λαμβάνουσιν τέλη (toll) ἢ κῆνσον (tribute); (Matt. 17:25)

1.17 Πᾶς οὖν ὅστις ἀκούει μου τοὺς λόγους τούτους καὶ ποιεῖ αὐτούς . . . (Mt. 7:24)

1.18 τότε λέγει τοῖς μαθηταῖς αὐτοῦ· ὁ μὲν θερισμὸς πολύς, οἱ δὲ ἐργάται (ἐργάτης) ὀλίγοι· (Mt. 9:37)

λέγει is _____ tense. If this sentence is from a narrative, λέγει needs to be _____ time in English. Thus, λέγει can be translated _____. This use is called the "_____ present."

1.19 τὰ πρόβατα (πρόβατον) τὰ ἐμὰ τῆς φωνῆς μου ἀκούουσιν, κἀγὼ γινώσκω αὐτὰ καὶ ἀκολουθοῦσίν μοι. (Jn. 10:27)

 **Vocabulary 12**

ἀγαπάω, *I love*

ἀκολουθέω, *I follow* (acolyte)

βασιλεύς, -έως, ὁ, *king* (basilica)

γεννάω, *I beget*

ζάω, ζήω, *I live*

ζητέω, *I seek*

καλέω, *I call* (Paraclete)

λαλέω, *I speak* (glossalalia)

μή, *no, not*

ὁράω, *I see* (panorama)

ὅστις, ἥτις, ὅτι, *who, whoever, which*

παρακαλέω, *I comfort, exhort, beseech* (Paraclete)

περιπατέω, *I walk* (peripatetic)

πληρόω, *I fulfill* (pleroma)

ποιέω, *I do, accomplish, produce* (poem)

ποῖος, -α, -ον, *which? what?*

πόσος, -α, -ον, *how much? how many?*

τίς, τί, *who? which?*

τις, τι, *someone, something, certain one, certain thing*

ὑπάρχω, *I am, be, exist*

φοβέομαι, *I am afraid of*

Vocabulary notes:

(1) The verb ἀκολουθέω takes a dative direct object.

(2) The verb ζάω also shows a dual formation as ζήω.

(3) Review interrogative (τίς, ποίος, πόσος), indefinite (τις), and indefinite relative (ὅστις) pronouns, pp. 120-22. Do not confuse correlatives οἷος and ὅσος (*as, as much as*) with interrogatives ποίος and πόσος.

(4) The verb ὑπάρχω functions as a copulative.

(5) The verb φοβέομαι actually has active voice forms (as φοβέω, *I frighten*) but these active forms never occur in the New Testament.

Language Lesson 3

Verb Morphology

Before we go farther with Greek tenses, we want to stand back and look at verb formation in general. At first, Greek verbs appear to be quite complicated in their forms. That makes them look intimidating. Greek verbs, however, can be handled much more easily than first appears by recognizing that *all* Greek verb formation operates on the basis of *six* basic morphological slots manipulated in various ways to create all Greek tenses, moods, and voices. Six is a manageable number. Divide and conquer!

Morphology Slots

Greek verb formation can be conquered by recognizing the six morphology slots that potentially can be used to create a tense, mood, and voice. Before we outline these slots, we give one qualification. Note: *compounds are independent elements always at the front of all slots*, regardless the total number involved in a given tense formation. Here are the six basic morphological slots:

(1) **Augmentation**—a time prefix indicating past time
(2) **Reduplication**—a tense prefix changing action kind
(3) **Tense stem**—a base indicating action kind
(4) **Tense suffix**—a tense suffix changing action kind
(5) **Thematic vowel**—a set o/ε pattern to join endings
(6) **Inflection**—endings indicating action performer

♦ *Compounds always precede all morphology slots.*

Table LL3.1—Verb Morphology

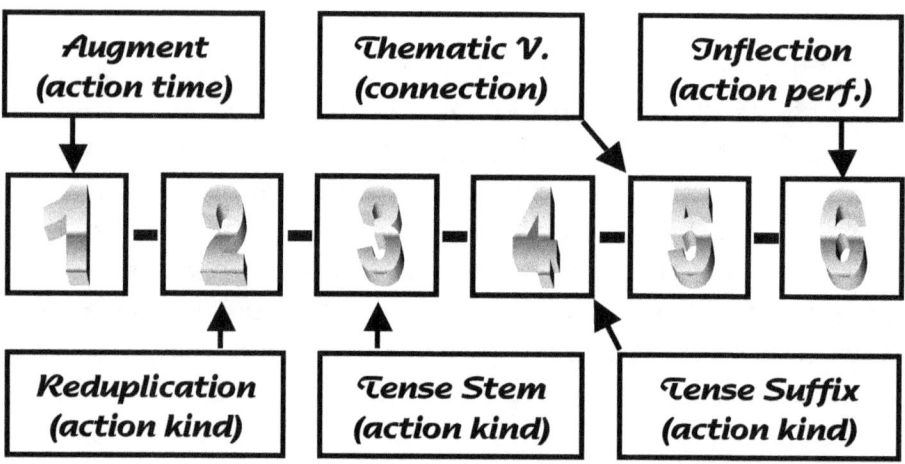

Morphology Mastery

Not every tense, mood, and voice formation will require all slots. Notice that present active indicative requires only slots 3, 5, and 6 (i.e., tense stem, thematic vowel, and inflection). So, for example, λύετε has the present tense stem, λυ-, thematic vowel, -ε-, and second person plural ending, -τε.

Table LL3.2—Morphology—Present Active Indicative

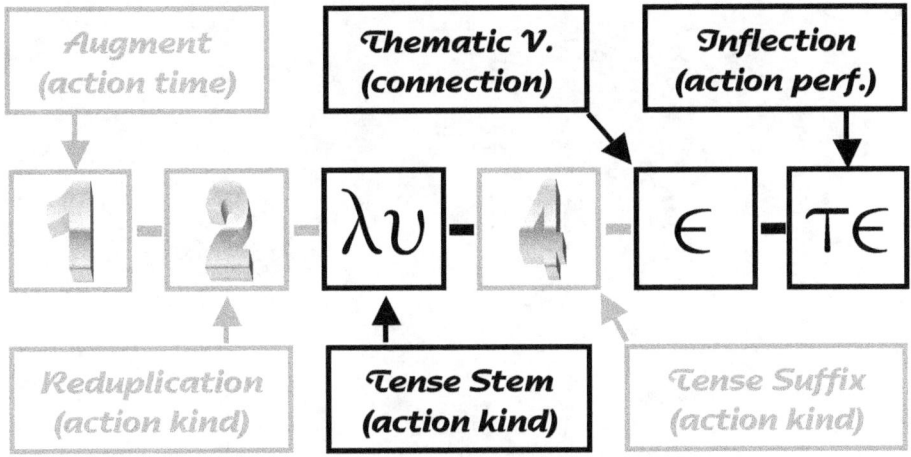

As is evident in the table above, the present tense stem, λυ-, provides the tense (action kind: durative), and the thematic vowel and ending, -ετε, provide the action potential (mood: indicative) and action performer (person: second; number: plural; and voice: active). Review pp. 466-67 and pp. 474-75, English 3, "Sentences," on these verb parameters of action performer and action potential.

Divide a given verb into these six morphology slots and you can master any Greek verb. Divide and conquer!

Photo © Gerald L. Stevens

Fig. 11. Hierapolis Theater. The ancient theater at Hierapolis in western Turkey is one of the few that has in tact the stage and backdrop area with the accompanying underground service tunnels. Sometimes the hollow ends of brass jars were sunken into the back walls of the theater stages, which created a natural amplification of the sound on the stage. Paul used this theater metaphor when he commended the Thessalonians that their faith had "sounded forth from you not only in Macedonia and Achaia, but in every place your faith in God has become known" (1 Thess. 1:8). Some ancient theaters are still used today. In this picture a troupe of actors is practicing for an upcoming performance of an ancient Greek play.

Hierapolis was part of a tri-city area that included Colossae 15 miles to the southeast on the Lycus river at the foot of Mount Cadmus and Laodicea 4 miles to the south. Hierapolis was famous for its natural warm springs, used for centuries as medicinal warm baths, especially by the Romans. The local spring water was rich in mineral content, so the flow over the mountainside evaporated into a white lime cascade arrested in time. The white cliffs of Hierapolis could be seen easily from Laodicea in the valley several miles away. (The modern Turkish name is Pamukkale, meaning, "Cotton Castle.") The church at Hierapolis probably was started under the work of Epaphras, one of Paul's co-workers during the Ephesian period of Paul's missionary labors (cf. Col. 4:13).

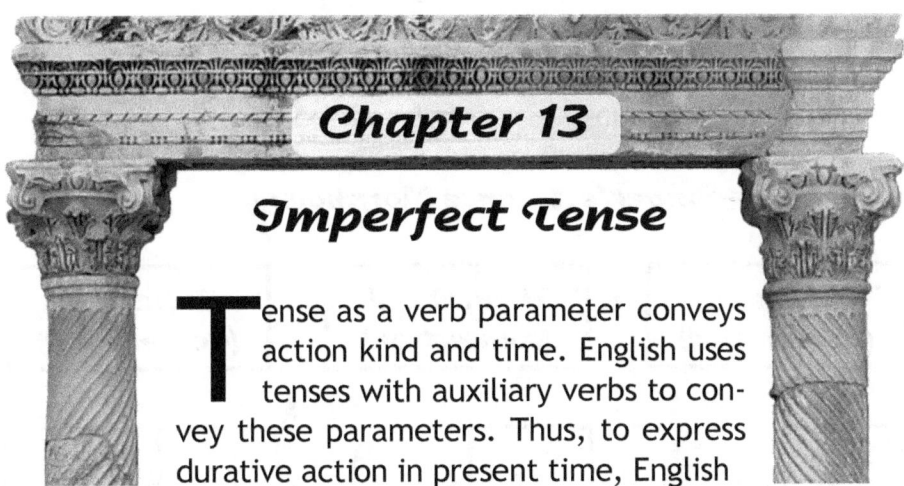

Chapter 13

Imperfect Tense

Tense as a verb parameter conveys action kind and time. English uses tenses with auxiliary verbs to convey these parameters. Thus, to express durative action in present time, English uses simple present tense: "I go." To make this action clearly durative, English invokes a form of the auxiliary verb "to be" and the present participle: "I *am* going." To put this durative action into past time, English retains the present participle for kind of action, but changes the auxiliary verb to past tense: "I *was* going."

Grammar of Time

In English, time is a function of tense, associated with the verb's tense stem. In Greek, time is a function of the indicative mood only, not associated with the tense stem. As a result, in Greek, a verb *must* be in the indicative mood to express the verb parameter of *action time*. Indicative mood is the default mood of a Greek verb—the assumed mood if other mood indicators are absent.

Imperfect Tense

Imperfect tense is durative action in past time. To make durative action in past time, Greek borrows the durative present tense stem with indicative mood. To make past time, Greek augments the tense stem, similar to English changing the auxiliary verb "am" to "was."

Table 13.1—Imperfect Tense Morphology

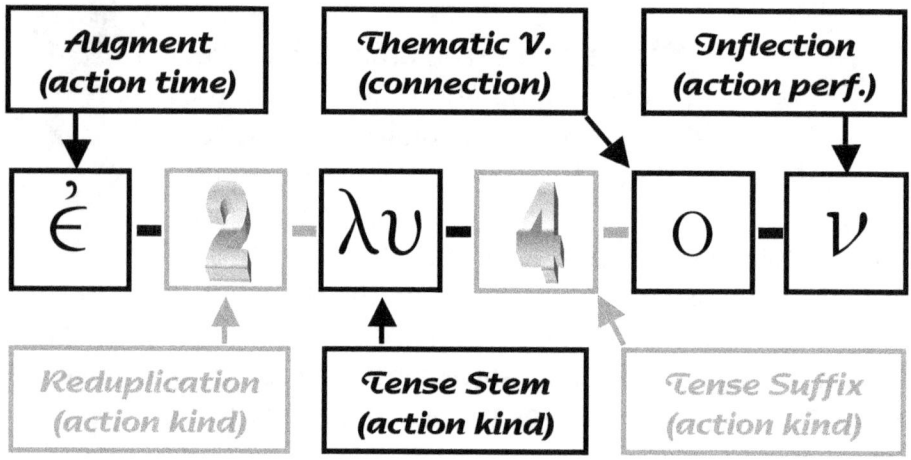

Durative Stem

Greek starts with the present tense stem, because this stem is durative action. Use of the present tense stem for the imperfect means that:

♦ *The Greek imperfect tense is the second of the two tenses of the first principal part.*

This durative action stem is easily derived from any verb in the dictionary by dropping the final -ω of the first person singular primary ending.

Time Augment

Use of an augment prefix signals past time. The type of augment depends upon the initial letter of the tense stem.

(1) Consonants
Tense stems beginning with a consonant have vowel augments using ε. Thus:

$$\dot{\dot{ε}}\text{-}λυ$$

The one exception is an initial rho, which doubles the rho to the form ἐρρ-.

(2) Vowels
Beginning short vowels α- and ε- lengthen to η-; short vowel ο lengthens to ω-. Initial rough breathing is retained. Infrequently, ε becomes ει- (cf. ἔχω); this augment is learned only by observation. The short vowels ι- and υ- lengthen to their vocalized long forms, but this sound leaves no visible change. (You would hear the change if you were speaking the language.)

Vowels already long (η, ω) do not change. Diphthongs may or may not change. Diphthong reactions simply have to be observed and noted per verb. Commonly, αι- and οι- lengthen the initial vowel and subscript the iota: ῃ- and ῳ-. Less common is ευ- to ηυ-, and ευα- to ευη-. Using ἄγω, ἐσθίω, ἔχω, ὀφείλω, αἰτέω, and οἰκέω as examples, the lengthened stems would look like this:

$$ἀγ\text{-} → ἠγ\text{-}$$
$$ἐσθι\text{-} → ἠσθι$$
$$ἐχ\text{-} → εἰχ\text{-}$$
$$ὀφειλ\text{-} → ὠφειλ\text{-}$$

$$\text{αἰτε-} \rightarrow \text{ᾐτε-}$$

$$\text{οἰκε-} \rightarrow \text{ᾠκε-}$$

(3) Compounds
Compounds always precede all morphology elements:

$$\text{ἐνδυ-} \rightarrow \text{ἐνεδυ-}$$

The compound may suffer phonetic change of a final consonant or loss of a final vowel in front of the augment:

$$\text{ἐκδυ-} \rightarrow \text{ἐξεδυ-}$$

$$\text{ἀναλυ-} \rightarrow \text{ἀνελυ-}$$

Here is one *practical* issue about this business of compounds:

♦ *Compounds hide augments!*

Thematic Vowel

(1) Use of ο/ε
The ο/ε set is used. Pattern is the same as present tense.

(2) Contract Verbs
Contract verbs contract like present with similar results. The ε contract is different in first singular (-ουν), ο contract in all singulars (-ουν, -ους, -ου), and α contract in second, third singular, with no subscripting iota (-ας, -α). Consult the endings summarized in the Paradigms index, p. 571.

Inflection

Inflection added on the end gives the subject parameters of person, number, and voice. Past tense invokes a new set of endings. Tenses of the past are called "historical tenses." All historical tenses are secondary tenses. Here is the dictum:

♦ *Secondary tenses take secondary endings.*

Table 13.2—Secondary Endings

Active	Middle
-ν	-μην
-ς	-ου (σο)
-- (εν)	-το
-μεν	-μεθα
-τε	-σθε
-ν, -σαν	-ντο

(1) Active Voice

Third singular has no ending, indicated with the dash. The resultant look is the thematic vowel with movable nu, -εν.

First and second plural endings -μεν and -τε are the same as present active. However, the imperfect has the *augment* for *past* time the present does not. Note carefully the difference between λύομεν and ἐλύομεν.

Third plural usually is -ν, sometimes -σαν. Since the -ν option is common, distinguishing first singular from third plural is by context alone.

(2) Middle/Passive Voice

First singular -μην might be confused with the *active* first plural -μεν. Note carefully the *long* vowel η in the middle form.

Second singular involves a sigma that slips out, leaving some vowels to contract to the result -ου. Learn the pattern with -σο also, because this ending will show up elsewhere.

Note that first and second plural endings -μεθα and -σθε are the same as present middle. Again, however, as with active voice, the imperfect middle has the *augment* for *past* time that the present does not. Note carefully the difference between λυόμεθα and ἐλυόμεθα.

Third plural has a "nu pattern," a descriptive phrase that takes note of the close similarity between middle third singular and plural for both primary and secondary endings. Each just throws in a nu to generate the third plural form. Primary forms are: -ται, -νται. Secondary forms are: -το, -ντο.

Passive forms are the same as middle. Passive translation is given in the paradigms, since middle voice is difficult to translate, as we have pointed out already; English has no equivalent. Middle expresses personal interest in the action. Assume that a middle/passive form is passive for translation; this works three-fourths of the time, except for lexical middle verbs.

For comparison, primary and secondary endings are given together below. Remember that the primary active was given as *resultant* endings (thematic vowel already lost to interactions with primitive endings), except in first and second plural.

Table 13.3—Primary and Secondary Endings

Primary		Secondary	
Active	Middle	Active	Middle
-ω	-μαι	-ν	-μην
-εις	-η (σαι)	-ς	-ου (σο)
-ει	-ται	-- (εν)	-το
-ομεν	-μεθα	-μεν	-μεθα
-ετε	-σθε	-τε	-σθε
-ουσι(ν)	-νται	-ν, -σαν	-ντο

Imperfect Paradigms

ἔ-λυ-ο-ν

Table 13.4—Imperfect Active Indicative

ἔλυον	I was loosing
ἔλυες	you were loosing (sg)
ἔλυε(ν)	he (she, it) was loosing
ἐλύομεν	we were loosing
ἐλύετε	you were loosing (pl)
ἔλυον	they were loosing

Table 13.5—Imperfect Midd/Pass Indicative

ἐλυόμην	I was being loosed
ἐλύου	you were being loosed (sg)
ἐλύετο	he (she, it) was being loosed
ἐλυόμεθα	we were being loosed
ἐλύεσθε	you were being loosed (pl)
ἐλύοντο	they were being loosed

Table 13.6—Imperfect Active Contract Verbs

ποιέω	πληρόω	ἀγαπάω
ἐποίουν	ἐπλήρουν	ἠγάπων
ἐποίεις	ἐπλήρους	ἠγάπας
ἐποίει	ἐπλήρου	ἠγάπα
ἐποιοῦμεν	ἐπληροῦμεν	ἠγαπῶμεν
ἐποιεῖτε	ἐπληροῦτε	ἠγαπᾶτε
ἐποίουν	ἐπλήρουν	ἠγάπων

Table 13.7—Imperfect Midd/Pass Contract Verbs

ποιέω	πληρόω	ἀγαπάω
ἐποιούμην	ἐπληρούμην	ἠγαπώμην
ἐποιοῦ	ἐπληροῦ	ἠγαπῶ
ἐποιεῖτο	ἐπληροῦτο	ἠγαπᾶτο
ἐποιούμεθα	ἐπληρούμεθα	ἠγαπώμεθα
ἐποιεῖσθε	ἐπληροῦσθε	ἠγαπᾶσθε
ἐποιοῦντο	ἐπληροῦντο	ἠγαπῶντο

Imperfect of Εἰμί

Remember that εἰμί does not have voice. Location does not inlude "active" or "passive." Thus, the -μην of the first singular looks middle in form but is not in fact. The ἦσθα and ἤμεθα are rare alternate forms. Note the third plural taking the -σαν option rather than the -ν. Some present tense forms of εἰμί are enclitic (minus accent), but not the imperfect. Finally, notice *smooth* breathing on monosyllable forms. Do *not* confuse these with relative pronoun forms, which always have *rough* breathing (remember: "relatives are rough"). You probably should treat εἰμί forms as just six different vocabulary words to learn.

Table 13.8—Imperfect Indicative of Εἰμί

ἤμην	I was
ἦς (ἦσθα)	you were
ἦν	he (she, it) was
ἦμεν (ἤμεθα)	we were
ἦτε	you were (pl)
ἦσαν	they were

Imperfect Translation

Imperfect Nuances

Imperfect translation can be nuanced several ways, context always the key. These nuances presented here help you to be alert to differences in various English translations.

(1) Inceptive Imperfect
Imperfect is durative, but emphasis may be on the *beginning* of the action. If so, "began to" could be used in translation. The Sermon on the Mount introduction is a classic example:

καὶ ἀνοίξας τὸ στόμα αὐτοῦ ἐδίδασκεν αὐτοὺς
"and opening his mouth, he *began to teach* them" (Mt. 5:2)

(2) Conative Imperfect
The adjective "conative" is about impulse or directed action. Expressions such as "was trying to" or "tried to" convey the idea. Attempted action not necessarily successful is the point. Paul described his former persecution of the church:

καὶ ἐπόρθουν αὐτήν
"and *I was trying to destroy* it" (Gal. 1:13)

Translating this imperfect as "I was destroying it" would not convey Paul's understanding of church. He did not mean to imply that he would have been successful in his efforts, so good thing God stopped him on the Damascus Road.

(3) Customary Imperfect
We all have habits and customs that continue over time. Thanksgiving is such a well-established tradition in American society that this season presents the heaviest commercial traffic of the entire year. Airlines always brace for the event. You might nostalgically look back on old times and muse, "Yeah, our

family *used to get together* every Thanksgiving. We always had fun—eating all that food and visiting with family."

This "used to" expression can be the sense for some uses of imperfect tense, called the customary imperfect. One classic example is the Passover custom of Jesus' family:

<u>ἐπορεύοντο</u> οἱ γονεῖς αὐτοῦ κατ' ἔτος εἰς Ἰερουσαλὴμ
"his parents *used to go* each year to Jerusalem" (Lk. 2:41)

Use of the clarifying phrase "each year" (κατ' ἔτος) and the phrase "according to their custom" (κατὰ τὸ ἔθος) in the next verse makes clear the nuance of this imperfect form.

Imperfect "Deponent"

If the present tense were so-called "deponent," then the imperfect would be too. However, middle Greek verbs are not truly deponent (minus middle meaning). The middle meaning is so dominant in the idea of the verb that active voice forms simply occur infrequently or not at all. Unfortunately, the middle sense is not translatable into English, so the Greek middle verb winds up sounding as if active voice in English. So ἔρχομαι as imperfect has an active voice "ring" in English:

<u>ἤρχοντο</u> πρὸς αὐτὸν
"they *were coming* to him" (Mk. 1:45)

Assume a middle/passive form is passive, since a majority are, then try middle if passive does not work well in context.

Exercise 13

1. Fill in the blank:

   1.1 _____ = The only Greek mood indicating the *action time* parameter.

Chapter 13: Imperfect Tense

1.2 _____ = The tense stem borrowed for creating the imperfect tense.

1.3 _____ = The *action kind* for imperfect tense.

1.4 _____ = The principal part to which the imperfect belongs.

1.5 _____ = The name of the verb prefix indicating past time.

1.6 _____ = Verbs showing only mid./pass. forms but "active" translation.

1.7 _____ = The other name for secondary tenses.

1.8 _____ = The time frame of all secondary tenses.

1.9 _____ = The pattern of endings for secondary tenses.

1.10 _____ = The imperfect translation nuanced as "used to."

1.11 _____ = The imperfect translation nuanced as "began to."

1.12 _____ = The imperfect translation nuanced as "tried to."

1.13 _____ = So-called "deponent" presents make what kind of imperfects?

2. Augment the following tense stems. Assume that all vowel forms are augmented as long vowels:

Present	Stem	Augmented Stem
2.1 ἀκούω →	ἀκου- →	_____
2.2 βάλλω →	βαλλ- →	_____
2.3 ἐγείρω →	ἐγειρ- →	_____

2.4 ὁδεύω → ὁδευ- → _____

2.5 ὀκνέω → ὀκνε- → _____

2.6 αἰνέω → αἰνε- → _____

2.7 ἠχέω → ἠχε- → _____

2.8 ἰσχύω → ἰσχυ- → _____

2.9 ἀποβλέπω, ἀποβλεπ- = _____

3. Provide the active and mid./pass. *secondary* endings and the imperfect of εἰμί:

Active	Mid./Pass.	Impf.: εἰμί	Gloss
___	___	___	___
___	___	___	___
___	___	___	___
___	___	___	___
___	___	___	___
___	___	___	___

4. Complete the imperfect *active* indicative conjugation for the verb ἀναβλέπω ("I look up"):

_____ = _____

_____ = _____

_____ = _____

_____ = _____

_____ = _____

_____ = _____

Chapter 13: Imperfect Tense

5. Complete the imperfect *passive* indicative conjugation for the verb αἰτέω ("I ask"):

_____ = _____
_____ = _____
_____ = _____
_____ = _____
_____ = _____
_____ = _____

6. Translate. Be ready to locate verbs. Look up any unknown words in your UBS dictionary. Some forms may look "unknown," but augmentation/compounds hide augments.

6.1 ἐσῴζοντο. (Mk. 6:56)

_____

6.2 ἠτοῦντο (αἰτέω) εἰρήνην. (Acts 12:20; middle voice)

_____

6.3 ἀλλ᾽ οὐκ ἦσαν ἐξ ἡμῶν· (1 Jn. 2:19)

_____

6.4 καὶ αὐτὴ ἀπέθνῃσκεν (Lk. 8:42)

_____

6.5 αἴρεται ἀπὸ τῆς γῆς ἡ ζωὴ αὐτοῦ. (Acts 8:33)

_____

6.6 καθὼς σὺ ἐν ἀληθείᾳ περιπατεῖς. (3 Jn. 1:3)

6.7 ὅτε ἤμην νήπιος, ἐλάλουν ὡς νήπιος (1 Cor. 13:11)

6.8 καὶ ἐν οἰκίᾳ οὐκ ἔμενεν ἀλλ᾽ ἐν τοῖς μνήμασιν (μνῆμα) (Lk. 8:27)

6.9 ἐν αὐτῷ ζωὴ ἦν, καὶ ἡ ζωὴ ἦν τὸ φῶς τῶν ἀνθρώπων (Jn. 1:4)

6.10 τοῦτο δὲ ἔλεγεν σημαίνων (signifying) ποίῳ θανάτῳ ἤμελλεν ἀποθνῄσκειν (infinitive form). (Jn. 12:33)

6.11 Αἱ μὲν οὖν ἐκκλησίαι ἐστερεοῦντο (στερεόω) τῇ πίστει καὶ ἐπερίσσευον (περισσεύω) τῷ ἀριθμῷ (ἀριθμός) καθ᾽ ἡμέραν.[1] (Acts 16:5)

---

[1] Here, καθ᾽ ἡμέραν is distributive = "from day to day," or "daily."

6.12 ἄνδρες (voc.) ἀδελφοί (voc.), ἐγὼ Φαρισαῖός εἰμι, υἱὸς Φαρισαίων, περὶ ἐλπίδος καὶ ἀναστάσεως (ἀνάστασις) νεκρῶν [ἐγὼ] κρίνομαι. (Acts 23:6)

 **Vocabulary 13**

αἴρω, *I take up, take away* (aorta)

αἰτέω, *I ask*

ἀλήθεια, ἡ, *truth, reality, faithfulness*

ἀποθνῄσκω, *I die* (cf. θάνατος)

ἐκκλησία, ἡ, *assembly, church* (ecclesiology)

ἤμην, *I was*

κρίνω, *I judge* (crisis, critic, hypocrite)

μέλλω, *I am about to, going to* (with infinitives)

μένω, *I remain, abide, stay*

οἶκος, ὁ, *house, home, family* (economy, ecology)

σῴζω, *I heal, preserve, save*

ὥρα, *hour, moment, time, occasion* (with infinitives)

Vocabulary notes:

(1) Compare masculine οἶκος with feminine οἰκία in Chapter 6. The masculine form seems preferred for referring to larger or official buildings (cf. Lk. 11:51; Mt. 11:8).

(2) The verb μέλλω often is used with infinitives, not yet studied. Until then, we will supply you with the indication that a form that follows the verb μέλλω is an infinitive.

Photo © Gerald L. Stevens

Fig. 12. Laodicea Inscription. Scattered about lying around in the ruins of ancient Laodicea in western Turkey are various architectural remains. One is this piece along the main road that has fallen from an arch or crossbeam to some columns. The visible part of the inscription reads:

[*Ε*]*ΞΟΥΣΙΑΣΤΟ*[*Μ*]

[ἐ]ξουσίας το[μ]

One clearly can make out the word [ἐ]ξουσίας, which is the accusative feminine plural form of the word "power" or "authority." Jesus promised the church at Laodicea that the one who "overcomes" would sit down with him on his throne as he overcame and sat down with his Father on his throne (Rev. 3:21).

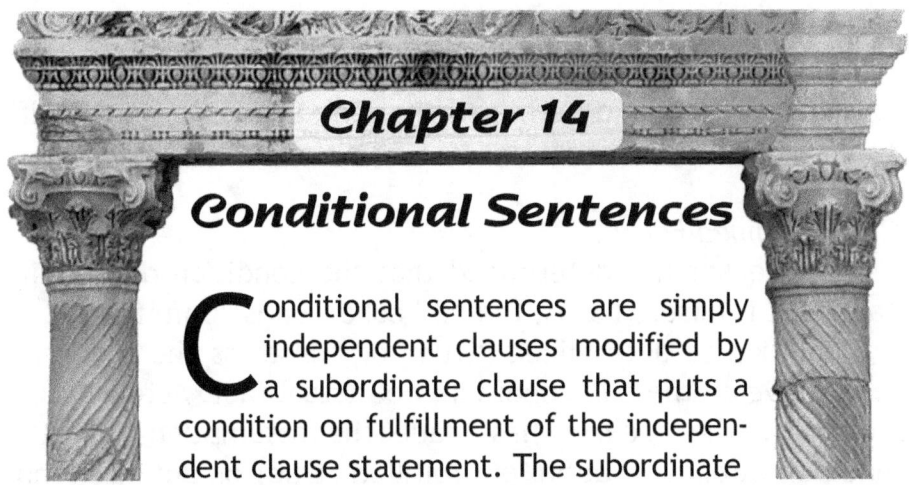

Chapter 14

Conditional Sentences

Conditional sentences are simply independent clauses modified by a subordinate clause that puts a condition on fulfillment of the independent clause statement. The subordinate clause is introduced by the subordinate conjunction "if." The main verb is the "then" statement—what would happen or be true if the condition were fulfilled. The "if" clause often comes first. The rhetorical thrust of the conditional sentence is up to the speaker, who reveals the nature of the conditional assumptions and their logic through the character of the grammar that is employed.

Logic of Conditions

The first subject to understand about "if" statements is the basic logic behind all conditions. This logic orbits around two foci—determined or undetermined. That is, either the speaker has *determined* the fulfillment of the condition, or the speaker has left the assessment of the fulfillment *undetermined*.

Logic: Determined

If the speaker already has a mind made up about fulfillment of the "if" condition, then the speaker's logic is characterized as *determined*. Determined logic has two correlatives, that is, the if already has been determined *true* or determined *false*.

(1) Determined True

The speaker has determined that the condition of the "if" statement is true. That is, the "if" condition is "fulfilled."

(2) Determined False

The speaker has determined that the condition of the "if" statement is false. That is, the "if" condition is "unfulfilled."

Condition as determined "true" or "false" is the *speaker's perspective* on the "if" condition, not actual fact. Actual fact is irrelevant. The speaker has made the assumption that the condition already is definitely fulfilled (true) or definitely not fulfilled (false). Either way, true or false, the condition already is *determined* in the speaker's mind.

Logic: Undetermined

If the speaker has not made a determination about fulfillment of the "if" condition, then such logic is characterized as undetermined. Similar to determined logic, undetermined logic also has two correlatives, undetermined yet still considered as *possible*, or undetermined but only *remote*.

(1) Undetermined, But Possible

The speaker has not made a determination about fulfillment of the "if" condition. That is, the "if" condition is "unfulfilled." However, the speaker considers fulfillment a *possibility*.

(2) Undetermined, And Remote

The speaker has not made a determination about fulfillment of the "if" condition. That is, the "if" condition is "unfulfilled." The speaker, however, considers fulfillment only *remote*.

Undetermined conditions assumed either as "possible" or as "remote" are the *speaker's perspective* on the "if" condition, not actual fact. Actual fact is irrelevant. The speaker has made the assumption that the condition is unfulfilled but possible or unfulfilled and only remote. Either way, possible or remote, the condition is left *undetermined* by the speaker.

These conditions, then, are the four types of conditional sentences: true, false, possible, remote. These logical assumptions made by the speaker about the nature of the fulfillment of the "if" clause also are called the four *classes* of conditional sentences: *first class* (true), *second class* (false), *third class* (possible), and *fourth class* (remote).

Grammar of Conditions

◆ *Grammar reflects the logic of conditional sentences.*

Logic Determined = Indicative Mood

Determined condition logically uses *indicative* mood. This mood makes sense because indicative is the mood of reality or assertion.[1] Whether an "if" statement is determined as true or false (first or second class) is by a contextual evaluation of the speaker's perspective. Would you say that the speaker assumes the "if" as fulfilled (true) or unfulfilled (false)?

Logic Undetermined = Contingency Moods

Undetermined condition logically uses moods of contingency).[2] Two contingency moods are enlisted: (1) subjunctive, of some probability, and (2) optative, only remote possibility.

---

[1] You would be well served to review the material on mood as the verb potential parameter, pp. 474-75.
[2] English has only two, the subjunctive and the imperative. The imperative as command, however, is not conducive to setting forth conditional logic. Greek has three potential moods, adding optative to the subjunctive.

Table 14.1—Conditional Sentences: Grammar, Logic, Assumption, Time

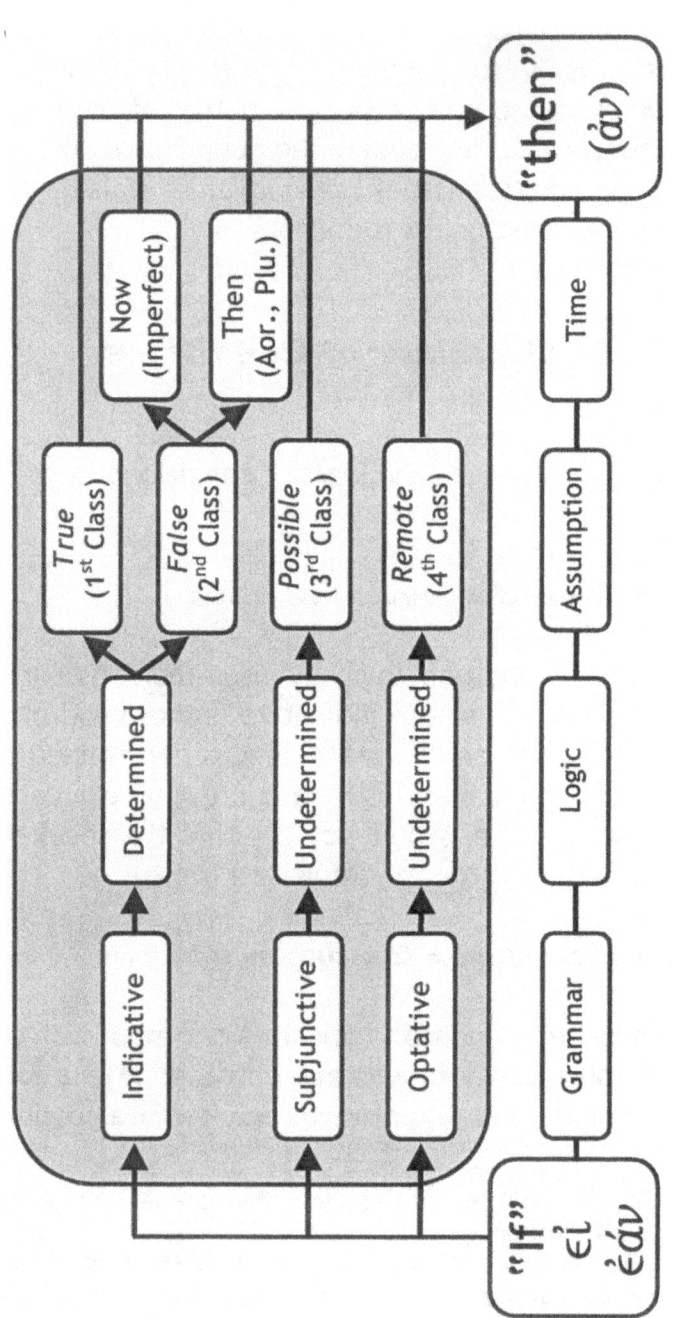

Logically, then, the third class conditional sentence, considered probable by the speaker, has an "if" clause expressed in the *subjunctive*. The fourth class conditional sentence, considered only remotely possible by the speaker, has an "if" clause expressed in the *optative*.

So, the Greek speaker tips off the reader as to the logic of the conditional sentence and the nature of the assumptions by the *mood* of the "if" clause. Thus, we have the dictum:

♦ *The mood of the "if" clause reveals the speaker's logic and assumptions in the conditional sentence.*

Thus, the first task when translating any conditional sentence is to determine the mood of the "if" verb. The mood of the "if" verb is crucial to interpreting the rhetoric of a Greek conditional sentence.

Analysis of Classes

In examples to follow, we underline the "if" verb. *Always note carefully the mood of this "if" verb.* Also, we use the expression the "then clause" by way of identification only. We do not infer that the word "then" must appear in all conditional sentence translations. For this lesson, study the first and second class conditional sentences, then do exercises. (The third and fourth class conditional sentences will be studied later.)

First Class (Indicative, True)

The "if" verb is indicative. The speaker has determined the "if" condition fulfilled. The "if" conjunction usually is εἰ. The "if" verb potentially could be in any tense, but frequently present. The "then" clause could be any tense, and any mood but optative. A particle of contingency can be found in the "then" clause, often ἄν, but not always translated. At other times an inferential conjunction, such as ἄρα, could be used. Note Mt. 12:28:

εἰ δὲ ἐν πνεύματι θεοῦ ἐγὼ ἐκβάλλω τὰ δαιμόνια,
ἄρα ἔφθασεν ἐφ᾽ ὑμᾶς ἡ βασιλεία τοῦ θεοῦ.

"But if by the Spirit of God *I am casting out* the demons
 then the kingdom of God has come upon you."

Notice that the "if" verb, ἐκβάλλω, is indicative mood. This indicative mood means that the speaker's logic is determined. The interpreter must decide whether this speaker would have determined already that this "if" condition was true or is false, fulfilled or unfulfilled. In this context, Jesus is arguing with his detractors. He would assume his actions were by the Spirit of God. Therefore, his "if" is determined already in his own mind to be fulfilled, or true. This statement, then, is an example of a first class conditional sentence.

One way to test the first class conditional sentence is to convert the "if" clause into an affirmative statement one could put in parentheses behind the "if" assertion. If the affirmation makes sense in context, that sensibility helps confirm that the "if" clause represents a first class (true) condition. In the case above, this conversion would be: "If by the Spirit of God I am casting out the demons (which I am), . . ."

Second Class (Indicative, False)

(1) False in Present Time
The "if" verb is indicative. The speaker has determined the "if" condition unfulfilled. The "if" conjunction usually is εἰ. The "if" verb potentially could be any past tense indicative, but frequently is imperfect. If the "if" condition is put in the negative, the "if" clause uses the alternate negative μή, not οὐ. The "then" clause could be any past tense indicative.

Since the condition is false, English idiom for second class conditional sentences requires a form of contingency in the "then" clause, either a contingent auxiliary verb, such as "could" or "would," or some other grammatical element that expresses contingency. English also expects the "then" clause to be present tense. So, in translating a second class conditional sentence, a contingency auxiliary verb often is inserted, and the Greek past tense is converted to a present tense to meet the English idiom. Our example is Jn. 5:46:

εἰ γὰρ <u>ἐπιστεύετε</u> Μωϋσεῖ, ἐπιστεύετε ἂν ἐμοί·
"For if you *believed* Moses, you *would believe* me."

Notice that the "if" verb, ἐπιστεύετε, is indicative mood. This indicative mood means that the speaker's logic is determined. The interpreter must decide whether this speaker would have determined already that this "if" condition was true or false, fulfilled or unfulfilled. In this context, Jesus is arguing with his opponents. He would assume they, in fact, did not really believe Moses, because Moses wrote about Jesus. Therefore, his "if" is determined already in his own mind to be unfulfilled, or false. His response, then, is an example of a second class conditional sentence. The "if" condition is false even as the speaker speaks (false *now*). That present reality is why the imperfect tense is used (think kind of action, i.e., durative action, ongoing). The conversion test in this case would be the assertion, "For if you believed Moses (which you obviously do not) . . ."

(2) False in Past Time
The "if" verb is indicative. The speaker has determined the "if" condition unfulfilled. The "if" conjunction usually is εἰ. The "if" verb usually is aorist or pluperfect, distinguishing this use from false in present time, which uses the imperfect tense. When stated in the negative, the "if" clause uses the alternate negative μή. The "then" clause could be any past tense indicative.

English also distinguishes tenses in the "if" clause of this condition-determined-false logic, based on whether present or past time is in view. For example, the expression "If I *were* hungry . . ." has present time in view, what the condition *now* is. In contrast, "If I *had been* hungry . . ." has past time in view, what the condition *then* was.

Since the condition is false, English requires contingency in the "then" clause. The auxiliary verb "would," therefore, or a similar auxiliary often is inserted into the translation to meet this English idiom, even though the Greek verb in the "then" clause is indicative mood. Our example is Jn. 15:22:

εἰ μὴ ἦλθον καὶ ἐλάλησα αὐτοῖς,
ἁμαρτίαν οὐκ εἴχοσαν.

"For if I *had not come* and *spoken* to them,
they would not have sin."

Third Class (Subjunctive, Possible)

The "if" verb is subjunctive. The "if" logic, then, is undetermined or unfulfilled. Fulfillment, however, is possible, or even probable. The "if" conjunction usually is ἐάν. The "if" verb potentially could be any tense. The "then" clause could be any tense, but frequently is future. A particle of contingency can be found in the "then" clause, often ἄν, but not always translated. At other times an inferential conjunction could be used, such as ἄρα. Our example is Mk. 1:40:

ἐὰν θέλῃς δύνασαί με καθαρίσαι.
"If *you choose*, you can make me clean."

Fourth Class (Optative, Remote)

The "if" verb is optative. The logic, then, is undetermined, or unfulfilled. Fulfillment, however is only remote. The "if" conjunction is εἰ. The "if" verb potentially could be any tense. The "then" clause could be any tense, but also would be optative mood. The particle of contingency, ἄν, is found in the "then" clause, but not translated.

No complete fourth class conditional sentence with both an "if" and a "then" clause is found in the New Testament. Either clause is left off, yielding grammatically incomplete statements that still rhetorically make sense as the reader can supply the other half—something similar to a parent scolding a child without finishing the statement, "If you *dare* do that!"

Koine Greek virtually had ceased using optative mood by New Testament times. For incomplete "if" statements, optative constructions using the conjunction εἰ occur 12 times (Acts, 8x; 1 Corinthians, 2x; 1 Peter, 2x).[3] For incomplete "then" statements, optative constructions with the particle ἄν occur only 9 times, all in Luke and Acts, save one in John.[4] Note 1 Pet. 3:14:

ἀλλ' εἰ καὶ πάσχοιτε διὰ δικαιοσύνην, μακάριοι.

"But even if you *should suffer* because of righteousness, [you would be] blessed."

Diagramming

Grammatical Analysis

The independent "then" clause contains the main verb of the sentence. The particle of contingency, ἄν, regardless its position, goes in parentheses immediately after the main verb. Conjunctions, such as ἄρα, go on a support at the beginning.

The dependent "if" clause is an adverbial modifier of the main verb in the "then" clause. The "if" clause takes an adverb

---

[3] Acts 17:11, 27 (twice); 20:16; 24:19; 25:20; 27:12, 39; 1 Cor. 14:10; 15:37; 1 Pet. 3:14, 17.
[4] Lk. 1:62; 6:11; 9:46; 15:26; Jn. 13:24; Acts 5:24; 8:31; 10:17; 17:18.

position under the main verb. The εἰ conjunction, and any postpositive, goes on the slanted line down to the "if" clause.

Conditional Sentences

εἰ δὲ ἐν πνεύματι θεοῦ ἐγὼ ἐκβάλλω τὰ δαιμόνια,
ἄρα ἔφθασεν ἐφ᾽ ὑμᾶς ἡ βασιλεία τοῦ θεοῦ.

"But if by the Spirit of God *I am casting out* the demons
then the kingdom of God has come upon you."

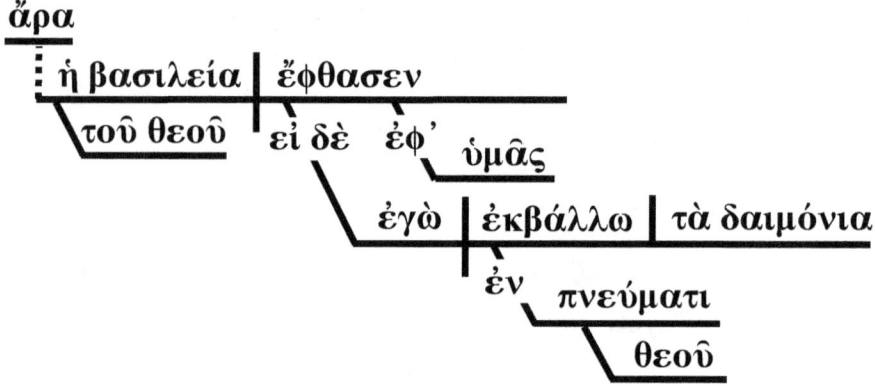

 **Exercise 14**

1. Fill in the blank:

   In conditional sentences, the _____ of the "if" verb reveals the logic and assumptions of the speaker. The logic of the "if" statement from the speaker's perspective is either _____ or _____. This logic reveals one of four assumptions about the "if" condition, that is,

Chapter 14: Conditional Sentences   217

that a condition is assumed _____, _____, _____, or _____. The first and second class conditional sentence will place the "if" verb in the _____ mood.

2. Review the imperfect indicative conjugation for the verb εἰμί by repeating its forms below (cf. p. 198):

_____ = _____
_____ = _____
_____ = _____
_____ = _____
_____ = _____
_____ = _____

3. Translate. Be ready to locate verbs. Look up any unknown words in your UBS dictionary. Remember: augmentation or compounds may hide past time augments.

   3.1 αὐτοὶ ὑμεῖς μοι μαρτυρεῖτε. (Jn. 3:28)

   3.2 ἔτι ἕνα εἶχεν[5] υἱὸν ἀγαπητόν. (Mk. 12:6)

   3.3 πίπτει πρὸς τοὺς πόδας (πούς) αὐτοῦ. (Mk. 5:22)

---

[5]In the imperfect, ἔχω augments for past time as ει-, not as η-. See this unusual form in the examples at the bottom of p. 193.

3.4 ἔπιπτεν ἐπὶ τῆς γῆς καὶ προσηύχετο. (Mk. 14:35)

_____

3.5 εἰ δὲ ἑαυτοὺς διεκρίνομεν (διακρίνω), οὐκ ἂν ἐκρινόμεθα. (1 Cor. 11:31)

_____

_____

_____ Identify the "if" verb.

_____ What is the "if" verb mood?

_____ Determined or undetermined?

_____ "If" assumption: true or false?

_____ What class conditional sentence?

3.6 εἰ οὖν Δαυὶδ καλεῖ αὐτὸν κύριον, πῶς υἱὸς αὐτοῦ ἐστιν; (Mt. 22:45)

_____

_____

_____ Identify the "if" verb.

_____ What is the "if" verb mood?

_____ Determined or undetermined?

_____ "If" assumption: true or false?

_____ What class conditional sentence?

Chapter 14: Conditional Sentences

3.7 ἔλεγεν αὐτοῖς ὁ Ἰησοῦς· εἰ ὁ θεὸς πατὴρ ὑμῶν ἦν ἠγαπᾶτε ἂν ἐμέ. (Jn. 8:42*)

_____

_____

_____ Identify the "if" verb.

_____ What is the "if" verb mood?

_____ Determined or undetermined?

_____ "If" assumption: true or false?

_____ What is the tense of the "if"?

_____ What is time of "if": now or then?

_____ What class conditional sentence?

3.8 ὁ οὖν διδάσκων (the one who teaches) ἕτερον σεαυτὸν οὐ διδάσκεις; (Rom. 2:21)

_____

_____

3.9 τί οὖν βαπτίζεις εἰ σὺ οὐκ εἶ ὁ χριστὸς οὐδὲ Ἠλίας (Elijah) οὐδὲ ὁ προφήτης; (Jn. 1:25)

_____

_____

3.10 ἔλεγεν αὐτοῖς ὁ Ἰησοῦς· εἰ τέκνα τοῦ Ἀβραάμ ἐστε, τὰ ἔργα τοῦ Ἀβραὰμ ἐποιεῖτε. (Jn. 8:39*)

_____

_____

_____

_____ Identify the "if" verb.

_____ What is the "if" verb mood?

_____ Determined or undetermined?

_____ "If" assumption: true or false?

_____ What class conditional sentence?

3.11 ἔλεγεν τοῖς μαθηταῖς αὐτοῦ ὁ Ἰησοῦς· εἰ ἐκ τοῦ κόσμου ἦτε, ὁ κόσμος ἂν τὸ ἴδιον ἠγάπα. (Jn. 15:19*)

_____

_____

_____ Identify the "if" verb.

_____ What is the "if" verb mood?

_____ Determined or undetermined?

_____ "If" assumption: true or false?

_____ What is the tense of the "if"?

_____ What is time of "if": now or then?

_____ What class conditional sentence?

3.12 ὁ τρώγων (the one who eats) μου τὴν σάρκα καὶ πίνων (drinks) μου τὸ αἷμα ἐν ἐμοὶ μένει κἀγὼ ἐν αὐτῷ. (Jn. 6:56)

3.13 λαμβάνομεν ἀπ' αὐτοῦ, ὅτι τὰς ἐντολὰς (ἐντολή) αὐτοῦ τηροῦμεν καὶ τὰ ἀρεστὰ (the things that are pleasing) ἐνώπιον αὐτοῦ ποιοῦμεν. (1 Jn. 3:22)

4. Diagram the following from above.

4.1 [3.7]

ἔλεγεν αὐτοῖς ὁ Ἰησοῦς· εἰ ὁ θεὸς πατὴρ ὑμῶν ἦν ἠγαπᾶτε ἂν ἐμέ.

 **Vocabulary 14**

αἷμα, -ματος, τό, *blood* (hematology, hemorrhage)

ἄν, (particle of contingency)

ἄρα, *then, therefore*

ἄρχω, *I rule* (anarchy, monarch), *begin* (middle voice)

διδάσκω, *I teach* (didactic)

εἰ, *if*

ἐνώπιον, *before, in the presence of*

ἕτερος, -α, -ον, *other, another, different* (heterodox)

ἔτι, *still, yet, more*

κἀγώ, *and I* (combining καί and ἐγώ)

μαρτυρέω, *I testify, witness* (martyr)

οὔτε, *and not, neither, nor*

πίπτω, *I fall, fall down* (symptom)

πούς, ποδός, ὁ, *foot* (podiatry, podium, tripod)

προσεύχομαι, *I pray*

τηρέω, *I keep*

Vocabulary notes:

(1) Remember all -μα, -ματ third declension nouns are neuter (αἷμα).

(2) ἄν is just a particle of contingency that identifies the "then" part of the conditional sentence when present. The ἄν is not translated and immediately follows the "then" verb in parentheses in diagramming.

(3) The verb ἄρχω has a different meaning as middle.

(4) ἕτερος is a variation of ἄλλος with the sense "another of a different kind," whereas the term ἄλλος means "other of the same kind."

(5) Note that προσεύχομαι is a compound verb. Compounds hide augments. The imperfect is προσηυχόμην.

Language Lesson 4

Tense Stems

The principal parts of a verb system in any language are the essential foundation of formation for creating all incarnations of the verb's tenses and voices. English has three principal parts: present, past, and past participle. From these three basic forms, one can generate the entire English verb system.[1]

Greek has six total principal parts: present, future (active, middle), aorist (active, middle), perfect active, perfect middle, and passive (aorist, future). These six parts are the formation foundation for all Greek tenses and voices. Understanding the nature of these principal parts is helpful for understanding the terminology used is discussing Greek verbs.

One key concept of principal parts is the "tense stem." One might think this term is just a synonym for "verb stem." Another term easily confused is "verb root." All three terms need to be distinguished to understand verbs in their formation and their meaning.

---

[1]English 4, "Sentence Sense," pp. 477-96.

Table LL4.1—Greek Tense Stems

Stem Terminology

Words develop over time. By custom and usage, a word's formation evolves. Like a snowflake that crystallizes over a microscopic particulate suspended in the atmosphere, a word has some kernel form. This early stage is usually what is meant by the word's "root." From this root various sentence functions are developed over time, such as nouns, verbs, and adjectives. Some word roots are easy to recognize: noun, ἀγάπη; verb, ἀγαπάω; adjective, ἀγάπητος.

Language Lesson 4: Tense Stems

A *verb stem* is the basic *verbal* development off the word root. This verb stem becomes the basis for crystallizing the branches of the tense stems. *Tense stems* are formulations off the verb stem using prefixes, infixes, and suffixes to generate principal parts. Thus, principal parts are not about tenses. Principal parts are more about prefixes and suffixes. As you will see, if a verb prefix or suffix creates a tense, that principal part is about tense (parts 1, 2, 3, 4). If a verb prefix or suffix creates a voice, that principal part is about voice (parts 5, 6).

A "regular" verb develops all tense stems from the same verb stem. We use λύω as our Greek paradigm verb because this verb's formation is "regular." That regularity of stem allows the verb's morphological parts to stand out clearly and easily to the beginning student.

However, morphological changes can alter the verb stem. The root of γινώσκω is γνο- (as in *gnostic*). The verb stem lengthens the root vowel to γνω-. Tense stems are developed from this γνω- verb stem (e.g., future stem = γνωσ-).

So why is the present tense γινώσκω? Well, the present tense often is the most changed of the tense stems in its formation! That change is why the dictionary form not always is going to tell you the verb's principal parts. That is to say, a complicated process is involved in forming the present tense form of γινώσκω.[2]

An "irregular" verb borrows its tense stem from another verb. Thus, the principal parts do not look the same. As a result, principal parts must be memorized. Like *go* has a past tense *went* that just has to be memorized to be known, λέγω has a future ἐρῶ that just has to be memorized to be known.

---

[2]Reduplication to γιγνω by repeating the initial γ consonant with ι vowel; then, the resulting γν combination changes for euphony to just ν.

Root Fallacy

One mistake often made in word study usually is referred to as "root fallacy." The problem is confusing word roots with word usage hundreds of years later. This problem is related to the "meaning" versus "usage" issue that we already have discussed.

Here is one form of "root fallacy" with verbs: cut up a verb into its component parts (compounds, prefixes, stem, suffixes, etc.). Assign "root" meanings to all these parts from a Greek dictionary. Add up these supposed "root" meanings into a composite mutant meaning for the word. For example, take ἀναγινώσκω. First, cut off the compound preposition, ἀνά; the root means "up." Then, add the root of γινώσκω, "know." So, ἀναγινώσκω means "I know up"? Not at all! Our word ἀναγινώσκω means "I read"! Thus, probing "roots" as if magically generating "meaning" is sorely misinformed.

Vocabulary Cards

Principal parts are the key to mastery of the Greek verb. As you develop your vocabulary cards, a practical suggestion is to record principal parts for verbs that are unlike λύω, that is, for verbs you cannot say what the other tense stems are just because you know the vocabulary word. Even a verb that is regular, such as γινώσκω, needs a notation about the verb stem that shows up in all the other parts, since the present tense form γινώσκω is so "manufactured" as to make other tense stems hard to recognize from the dictionary form.

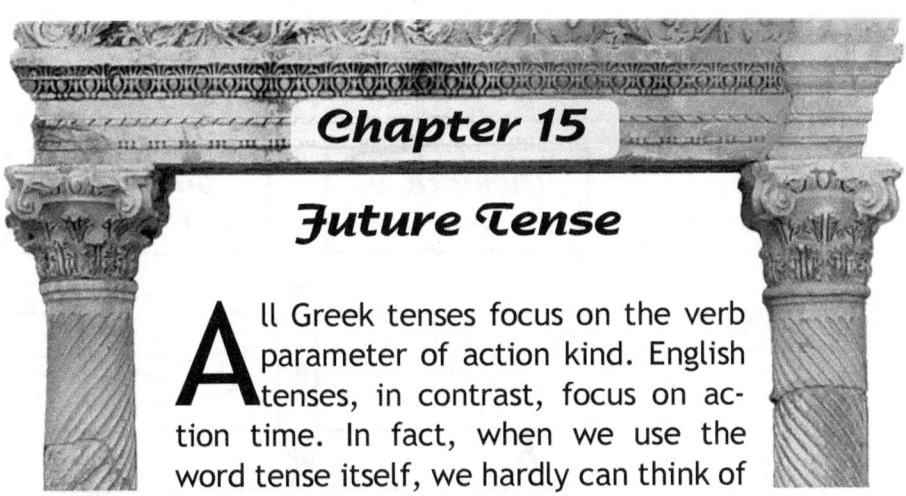

Chapter 15

Future Tense

All Greek tenses focus on the verb parameter of action kind. English tenses, in contrast, focus on action time. In fact, when we use the word tense itself, we hardly can think of anything but time. That is to say, the knee-jerk reaction of an English speaking person to the idea "verb tense" is action time. The grammar of time in English is tense.

In contrast, the grammar of time in Greek is mood. That is, a Greek verb *must* be in the *indicative* mood to express action *time*. Indicative mood is the default Greek mood. Thus, if we are talking about *time* with any Greek tense, we have to be assuming the indicative mood.

A key to understanding any Greek tense is to remold your thinking to action kind. That is, any time a new Greek tense is introduced to you, your *first* question ought to be, "What *kind of action* are we talking here?"

Future Tense

Future tense typically is *undefined* action. Thus, the present tense stem, which is durative, cannot be used. Another tense stem must be developed, creating a second principal part. This new stem is the future tense stem. Sometimes a future tense stem might clone the *look* of a present tense stem, but *a tense suffix changes the stem*. The tense suffix formation pattern is the foundation of calling future tense the second principal part.

Table 15.1—Future Tense Morphology

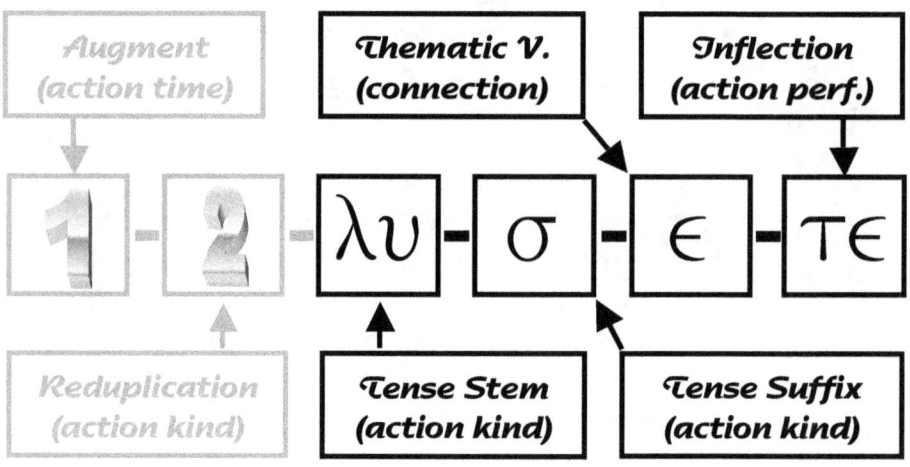

Future Tense Stem

Greek manufactures a new tense stem for future tense, because this tense needs to express *undefined* action. This process includes modification with a tense suffix. This use of the tense suffix for the future tense means that:

♦ *The Greek future tense is the second principal part.*

This future undefined action stem sometimes can be derived from the dictionary present tense form by dropping the first person singular primary ending, -ω, and adding the tense suffix. However, in other cases the future tense stem looks different from the present stem. The bottom line is this: verb principal parts have to be memorized. For some verbs, you will just have to memorize the second principal part.[1] Study the table below.

---

[1] Verb principal parts have to be memorized in *any* language. Review English 4, "Sentence Sense," pp. 484-85, about English principal parts.

Table 15.2—Future Stems

Present	Future
ἀναβαιν-	ἀναβη-
ἀποθνησκ-	ἀποθαν-
γιν-	γενη-
γινωσκ-	γνω-
καταβαιν-	καταβη-
εὑρισκ-	εὑρη-

Tense Suffix

(1) Future Stems Like Present Stems

Use of a tense suffix signals different action kind. The future tense suffix is sigma. For a verb such as λύω, the suffix is just added on after dropping the inflection:

$$\lambda \upsilon \text{-} \sigma$$

(2) Future Stems Unlike Present Stems

For some verbs, the *future stem* is not the same as the present stem. The future of εὑρίσκω is εὑρήσω, and of γινώσκω is γνώσομαι ("deponent"). One has to know the *future stem*:

$$\gamma \nu \omega \text{-} \sigma$$

(3) "Irregular" Stems

Greek has "irregular" verbs like English.[2] Memorize these.

---

[2] You may want to review the discussion of "irregular" verbs. English 4, "Sentence Sense," pp. 485-86.

Table 15.3—Irregular Futures

Present	Future
ἔρχομαι	ἐλεύσομαι
λέγω	ἐρῶ
ὁράω	ὄψομαι
πίνω	πίομαι
πίπτω	πεσοῦμαι
φέρω	οἴσω

(4) Consonant Stems

Consonant stems react to the σ. We give types of reactions.

a.) Consonant Reactions—Stops

When studying third declension nouns, we had to learn the following chart for inflection patterns involving a sigma.

Table 15.4—Sigma Stop Interactions

labials: π, β, φ + σ = ψ
palatals: κ, γ, χ + σ = ξ
dentals: τ, δ, θ + σ = σ

This reaction also happens with the future suffix. For example, βλέπω, ἔχω, and πείθω will change like this for future tense:

$$\beta\lambda\epsilon\pi\text{-}\sigma = \beta\lambda\epsilon\psi\text{-}$$

$$\dot{\epsilon}\chi\text{-}\sigma = \dot{\epsilon}\xi\text{-}$$

$$\pi\epsilon\iota\theta\text{-}\sigma = \pi\epsilon\iota\sigma\text{-}$$

b.) Consonant Reactions—"Hidden" Stems

Some verbs have "hidden" stems in that the present tense stem hides the actual consonant of the verb stem. Most of these types have present tense forms that end in zeta (σῴζω), double sigmas (κηρύσσω), double lambdas (βάλλω), and certain sigma kappas (διδάσκω).

Zeta Stems (ζ-). Any zeta stem present is a formation from an original verb stem that ended in delta or gamma. The future suffix is added to *that original* delta or gamma stem. Delta is a dental, so suffers the standard dental stop reaction of dropping. Likewise, the guttural gamma becomes xi:

$$\beta\alpha\pi\tau\acute{\iota}\zeta\omega, \beta\alpha\pi\tau\iota\delta\text{-}\sigma = \beta\alpha\pi\tau\iota\sigma\text{-}$$

$$\kappa\rho\acute{\alpha}\zeta\omega, \kappa\rho\alpha\gamma\text{-}\sigma = \kappa\rho\alpha\xi\text{-}$$

Double Consonant Stems (σσ-, λλ-). A double consonant present stem always hides an original single consonant. Double sigma, for example, hides an original palatal (κ, γ, χ). Thus:

$$\pi\rho\acute{\alpha}\sigma\sigma\omega, \pi\rho\alpha\gamma\text{-}\sigma = \pi\rho\alpha\xi\text{-}$$

Sigma Kappa Stems (σκ-). A sigma kappa present stem at times hides an original palatal stem (κ, γ, χ). Thus:

$$\text{διδάσκω, διδακ-σ = διδαξ-}$$

Thematic Vowel

(1) Use of o/ε
The o/ε set is used. Pattern is the same as present tense.

(2) Contract Verbs
Good news! The thematic vowel interaction of the contract verb is much simpler outside the first principal part. Here are two mutual dictums to nail down about contract verbs:

♦ *Contract verbs contract in first principal part.*

♦ *Contract verbs lengthen in all other principal parts.*

The lengthening process always is ε/α → η, and o → ω. So:

$$\text{ποιε-σ = ποιησ-}$$
$$\text{πληρο-σ = πληρωσ-}$$
$$\text{ἀγαπα-σ = ἀγαπησ-}$$

Inflection

Future tense is a primary tense. Primary tenses take primary endings. The future tense takes the same endings as the present tense. You have no new endings to learn![3]

A (so-called) *deponent future* shows only middle voice. If we say, "translate as active," we really are saying that the middle voice component simply is not conveyed easily into English.

Future Paradigms

$$\lambda\upsilon\text{-}\sigma\text{-}\epsilon\text{-}\tau\epsilon$$

Table 15.5—Future Active Indicative

λύσω	I shall loose
λύσεις	you will loose (sg)
λύσει	he (she, it) will loose
λύσομεν	we will loose
λύσετε	you will loose (pl)
λύσουσι(ν)	they will loose

Table 15.6—Future Middle Indicative

λύσομαι	I shall loose *(for myself)*
λύσῃ	you will loose *(for yourself)*
λύσεται	he (she, it) will loose *(for himself)*
λυσόμεθα	we will loose *(for ourselves)*
λύσεσθε	you will loose *(for yourselves)*
λύσονται	they will loose *(for themselves)*

---

[3] The future *passive* is built on a different tense stem, studied later. Thus, paradigms give only future "middle," not future "middle/passive."

Table 15.7—Future Active Contract Verbs

ποιέω	πληρόω	ἀγαπάω
ποιήσω	πληρώσω	ἀγαπήσω
ποιήσεις	πληρώσεις	ἀγαπήσεις
ποιήσει	πληρώσει	ἀγαπήσει
ποιήσομεν	πληρώσομεν	ἀγαπήσομεν
ποιήσετε	πληρώσετε	ἀγαπήσετε
ποιήσουσι(ν)	πληρώσουσι(ν)	ἀγαπήσουσι(ν)

Table 15.8—Future Middle Contract Verbs

ποιέω	πληρόω	ἀγαπάω
ποιήσομαι	πληρώσομαι	ἀγαπήσομαι
ποιήσῃ	πληρώσῃ	ἀγαπήσῃ
ποιήσεται	πληρώσεται	ἀγαπήσεται
ποιησόμεθα	πληρωσόμεθα	ἀγαπησόμεθα
ποιήσεσθε	πληρώσεσθε	ἀγαπήσεσθε
ποιήσονται	πληρώσονται	ἀγαπήσονται

Table 15.9—Future Consonant Examples

ἔχω	πείθω	βαπτίζω
ἕξω	πείσω	βαπτίσω
ἕξεις	πείσεις	βαπτίσεις
ἕξει	πείσει	βαπτίσει
ἕξομεν	πείσομεν	βαπτίσομεν
ἕξετε	πείσετε	βαπτίσετε
ἕξουσι(ν)	πείσουσι(ν)	βαπτίσουσι(ν)

Future of Εἰμί

Table 15.10—Future Indicative of Εἰμί

ἔσομαι	I shall be
ἔσῃ	you will be (sg)
ἔσται	he (she, it) will be
ἐσόμεθα	we shall be
ἔσεσθε	you will be (pl)
ἔσονται	they will be

As a copulative, εἰμί exists only in the present, imperfect, and future tenses—that is, the three basic time frames. The future paradigm, then, completes εἰμί in the indicative mood.

Future Translation

Future Nuances

Use of the future is intuitively obvious. One predictable use is within a prophetic context, as *futuristic* or *predictive*:

αὐτὸς δὲ <u>βαπτίσει</u> ὑμᾶς ἐν πνεύματι ἁγίῳ.
"but he *will baptize* you with the Holy Spirit" (Mk. 1:8)

Another use is the *deliberative*, that is, when someone puts forth a question of what to do:

ἕως πότε μεθ᾽ ὑμῶν <u>ἔσομαι</u>;
"How much longer *must I put up* with you?" (Mt. 17:17)

Literally, this is: "Until when with you will I be?" Jesus was frustrated with his disciples' lack of understanding. You can see how translation has to become less literal and more dynamic if you wants to convey the idea expressed above adequately.

One special use of future tense is as an *imperative*, that is, giving a command. For this use, you drop the "will" auxiliary:

ἀγαπήσεις τὸν πλησίον σου.
"*Love* your neighbor." (Mt. 5:43)

Future Middle "Deponent"

Table 15.11—So-Called "Deponent Future"

Present	Future Middle
γινώσκω	γνώσομαι
λαμβάνω	λήμψομαι
ὁράω	ὄψομαι

Some future verbs showing no active voice forms traditionally were described as *deponent futures*. Students were told to "translate actively." Three verbs in your vocabulary that have (so-called) "future deponent" forms are given above.

Actually, the Greek middle voice nuance is present in Greek but simply does not translate very well into English. Thus, for example, the verb γινώσκω *as future* would be encountered in the New Testament *in middle forms only*. Practically speaking, the middle nuance of this verb is so strong that active voice forms simply are not used. English translation, however, cannot communicate this middle voice, so English translation sounds as if active voice.[4] Observe:

ἐν τούτῳ γνώσονται πάντες ὅτι ἐμοὶ μαθηταί ἐστε.
"By this all *will know* that you are my disciples." (Jn. 13:35)

---

[4]Our translation difficulty for the Greek middle voice in the past has been confused with a legitimate grammatical category of some Latin verbs, from which we derived the traditional use of the word "deponent." Greek verbs, however, probably are not genuinely "deponent" in the Latin sense (actually minus a middle meaning). You also might notice that two of the verbs above, λαμβάνω and ὁράω, also are "irregular" verbs.

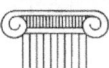

Exercise 15

1. Fill in the blank:

    1.1 _____ = The future tense is what principal part?

    1.2 _____ = The future stem is what action kind?

    1.3 _____ = What morphological component makes the future stem?

    1.4 _____ = The future suffix is what Greek letter?

    1.5 _____ = Contract verbs do what in principal parts outside the first?

2. Complete the following chart of sigma stop reactions:

    labials: ____, ____, ____ + σ = ____

    palatals: ____, ____, ____ + σ = ____

    dentals: ____, ____, ____ + σ = ____

3. Stop stems react with the sigma tense suffix. Provide the resultant future tense stem of the following:

Present	Stop Stem	With future suffix
3.1 βλέπω →	βλεπ- →	_____
3.2 γράφω →	γραφ- →	_____
3.3 πέμπω →	πεμπ- →	_____
3.4 ἄγω →	ἀγ- →	_____

4. "Hidden stems" hide a letter in the present tense form that reacts in other tense formations. Provide the resultant future tense stem of the following:

	Present	Hidden Stem	With future suffix
4.1	βαπτίζω →	βαπτιδ- →	_____
4.2	διδάσκω →	διδακ- →	_____
4.3	σῴζω →	σωδ- →	_____

5. Contract verbs:

	Present	Vowel	With future suffix
5.1	αἰτέω →	αἰτε- →	_____
5.2	γεννάω →	γεννα- →	_____
5.3	πληρόω →	πληρο- →	_____

6. Identify the following morphological components of the future tense verb:

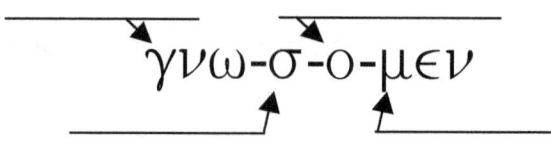

γνω-σ-ο-μεν

Chapter 15: Future Tense

7. Complete the future *active* indicative conjugation for the verb πέμπω ("I send"):

_____ = _____
_____ = _____
_____ = _____
_____ = _____
_____ = _____
_____ = _____

8. Complete the future *middle* indicative conjugation for the verb αἰτέω ("I ask"):

_____ = _____
_____ = _____
_____ = _____
_____ = _____
_____ = _____
_____ = _____

9. Translate. Be ready to locate verbs. Look up any unknown words in your UBS dictionary. "Unknown" forms may be future tense stems different than present, consonant and hidden stems that have reacted with the future tense sigma suffix, or an irregular verb.

9.1 δῶρα (δῶρον) πέμψουσιν ἀλλήλοις. (Rev. 11:10)

_____

9.2 ἐγὼ ὑπάγω καὶ ζητήσετέ με. (Jn. 8:21)

_____

9.3 οὐκ ἀνοίγει τὸ στόμα αὐτοῦ. (Acts 8:32)

9.4 τί καὶ βαπτίζονται ὑπὲρ αὐτῶν; (1 Cor.15:29)

9.5 τίς ἀναβήσεται (ἀναβαίνω) εἰς τὸν οὐρανόν; (Rom. 10:6)

9.6 ὁ δὲ δίκαιος ἐκ πίστεως ζήσεται. (Rom. 1:17)

9.7 ὥστε οὐκέτι εἶ δοῦλος ἀλλὰ υἱός. (Gal. 4:7)

9.8 καὶ ἔσονται οἱ δύο εἰς σάρκα μίαν. (Mt. 19:5)

9.9 ἑκάστου τὸ ἔργον φανερὸν (manifest) γενήσεται (γίνομαι). (1 Cor. 3:13)

9.10 ὅτι αὐτὸς ὁ κύριος . . . καταβήσεται (καταβαίνω) ἀπ' οὐρανοῦ (οὐρανός). (1 Thess.4:16)

9.11 Μωϋσῆς λέγει· ἐγὼ παραζηλώσω (παραζηλόω) ὑμᾶς ἐπ' οὐκ ἔθνει (ἔθνος, Table 7.11). (Rom. 10:19)

9.12 ἡ δὲ ἄνω Ἰερουσαλὴμ ἐλευθέρα (ἐλεύθερος) ἐστίν, ἥτις ἐστὶν μήτηρ ἡμῶν. (Gal. 4:26)

9.13 ὁ πονηρὸς ἄνθρωπος ἐκ τοῦ πονηροῦ θησαυροῦ (θησαυρός) ἐκβάλλει πονηρά. (Mt. 12:35)

 **Vocabulary 15**

ἀναβαίνω, *I go up*

ἀνοίγω, *I open*

ἀπόστολος, ὁ, *apostle, messenger*

βαπτίζω, *I baptize* (baptism)

δίκαιος, -α, -ον, *upright, just, righteous* (syndicate)

ἕκαστος, -η, -ον, *each, every*

ἐκβάλλω, *I throw out, drive out, bring forth*

ἔσομαι, *I shall be*

Ἰερουσαλήμ, ἡ, *Jerusalem*

καταβαίνω, *I go down*

μήτηρ, μητρός, ἡ, *mother* (metropolis)

Μωϋσῆς, -εως, ὁ, *Moses*

πέμπω, *I send*

πονηρός, -ά, -όν, *evil, wicked, bad, sick*

στόμα, -ματός, τό, *mouth* (stomach)

ὑπάγω, *I go away* (cf. ἄγω)

ὥστε, *so that, therefore*

Vocabulary notes:

(1) Future tense stems: ἀναβαίνω, ἀναβήσω; βαπτίζω, βαπτίσω; καταβαίνω, καταβήσω; πέμπω, πέμψω; ἀνοιγω, ἀνοίξω.

(2) Perhaps approach the future of εἰμί, ἔσομαι, as simply six different vocabulary words to learn.

(3) Note the third declension nouns: μήτηρ has a genitive singular μητρός; στόμα has a genitive singular στοματός; remember that all -μα, -ματ nouns are neuter.

(4) The conjunction ὥστε often is followed by an infinitive as a result clause.

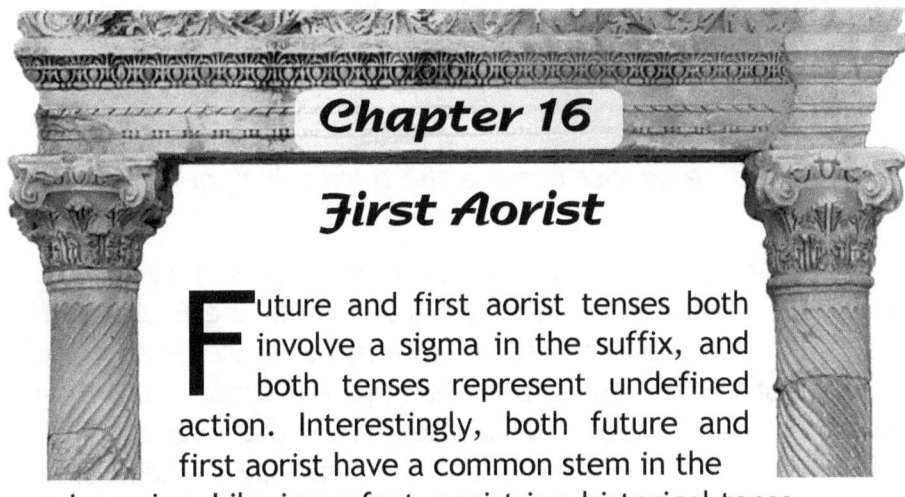

Chapter 16

First Aorist

Future and first aorist tenses both involve a sigma in the suffix, and both tenses represent undefined action. Interestingly, both future and first aorist have a common stem in the passive voice. Like imperfect, aorist is a historical tense.

First Aorist Tense

Aorist tense is undefined action, and, when indicative, past time. Another tense stem was developed, creating the third principal part. The formation uses a tense suffix, which sets up the aorist tense as the third principal part.

Table 16.1—First Aorist Tense Morphology

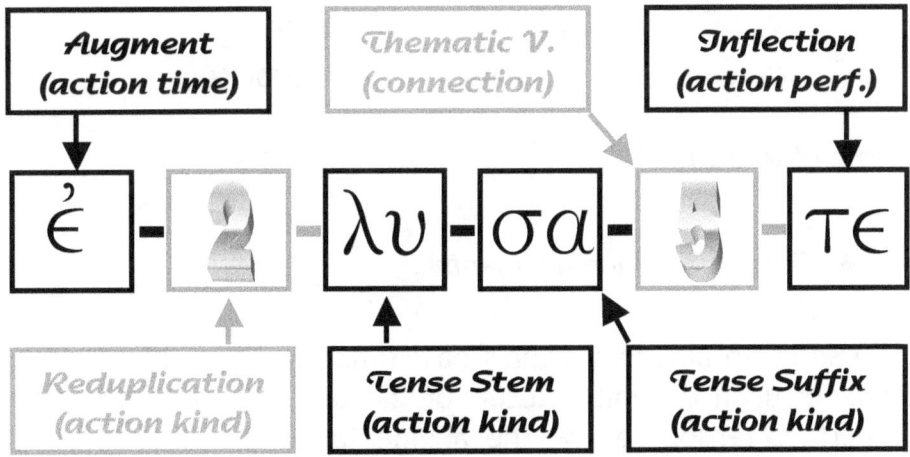

Aorist Tense Stem

♦ *The Greek aorist tense is the third principal part.*

Some aorist stems look like present tense stems, only with the suffix added. This formation is similar to the English suffix "-ed" added to make a past tense from the present tense. Other aorist stems are not exactly like present tense counterparts before adding the tense suffix. Stem types that regularly differ from the present tense include stop consonants, hidden stems, and irregular verbs. (Review the related discussion of various stem types and their future tense formation, pp. 229-32. The resultant look will be similar.)

Table 16.2—First Aorist Stem Formative

Present	Aorist Form.	Aor. 1st Sg.
βαπτιζ-	βαπτιδ-	ἐβάπτισα
θελ-	θελη-	ἠθέλησα
διδασκ-	διδακ-	ἐδίδαξα
κηρυσσ-	κηρυκ-	ἐκήρυξα
κραζ-	κραγ-	ἔκραξα
σῳζ-	σωδ-	ἔσωσα

Time Augment

♦ *Compounds hide augments!*

Use of an augment signals past time. The type of augment depends upon the initial letter of the tense stem, as with the imperfect tense. Review the augmentation patterns given in Chapter 13, pp. 193-94.

Tense Suffix

(1) First Aorist Stems Like Present Stems
The first aorist suffix is -σα-. Note carefully that the suffix vowel (α) eliminates the need for a thematic vowel. For a verb such as λύω, the suffix is just added on after dropping the inflection:

$$ἐ\text{-}λυ\text{-}σα$$

(2) First Aorist Stems Unlike Present Stems
The first aorist suffix is added to the stem formative. Depending on the type of stem, the first aorist suffix may invite change, exactly as with future tense. Review those future paradigms for typical reactions covered there. Note:

$$ἐδιδακ\text{-}σα \rightarrow ἐδίδαξα$$

(3) "Irregular" Stems
Irregular aorists create a special category called "second aorists." These verbs are treated in the next chapter. They do not use the aorist σα suffix. Verbs that do use the σα suffix, as is true of the verbs in this chapter, are called "first aorists."

Thematic Vowel

The ο/ε set is *not* used. The first aorist tense suffix has a vowel already. What about contract verbs? They contract in the *first* principal part *only*. Otherwise, their reaction is this:

♦ *Contract verbs lengthen in all other principal parts.*

The lengthening process always is ε/α → η, and ο → ω. So: ἐποιε-σα = ἐποιησα-; ἐπληρο-σα = ἐπληρωσα-; ἠγαπα-σα = ἠγαπησα-.

Inflection

Aorist tense is a historical tense. Historical tenses are secondary tenses. Secondary tenses take secondary endings. The aorist tense takes the same endings as the imperfect, that is, secondary active: -ν, -σ, --, -μεν, -τε, -ν or -σαν; secondary middle: -μην, -σο, -το, -μεθα, -σθε, -ντο.

A few comments on forms need to be made. In active voice, the first singular is supposed to be -ν. The first aorist simply drops the ending, which leaves only the tense suffix, -σα. The third singular shows up as -σε(ν). As with the imperfect, the third plural and first singular are the same (-ν). Oddly, because the aorist tense suffix is σα, the look is the same as using the *alternate* secondary active ending of -σαν.

Note the middle second singular (-σω) carefully![1] This is *not* a first singular primary active ending ("I"). Rather, this -σω is *second* person ("you"). Notice the *augment* indicates clearly *past time*, not present (i.e., -ω) or future (i.e., -σω).

As with the future tense, aorist passive uses a different stem than the aorist middle and will be studied later. You will note that, as with the future tense, the paradigms mention only aorist "middle," not aorist "middle/passive."

A so-called *"middle deponent"* traditionally is an *aorist* verb that has only middle forms, translated as if active. You now have met three terms used for so-called "deponents." Notice that the terminology used is an attempt to distinguish "deponents" in different principal parts: *deponent* (first), *deponent future* (second), *middle deponent* (third). However, Greek verbs are not truly deponent (see p. 249).

---

[1] The -σασο undergoes a sigma reaction in which the σ of the ending drops between the two vowels (-σαο), and the resulting vowels contract.

First Aorist Paradigms

$$\overset{\text{'}}{\epsilon}\text{-}\lambda\upsilon\text{-}\sigma\alpha\text{-}\tau\epsilon$$

Table 16.3—First Aorist Active Indicative

ἔλυσα	I loosed
ἔλυσας	you loosed (sg)
ἔλυσε(ν)	he (she, it) loosed
ἐλύσαμεν	we loosed
ἐλύσατε	you loosed (pl)
ἔλυσαν	they loosed

Table 16.4—First Aorist Middle Indicative

ἐλυσάμην	I loosed *(for myself)*
ἐλύσω	you loosed *(for yourself)*
ἐλύσατο	he (she, it) loosed *(for himself)*
ἐλυσάμεθα	we loosed *(for ourselves)*
ἐλύσασθε	you loosed *(for yourselves)*
ἐλύσαντο	they loosed *(for themselves)*

Aorist Translation

Aorist Nuances

Aorist is undefined action. Use of the aorist is by default when action kind is not emphasized. Aorist, then, is used often, especially in narrative, since narrative usually is a report of past events. The action is simply reported as having happened, that is, *that* events happened, not *how*.

The aorist tense can be used in a punctiliar sense (a specific point in time), but aorist tense is not inherently punctiliar action. Punctiliar action is contextually perceived, not grammatically conceived, and is not confined to the aorist tense.

(1) Ingressive and Culminative

Sometimes context implies specific nuances. One might have emphasis on the beginning (*ingressive*) or the end (*culminative*) of the action. Auxiliary verbs must be used in English if this context needs to be brought out in translation. One might use *came*, *became*, or *began* for the ingressive nuance, or *have* or *has* for the culminative nuance. For the ingressive, compare Mt. 9:9: "and after he got up, he *began to follow him*" (cf. Jn. 4:52; Acts 11:28). For the culminative nuance:

ἐγὼ ἐβάπτισα ὑμᾶς ὕδατι.
"I *have baptized* you with water." (Mk. 1:8)

(2) Dramatic, Prophetic, Gnomic

Some contexts call for a *present* translation. The author has used aorist for emphasis. *Dramatic* use is when something dramatic has just taken place: "He is alive!" (Lk. 15:32). *Prophetic* use is with prophetic surety, that is, as if the event already has happened: "Babylon is fallen!" (Rev. 18:2). *Gnomic* use covers generalized truisms: "for all sin" (Rom. 3:23).

(3) Epistolary

How we refer to the process of writing a letter is idiomatic: English chooses to relate the process from the perspective of the author at the time of composition, so uses present tense: "I *am writing* this letter to you because . . ." In contrast, Greek chooses to refer to the process of writing from the perspective of the reader later, so uses past tense; this use is called the "epistolary aorist." On the one hand, one could use a culminative aorist to translate: "have written." Such a reference would be more toward the end of the letter as the author is making closing remarks.

On the other hand, if the reference is understood as the typical reference to the *actual process* of writing, such as would occur more at the beginning or in the middle of a letter, one probably would consider this aorist an "epistolary aorist" and need to put this usage into proper English idiom, which requires a present tense: "am writing." Compare 1 Jn. 2:14:

<u>ἔγραψα</u> ὑμῖν, παιδία, ὅτι . . .
"I *am writing* to you, children, because . . ."

"Middle Deponent"

So-called "middle deponents" are not common in the New Testament, especially of those that occur fifty or more times, the delimitation for this grammar. These aorist verbs that are found only as middle probably have middle sense inherently, such as ἀσπάζομαι, "I greet." This middle sense, however, is difficult or awkward to represent in translation. Other verbs that occur only in middle or passive forms in the New Testament still have active forms in the wider Hellenistic world (as πορεύομαι). Thus, our trying to say Greek verbs are "deponent" (like Latin verbs) is chasing illusive butterflies: the more we try to catch them in our grammar nets, the more the specimens elude us. We perhaps should quit trying to snare so-called Greek deponents with a Latin grammar net. These Greek middle verbs are not deponent. They simply show dominantly middle forms with true middle meanings that frustrate most of our attempts at English translation.

 **Exercise 16**

1. Fill in the blank:

    1.1 _____ = The aorist tense is what principal part?

    1.2 _____ = The aorist stem is what action kind?

    1.3 _____ = What morphological component makes the aorist stem?

    1.4 _____ = What suffix vowel shows up instead of thematic vowels?

    1.5 _____ = Contract verbs do what in principal parts outside the first?

2. Contract verbs. Show stems first as modified by the augment and then with the aorist tense suffix:

Present	Augment	Aorist suffix
2.1 αἰτέω →	_____	_____
2.2 γεννάω →	_____	_____
2.3 πληρόω →	_____	_____
2.4 ἐπερωτάω →	_____	_____

3. Identify the following morphological components of the first aorist tense verb:

    ἐ-λυ-σα-τε

Chapter 16: First Aorist

4. Complete the aorist *active* indicative conjugation for the verb πέμπω ("I send"):

   _____ = _____
   _____ = _____
   _____ = _____
   _____ = _____
   _____ = _____
   _____ = _____

5. Complete the aorist *middle* indicative conjugation for the verb αἰτέω ("I ask"):

   _____ = _____
   _____ = _____
   _____ = _____
   _____ = _____
   _____ = _____
   _____ = _____

6. Translate. Be ready to locate verb forms and to explain morphological elements of formation.

    6.1 ἠγάπησας αὐτούς. (Jn. 17:23)

    _____

    6.2 τὸ ποτήριον ὃ ἐγὼ πίνω πίεσθε. (Mk. 10:39)

    _____

    6.3 ἔκραξεν οὖν ἐν τῷ ἱερῷ ὁ Ἰησοῦς. (Jn. 7:28*)

    _____

6.4 οἱ δὲ πατέρες ὑμῶν ἀπέκτειναν² αὐτούς. (Lk. 11:47)

6.5 καὶ ἐν τούτῳ χαίρω. Ἀλλὰ (Yes,) καὶ χαρήσομαι.³ (Phil. 1:18)

6.6 πολλάκις γὰρ πίπτει εἰς τὸ πῦρ καὶ πολλάκις εἰς τὸ ὕδωρ. (Mt. 17:15)

6.7 ἰδοὺ ἐγὼ ἀποστέλλω τὸν ἄγγελόν μου πρὸ προσώπου σου. (Mt. 11:10)

6.8 ἠγάπησαν οἱ ἄνθρωποι μᾶλλον τὸ σκότος ἢ τὸ φῶς· ἦν γὰρ αὐτῶν πονηρὰ τὰ ἔργα. (Jn. 3:19)

---

²This verb is from your vocabulary. Where is the augment in this form? The verb is called a "liquid aorist" (next chapter) because the stem ends in a liquid consonant, ν. This liquid consonant causes the σ of the σα aorist suffix to drop, yielding the -αν ending you see. The original ending is -σαν. What person and number is this inflection?

³A (so-called) "deponent future" (p. 236; cf. principal parts, p. 560).

6.9 παντὸς ἀνδρὸς ἡ κεφαλὴ ὁ Χριστός ἐστιν, κεφαλὴ δὲ γυναικὸς ὁ ἀνήρ, κεφαλὴ δὲ τοῦ Χριστοῦ ὁ θεός. (1 Cor. 11:3)

 **Vocabulary 16**

Ἀβραάμ, ὁ, *Abraham*

ἀποκτείνω, *I kill, put to death*

δώδεκα, *twelve*

ἱερόν, τό, *temple, sanctuary* (hierarchy)

Ἰσραήλ, ὁ, *Israel*

κεφαλή, ἡ, *head* (encephalitis)

πίνω, *I drink* (symposium)

πλοῖον, τό, *ship, boat*

πρόσωπον, τό, *face, appearance, presence*

πῦρ, πυρός, τό, *fire* (pyre, pyromania, Pyrex)

Σίμων, -ωνος, ὁ, *Simon*

ὕδωρ, -ατος, τό, *water* (hydrant, dehydrate, hydraulic)

φῶς, φωτός, τό, *light, fire* (phosphorus, photograph)

χαίρω, *I rejoice, am glad*

Vocabulary notes:
(1) Notes on tense stems:
- ἀποκτείνω is a special future stem, as well as a second aorist (both studied in the next chapter)
- χαίρω is a (so-called) deponent future: χαρήσομαι
- πίνω has a (so-called) deponent future: πίομαι; the aorist is a second aorist (next chapter)

(2) Note the third declension nouns: ὕδωρ, φῶς, and πῦρ.

Photo © Gerald L. Stevens

Fig. 13. Thessaloniki Inscription. This inscription appears on the base of a second-century A.D. statue of Thessaloniki, wife of King Cassander, who gave his wife's name to the city he founded in Macedonia in 315 B.C. Even though Thessaloniki was a sister of Alexander the Great, the rest of her family faired poorly at the hands of her husband. After the death of Alexander the Great, Cassander murdered Alexander's wife, Roxana, along with Roxana's son, Alexander IV, in the process of wresting control of Macedonia from other generals competing for the remnants of Alexander's kingdom. The inscription reads:

ΘΕΣΣΑΛΟΝΙΚΗΝ
ΦΙΛΙΠΠΟΥ
ΒΑΣΙΛΙΣΣΑΝ

Θεσσαλονικην
Φιλιππου
Βασιλισσαν

The translation is: "Queen Thessaloniki, daughter of Philip." From the Archaeological Museum Thessaloniki, Thessalonica, Macedonia, Greece.

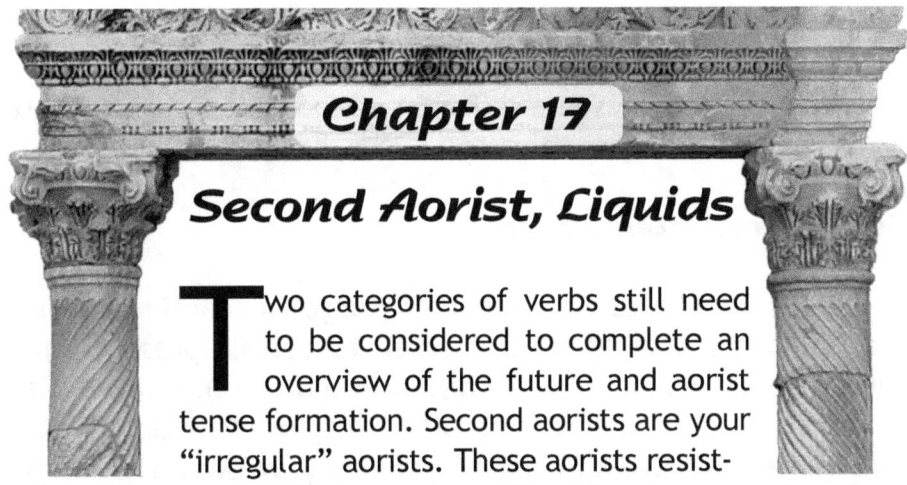

Chapter 17

Second Aorist, Liquids

Two categories of verbs still need to be considered to complete an overview of the future and aorist tense formation. Second aorists are your "irregular" aorists. These aorists resisted development with the aorist suffix. Liquids are verbs whose stems end in a liquid consonant. These stems react to the sigma suffix involved in both tenses.

Second Aorists

Table 17.1—Second Aorist Morphology

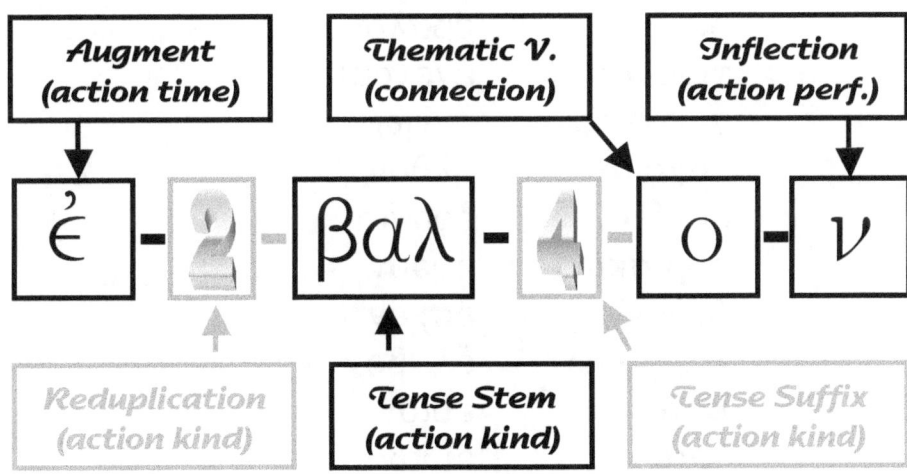

Some past tense verbs in English do not add an "-ed" suffix. They draw their past tense elsewhere—a different form, another verb—like *go* uses *went*. Greek is similar. Verbs that refused to take a σα suffix used a different stem for the aorist. These verbs are called "second aorists."

Second Aorist Tense Stem

Like *went* has to be connected to *go* in learning English, second aorists have to be connected to certain present tense verbs in Greek (a memorized third principal part). Here is a list of verbs with second aorists occurring fifty or more times in the New Testament, except compound forms (ἀναβαίνω, ἀνέβην, etc).

Table 17.2—Second Aorist Stems

Present	Second Aorist
ἄγω	ἤγαγον
ἀποθνῄσκω	ἀπέθανον
βαίνω	ἔβην
βάλλω	ἔβαλον
γίνομαι	ἐγενόμην
γινώσκω	ἔγνων
ἔρχομαι	ἦλθον
ἐσθίω	ἔφαγον
εὑρίσκω	εὗρον
ἔχω	ἔσχον
λαμβάνω	ἔλαβον
λέγω	εἶπον
ὁράω	εἶδον
πίνω	ἔπιον
πίπτω	ἔπεσον
φέρω	ἤνεγκα

Time Augment

Augments signal past time. Second aorist is augmented.

$$\overset{\text{'}}{\varepsilon}\text{-}\beta\alpha\lambda\text{-}$$

Tense Suffix

None is used. *Recognition depends upon stem alone.*

Thematic Vowel

$$\overset{\text{'}}{\varepsilon}\text{-}\beta\alpha\lambda\text{-o-}$$

The o/ε set is used, just like imperfect. Second aorists do not have contract vowels.

Inflection

Second aorist tense takes the same endings as imperfect tense—secondary active: -ν, -σ, --, -μεν, -τε, -ν or -σαν; secondary middle: -μην, -σο, -το, -μεθα, -σθε, -ντο. The sigma drops between two vowels in the middle second singular (-εσο → -εο → -ου). Perhaps you can see by now:

- *Second aorist looks just like the imperfect except for stem alone.*

As with the future and first aorist, the second aorist passive uses a different stem than second aorist middle; this is the sixth principal part. Notice the paradigms mention only second aorist "middle," not second aorist "middle/passive." Present and imperfect tenses have middle and passive forms that are the same. The aorist does not.

Second Aorist Paradigms

$$\dot{\dot{\epsilon}}\text{-}\beta\alpha\lambda\text{-}o\text{-}\nu$$

Table 17.3—Second Aorist Active Indicative

ἔβαλον	I threw
ἔβαλες	you threw (sg)
ἔβαλεν	he (she, it) threw
ἐβάλομεν	we threw
εβάλετε	you threw (pl)
ἔβαλον	they threw

Table 17.4—Second Aorist Middle Indicative

ἐβάλομην	I threw (for myself)
ἐβάλου	you threw (for yourself)
ἐβάλετο	he (she, it) threw (for himself)
ἐβαλόμεθα	we threw (for ourselves)
ἐβάλεσθε	you threw (for yourselves)
ἐβάλοντο	they threw (for themselves)

Liquid Verbs

Liquid verbs are verbs whose future and aorist tense stems end in a liquid consonant (λ, μ, ν, or ρ) that react to the sigma of future and aorist suffixes. Verbs such as αἴρω, ἀπαγγέλλω, ἀποθνῄσκω, ἀποκρίνομαι, ἀποκτείνω, ἀποστέλλω, βάλλω, ἐγείρω, κρίνω, μένω, and σπείρω, are liquid verbs, because these verbs have liquid consonant tense stems that react to sigmas in tense suffixes.

Not all verbs that have stems ending in a liquid consonant, however, are liquid verbs. Such verbs do not show liquid reactions to the sigma suffix. Examples of such non-liquid verbs are γίνομαι, θέλω, μέλλω, ὀφείλω, and χαίρω. The verb πίνω is just off to itself in its own special category of oddball formation (future: πίομαι; second aorist: ἔπιον).

The table below provides liquid forms for verbs occurring fifty or more times in the New Testament, not including compounds (e.g., ἐκβάλλω) and not -μι verbs (e.g., ἀπόλλυμι). A dash means no forms of that verb occur in that principal part, and an asterisk indicates a second aorist form rather than a liquid aorist is used in the third principal part.

Table 17.5—Liquid Verbs

Present	Future	Aorist
αἴρω	ἀρῶ	ἦρα
ἀπαγγέλλω	ἀπαγγελῶ	ἀπήγγειλα
ἀποθνῄσκω	ἀποθανοῦμαι	ἀπέθανον*
ἀποκρίνομαι	-------	ἀπεκρινάμην
ἀποκτείνω	ἀποκτεινῶ	ἀπέκτεινα
ἀποστέλλω	ἀποστελῶ	ἀπέστειλα
βάλλω	βαλῶ	ἔβαλον*
ἐγείρω	ἐγερῶ	ἤγειρα
κρίνω	κρινῶ	ἔκρινα
μένω	μενῶ	ἔμεινα
σπείρω	-------	ἔσπειρα

Liquid Future

By studying the table above, you should be able to see the issue with liquid verbs:

♦ *Liquid verbs loose the sigma tense suffix indicator.*

Slipping on a liquid is easy. Sometimes a circumflex accent alerts you that something has happened, especially with liquid futures. What is going on?

(1) Different Tense Suffix
   A liquid future uses an *alternate -εσ tense suffix*, not just -σ. Sigma has the habit of falling out when between two vowels. The thematic vowel of future tense formation always causes the suffix sigma to drop out (εσο → εο; εσε → εε).

(2) Contraction
   Once the sigma drops, the leftover ε of the original future tense suffix and the thematic vowel contract like a present tense epsilon contract verb (εο → οῦ; εε → εῖ; study Tables 12.1 and 12.2). The result generates this confusion:

♦ *A liquid future looks like a present tense epsilon contract verb.*

However, think about this result. Supposing the verb to be a present tense contract has to be wrong, because *a verb ending in a consonant would not contract in the first principal part.*

(3) Accenting Distinctions
   A liquid future also is confused easily with present tense. The only difference in some forms is accent. Note well:

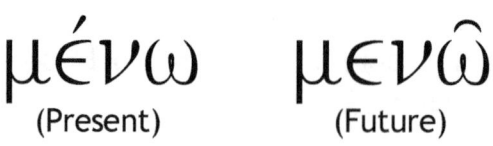

Liquid Aorist

(1) Dropping the Sigma

A liquid aorist also looses its sigma from the aorist tense suffix, but for a different reason than in the future tense; a sigma often drops before a liquid consonant. This form can be called the "asigmatic" aorist, because the sigma is missing:

$$κρίνω \rightarrow ἔκρινα$$

A *non-liquid* move is to *insert a vowel* between the liquid and the sigma, such as an eta, so that the sigma can remain:

$$θέλω \rightarrow ἠθέλησα$$

This insert has no effect on recognizing the σα aorist suffix.

(2) Compensatory Lengthening

For a liquid verb that *does* lose its sigma, a stem may "compensate" for the loss of a letter by lengthening a short vowel in the stem to a long vowel or diphthong. Thus:

$$μένω \rightarrow ἔμεινα$$

(3) Recognition of Forms

Such morphological changes as the loss of a sigma and the lengthening of the stem vowel make recognizing the liquid aorist as a verb you actually already know a little difficult. What verbs lengthen the stem vowel? Not many, really. Of verbs given in vocabulary in this grammar, only the diphthong ει is involved (see Table 17.5). Further, if a verb is not a known alpha contract, *an alpha in the ending has to be guessed first as an aorist*, because very few formation patterns can account for the alpha—even more so if a liquid consonant is right there!

Exercise 17

1. True or False

    1.1 ____ = The second aorist tense is built on the first aorist stem.
    1.2 ____ = The second aorist uses the σα aorist tense suffix.
    1.3 ____ = The second aorist uses the thematic vowel in the ending pattern.
    1.4 ____ = The second aorist looks just like the imperfect except for stem.
    1.5 ____ = All verbs that end in a liquid consonant are liquid verbs.
    1.6 ____ = Liquid futures use the same tense suffix as do non-liquid stem futures.
    1.7 ____ = Liquid futures have a resultant look like present tense alpha contracts.
    1.8 ____ = Liquid aorists result from a tense suffix sigma dropping before liquids.
    1.9 ____ = Short stem vowels often become ει in the process of compensatory lengthening.
    1.10 ____ = An alpha in the verb ending, if not a contract verb, likely is an aorist.

2. Identify the following morphological components of the second aorist verb:

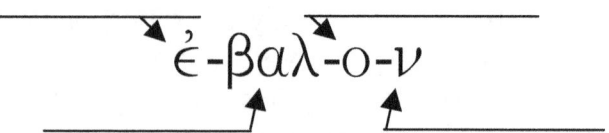

3. Complete the second aorist *active* indicative conjugation for the verb ἔρχομαι ("I come/go"):

   _____ = _____
   _____ = _____
   _____ = _____
   _____ = _____
   _____ = _____
   _____ = _____

4. Complete the future active indicative conjugation for the verb κρίνω ("I judge"):

   _____ = _____
   _____ = _____
   _____ = _____
   _____ = _____
   _____ = _____
   _____ = _____

5. Complete the aorist active indicative conjugation for the verb μένω ("I remain"):

   _____ = _____
   _____ = _____
   _____ = _____
   _____ = _____
   _____ = _____
   _____ = _____

6. Translate. Be ready to locate and explain verbs.

6.1 Πιστὸς δέ ἐστιν ὁ κύριος. (2 Thess. 3:3)

6.2 νῦν ἀπολύεις τὸν δοῦλόν σου. (Lk. 2:29)

6.3 ἐγενόμην τοῖς Ἰουδαίοις ὡς Ἰουδαῖος. (1 Cor. 9:20)

6.4 ἀπὸ τῶν καρπῶν αὐτῶν ἐπιγνώσεσθε (ἐπιγινώσκω) αὐτούς. (Mt. 7:16)

6.5 ταύτην τὴν ἐντολὴν ἔλαβον παρὰ τοῦ πατρός μου. (Jn. 10:18)

6.6 ὃν γὰρ ἀπέστειλεν ὁ θεὸς τὰ ῥήματα τοῦ θεοῦ λαλεῖ. (Jn. 3:34)

6.7 καὶ πολλάκις καὶ εἰς πῦρ αὐτὸν ἔβαλεν καὶ εἰς ὕδατα. (Mk. 9:22)

6.8 καὶ ἐγένετο μετὰ ἡμέρας τρεῖς εὗρον αὐτὸν ἐν τῷ ἱερῷ. (Lk. 2:46)

_____

_____

6.9 τῇ τε ἡμέρᾳ τῶν σαββάτων ἐξήλθομεν ἔξω τῆς πύλης (πύλη) παρὰ ποταμὸν (ποταμός). (Acts 16:13)

_____

_____

6.10 ἀπήγγειλαν ὅσα (ὅσος) πρὸς αὐτοὺς οἱ ἀρχιερεῖς καὶ οἱ πρεσβύτεροι εἶπαν (= εἶπον). (Acts 4:23)

_____

_____

 **Vocabulary 17**

Second Aorist Recognition:

ἠγαγ-, ἄγω, *I lead, bring, go*
　(synagogue, demagogue)

-θαν-, ἀποθνῄσκω

-βη-, βαίνω, (always compounded)

-βαλ-, βάλλω

-γεν-, γίνομαι

-γνω-, γινώσκω

ἠλθ-, ἔρχομαι

-φαγ-, ἐσθίω

εὑρ-, εὑρίσκω

-σχ-, ἔχω

-λαβ-, λαμβάνω

εἰπ-, λέγω

εἰδ-, ὁράω

-πι-, πίνω

-πεσ-, πίπτω

ἠνεγκ-, φέρω, *I carry, lead bring*, (euphoria, metaphor)

Other Vocabulary:

ἀπολύω, *I set free, send away, release, divorce*

ἐντολή, ἡ, *commandment, law*

καρπός, ὁ, *fruit, crop, result* (carpology)

πιστός, ή, -όν, *faithful, reliable, trusting*

πρεσβύτερος, -α, -ον, *older person, ancestor, elder* (presbyter)

ῥῆμα, -ματος, τό, *word, saying, report* (cf. rhetoric)

σάββατον, τό, *Sabbath* (sabbatical)

Vocabulary notes:

(1) The vocabulary burden for this lesson is recognizing second aorist stems. Treat second aorist stem formatives as vocabulary words to be connected to the present tense form. Two new verbs with second aorists are given glosses.

(2) Translation of γίνομαι as an aorist has to be flexible, according to context. The word can vary from "happened," "came about that," to "was," "became." The particular second aorist form, ἐγένετο δὲ, frequently is used in narrative to link units or to make transitions in stories, often translated like: "Now it happened that . . . ," or "And it came about that . . . ," etc.

(3) The noun σάββατον sometimes is found in the plural but translated as singular. This construction usually is in a context of habitual action. Notice:

εἰσῆλθεν κατὰ τὸ εἰωθὸς αὐτῷ <u>ἐν τῇ ἡμέρᾳ τῶν σαββάτων</u> εἰς τὴν συναγωγὴν.

"He went, as was his custom *on the sabbath day*, to the synagogue." (Lk. 4:16)

The sense perhaps is something similar to someone saying: "When I was growing up, we went to church *on Sundays*."

Chapter 18

The Passive System

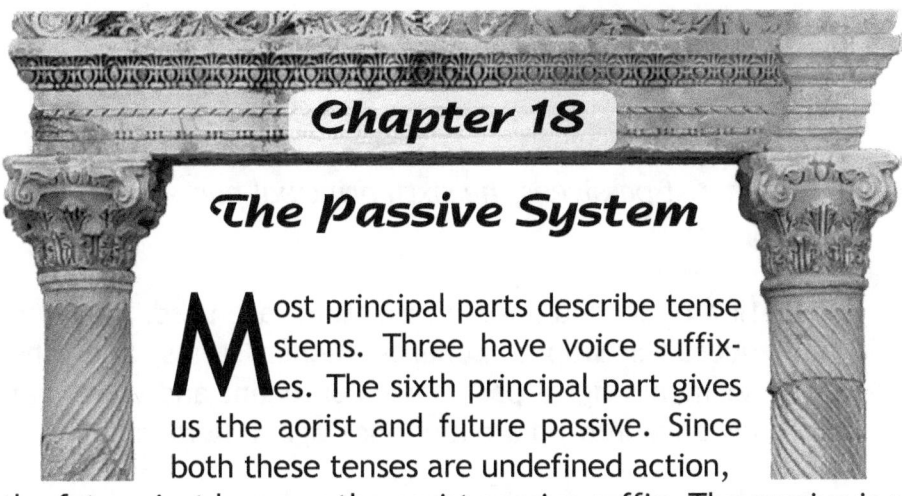

Most principal parts describe tense stems. Three have voice suffixes. The sixth principal part gives us the aorist and future passive. Since both these tenses are undefined action, the future just borrows the aorist passive suffix. The passive is a "system" because the formation involves two related patterns, one called the first passive, and the other the second passive.

Aorist First Passive

Aorist first passive is undefined action, and past time in the indicative. A *voice stem* was developed by using a *voice suffix*, creating the sixth principal part.

Table 18.1—Aorist First Passive Morphology

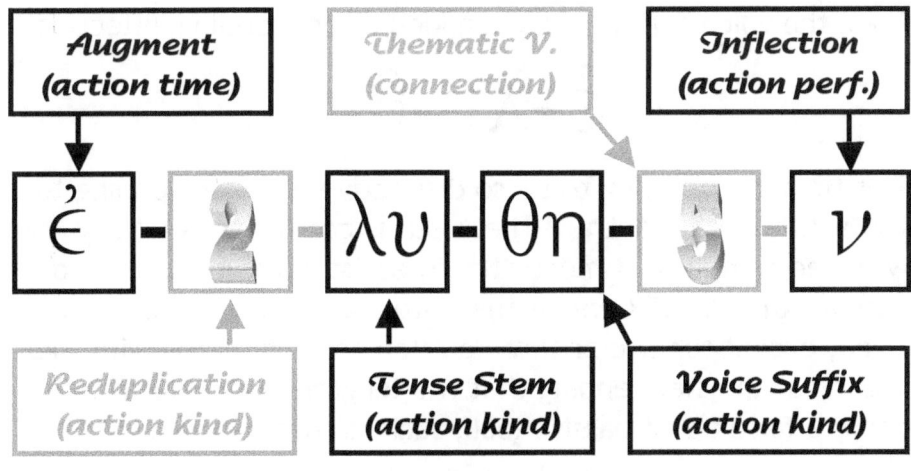

Aorist Stem and Augment

♦ *The aorist passive is the sixth principal part.*

Either first or second aorist tense stems are used. Reactions can be expected in stop consonants, hidden stems, and other patterns. Augments signal past time. Consonant and vowel patterns already encountered are met once again. Remember:

♦ *Compounds hide augments!*

$$\overset{\text{'}}{\epsilon}\text{-}\lambda\upsilon\text{-}$$

Voice Suffix

(1) Aorist Stems Like Present Stems
The aorist passive voice suffix is -θη-. The voice suffix vowel (η) eliminates the need for a thematic vowel. For a verb such as λύω, the voice suffix simply is added after dropping inflection:

$$\overset{\text{'}}{\epsilon}\text{-}\lambda\upsilon\text{-}\theta\eta$$

This θη suffix is going to be so distinctive as a verb ending that you will learn a mantra: "Theta eta is aorist passive." Say that with me a million times: "θη is aorist passive. θη is aorist passive. θη is . . ." Cement that into your brain. You can't miss. (Well, except for two or three epsilon contract verbs with theta epsilon at the stem ending that will lengthen the epsilon to eta, giving a false aorist passive look, such as ἀκολουθέω.)

- *θη is aorist passive!*

(2) Theta Stop Interactions
   Whoops. Sorry. Theta is a consonant, and consonants just do not always get along. (Is that why vowels were invented?) Theta reacts against other stops and liquids.

Table 18.2—Theta Stop Interactions

$$\text{labials: } \pi, \beta, -- + \theta = \phi\theta$$
$$\text{palatals: } \kappa, \gamma, \chi + \theta = \chi\theta$$
$$\text{dentals: } \tau, \delta, \theta + \theta = \sigma\theta$$

   The reaction is patterned. The first two labials become the third. The first two palatals become the third. The last labial combo, $\phi\theta$-, causes the theta to drop, leaving just ϕ-. The last palatal combo, $\chi\theta$-, remains the same. All dentals convert to sigma.

Table 18.3—Theta Liquid Interactions

$$\lambda + \theta = \lambda\eta\theta, \lambda\theta$$
$$\mu + \theta = \mu\eta\theta$$
$$\nu + \theta = \nu\eta\theta, \nu\theta, \theta$$
$$\rho + \theta = \rho\epsilon\theta, \rho\theta$$

   Theta liquid reactions are easy. (Really.) Either the vowel η or ϵ is inserted, or no reaction occurs, or ν might drop.
   What does this theta reaction pattern mean? Not too hard. You do not have to memorize these theta reactions, but you do

want to *recognize the result* as a "theta reaction." That is to say, adding the θη (knee-jerk: "aorist passive!") suffix can slightly change the spelling of an aorist tense stem immediately before the voice suffix. The stem appearance changes a letter:

πέμπω → ἐπεμφθη-

βούλομαι → ἐβουληθη-

κρίνω → ἐκριθη-

This change is more of a problem with *short tense stems*, because so little is left after augmentation, and even more so for a compound in which the augment already is hidden behind the compound. You may even loose every tense stem letter with which you started! For example:

συνάγω → συνηχθη-

Such a result probably best should be treated simply as a new vocabulary word to learn. Often the shorter the tense stem, the more problematic recognition can become.

Thematic Vowel

The ο/ε set is *not* used, since the aorist passive voice suffix already has a vowel. Contract verb interaction is the same:

◆ *Contract verbs lengthen the contract vowel in all other principal parts outside the first.*

The lengthening process always is ε/α → η, and ο → ω. The patterns, then, look like: ἐποιε-θη- = ἐποιηθη-; ἐπληρο-θη- = ἐπληρωθη-; ἠγαπα-θη- = ἠγαπηθη-.

Inflection

Aorist tense takes secondary endings. However, secondary *active* endings are used (-ν, -ς, --, -μεν, -τε, -ν or -σαν). The third plural takes the -σαν option. Use of *active* endings does *not* confuse *passive* location, *because*:

◆ *θη is aorist passive!*

Aorist First Passive Paradigm

$$\overset{\text{'}}{\epsilon}\text{-}\lambda\upsilon\text{-}\theta\eta\text{-}\nu$$

Table 18.4—Aorist First Passive Indicative

ἐλύθην	I was loosed
ἐλύθης	you were loosed (sg)
ἐλύθη	he (she, it) was loosed
ἐλύθημεν	we were loosed
ἐλύθητε	you were loosed (pl)
ἐλύθησαν	they were loosed

A so-called *"passive deponent"* traditionally is an *aorist* verb whose passive forms are translated as if active. We have met "deponent" terms four times, an effort of outdated grammars to distinguish by principal parts a false category of "deponency" in Greek verbs: *deponent* (first), *deponent future* (second), *middle deponent* (third), *passive deponent* (sixth). Note that both "middle deponents" and "passive deponents" involve aorists translated "actively," so their translation comes out the same (i.e., γίνομαι: ἐγενόμην and ἐγενήθην = "I became"). Greek verbs, however, are not truly deponent like Latin verbs. They did not "loose" their middle voice along the way.

Future First Passive

Future first passive is undefined action, and if indicative, future time. The future first passive borrows the aorist first passive stem from the sixth principal part. The future passive formation, then, has the aorist passive *voice suffix* combined with the future *tense suffix*.

Table 18.5—Future First Passive Morphology

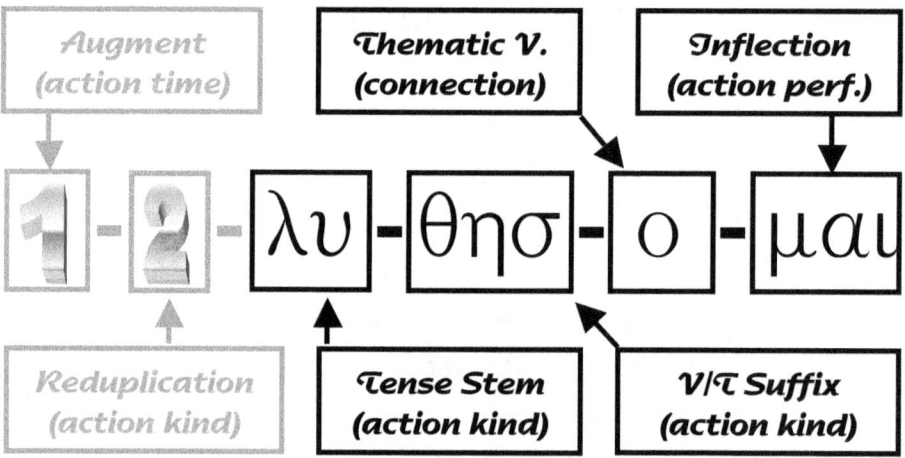

Aorist First Passive Stem

The aorist first passive stem of the sixth principal part is used. Stop consonants, hidden stems, and other reactions can be expected.

Chapter 18: The Passive System

$$\lambda\upsilon\theta\eta\text{-}$$

Time Augment

Future tense does not use an augment. The lack of an augment is another indicator that this formation is not aorist.

Tense Suffix

The future tense suffix is -σ-. For a verb such as λύω, this tense suffix is just added on after the voice suffix:

$$\lambda\upsilon\theta\eta\text{-}\sigma$$

This combination θησ suffix is distinctive. Thus:

♦ *θησ is future passive!*

You still have your theta reactions with stops and liquids.

Thematic Vowel

The ο/ε set is used. Contract verb interaction applies:

♦ *Contract verbs lengthen the contract vowel in all other principal parts outside the first.*

The lengthening process always is ε/α → η, and ο → ω. The patterns will look like: ποιε-θησ- = ποιηθησ-; πληρο-θησ- = πληρωθησ-; ἀγαπα-θησ- = ἀγαπηθησ-.

Inflection

Future tense takes *primary* endings. Future middle uses primary middle endings: -μαι, -ῃ, -ται, -μεθα, -σθε, -νται.

Future First Passive Paradigm

$$\lambda υθη\text{-}σ\text{-}ο\text{-}μαι$$

Table 18.6—Future First Passive Indicative

λυθήσομαι	I shall be loosed
λυθήσῃ	you will be loosed (sg)
λυθήσεται	he (she, it) will be loosed
λυθησόμεθα	we will be loosed
λυθήσεσθε	you will be loosed (pl)
λυθήσονται	they will be loosed

Aorist Second Passive

Aorist second passive as sixth principal part has the same morphological components as the first passive, with one simple change:

♦ *Second passives loose the θ of the θη voice suffix.*

The result is a passive voice suffix that shows only the vowel eta:

$$\overset{\text{'}}{ε}γραφ\text{-}θη \rightarrow \overset{\text{'}}{ε}γραφη\text{-}$$

Aorist Second Passive Paradigm

$$\dot{\dot{\epsilon}}\text{-}\gamma\rho\alpha\phi\text{-}\eta\text{-}\nu$$

Table 18.7—Aorist Second Passive Indicative

ἐγράφην	I was written
ἐγραφης	you were written (sg)
ἐγράφη	he (she, it) was written
ἐγράφημεν	we were written
ἐγράφητε	you were written (pl)
ἐγράφησαν	they were written

"That's it?" you ask. Yes, that's it—but that's not all.

Did you notice we deftly changed the order of adjectives in the headers for this chapter? (In other words, not "First Aorist Passive," but "Aorist First Passive," and so forth.) Why did we do that? Well, that's the "that's not all" part.

We changed the adjective order because "first aorist" and "second aorist" refer to *tense stems* of the *third* principal part. In contrast, the terms "first passive" and "second passive" refer to *voice suffixes* of the *sixth* principal part, *not aorist tense stems*. "First aorist" is a tense stem designation. "First passive" is a voice suffix designation. One is tense, the other is voice.

As aorist passive formations turn out, one will be able to observe that:

- a *first aorist* tense stem (third principal part) can have a *second passive* voice suffix (sixth principal part)
- a *second aorist* tense stem (third principal part) can have a *first passive* voice suffix (sixth principal part).

Thus, γράφω, which has a first aorist tense stem formation in the third principal part, ἔγραψα, has a second passive voice suffix formation in the sixth principal part:

$$\overset{\text{'}}{\epsilon}\gamma\rho\alpha\phi\text{-}\theta\eta \rightarrow \overset{\text{'}}{\epsilon}\gamma\rho\alpha\phi\eta\text{-}$$

Likewise, βάλλω, which has a second aorist tense stem in the third principal part, ἔβαλον, has a first passive formation in the sixth principal part. (The alpha vowel of the second aorist stem also is lost in a process called "vowel gradation"; further, the letter eta is added to the stem) Thus:

$$\overset{\text{'}}{\epsilon}\beta\alpha\lambda\text{-}\theta\eta \rightarrow \overset{\text{'}}{\epsilon}\beta\lambda\eta\theta\eta\text{-}$$

Confusing? You bet. Simply put, you cannot predict what passive configuration, first or second, an aorist verb will take. You simply observe what you see over time and take note. Only if a second aorist looses the theta of the aorist passive voice suffix is a second aorist (third principal part) also a second passive (sixth principal part).

Future Second Passive

Future passive is built on the aorist passive stem. Therefore, an aorist second passive, by default, also creates a future second passive:

- ♦ *Aorist second passive makes a future second passive.*

$$\gamma\rho\alpha\phi\text{-}\theta\eta\sigma \rightarrow \gamma\rho\alpha\phi\eta\sigma\text{-}$$

The rest of the formation is just what you would expect. You have *no augment* on the front, because the future is a primary tense. On the backside, you have your standard *thematic vowel* pattern, followed by your *primary* middle endings.

Future Second Passive Paradigm

γραφη-σ-ο-μαι

Table 18.8—Future Second Passive Indicative

γραφήσομαι	I shall be written
γραφήσῃ	you will be written (sg)
γραφήσεται	he (she, it) will be written
γραφησόμεθα	we will be written
γραφήσεσθε	you will be written (pl)
γραφήσονται	they will be written

Exercise 18

1. True or False

    1.1 ____ = The consonant theta can alter the look of a verb before the passive suffix.

    1.2 ____ = The passive system is one exception to contract vowel lengthening.

    1.3 ____ = So-called "middle" and "passive deponents" of a verb require different translations.

    1.4 ____ = The aorist passive uses secondary middle endings.

    1.5 ____ = A second passive drops the theta of the aorist passive voice suffix.

    1.6 ____ = The future passive has an augment because the aorist passive does.

    1.7 ____ = The future passive, like the aorist, does not use a thematic vowel.

2. Contract verbs. Show contract formation, first as modified by the augment, and then with the aorist passive suffix:

	Present	Augment	Passive suffix
2.1	αἰτέω →	_____	_____
2.2	γεννάω →	_____	_____
2.3	πληρόω →	_____	_____
2.4	ἐπερωτάω →	_____	_____

3. Identify the following morphological components of the aorist first passive verb:

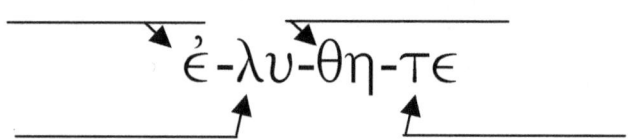

ἐ-λυ-θη-τε

4. Write out an *aorist passive* indicative conjugation for the verb πέμπω ("I send"; see p. 270):

_____ = _____
_____ = _____
_____ = _____
_____ = _____
_____ = _____
_____ = _____

5. Complete the *future passive* indicative conjugation for the verb καλέω ("I call"; looses stem vowel):

_____ = _____
_____ = _____
_____ = _____
_____ = _____
_____ = _____
_____ = _____

6. Translate. Be ready to locate verbs and explain morphological elements of formation.

   6.1 Τί ὑμῖν δοκεῖ; (Mt. 18:12)

   _____

   6.2 καὶ ὄρη[1] οὐχ εὑρέθησαν. (Rev. 16:20)

   _____

   6.3 ὁ δὲ ἔφη· πιστεύω, κύριε (vocative). (Jn. 9:38)

   _____

   6.4 διὰ τὸ θέλημά σου ἦσαν καὶ ἐκτίσθησαν (κτίζω). (Rev. 4:11)

   _____

   6.5 οἱ γραμματεῖς καὶ οἱ πρεσβύτεροι συνήχθησαν (συνάγω). (Mt. 26:57)

   _____

---

[1] A *plural* form; see Table 7.11.

6.6 νῦν ὁ ἄρχων τοῦ κόσμου τούτου ἐκβληθήσεται (ἐκβάλλω) ἔξω. (Jn. 12:31)

6.7 Καὶ ἐπηρώτησεν αὐτὸν ὁ Πιλᾶτος· σὺ εἶ ὁ βασιλεὺς τῶν Ἰουδαίων; (Mk. 15:2)

6.8 Εἴτε οὖν ἐσθίετε εἴτε πίνετε εἴτε τι ποιεῖτε, πάντα εἰς δόξαν θεοῦ ποιεῖτε. (1 Cor. 10:31)

6.9 ἐξῆλθεν ἀπ᾽ αὐτοῦ τὸ δαιμόνιον καὶ ἐθεραπεύθη ὁ παῖς ἀπὸ τῆς ὥρας ἐκείνης. (Mt. 17:18)

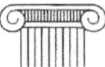 **Vocabulary 18**

γραμματεύς, -έως, ὁ, *scribe, secretary* (grammatical)

δαιμόνιον, τό, *demon, evil spirit* (demon, demoniac)

δοκέω, *I think, suppose, seem* (dogma, Docetism)

εἴτε, *if, whether*

ἔξω, *outside, outer* (exotic)

ἐπερωτάω, *I ask, ask for*

ἐρωτάω, *I ask, request*

θέλημα, -ματος, τό, *will, desire, wish*

ὄρος, -ους, τό, *mountain, hill* (ore)

φημί, *I say* (blasphemy, emphasis, euphemism)

φησίν, *he (she) says*

φασίν, *they say*

ἔφη, *he (she) was saying*

Vocabulary notes:

(1) The verb φημί occurs frequently in the New Testament, but only in the four forms given in this vocabulary. This verb, like εἰμί, is from the "-μι verb" conjugation, the other of the two Greek verb conjugations.

(2) The verb δοκέω often occurs in the form of a question with the pronoun τί at the beginning of the clause, meaning, "what do you think . . . ?" The idea is, "How does it appear to you?" or "What does it seem to you?"

(3) The conjunction εἴτε obviously is a combination of εἰ and τέ.

(4) The verb ἐρωτάω and its compound, ἐπερωτάω, are almost synonyms.

(5) The noun ὄρος is third declension that follows the peculiar ἔθνος pattern (Table 7.11, p. 83).

Photo © Gerald L. Stevens

Fig. 14. Commander Token. A terracotta token. The inscription reads:

ΙΠΠΑΡΧΟΝ
ΕΙΣΛΗΜΝΟΝ
ΦΕΙΔΩΝΑΘΡΙ

ἱππαρχον
εἰς λημνον
Πειδωνα θρι

The translation is: "Pheidon of Thriasos, cavalry commander at Lemnos." Pheidon was a famous cavalry trainer in Athens. Thriasos was his Deme, or, home territory. Lemnos is a Greek island in the Aegean. The discovery of this token and others establishes a rare conjunction of archaeology and literature. The comic poet Mnesimachos (4th cent. B.C.) mentions the famous cavalry trainer Pheidon (*Athenaeus* 9.402). Fighting on horseback was a privilege of the upper class Athenian military, a tradition that carried into the knight system of Europe's Middle Ages. For more details, see John M. Camp, *The Athenian Agora: Excavations in the Heart of Classical Athens*, with 200 illustrations, 11 in color (New York: Thames and Hudson, Inc., 1986; paperback 1992; reprinted 1998), pp. 18–19. Attalos Stoa Museum, Ancient Agora, Athens, Greece.

Vocabulary Review 3

The following list summarizes words introduced since Review 2, generally by frequency of occurrence. The number is the chapter. (Check the next page too.)

Vocabularies 12–18

Ἀβραάμ 16
ἀγαπάω 12
ἄγω 17
αἷμα 14
αἴρω 13
αἰτέω 13
ἀκολουθέω 12
ἀλήθεια 13
ἄν 14
ἀναβαίνω 15
ἀνοίγω 15
ἀποθνῄσκω 13
ἀποκτείνω 16
ἀπολύω 17
ἀπόστολος 15
ἄρα 14
ἄρχω 14
βαπτίζω 15
βασιλεύς 12
γεννάω 12
γραμματεύς 18
δαιμόνιον 18

διδάσκω 14
δίκαιος 15
δοκέω 18
δώδεκα 16
εἰ 14
εἴτε 18
ἕκαστος 15
ἐκβάλλω 15
ἐκκλησία 13
ἐντολή 17
ἐνώπιον 14
ἔξω 18
ἐπερωτάω 18
ἐρωτάω 18
ἔσομαι 15
ἕτερος 14
ἔτι 14
ζάω, ζήω 12
ζητέω 12
ἤμην 13
θέλημα 18
ἱερόν 16

Ἰερουσαλήμ 15
Ἰσραήλ 16
κἀγώ 14
καλέω 12
καρπός 17
καταβαίνω 15
κεφαλή 16
κρίνω 13
λαλέω 12
μαρτυρέω 14
μέλλω 13
μένω 13
μή 12
μήτηρ 15
Μωϋσῆς 15
οἶκος 13
ὁράω 12
ὄρος 18
ὅστις 12
οὔτε 14
παρακαλέω 12
πέμπω 15

περιπατέω 12
πίνω 16
πίπτω 14
πιστός 17
πληρόω 12
πλοῖον 16
ποιέω 12
ποῖος 12
πονηρός 15
πόσος 12
πούς 14
πρεσβύτερος 17
προσεύχομαι 14
πρόσωπον 16
πῦρ 16
ῥῆμα 17
σάββατον 17
Σίμων 16
στόμα 15
σῴζω 13
τηρέω 14
τίς 12

τις 12   ὑπάρχω 12   φοβέομαι 12   ὥρα 13
ὕδωρ 16   φέρω 17   φῶς 16   ὥστε 15
ὑπάγω 15 φημί 18   χαίρω 16

Photo © Gerald L. Stevens

Fig. 15. The Via Egnatia. Sometimes called the "Egnatian Way," this ancient Roman road ran west to east through the province of Macedonia connecting Dyrrhachium and the Adriatic Sea on Macedonia's west coast to Neapolis and the Aegean Sea on Macedonia's east coast. Neapolis was the port city for Philippi, which lay on the Via Egnatia about 8 km inland. Paul and his associates traveled this road on the Second Missionary Journey (Acts 16:11-12). The author is seen here on the actual pavement stones of the ancient Via Egnatia that runs through the ruins of Philippi near the modern city of Krenides. The modern road follows immediately alongside the ancient road about ten feet up the hill to the author's right.

Chapter 19

The Perfect System

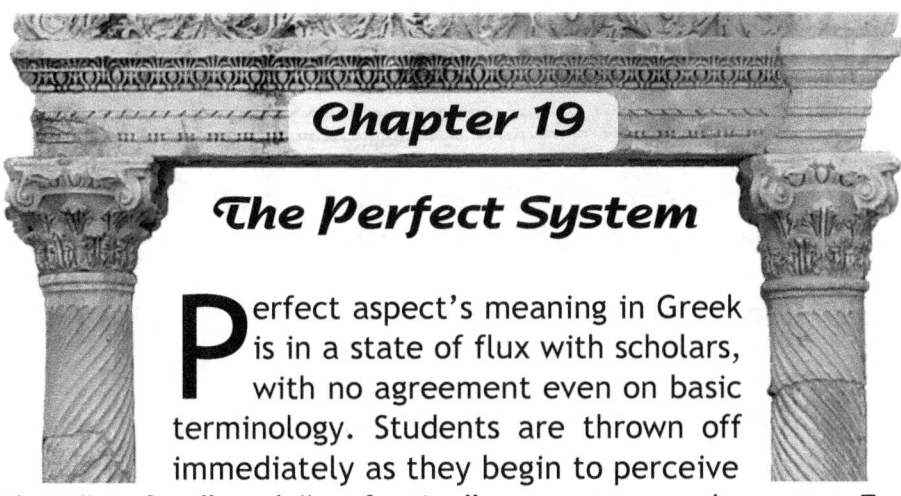

Perfect aspect's meaning in Greek is in a state of flux with scholars, with no agreement even on basic terminology. Students are thrown off immediately as they begin to perceive that "perfect" and "perfective" are not even the same. For the purposes of this primer, know that Greek perfect active is the fourth principal part and middle/passive the fifth.

Perfect First Active

Table 19.1— Perfect First Active Morphology

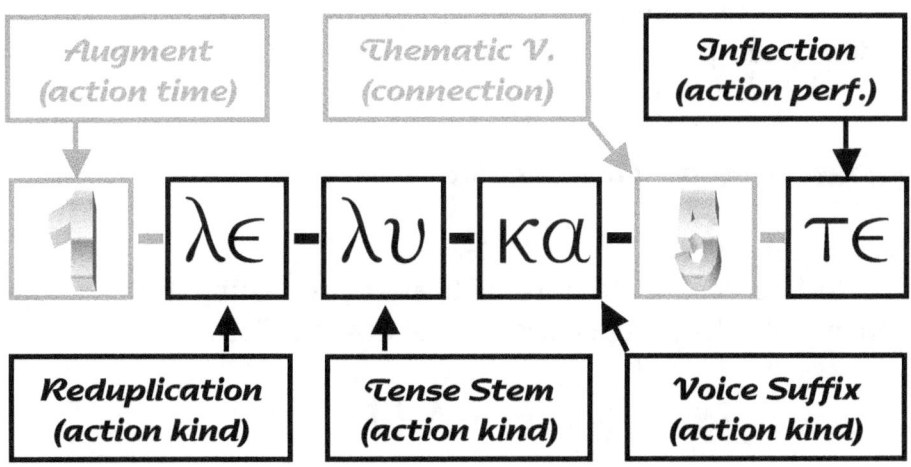

Perfect tense has a hybrid aspect that combines the action kind of aorist (undefined) and present (durative). Undefined means an event taken as a whole, beginning to end, expressing *what* but not *how*. Durative means inclusion of some thought of *afterwards*. Another tense stem developed, creating the fourth principal part. Formation with *both* a tense *prefix* and an active voice *suffix* makes identification a snap.

Perfect Tense Stem

♦ *The perfect active is the fourth principal part.*

Some perfect stems look like present tense stems, only with a prefix and suffix added. Other perfect stems are not like present stems before adding these formatives. These stems include stop consonants, hidden stems, and irregular verbs.

Tense Prefix

Perfect tenses use a tense stem *prefix*. This tense prefix is generated by a process called *reduplication*. The nature of the reduplicated prefix varies, based upon whether a stem begins with a consonant or a vowel.

(1) Reduplication—Consonant Stems

Single Consonants
Most consonant stems reduplicate by repeating the first consonant with the reduplication vowel epsilon. Thus, λύω is:

$$λε-λυ-$$

Rough Stops
The rough stop (right column of Table of Stops, Table 1.5, p. 8) reduplicates with its corresponding smooth stop (left). The

process of smoothing out the pronunciation in this way prevents trying to sound out two rough stops together.[1] So, φιλέω is:

$$\pi\epsilon\text{-}\phi\iota\lambda\epsilon\text{-}$$

Multiple Consonants

Multiple consonants simply are too cumbersome to reduplicate. Only the reduplication vowel is used. So, σταυρόω is:

$$\dot{\epsilon}\text{-}\sigma\tau\alpha\upsilon\rho o\text{-}$$

Stop/Liquid Exceptions

The one multiple consonant exception would be stops followed by either lambda or rho (liquids), such as βλέπω. These stems reduplicate as if single consonants; that means their reduplicated forms almost look "normal" if ignoring the liquid:

$$\beta\epsilon\text{-}\beta\lambda\epsilon\pi\text{-}$$

Complex Sibilants

The complex sibilants are all sibilants but sigma: ζ, ξ, and ψ. These also just use the reduplication vowel. So, ξηραίνω is:

$$\dot{\epsilon}\text{-}\xi\eta\rho\alpha\nu\text{-}$$

Rho Stems

Stems beginning with rho *sometimes* reduplicate the initial rho, but doubled *after* the vowel for pronunciation. So, ῥέω is:

$$\dot{\epsilon}\text{-}\rho\rho\upsilon\text{-}$$

---

[1] The process technically is called *deaspiration*.

Confusing Result

The confusing result of some consonant reduplication that leaves an epsilon on the front of a verb is this: a *reduplicated* perfect stem can look like an *augmented* aorist stem. So how do you discriminate between perfect and aorist in such stems? Fortunately, the perfect tense stem has *two* formatives: *both* a prefix *and* a suffix (see Table 19.1). The perfect *voice suffix* is a distinctive -κα. Thus, as aorist, one would have ἐσταύρωσα, but as perfect, ἐσταύρωκα. Notice the different *suffixes*: the perfect -κα- versus the aorist -σα-. So:

♦ *Depend more on the perfect voice suffix than on tense prefix for tense identification.*

(2) Reduplication—Vowel Stems

Lengthening

Vowel stems can lengthen to reduplicate. So ἀγαπάω is:

$$\dot{\eta}\gamma\alpha\pi\alpha\text{-}$$

This result can be confusing. The verb looks as if augmented for past time, but, again, *note the suffix:* ἠγαπήκα.

Vowel Variations

Other vowel stems present variations that just have to be observed. Some epsilon stems may insert an iota: ἐργάζομαι, εἴργασμαι. Some omicron stems simply add the ε reduplication vowel, which yields a form that looks like the past time augment: ὁράω, ἑόρακα (or ἑώρακα)—but note the suffix!

Attic Reduplication

Attic reduplication is a rare form, but shows up on common verbs. A *syllable* is doubled (not just a letter), and at the same time a stem vowel is *lengthened*. For example, ἀκούω:

$$\dot{\alpha}\kappa\text{-}\eta\kappa o\text{-}$$

(3) Reduplication—Compounds
Lest we ever forget, compounds go before *all* tense stem formatives, including perfect reduplication. So remember:

♦ *Compounds hide perfect reduplication!*

Voice Suffix

(1) Suffix—Perfect Stems Like Present Stems
The perfect *active voice* suffix is -κα-. Note carefully that the suffix vowel (α) eliminates the need for a thematic vowel. For a verb such as λύω, the suffix is simply added on to the reduplicated stem:

$$\lambda\epsilon\text{-}\lambda\upsilon\text{-}\kappa\alpha$$

(2) Suffix—Vowel Insert Stems
Some verbs insert either an η or ω in front of the κ of the perfect active voice suffix. For example:

$$\mu\acute{\epsilon}\nu\omega \rightarrow \mu\epsilon\mu\epsilon\nu\eta\kappa\alpha\text{-}$$

(3) Suffix—Dental Stems
Tense stems that end with a dental will drop the dental in front of the κ of the perfect active voice suffix. As one common example, remember that dental stems often can be "hidden" behind a present tense zeta verb (-ζω). Thus, the verb ἐλπίζω,

with its hidden stem ἐλπιδ-, is reduplicated by vowel lengthening, and looses a delta at the end of the stem:

$$\text{ἐλπίζω} \rightarrow \text{ἠλπικα-}$$

Thematic Vowel

The ο/ε set is *not* used. The perfect active voice suffix already has a vowel. Contract verb interaction applies:

- ♦ *Contract verbs lengthen the contract vowel in all other principal parts outside the first.*

The lengthening process always is ε/α → η, and ο → ω. Thus: πεποιε-κα- = πεποιηκα-; πεπληρο-κα- = πεπληρωκα-; ἠγαπα-κα- = ἠγαπηκα-.

Inflection

Perfect tense is a primary tense. Usually, primary tenses will take primary endings. Yet, perfect active takes *secondary* active endings. This feature should not be confusing for location because the perfect tense stem is so distinctive, either with the reduplicated prefix or the kappa suffix pattern. Like the aorist, the first singular uses no ending, leaving only the -κα voice suffix. Third plural sometimes is the standard -ν ending, but most often is an alternate -σι(ν) ending. In fact, you have seen this alternate third plural -σι ending before—remember εἰμί and φημί? So, we have: -ν, -σ, --, -μεν, -τε, -ν (-σι).

Perfect First Active Paradigm

$$\text{λε-λυ-κα-τε}$$

Chapter 19: The Perfect System

Table 19.2—Perfect First Active Indicative

λέλυκα	I have loosed
λέλυκας	you have loosed (sg)
λέλυκεν	he (she, it) has loosed
λελύκαμεν	we have loosed
λελύκατε	you have loosed (pl)
λέλυκασι	they have loosed

Perfect Second Active

Morphology

Perfect second active is still the fourth principal part, so the morphological components are the same, but with one relatively minor change:

- ♦ *The perfect second active looses the κ of the κα active voice suffix.*

The result is an active voice suffix that has only the alpha vowel. Notice how the φ in γράφω causes the suffix κ to drop:

$$\gamma\epsilon\gamma\rho\alpha\phi\text{-}\kappa\alpha \rightarrow \gamma\acute{\epsilon}\gamma\rho\alpha\phi\alpha$$

"That's it?" you ask. Yes, that's it—and that's all.

Perfect Second Active Paradigm

$$\gamma\epsilon\text{-}\gamma\rho\alpha\phi\text{-}\alpha\text{-}\tau\epsilon$$

Table 19.3—Perfect Second Active Indicative

γέγραφα	I have written
γέγραφας	you have written (sg)
γέγραφεν	he (she, it) has written
γεγράφαμεν	we have written
γεγράφατε	you have written (pl)
γεγράφασι	they have written

Terminology

These perfect active systems often are called "first perfect" and "second perfect." However, the perfect tense does *not* have the *tense stem* distinctions that generate the terms "first aorist" and "second aorist" in the third principal part. For the perfect system, the descriptions "first" and "second" are *voice* distinctions, not *stem* distinctions. Some common perfect second active verbs are given in the table below.

Table 19.4—Perfect Second Active Verbs

Present	Perf. Sec. Act.
ἀκούω	ἀκήκοα
γίνομαι	γέγονα
γράφω	γέγραφα
ἔρχομαι	ἐλήλυθα
λαμβάνω	εἴληφα
πείθω	πέπονθα
πέμπω	πέπομφθα

This terminology issue is similar to the aorist passive formation (sixth principal part). We had "first passive" and "second passive" formation patterns. Yet, *both* of these voice formation patterns occur on *either* "first aorist" or "second aorist" *tense* stems (third principal part). For analytical clarity, we have used the adjectives "first" and "second" when describing both fourth (perfect active) and sixth (aorist passive) principal parts for the *voice parameter* rather than the tense stem.

Perfect Middle/Passive

Perfect middle/passive does *not* use the active voice suffix. Thus, another tense formulation was developed, creating the fifth principal part. Since the perfect active voice suffix, -κα, is not used, the fifth principal part by default has no "perfect first middle" or "perfect second middle" formation systems. As with both present and imperfect tenses, the perfect passive voice clones the form of the perfect middle voice. The morphological slots used are indicated in the table below.

Table 19.5—Perfect Middle/Passive Morphology

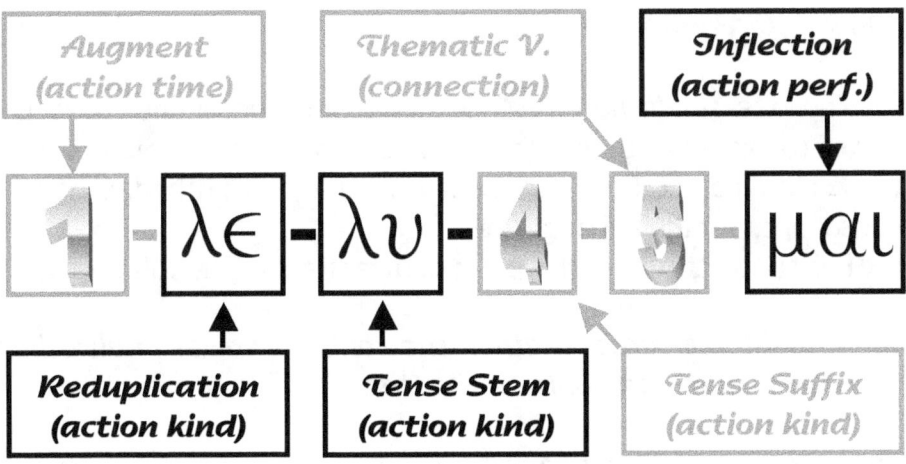

Perfect Tense Stem

♦ *The perfect middle is the fifth principal part.*

Some perfect middle/passive stems look like their present tense counterparts, only with the perfect prefix added. Other perfect stems, however, do not look like their present stems.

Tense Prefix

Perfect middle/passive uses the same reduplication prefix as does the perfect active, making reduplication the quintessential perfect tense feature. Reduplication patterns are the same.

Voice Suffix

Perfect middle/passive does *not* use the -κα- *active voice* suffix. However, no thematic vowel is used either! This oddity, unfortunately, will generate some stem spelling changes.

Thematic Vowel

The ο/ε set is *not* used, so combined consonants have no vowel to separate them. Thus, any consonant that might end a tense stem can collide with a personal ending that begins with a consonant. Spelling changes result.

For contract verbs, the basic contract principle still applies:

♦ *Contract verbs lengthen the contract vowel in all other principal parts outside the first.*

The lengthening process always is ε/α → η, and ο → ω. So, we have the results: πεποιε-μαι = πεποίημαι; πεπληρο-μαι = πεπλήρωμαι; ἠγαπα-μαι = ἠγάπημαι.

Inflection

Primary Middle/Passive Endings

Primary tenses take primary endings. The fifth principal part uses primary middle/passive endings. Note that the second singular -σαι does *not* morph into η, as in other tense formation patterns. Thus, we have: -μαι, -σαι, -ται, -μεθα, -σθε, -νται.

Perfect Middle/Passive Reactions

With *no thematic vowel*, however, consonant reactions occur in a way similar to consonant reactions with the aorist passive suffix. Several different consonants are involved, though, yielding more complex results. The bottom line? The consonant just before the ending may change, as with γράφω:

$$\gamma\epsilon\gamma\rho\alpha\varphi\text{-}\mu\alpha\iota \rightarrow \gamma\acute{\epsilon}\gamma\rho\alpha\mu\mu\alpha\iota$$

Or, either an η or σ might be *inserted*, as with γινώσκω:

$$\check{\epsilon}\gamma\nu\omega\text{-}\mu\alpha\iota \rightarrow \check{\epsilon}\gamma\nu\omega\sigma\mu\alpha\iota$$

Recognition Issue

Good news. You do not have to memorize these perfect middle reaction patterns. We style all these annoying stem changes simply "perfect middle reactions." Anytime you recognize a perfect tense stem in general but encounter an unknown consonant just before the middle ending, when asked, just describe the peculiar spelling as a "perfect middle reaction." Practically speaking, you instantly know the form is perfect due to the reduplication on the front; you also know the form is middle due to the primary middle ending on the back. That odd consonant before the ending is simply a "perfect middle reaction." Just remember this happened because no thematic vowel is used.

Perfect Middle/Passive Paradigm

λε-λυ-μαι

Table 19.6—Perfect (Middle) Passive Indicative

λέλυμαι	I have been loosed
λέλυσαι	you have been loosed (sg)
λέλυται	he (she, it) has been loosed
λελύμεθα	we have been loosed
λέλυσθε	you have been loosed (pl)
λέλυνται	they have been loosed

Pluperfect Active

Pluperfect tense in the indicative mood includes a *past* time frame. Fourth and fifth principal parts are used. Two distinctions from the perfect tense morphology are: (1) a modified vowel in the voice suffix and (2) an augment to signal past time.

Table 19.7— Pluperfect First Active Morphology

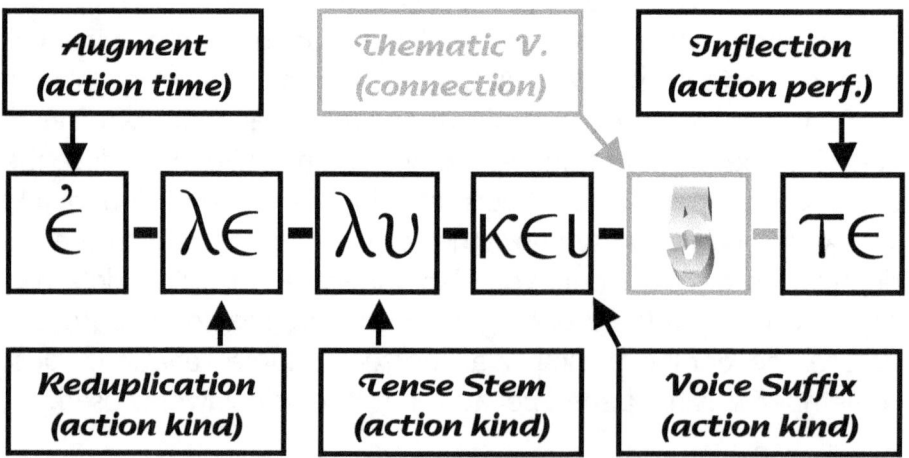

Reduplication

The basic tense stem formative of the perfective system is reduplication, its most characteristic feature. The reduplication is based on the patterns already presented. Thus:

$$\lambda\epsilon\text{-}\lambda\upsilon$$

Augment

Augments signal past time. Augmentation is based on the familiar process regarding consonants and vowels. Thus:

$$\dot{\epsilon}\text{-}\lambda\epsilon\text{-}\lambda\upsilon$$

A vowel stem already lengthened for reduplication, however, cannot lengthen any further to show past time augmentation. So, the pluperfect past time augment is ignored. Thus:

$$\dot{\alpha}\gamma\alpha\pi\alpha\text{-} \longrightarrow \dot{\eta}\gamma\alpha\pi\alpha\text{-}$$

Formally speaking, one would say the pluperfect takes an augment as a historical tense. Practically speaking, though, in the New Testament we actually have this observation:

♦ *The pluperfect augment often is dropped.*

If so, how will you know you have a past time tense? Easy! Perfective *reduplication* and the distinct active *voice suffix*.

Voice Suffix

The pluperfect *first active* suffix is the distinct -κει. Thus:

$$\overset{\text{᾿}}{\epsilon}\text{-}\lambda\epsilon\text{-}\lambda\upsilon\text{-}\kappa\epsilon\iota$$

The *second active* drops the kappa of the voice suffix, as with the perfect. Thus, for ἔρχομαι, which is irregular:

$$\overset{\text{᾿}}{\epsilon}\lambda\eta\lambda\upsilon\theta\text{-}\kappa\epsilon\iota \longrightarrow \overset{\text{᾿}}{\epsilon}\lambda\eta\lambda\upsilon\theta\epsilon\iota\text{-}$$

A first active perfect will be a first active pluperfect, and a second active perfect will be a second active pluperfect. In fact, though, pluperfect is uncommon in the New Testament, with about 86 total occurrences. Only three of our vocabulary words have a pluperfect second active: γίνομαι, ἐγεγόνειν; ἔρχομαι, ἐληλύθειν; and πείθω, ἐπεποίθειν.

Thematic Vowel

The ο/ε set is *not* used. The voice suffix diphthong, ει, renders a theme vowel unnecessary. The contract principle still applies:

◆ *Contract verbs lengthen the contract vowel in all other principal parts outside the first.*

The lengthening process always is ε/α → η, and ο → ω. So, we will encounter typical patterns: ἐπεποιε-κει- = ἐπεποιηκει-; ἐπεπληρο-κει- = ἐπεπληρωκει-; ἠγαπα-κει- = ἠγαπηκει-.

Inflection

Secondary tenses take secondary endings. The pluperfect active uses secondary active endings. One distinction is that the third plural takes the -σαν option. Thus, we have the standard forms: -ν, -ς, --, -μεν, -τε, -σαν.

Chapter 19: The Perfect System

Pluperfect First Active Paradigm

$$\dot{ε}\text{-}λε\text{-}λυ\text{-}κει\text{-}τε$$

Table 19.8—Pluperfect First Active Indicative

ἐλελύκειν	I had loosed
ἐλελύκεις	you had loosed (sg)
ἐλελύκει	he (she, it) had loosed
ἐλελύκειμεν	we had loosed
ἐλελύκειτε	you had loosed (pl)
ἐλελύκεισαν	they had loosed

Pluperfect Second Active Paradigm (ἔρχομαι)

$$\dot{ε}ληλυθ\text{-}ει\text{-}τε$$

Table 19.9—Pluperfect Second Active Indicative

ἐληλύθειν	I had come
ἐληλύθεις	you had come (sg)
ἐληλύθει	he (she, it) had come
ἐληλύθειμεν	we had come
ἐληλύθειτε	you had come (pl)
ἐληλύθεισαν	they had come

Pluperfect Middle/Passive

Pluperfect middle/passive uses the fifth principal part. Passive voice clones the middle voice, as in the present, imperfect, future, and perfect tenses.

Table 19.10—Pluperfect Middle/Passive Morphology

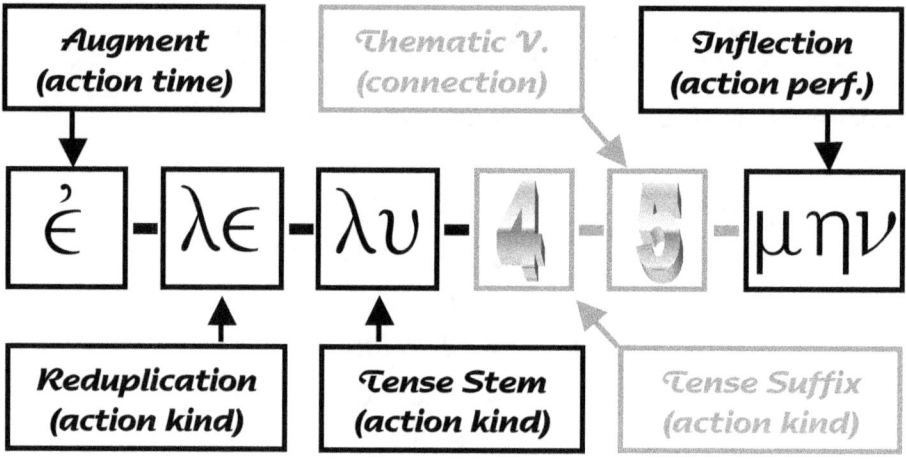

Voice Suffix

The pluperfect middle/passive does *not* use the -κει- *active voice* suffix. However, no thematic vowel is used either!

Thematic Vowel

The ο/ε set is *not* used. The pluperfect middle/passive has no vowel separating personal endings from consonants at the end of tense stems. The contract principle still applies:

♦ *Contract verbs lengthen the contract vowel in all other principal parts outside the first.*

The lengthening process always is ε/α → η, and ο → ω. So, we will encounter typical patterns: ἐπεποιε-μην = ἐπεποιήμην; ἐπεπληρο-μην = ἐπεπληρώμην; ἠγαπα-μην = ἠγαπήμην.

Inflection

Secondary tenses take secondary endings. The pluperfect uses secondary middle/passive endings. One distinction is that the second singular -σο does *not* change to -ου. Thus, we have: -μην, -σο, -το, -μεθα, -σθε, -ντο. A few verbs show the fifth principal part's middle reactions, such as a typical stop reaction (ἐπιγράφω, ἐπεγεγράμμην) or a letter insert reaction, such as using an η (βάλλω, ἐβεβλήμην).

Pluperfect Middle/Passive Paradigm

$$\dot{\epsilon}\text{-}\lambda\epsilon\text{-}\lambda\upsilon\text{-}\mu\eta\nu$$

Table 19.11—Pluperfect (Middle) Passive Indicative

ἐλελύμην	I had been loosed
ἐλέλυσο	you had been loosed (sg)
ἐλέλυτο	he (she, it) had been loosed
ἐλελύμεθα	we had been loosed
ἐλέλυσθε	you had been loosed (pl)
ἐλέλυντο	they had been loosed

Future Perfect

We can deal with this tense with dispatch. First, the future perfect is rare in the New Testament. Second, almost all those forms that occur are constructed using participles, which we have not covered. Third, only one form is not a participle, that of εἰδήσουσιν ("they will know") in Heb. 8:11, using the old second perfect base of οἶδα, whose perfective force has worn out due to overuse.

Perfect Translation

Distinguishing Action Kind

English and Greek differ on perfect action. English perfect is "completed" action.[2] The Greek perfect is more complex. For Greek, an event taken as a whole beginning to end (undefined) then includes resultant *state, completion,* or *consequences.*

Were I to say, "I have written a new praise song for our worship celebration," the English focus would be on the completed manuscript you could see. The Greek focus, however, might be on the durative impact upon our worship experiences the song presently could offer. Thus, Paul could write that Jesus "has been raised" using perfect tense. Given context, his focus could be not on the completed past action of Jesus' exit from the tomb as much as on the possible on-going theological and spiritual consequences for believers' present experience that a past resurrection event implies (cf. Rom. 7:4; 1 Cor. 15:20).[3]

Perfect Tense Nuances

Auxiliary Verb Constructions

English uses auxiliary verbs and the past participle to create the perfect tense. The auxiliary verb "had" is used for the pluperfect (English past perfect), "have" or "has" for the perfect (English present perfect), and "will have" for the English future perfect: "had gone," "have gone," "will have gone." If contextual focus is on the on-going effects, by tense then:

- **Pluperfect**—effects *completed* (e.g., "I *had cleaned* your shirt, but you got it dirty again.")

---

[2]For the English perfect, see the English appendix, p. 472.
[3]Truth in advertising requires that the student be appraised that the essence and meaning of the Greek perfect and its aspectual interaction both with the inherent meaning of a verb stem (lexical) and its grammatical context (semantic) needs nuancing. Consult the advanced grammars.

- **Perfect**—effects *continuing* ("I *have cleaned* your shirt, and it is hanging in your closet.")
- **Future perfect**—future action with *future* effects ("I *will have cleaned* your shirt by the time you return, and you will find it hanging in your closet.")

Present Tense Emphasis

Two uses of the perfect have focus on present reality. The English *present tense*, then, could be used in translation. One use is the *intensive perfect*, focused on the existing state:

πέποιθεν ἐπὶ τὸν θεόν.
"He *trusts* in God." (Mt. 27:43)

Another use is the *dramatic perfect*, which gives narration vivid emphasis or underscores some dramatic declaration:

νῦν ἐγνώκαμεν ὅτι δαιμόνιον ἔχεις.
"Now *we know* that you have a demon!" (Jn. 8:52)

Exegetical Significance

The Greek emphasis on the *on-going effects* of completed action renders the use of perfective action exegetically significant in most instances. However, Greek perfect meaning often cannot be brought out fully by translation. Translation, then, is not the be all and end all of exegesis. Where translation falters, explanation needs to pick up. Use of the perfect tense regularly should be noted in Bible study and sermon preparation. The attentive student should be alert to possible ramifications of an author's choice of this tense. A good example is the illustration a study of Paul offers regarding the historical significance of the resurrection, which is not so much in an empty tomb as a Spirit-filled room. At the same time, try to avoid the temptation of oversqueezing the fruit and serving up more seeds than juice as you wax eloquent in developing your late Saturday night three points and a poem.

Exercise 19

1. Fill in the blank:

    1.1 _____ = Perfect active is what principal part?
    1.2 _____ = Perfect middle is what principal part?
    1.3 _____ = The perfect stem is what action kind?
    1.4 _____ = What type of prefix makes the perfect stem?
    1.5 _____ = What type of suffix makes the perfect active voice?
    1.6 _____ = What active suffix vowel replaces thematic vowels?
    1.7 _____ = What pluperfect vowels replace thematic vowels?
    1.8 _____ = Loss of what consonant makes a second active form?
    1.9 _____ = What pluperfect prefix, if present, shows past time?
    1.10 _____ = On what should you depend for perfect tense identification?
    1.11 _____ = Contract verbs do what in principal parts outside the first?

2. Reduplication. Show perfect stems as modified by reduplication, then with the perfect tense active voice suffix for μένω (μεν-), βαπτίζω (βαπτιδ-), γινώσκω (γνω-), and αἰτέω (αἰτε-; the iota subscripts):

Present	Reduplication	Voice Suffix
2.1 μένω →	_____	_____

2.2 βαπτίζω → _____ _____

2.3 γινώσκω → _____ _____

2.4 αἰτέω → _____ _____

3. Identify the following morphological components of the perfect first active tense verb:

$$\lambda\epsilon\text{-}\lambda\upsilon\text{-}\kappa\alpha\text{-}\tau\epsilon$$

4. Complete the perfect *first active* indicative conjugation for the verb αἰτέω ("I ask"):

_____ = _____
_____ = _____
_____ = _____
_____ = _____
_____ = _____
_____ = _____

5. Complete the perfect *passive* indicative conjugation for the verb φανερόω ("I manifest," "reveal"):

_____ = _____
_____ = _____
_____ = _____
_____ = _____
_____ = _____
_____ = _____

6. Complete the *pluperfect first active* indicative conjugation for the verb κρίνω ("I decide"; the liquid stem looses its ν in front of the voice suffix):

   _____ = _____
   _____ = _____
   _____ = _____
   _____ = _____
   _____ = _____
   _____ = _____

7. Translate. Be ready to locate verbs and explain morphological elements of formation.

   7.1 δεδόξασμαι ἐν αὐτοῖς. (Jn. 17:10)

   7.2 οὐκ ἔστιν ὧδε, ἀλλὰ ἠγέρθη (ἐγείρω). (Lk. 24:6)

   7.3 μὴ καὶ σὺ ἐκ τῆς Γαλιλαίας εἶ; (Jn. 7:52)

   7.4 τὰ ἱμάτια ὑμῶν σητόβρωτα (σητόβρωτος) γέγονεν (dramatic). (Jas. 5:2)

   7.5 ἡμεῖς ἐγνώκαμεν καὶ πεπιστεύκαμεν. (1 Jn. 4:16)

Chapter 19: The Perfect System

7.6 ἀγαπητοί (vocative), νῦν τέκνα θεοῦ ἐσμεν. (1 Jn. 3:2)

7.7 τοῦτ' ἔστιν τὸ ῥῆμα τῆς πίστεως ὃ κηρύσσομεν. (Rom. 10:8)

7.8 κηρυχθήσεται τοῦτο τὸ εὐαγγέλιον τῆς βασιλείας. (Mt. 24:14)

7.9 Νυνὶ δὲ χωρὶς νόμου δικαιοσύνη θεοῦ πεφανέρωται. (Rom. 3:21)

7.10 οἶδα ποῦ κατοικεῖς (κατοικέω), ὅπου ὁ θρόνος τοῦ σατανᾶ [ἐστίν]. (Rev. 2:13)

7.11 Ἤκουσαν δὲ οἱ ἐν Ἱεροσολύμοις ἀπόστολοι ὅτι δέδεκται (δέχομαι) ἡ Σαμάρεια τὸν λόγον τοῦ θεοῦ. (Acts 8:14*; indirect discourse shifts one tense back in time)

7.12 οὗτος ἦλθεν πρὸς αὐτὸν νυκτὸς καὶ εἶπεν αὐτῷ· ῥαββί (vocative), οἴδαμεν ὅτι ἀπὸ θεοῦ ἐλήλυθας διδάσκαλος. (Jn. 3:2)

 **Vocabulary 19**

Perfect Second Active:
ἀκήκοα, ἀκούω
γέγονα, γίνομαι
γέγραφα, γράφω
ἐλήλυθα, ἔρχομαι
εἴληφα, λαμβάνω
οἶδα, I know
πέπονθα, πάσχω

Pluperfect Second Active:
ᾔδειν, I was knowing
ἐγεγόνειν, γίνομαι
ἐληλύθειν, ἔρχομαι
ἐπεποίθειν, πείθω

Other Vocabulary:

ἀγαπητός, -ή, -όν, beloved, dear
Γαλιλαία, ἡ, Galilee
δοξάζω, I glorify, praise (doxology, orthodox)
ἤδη, now, already
θρόνος, ὁ, throne (throne)
Ἱεροσόλυμα, τά and ἡ, Jerusalem
ἱμάτιον, τό, garment, cloak, coat, clothing
κηρύσσω, I proclaim, announce, preach (kerygma)
νύξ, νυκτός, ἡ, night
ὧδε, here, to this place

Vocabulary notes:

(1) Perfect and pluperfect second active forms hide the kappa of the suffix, thereby disguising the tense stems. The forms are given for purposes of recognition of verbs in common use in the New Testament. For example, you do not have to be able to produce from memory the perfect second active of ἔρχομαι, but you *do* have to recognize ἐληλυθ- when you encounter that form as the *perfect tense stem* of ἔρχομαι.

(2) The verb οἶδα is an old perfect second active form (notice the loss of the kappa in the suffix) that has lost its perfective force and translates simply as present tense, "I know," not "I have known." A similar loss of perfective force is also true for its pluperfect second active form of ᾔδειν. This form just translates like an imperfect, "I was knowing" or "I knew."

(3) The verb κηρύσσω is a hidden stem; the tense stem formative is κηρυκ-.

Photo © Gerald L. Stevens

Fig. 16. Asklepios Inscription. This inscription found at the Asklepion of Pergamum and held in the Bergama Museum, Bergama, Turkey, reads:

ΑΣΚΛΗΠΙΩ ΣΩ-
ΤΗΡΙ ΦΑΒΙΑ ΣΕΚΟΥΝ-
ΔΑ ΚΑΤ ΟΜΕΙΡΟΝ

ασκληπιῳ σω-
τηρι φαβια σεκουν-
δα κατ ομειρον

The translation is: "To Asklepios, Savior, Fabia Sekounda, according to her strong desire." Such votive offerings were dedicated to the gods of healing, using likenesses of the body part healed. Galen (d. 212), personal physician to Emperor Marcus Aurelius (d. 180), taught at this Asklepion. Galen's physiological theories dominated Europe until the Renaissance.

The inscription's last word is the noun ὁμείρος. The verb ὁμείρομαι occurs only once in the LXX (Job 3:21) and only once in the New Testament as Paul described his strong yearning for the Thessalonians (1 Thess. 2:8). In the inscription the supplicant is indicating she had a strong desire for the healing. One recalls how Paul described Luke as "the beloved physician" (Col. 4:14). While physical healing was important to Jesus' ministry, and he performed many healing miracles, Jesus said true healing was not complete until spiritual sickness was addressed (Mk. 2:17).

Language Lesson 5

Indicative Verb Summary

We now have completed the six principal parts of the Greek indicative verb system. Our journey has been a long one. A summary of results would be helpful before moving on to the other Greek moods. We focus on two areas: indicative mood and action time.

Indicative Mood—Patterns and Morphology

Recognizing a verb form as one translates is a complex interaction based on vocabulary acquisition and a knowledge of verbal patterns and morphology. "Verbal patterns" are indicative mood principal parts with their tenses. Verb morphology would include all tense stem formative components and their endings. We provide a table summarizing

the Greek indicative verb system in these terms of its six verbal patterns and their morphological formatives and endings.

Table LL5.1 Greek Indicative Verb System

Greek Indicative Verb System									
Patterns		Morphology							
^		Formatives				Endings			
Part	Ten	Aug	Redu	Stem	Suff	Vow	Act	Mid	Pass
1	Pres			Pres		ο/ε	ω	μαι	μαι
	Impf	ἐ		Pres		ο/ε	ν	μην	μην
2	Fut			Fut	σ	ο/ε	ω	μαι	
3	1Aor	ἐ		1Aor	σα		ν	μην	
	2Aor	ἐ		2Aor		ο/ε	ν	μην	
4	Plup	ἐ	λε	Perf	κει		ν		
	Per		λε	Perf	κα		ν		
	FutP		λε	Perf	σ	ο/ε	ω		
5	Plup	ἐ	λε	Perf				μην	μην
	Perf		λε	Perf				μαι	μαι
	FutP		λε	Perf	σ			μαι	μαι
6	Aor	ἐ		Aor	θη				ν
	Fut			Aor	θησ	ο/ε			μαι

Tense Parameter—Action Kind, Action Time

After indicative mood, the second area of focus is the verbal parameter of *tense* as a composite of two components: *action kind* and *action time*.[1] Note, however, that the component of action time occurs *in indicative mood only*. Exactly what is the

---

[1] Review English 3, "Sentences," pp. 471-74.

relationship of action kind and time among the Greek tenses? This relationship is summarized in the table below.

Table LL5.2—Tense (Kind, Time)

(1) English Auxiliaries

	Past	Present	Future
Undefined:	I went.	I go.	I will go.
Durative:	I was going.	I am going.	I will be going.
Perfect:	I had gone.	I have gone.	I will have gone.

(2) Greek Tenses

	Past	Present	Future
Undefined:	Aorist	Present	Future
Durative:	Imperfect	Present	Future
Perfect:	Pluperfect	Perfect	Future Perfect

Notice how action kind *requires auxiliary verbs* in English but not Greek. Why? Because action kind is built into the Greek verb itself. Whereas English has action *time* built into its verb, Greek has action *kind* built into its verb—and that distinction is critical to understanding the difference between English and Greek tenses. The point is this: *action time is a mood in Greek*, not a tense. In the other Greek moods outside the indicative we have this dictum:

♦ *Greek tense expresses only action kind in moods other than the indicative.*

Thus, in Greek, *action kind* is a tense component that *always* is present within the tense stem, and, in the other moods, is the *only* component present. What is the import of this dictum?

In the next two chapters we will be taking up the moods of contingency—subjunctive, optative, and imperative. Retraining your thinking patterns away from an English habit of mind when dealing with the parameter of tense will be very important to getting a handle on translating moods of contingency. English habit is to think tense equals *time*. Greek habit is tense equals *kind*. So, in the coming chapters, if you hear the words "aorist subjunctive" and have a knee-jerk reaction that we must be talking about *past time* just because we used the word "aorist," you are not thinking Greek and already have missed the boat in dealing with the Greek moods of contingency.

What are some practical implications for grammar and morphology? Several implications surface immediately:
- *Aorist will not be past time, nor present present.*
- *Primary and secondary patterns do not apply.*
- *Augments are a thing of the past.* ☺

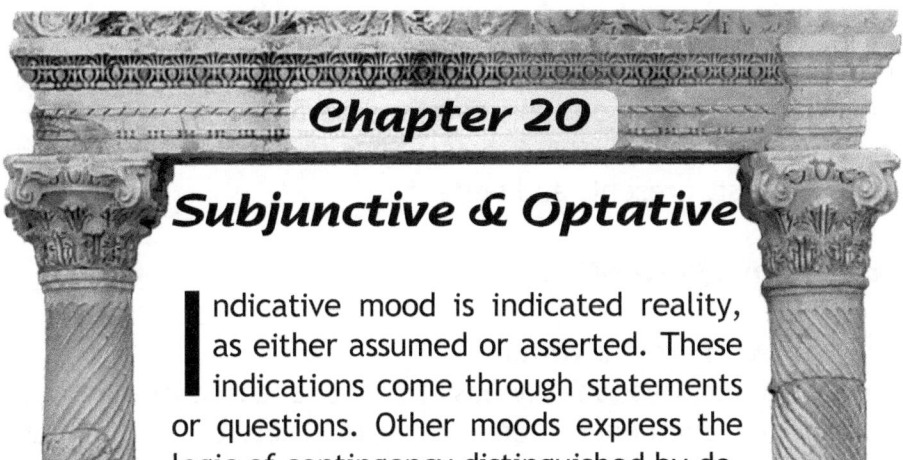

Chapter 20
Subjunctive & Optative

Indicative mood is indicated reality, as either assumed or asserted. These indications come through statements or questions. Other moods express the logic of contingency distinguished by degrees of potential realization. The subjunctive is probable. Optative is possible. Imperative (command) is anyone's guess.

English has two contingency moods, the subjunctive and the imperative. Greek adds a third, the optative, a nuance of the subjunctive common in Classical Greek. By the first century, the optative had all but disappeared in forms of spoken Hellenistic Greek and was uncommon even in literary traditions.

Greek Subjunctive

English subjunctive mood expresses the contingency of wish, doubt, and contrary-to-fact condition. English constructions use verbs of wishing, contingency auxiliaries such as *should, could, would, might*, etc., or the past tense *were*:

- **Wish:** "He *wishes* he could go."
- **Doubt:** "He *might* go."
- **Condition False:** " If he *were* here, he could go."

(Note the inflection of "go" for the third singular subject.)

Nature of Contingency Moods

Greek tense outside the indicative is focused on action kind. The Greek subjunctive, therefore, does not express action time.

The Greek subjunctive, instead, communicates action kind in its three forms: undefined, durative, and perfect. To encode these three kinds of action, the Greek subjunctive makes use of three tenses: aorist, present, and perfect.

Subjunctive Formation

Lengthened Thematic Vowel
The subjunctive is fairly easy to spot, because its formation is simple: a lengthened thematic vowel. Thus, the ο → ω, and the ε → η. We then have this dictum:

- ♦ *The signature of the subjunctive is a lengthened thematic vowel.*

Primary Endings
Since time is not a factor in subjunctive mood, only one set of endings is required, regardless of tense. The coin toss landed on primary endings. The so-called "deponent" is treated as in indicative (translate active). With lengthened vowel, we have:

- active: -ω, -ῃς, -ῃ, -ωμεν, -ητε, -ωσιν
- mid/pass.: -ωμαι, -ῃ, -ηται, -ώμεθα, -ησθε, -ωνται

Tense Distinctives
Aorist Tense
Since time is not a factor, two formulation characteristics of the aorist active *indicative* verb *no longer apply:* (1) augment for past time, (2) secondary endings of historical tenses. Aorist subjunctive *has no augment* and uses *primary* endings.

This aorist subjunctive formulation creates a huge problem: some regular first aorist subjunctives look as if they are future indicative. However, with the lengthened thematic vowel, you must learn to squelch the urge ever to say "future subjunctive"! Always remember before uttering that futile formulation:

Chapter 20: Subjunctive & Optative

♦ *There is no future subjunctive!*

Perfect Tense

The perfect subjunctive is a rare bird in the New Testament. Of the twenty occurrences, half are in the form of participles. The other ten are all from one verb, οἶδα, and even six of these are the one form εἰδῆτε, "you (pl) may know."

Subjunctive Paradigms

Table 20.1—Active Subjunctive

Present	2ⁿᵈ Aorist	1ˢᵗ Aorist
λύω	βάλω	λύσω
λύῃς	βάλῃς	λύσῃς
λύῃ	βάλῃ	λύσῃ
λύωμεν	βάλωμεν	λύσωμεν
λύητε	βάλητε	λύσητε
λύωσι(ν)	βάλωσι(ν)	λύσωσι(ν)

Table 20.2—Middle Subjunctive

Present	2ⁿᵈ Aorist	1ˢᵗ Aorist
λύωμαι	βάλωμαι	λύσωμαι
λύῃ	βάλῃ	λύσῃ
λύηται	βάληται	λύσηται
λυώμεθα	βαλώμεθα	λυσώμεθα
λύησθε	βάλησθε	λύσησθε
λύωνται	βάλωνται	λύσωνται

Table 20.3—Passive Subjunctive

Present	Aor. 2nd Pass.	Aor. 1st Pass.
λύωμαι	γραφῶ	λυθῶ
λύῃ	γραφῇς	λυθῇς
λύηται	γραφῇ	λυθῇ
λυώμεθα	γραφῶμεν	λυθῶμεν
λύησθε	γραφῆτε	λυθῆτε
λύωνται	γραφῶσι(ν)	λυθῶσι(ν)

Perfect subjunctive is rare, so not included here (see p. 574 for forms). The aorist is distinguished by first and second aorist forms. For active and middle voice, second aorist subjunctive is exactly like present subjunctive save stem alone.

The alpha of the first aorist active and middle tense suffix is lost. That lost vowel is what makes any first aorist subjunctive look like future tense, but: "There is no future subjunctive!"

The aorist first passive subjunctive suffix is θε, not the θη of the indicative. The epsilon in the voice suffix is swallowed up in contraction in all forms. The *result* of this contraction on half the forms is that the old indicative dictum, "theta eta is aorist passive," still is *practically* true even in the subjunctive.

The aorist second passive looses the θ of the θε voice suffix. Our paradigm showing this aorist second passive feature of the loss of the θ is γράφω. (Second aorist βάλλω is a *first* passive.)

Contract Subjunctives

Study the boldface forms in the table below. If you compare indicative and subjunctive, you will see that forms wind up the same in these patterns: epsilon contracts in only first person singular; omicron contracts in all singular forms; alpha contracts in *all* forms, singular and plural. With middle voice, only second person singular is the same for epsilon and omicron contracts (ποιῇ; πληροῖ). Once again, alpha contracts are the same in *all* forms. Why point out these morphological clones between the two moods? Because only context can distinguish these identical forms and their mood. Translation is impacted significantly.

Table 20.4—Present Active Contracts

ποιέω

Indicative	Subjunctive
ποιῶ	ποιῶ
ποιεῖς	ποιῇς
ποιεῖ	ποιῇ
ποιοῦμεν	ποιῶμεν
ποιεῖτε	ποιῆτε
ποιοῦσι(ν)	ποιῶσι(ν)

πληρόω

Indicative	Subjunctive
πληρῶ	πληρῶ
πληροῖς	πληροῖς
πληροῖ	πληροῖ
πληροῦμεν	πληρῶμεν
πληροῦτε	πληρῶτε
πληροῦσι(ν)	πληρῶσι(ν)

ἀγαπάω

Indicative	Subjunctive
ἀγαπῶ	ἀγαπῶ
ἀγαπᾷς	ἀγαπᾷς
ἀγαπᾷ	ἀγαπᾷ
ἀγαπῶμεν	ἀγαπῶμεν
ἀγαπᾶτε	ἀγαπᾶτε
ἀγαπῶσι(ν)	ἀγαπῶσι(ν)

The Negative μή

All moods outside the indicative use the negative μή. We already have seen this negative μή for the expected "no" answer to rhetorical questions. The double negative οὐ μή is emphatic, with the sense "never," "not at all," and so forth.

Εἰμί As Subjunctive

Εἰμί occurs as a subjunctive. Plural forms are easy to recognize, but singular forms are short and easily confused with other words, especially relative pronouns. However, remember: "relatives are rough." The glosses provided in the paradigm are loose approximations. Context is your best guide as to how to translate the verb εἰμί as a subjunctive form.

Table 20.5—Present Subjunctive of Εἰμί

ὦ	I (might) be
ᾖς	you (might) be
ᾖ	he (she, it) (might) be
ὦμεν	we (might) be
ἦτε	you (might) be (pl)
ὦσι(ν)	they (might) be

Greek Optative

The optative mood is just a weaker form of the subjunctive. A traditional description is as the mood of wish. (The Latin verb *opto* means "I wish.") The three main uses in the New Testament are (1) Paul's habitual rhetorical phrase "May it not be!" (μὴ γένοιτο), (2) use in prayers and benedictions with the third singular form εἴη, from εἰμί, and (3) fourth class conditional sentences. The optative occurs a total of only about 68 times in the New Testament.

Optative Formation

Optative occurs only as present or aorist tense in the New Testament. Remember, though, that any non-indicative tense is action kind, not time. The optative coin toss landed on secondary endings, even for present tense, except the first singular -μι ending (εἰμί). The present tense thematic vowel is always omicron. Aorist is *not augmented* and uses the tense suffix -σα.

The optative mood sign is easy to spot—an iota after the thematic vowel or tense suffix. This iota vowel mood sign creates a characteristic οι diphthong in both present and second aorist tenses and a (σ)αι diphthong in the first aorist. Aorist first passive varies this formulation slightly to (θε)ίη, but notice even here that the iota still shows up.

- *The signature of the optative is iota after the thematic vowel or tense suffix.*

Optative Paradigms

Notice how the iota mood sign is easy to spot. Second aorist is exactly like the present save for stem alone. As we have seen before, a secondary *middle*, second singular, -σο, reacts. Sigma when between two vowels slips out. The leftover vowels (οιο or αιο), however, do not contract in the optative as they do in the indicative. The blank column in the passive optative is because no aorist second passive optative occurs in the New Testament.

Table 20.6—Active Optative

Present	2ⁿᵈ Aorist	1ˢᵗ Aorist
λύοιμι	βάλοιμι	λύσαιμι
λύοις	βάλοις	λύσαις
λύοι	βάλοι	λύσαι
λύοιμεν	βάλοιμεν	λύσαιμεν
λύοιτε	βάλοιτε	λύσαιτε
λύοιεν	βάλοιεν	λύσαιεν

Table 20.7—Middle Optative

Present	2nd Aorist	1st Aorist
λυοίμην	βαλοίμην	λυσαίμην
λύοιο	βάλοιο	λύσαιο
λύοιτο	βάλοιτο	λύσαιτο
λυοίμεθα	βαλοίμεθα	λυσαίμεθα
λύοισθε	βάλοισθε	λύσαισθε
λύοιντο	βάλοιντο	λύσαίτο

Table 20.8—Passive Optative

Present	Aor. 2nd Pass.	Aor. 1st Pass.
λυοίμην	-----------	λυθείην
λύοιο	-----------	λυθείης
λύοιτο	-----------	λυθείη
λυοίμεθα	-----------	λυθείημεν
λύοισθε	-----------	λυθείητε
λύοιντο	-----------	λυθείησαν

Translating Contingency Moods

Translating Subjunctive Mood

Greek moods outside the indicative are focused on action kind. Greek action kind, however, not always is expressible in English translation. Thus, with the non-indicative Greek tense not expressing the component of action *time*, and the Greek tense component of action *kind* not always translatable, then the student needs to remember in translating subjunctives:

♦ *Aorist, present, and perfect subjunctives may translate the same into English.*

Independent Clauses

As an independent clause, the subjunctive is used to:

- **ask** what to do ("Shall we?"; in deliberative questions, often with interrogative adverbs: πόθεν, πότε, τί)
- **exhort** what to do ("Let us"; always first plural)
- **command** not to do ("Do not"; μή with aorist)
- **deny** emphatically ("Never"; use of οὐ μή)

Study the following illustrations of these uses. Notice that these subjunctive verbs create independent clauses. Often, the Greek *aorist* subjunctive translates with English *present* tense. In the last example (emphatic negation), note that sometimes a *future tense* in English even can be appropriate.

(1) Ask (deliberative):

λέγει αὐτοῖς ὁ Πιλᾶτος· τί οὖν ποιήσω[1] Ἰησοῦν;
"Pilate said to them: 'What then *should I do* with Jesus?'"
(Mt. 27:22)

(2) Exhort (hortatory):

ἀλλὰ ἄγωμεν πρὸς αὐτόν.
"But *let us go* to him." (Jn. 11:15)

(3) Command (prohibition):

Μὴ οὖν φοβηθῆτε αὐτούς.
"Therefore, *do not fear* them." (Mt. 10:26)

(4) Deny (negation):

οὐ μὴ πιστεύσητε.
"You *never* will believe." (Lk. 22:67)

---

[1] An aorist subjunctive first singular and future indicative look exactly the same in an epsilon contract verb.

Dependent Clauses

As a part of a dependent clause, the subjunctive verb is tied to a main verb in the independent clause. The subjunctive dependent clause functions as a noun, adjective, or adverb.

Noun Clause

The noun clause takes a noun role as subject or object. The subjunctive noun clause is introduced by conjunctions, such as ὅπως or ἵνα. The subjunctive also can be constructed with the relative pronoun, ὅς, ὅ, ἥ, for a noun clause with the meaning "whoever," "whatever," etc.

(1) Subject clause:

<u>ὃς ἂν</u> ἐμὲ <u>δέχηται</u>
"<u>whoever</u> *receives* me" (Mk. 9:37)

(2) Direct object clause:

<u>ὅ τι ἂν</u> λέγῃ ὑμῖν ποιήσατε.
"Do <u>whatever</u> *he tells* you." (Jn. 2:5)

δεήθητε . . . <u>ὅπως</u> ἐκβάλῃ ἐργάτας
"ask . . . <u>that</u> *he send out* laborers" (Mt. 9:38)

Adjective Clause

The subjunctive as an adjective clause is used to set forth comparison. The key is the conjunction ὡς in its usage as the comparative "as" rather than as an adverbial "when":

ἐστὶν ἡ βασιλεία τοῦ θεοῦ <u>ὡς</u> ἄνθρωπος <u>βάλῃ</u> τὸν σπόρον
"The kingdom of God is <u>as</u> a man who *scatters* seed" (Mk. 4:26)

Adverb Clause

The subjunctive as an adverb clause is the most dominant form of subjunctive use. The subjunctive will be introduced by a dependent conjunction. Typical functions are:

- **purpose** (ἵνα, ὅπως)
- **result** (ἵνα)

- **temporal** (ὅταν, ἕως, ἄχρι, μέχρι)
- **concession** (ἐάν; κἄν = καὶ ἐάν)

Study the following illustrations of these functions.

(1) Purpose clause:

<u>ἵνα</u> ἐπιγνῷς
"<u>in order that</u> *you might know*" (Lk. 1:4)

<u>ὅπως</u> λάβωσιν πνεῦμα ἅγιον
"<u>so that</u> *they might receive* the Holy Spirit" (Acts 8:15)

(2) Result clause:

<u>ἵνα</u> σκοτισθῇ τὸ τρίτον αὐτῶν
"<u>as a result</u> a third of their (light) *was darkened*" (Rev. 8:12)

(3) Temporal clause:

<u>ὅταν</u> ἀκούσωσιν τὸν λόγον
"<u>whenever</u> *they hear* the word" (Mk. 4:16)

<u>ὡς ἂν</u> πορεύωμαι εἰς τὴν Σπανίαν
"<u>when</u> *I go* to Spain" (Rom. 15:24)

(4) Concession clause:

<u>κἂν</u> ἐμοὶ μὴ πιστεύητε
"<u>even though</u> *you do not believe* me" (Jn. 10:38)

Translating Optative Mood

Optative is a weakened form of the subjunctive, so increases contingency from probable to possible, from objective consideration to subjective abstraction. Expressions of will ("what he wanted to do"), possible future events ("what might happen"), and indirect questions ("what might this be?") can be phrased in the optative. Again, the so-called "deponent" is treated as in indicative (translate active). An optative example would be:

τί ἂν γένοιτο τοῦτο
"what *might happen* because of this" (Acts 5:24)

Optative use in prayers and benedictions is conventional. That is to say, this polite form does not indicate doubt of fulfillment.

Being few, you almost can conquer optatives just by memorizing a select group of inflected forms. Of these, two forms:

- γένοιτο, sec. aor. mid. opt., third sing., γίνομαι
- εἴη, pres. opt., third sing., εἰμί

together account for almost half of all the New Testament optatives. Then add just the three forms:

- δῴη, "may he give" (δίδωμι)
- θέλοι, "he might want" (θέλω)
- ἔχοι, "he might have" (ἔχω)

and you have over half of all New Testament optatives!

Conditional Sentences

Table 20.9—Conditional Sentence Diagram

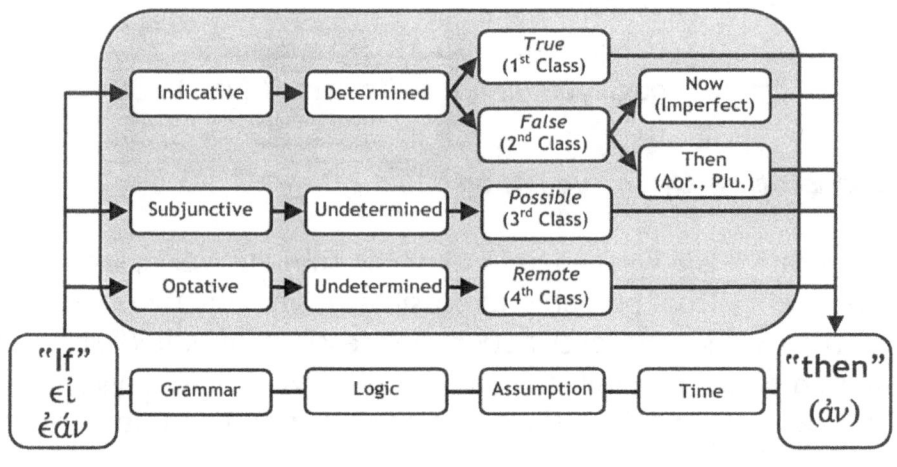

We have covered first class and second class conditional sentences.[2] In this chapter on subjunctive and optative moods, we now complete our overview of Greek conditional sentences.

Second Class: False in Past Time

Go back and now read what was skipped over in Chapter 14, that is, second class false in past time, pp. 212-13. Return here when you are done. Other examples of false in past time are:

(1) False, Past Time, Aorist:

εἰ κακῶς ἐλάλησα, μαρτύρησον περὶ τοῦ κακοῦ.
"If *I spoke* wrongly, testify concerning the wrong!" (Jn. 18:23)

(2) False, Past Time, Pluperfect:

εἰ ἐμὲ ᾔδειτε, καὶ τὸν πατέρα μου ἂν ᾔδειτε.
"If *you knew* me, you would know my Father also." (Jn. 8:19)

Third Class: Undetermined but Possible

When the "if" logic is undetermined but thought possible, the "if" verb is subjunctive. The "if" often is the conjunction ἐάν, which sometimes is your clue that the "if" verb is subjunctive and not some identical indicative form.[3] The following is a nice illustration of the exegetical sense of *both* a first class assumed true and a third class undetermined but possible rolled neatly into one statement:

εἰ ταῦτα οἴδατε, μακάριοί ἐστε ἐὰν ποιῆτε αὐτά.
"If *you know* these things, you are blessed if *you do* them."
(Jn. 13:17)

---

[2]Chapter 14, "Conditional Sentences," p. 212.
[3]However, not all third class sentences use ἐάν, so do *not* fall into the trap of assuming that the conjunction determines the class! Mood is key.

That is, in effect, Jesus has told the disciples: "If you know these things, *which I am confident that you do know them*, you are blessed if you do them, *which you might do, but that remains to be seen*." Knowing the Word is not enough. We have to do the Word. James echoed this truth (James 1:22).

Fourth Class: Undetermined and Remote

The fourth class conditional sentence is both rare and incomplete in the New Testament. However, you now at least can locate these optative forms and follow commentary discussion of the matter.

Exercise 20

1. True or False

   1.1 ____ = The signature of the subjunctive mood is a lengthened thematic vowel.
   1.2 ____ = Regardless of tense, the subjunctive mood takes secondary endings.
   1.3 ____ = The aorist subjunctive has an augment.
   1.4 ____ = There is a future subjunctive.
   1.5 ____ = Aorist first passive subjunctive has a theta in the suffix.
   1.6 ____ = Alpha contract forms are all the same for indicative and subjunctive.
   1.7 ____ = The signature of the optative is an iota after a thematic vowel or tense suffix.
   1.8 ____ = Aorist, present, perfect subjunctive translations always are distinguished.

1.9 ____ = The main use of the subjunctive is within dependent adverb clauses.

1.10 ____ = Forms of the verb εἰμί as subjunctive can be confused with the relative pronoun.

2. Identify the morphological components of the following:

$$\overline{\lambda υ\text{-}σ\text{-}ω\text{-}μεν}$$

3. Complete the *present active* subjunctive conjugation for the verb πέμπω ("I send"):

_____ = _____

_____ = _____

_____ = _____

_____ = _____

_____ = _____

_____ = _____

4. Complete the *aorist active* subjunctive conjugation for the verb πέμπω ("I send"):

_____ = _____

_____ = _____

_____ = _____

_____ = _____

_____ = _____

_____ = _____

5. Complete the *aorist passive* subjunctive conjugation for the verb σῴζω ("I save"). Assume the verb stem is σω-:

_____	=	_____
_____	=	_____
_____	=	_____
_____	=	_____
_____	=	_____
_____	=	_____

6. Translate. Be ready to locate verbs and explain subjunctive use.

   6.1 ἄχρι ἔλθῃ (1 Cor. 11:26*)

   6.2 ἠσπάζοντο αὐτόν. (Mk. 9:15)

   6.3 διδάσκαλε, τί ποιήσωμεν; (Lk. 3:12)

   6.4 ἠσπάσατο (subject is fem.) τὴν Ἐλισάβετ. (Lk. 1:40)

   6.5 γένοιτό μοι κατὰ τὸ ῥῆμά σου. (Lk. 1:38)

   6.6 Ἰωσὴφ υἱὸς Δαυίδ, μὴ φοβηθῇς. (Mt. 1:20)

6.7 ὅταν ἐν τῷ κόσμῳ ὦ, φῶς εἰμι τοῦ κόσμου. (Jn. 9:5)

6.8 καὶ μηδένα (μήδε + ἕνα) κατὰ τὴν ὁδὸν ἀσπάσησθε. (Lk. 10:4)

6.9 σὺ οὖν ἐὰν προσκυνήσῃς ἐνώπιον ἐμοῦ, ἔσται σοῦ (possessive) πᾶσα. (Lk. 4:7)

6.10 καὶ ἐὰν ἀσπάσησθε τοὺς ἀδελφοὺς ὑμῶν μόνον, τί περισσὸν ποιεῖτε; (Mt. 5:47)

6.11 τοῦτο δὲ ὅλον γέγονεν (γίνομαι) ἵνα πληρωθῶσιν αἱ γραφαὶ τῶν προφητῶν. (Mt. 26:56)

6.12 εἰ τὰ ἐπίγεια (ἐπί + γῆ) εἶπον ὑμῖν καὶ οὐ πιστεύετε, πῶς ἐὰν εἴπω ὑμῖν τὰ ἐπουράνια (ἐπί + οὐρανός) πιστεύσετε; (Jn. 3:12)

 **Vocabulary 20**

ἀσπάζομαι, *I greet, welcome*

ἄχρι, *until*

Δαυίδ, ὁ, *David*

διδάσκαλος, ὁ, *teacher*

ἐάν, *if, when, although*

ἵνα, *in order that, that*

κἄν, *even though* (= καί + ἐάν)

μηδέ, *but not, nor, not even*

μήτε, *but not, nor, not even*

μηδείς, *no one, nothing*

ὅπως, *in order that, so that*

ὅταν, *when, whenever*

προσκυνέω, *I worship, do reverence*

ᾖ, *he (she, it) might be* (subjunctive of εἰμί)

Vocabulary notes:

(1) The various conjunctions in this vocabulary coordinate with the grammar of contingency moods.

(2) In the New Testament, the verb ἀσπάζομαι almost half the time is in the *imperative* mood making requests at letter closings. The form usually is second plural, and looks like an indicative: ἀσπάσασθε, "you (pl) greet (so and so)."

(3) Make a note: the verb προσκυνέω takes a *dative direct object* (something similar in English to saying "giving worship *to*" or "do obeisance *to*").

(4) More than half the time, διδάσκαλος occurs with the vocative singular inflection: διδάσκαλε, "Teacher, . . ."

(5) The verb εἰμί as a subjunctive is hard to distinguish in its singular forms from the relative pronoun. Remember, on the other hand, that "relatives are rough" (rough breathing).

(6) The particle of contingency, ἄν, used as a grammatical marker in conditional sentences, was introduced in Chapter 14. See the vocabulary note, p. 222.

Chapter 21

Imperative

Degrees of contingency are the heart of Greek moods. Of all the moods, imperative has the highest contingency due to the nature of commands. Inherently, command does not exist in first person.[1] Since English has only second person command, English has no real slot for translating Greek third person commands. A fairly distinct set of endings mark off Greek imperative forms from other moods.

Imperative Formation

Table 21.1—Imperative Endings

Active	Middle/Passive
-------	-------
--- (= ε), -ς, θι (ον*)	-σο (= ου), (αι*)
-τω	-σθω
-------	-------
-τε	-σθε
-τωσαν	-σθωσαν

Imperative has its own set of endings. Thus:

♦ *The signature of the imperative is a distinct set of imperative endings.*

---

[1] Greek *subjunctive* does have a first plural exhortation ("Let us").

Imperative Endings

Imperative endings are *unique in third person*, but only partially distinct in second person; some second person forms have primary and secondary indicative twins. Such endings can make identifying the imperative a little pesky sometimes, but contextual clues often help. The so-called "deponent" is treated as in indicative (translate active). Note the following comments.

Second singular active has three optional endings. When the no-ending option is used, the thematic vowel is left exposed (-ε). The second singular active ending, -θι, is distinct. The aorist *first passive* uses this *active* ending, but alters pronunciation to the -τι to avoid two thetas together (θηθι → θητι). The -ον ending (in parentheses) is *first aorist only* and unexplained; note carefully the circumflex accent (λῦσον).

Second singular middle -σο ending will drop out between vowels and vowels contract to -ου, a familiar pattern. Like the -ον, the -αι ending (in parentheses) is *first aorist only* and unexplained; note carefully circumflex accent (λῦσαι).

Second plural endings *clone the indicative. Cloned forms make second person plural imperatives harder to identify.* Only context can distinguish indicative and imperative forms.

Third person endings are unique. That is, the "τω, σθω" style is easy to spot and identify.

Contract verbs create contraction forms as expected, so confusion with indicative is predictable. Often, a circumflex accent will result.

Tense Stems and Theme Vowel

Tense communicates *action kind*. As in the subjunctive, the *aorist imperative is not augmented*. The imperative uses an *epsilon* thematic vowel like the optative uses omicron. *Perfect imperatives* are extremely rare. Consult an intermediate grammar for this form and its meaning.

Imperative Paradigms

Table 21.2—Active Imperative

Present	2nd Aorist	1st Aorist
------	------	------
λῦε	βάλε	λῦσον*
λυέτω	βαλέτω	λυσάτω
------	------	------
λύετε	βάλετε	λύσατε
λυέτωσαν	βαλέτωσαν	λυσάτωσαν

Table 21.3—Middle Imperative

Present	2nd Aorist	1st Aorist
------	------	------
λύου	βαλοῦ	λῦσαι*
λυέσθω	βαλέσθω	λυσάσθω
------	------	------
λύεσθε	βάλεσθε	λύσασθε
λυέσθωσαν	βαλέσθωσαν	λυσασθωσαν

Table 21.4—Passive Imperative

Present	Aor 2nd Pass.	Aor 1st Pass.
------	------	------
λύου	γράφηθι	λύθητι
λυέσθω	γραφήτω	λυθήτω
------	------	------
λύεσθε	γράφητε	λύθητε
λυέσθωσαν	γραφήτωσαν	λυθήτωσαν

The Negative μή

All moods outside the indicative use the negative μή. The imperative forms that are like the indicative sometimes are revealed by use of this negative rather than the οὐ.

Εἰμί As Imperative

Εἰμί occurs as an imperative. One form, the second plural ἔστε, is similar to the indicative, but note its accent (indicative form is enclitic = no accent). Glosses provided in the paradigm are loose approximations. Context is your guide as to how to translate the verb εἰμί as imperative. English has no third person imperative. Use of "must" in the gloss is a work-a-round. You could use the helping verb "let," but that strategy changes the Greek subject into a direct object.

Table 21.5—Present Imperative of Εἰμί

------	------
ἴσθι	you be
ἔστω (ἤτω)	he (she, it) must, (let him, etc.)
------	------
ἔστε	you be
ἔστωσαν	they must (let them)

Imperative Translation

For reasons like the subjunctive:

♦ *Aorist, present, and perfect imperatives may translate the same into English.*

Command

Command is the obvious use of the imperative. In English, the subject can be unexpressed: "Go!" assumes "You go!"

λέγω τούτῳ· <u>πορεύθητι</u>, καὶ πορεύεται.
"I say to this one, '*Go!*' and he goes." (Mt. 8:9)

Prohibition

One can prohibit an action using the present imperative. The negative will be μή. This imperative use is the durative counterpart to the undefined aorist subjunctive with μή.

Distinctions between the uses of the two types of prohibition have been overworked. The idea was that present tense prohibition infers action *already in progress*, and aorist prohibition forbids *initiating an action*. In fact, these supposed distinctions are more a function of context than grammar. Deciding whether an author means to infer by using present imperative that some action already is in progress is impossible without evaluating the context. A good example is:

<u>Μὴ κρίνετε</u>, ἵνα μὴ κριθῆτε.
"*Do not judge*, in order that you not be judged." (Mt. 7:1)

Whether Jesus is forbidding specific action already in progress, as in some particular relationship among those attending in the crowd, or is simply giving a moral maxim always true is decided more by context than by grammatical appeal to the use of the present imperative of prohibition.

On the other hand, context *may* reveal that a present imperative *does* imply some particular action already in progress needs to stop. A translation using "stop (so and so)" would be appropriate. Action in progress is clear, for example, in the following context:

<u>μὴ ποιεῖτε</u> τὸν οἶκον τοῦ πατρός μου οἶκον ἐμπορίου.
"*Stop making* my Father's house a marketplace!" (Jn. 2:16)

Request

Another imperative use is polite request, similar to our use of "please." In ancient society, social rank was important and carefully observed. An inferior addressing a superior would use imperative as a polite mode of supplication. For example:

κύριε, σῶσόν με.
"Lord, *save* me!" (Mt. 14:30)

Permission

One may give permission in the imperative. English would use the auxiliary "may."

προσκαλεσάσθω τοὺς πρεσβυτέρους τῆς ἐκκλησίας
"*he may call upon* the elders of the church" (James 5:14)

Dramatic Ἰδού and Ἴδε

Story tellers traditionally heightened dramatic impact with the two aorist imperatives ἰδού and ἴδε ("behold," "look"). These imperatives grammatically function as interjections, but often they are dropped in translation due to formulaic overuse. Sometimes context seems to justify retention of the idea:

ἰδοὺ ὁ βασιλεύς σου ἔρχεταί σοι
"*Behold,* your king comes to you" (Mt. 21:5)

 **Exercise 21**

1. Multiple Choice

    1.1 The personal ending with no imperative form:

    a. first singular
    b. second singular
    c. second plural
    d. third singular

Chapter 21: Imperative

1.2 A personal ending *not* an imperative form:

a. -τω
b. -σο
c. -θι
d. -ουσιν

1.3 What diphthong results when -σο drops its sigma?

a. -οι
b. -αι
c. -ου
d. -η

1.4 Which ending is middle third plural?

a. -σθωσαν
b. -σθω
c. -τε
d. -τω

1.5 Which tense as an active imperative looks exactly like the present tense, save stem alone?

a. imperfect
b. second aorist
c. perfect
d. none of the above

1.6 The present imperative as prohibition is a counterpart to what subjunctive tense with μή?

a. imperfect
b. perfect
c. aorist
d. pluperfect

2. Translate. Notate imperative forms with indicative counterparts and specify the indicative location.

2.1 καὶ ἰδοὺ ἔκραξαν. (Mt. 8:29)

2.2 εἰμι ἐν μέσῳ αὐτῶν. (Mt. 18:20)

2.3 ἐὰν ἔλθῃ πρὸς ὑμᾶς, δέξασθε αὐτόν. (Col. 4:10)

2.4 εἰπὲ τῷ λίθῳ τούτῳ ἵνα γένηται ἄρτος. (Lk. 4:3)

2.5 ἔστω δὲ ὁ λόγος ὑμῶν ναὶ ναί, οὒ οὔ. (Mt. 5:37)

2.6 εἴσελθε εἰς τὴν χαρὰν τοῦ κυρίου σου. (Mt. 25:21)

2.7 συνάχθητε εἰς τὸ δεῖπνον τὸ μέγα τοῦ θεοῦ (Rev. 19:17)

2.8 ὑμεῖς ὃ ἠκούσατε ἀπ' ἀρχῆς, ἐν ὑμῖν μενέτω. (1 Jn. 2:24)

2.9 Τὸ λοιπὸν[2] προσεύχεσθε, ἀδελφοί, περὶ ἡμῶν (2 Thess. 3:1)

2.10 ἐάν τις τὸν ἐμὸν λόγον τηρήσῃ, θάνατον οὐ μὴ θεωρήσῃ εἰς τὸν αἰῶνα. (Jn. 8:51)

---

[2] Consult vocabulary; here, the meaning probably is close to "finally."

2.11 ὁ δὲ εἶπεν αὐτοῖς· βάλετε εἰς τὰ δεξιὰ (δεξιός) μέρη (μέρος) τοῦ πλοίου τὸ δίκτυον. (Jn. 21:6)

2.12 εἶπεν· πάτερ, ἐλήλυθεν ἡ ὥρα· δόξασόν σου τὸν υἱόν, ἵνα ὁ υἱὸς δοξάσῃ σέ. (Jn. 17:1)

 *Vocabulary 21*

ἀρχή, ἡ, *beginning, origin, ruler* (archangel, archetype)

δεξιός, -ά, -όν, *right, right hand, right side*

δέχομαι, *I receive, welcome*

θεωρέω, *I look at, observe* (theory)

ἴδε *behold!*

ἴσθι, *you be!*

κράζω, *I cry out, call out*

λίθος, ὁ, *stone* (monolith, Neolithic, Paleolithic)

λοιπός, -ή, -όν, *remaining, rest, finally*

μέσος, -η, -ον *middle, in the middle of* (Mesopotamia, Mesozoic)

Πιλᾶτος, ὁ, *Pilate*

συνάγω, *I gather, bring together*

συναγωγή, ἡ, *synagogue, assembly*

χαρά, ἡ, *joy, gladness*

Vocabulary note: Imperatives ἰδού and ἴδε are interjections.

Fig. 17. Cuirass of Hadrian. This statue shows a stylized representation of the cuirass of the emperor Hadrian (A.D. 117-38). The armor depicts selected elements of Roman imperial propaganda. The empire reached its greatest expanse under Hadrian, but Jews revolted for the final time following the Jewish leader Simon bar Kochba (A.D. 133-35). Akiba, a famous rabbi of the day, had declared Simon as messiah during the revolt. Ancient Agora, Athens, Greece.

Chapter 22

Infinitives

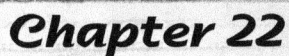

Verbals can be described as verbs grammatically transformed into other parts of speech but not having formal subjects of their own. Thus, they cannot function as the main verb. Infinitives and participles are the two main verbals. Infinitives are verbs transformed to act as nouns, adjectives, or adverbs. Infinitives do not need to show mood or person and number, since they have no subjects. Thus, infinitives are not inflected for mood, person, or number. Such grammatical features render infinitive morphology quite simple.

English infinitives are formed with a verb's present tense fronted by the preposition "to," as in "to go." (An uncommon perfect tense has a different form, "to have gone"). Actually, English present tense infinitives can be used with any tense:

- **past:** "She <u>studied</u> *to make* good grades."
- **present:** "She <u>studies</u> *to make* good grades."
- **future:** "She <u>will study</u> *to make* good grades."
- **perfect:** "She <u>has studied</u> *to make* good grades."

Some English verbs have established patterns in which the preposition "to" is left off the infinitive form constructed with them, such as *bid, dare, help, let, make, must, need, see*. For example: "I will <u>help</u> you *learn* the alphabet." This also could be: "I will <u>help</u> you *to learn* the alphabet."

As a verbal, the infinitive can be set up as a noun phrase, an adjective phrase, and an adverb phrase. This chapter covers the use of infinitives as nouns and adjectives. Infinitives as adverbs will be taken up in the next chapter. Review the grammatical principles in the table below (from English 2, "Word Groups").

Table 22.1—Word Group Junctions

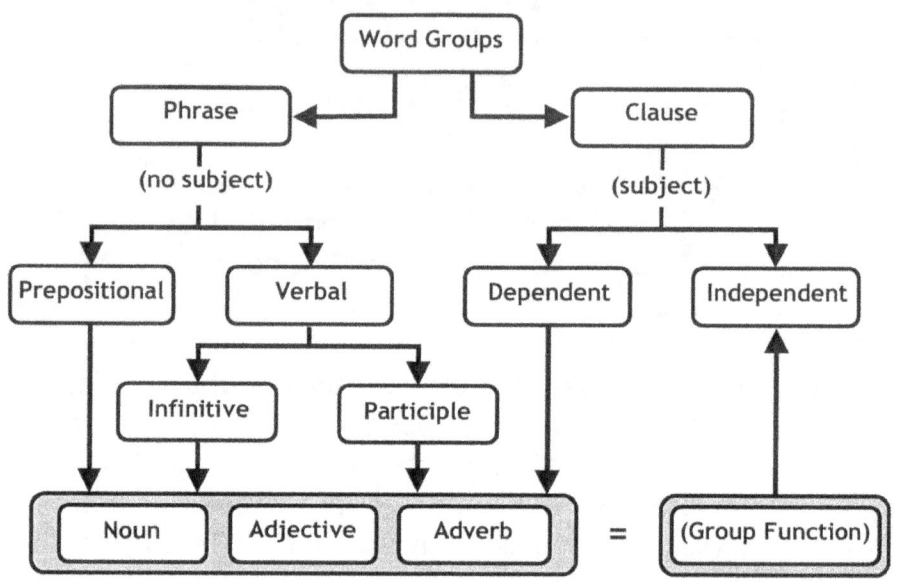

Infinitive Mophology

Table 22.2—Infinitive Endings

Always Active	Always Mid/Pass	Act or Pass
-ειν, -σαι	-σθαι	-ναι

Table 22.3—Infinitive Paradigms

	Present	2ⁿᵈ Aor	1ˢᵗ Aor	Perfect
act:	λύειν	βαλεῖν	λῦσαι	λελυκέναι
mid:	λύεσθαι	βαλέσθαι	λύσασθαι	λελύσθαι
pass:	λύεσθαι	γραφῆναι	λυθῆναι	λελύσθαι

Infinitive Construction

Inflection—What You See

Greek infinitives have four inflected endings: -ειν, -ναι, -σαι, and -σθαι. These endings are fairly distinct. Perhaps -σαι offers the most confusion with other verb endings—for example, the perfect middle form, λέλυσαι. Note that:

- -ειν and -σαι are always active
- -σθαι is always middle/passive
- -ναι is either active or passive

Aorist infinitives do not have augments, since time is not a factor (non-indicative). Remember patterns: (1) *contracts*: contraction—φιλεῖν; lengthening—φιλῆσαι; (2) *liquids*: drop aorist suffix sigma—ἀπαγγεῖλαι; (3) *stops*: aorist suffix reactions—πέμψαι and πεμφθῆναι. Unlike English, Greek infinitives have voice; however, the so-called "deponent" translates as active.

Inflection—What You Do Not See

English proper nouns have case function without case inflection. Thus, the spelling "John" can serve for subject or object. Greek infinitives similarly are not inflected. They look like indeclinable neuter nouns. In composition with infinitives, articles and prepositions reveal the infinitive's grammatical function.

Article

An infinitive's neuter noun similarity is evidenced when constructed with the article: always neuter singular (τό, τοῦ, τῷ, τό). So, you will encounter: τὸ λύειν (nom.), τοῦ λύειν, τῷ λύειν, and τὸ λύειν (acc.). Remember: the article does not have to be immediately adjacent to the infinitive to be in construction with the infinitive: καλὸν τὸ μὴ φαγεῖν κρέα (Rom. 14:21). The article reveals the infinitive's substantival character and can require prepositional phrasing of the interior cases (τοῦ: *of, from*; τῷ: *to, in, by, with*). For example:

περιῃρεῖτο ἐλπὶς πᾶσα <u>τοῦ σῴζεσθαι ἡμᾶς</u>
"all hope *of our being saved* was taken away" (Acts 27:20)

ἐνεκοπτόμην . . . <u>τοῦ ἐλθεῖν</u> πρὸς ὑμᾶς
"I have been hindered . . . *from coming* to you" (Rom. 15:22)

<u>ἐν τῷ λέγειν</u> καινὴν πεπαλαίωκεν τὴν πρώτην
"*in speaking* of the new he made obsolete the first" (Heb. 8:13)

Prepositions

The substantival infinitive can be constructed with prepositions (always with the article); for example: ἐν τῷ λέγειν. Such constructions create adverbial functions studied in the next chapter. Articular infinitives and prepositional infinitives always work together as *word groups* with a common function. That is, they find their translation only when taken together as one entire grammatical unit.

Infinitive Action Kind

Greek infinitives occur in four tenses: aorist, present, perfect, and future.[1] These tenses are used to show the three kinds of action: durative, undefined, perfect. As usual though, as for subjunctive, optative, and imperative moods, infinitive action kind does not come across always in translation.

Infinitive Relationships

Taking Objects

An infinitive can be part of an entire phrase having other related grammatical elements. Thus, an infinitive can take its own objects, both direct and indirect:

---

[1] Future only five times: a compound εἰσέρχομαι as εἰσελεύσεσθαι, and ἔσεσθαι from εἰμί (Heb. 3:18; Acts 11:28; 23:30; 24:15; 27:10).

ἐγεῖραι <u>τέκνα</u> <u>τῷ Ἀβραάμ</u>
"to raise up <u>children</u> <u>to Abraham</u>" (Lk. 3:8)

Being Modified

The infinitive itself also can be modified by an adverb, prepositional phrase, or even an adjective. Thus:

εὐχαριστεῖν τῷ θεῷ <u>πάντοτε</u> <u>περὶ ὑμῶν</u>
"to thank God <u>always</u> <u>for you</u>" (2 Thess. 2:13)

πολλὰ ἔχω <u>περὶ ὑμῶν</u> λαλεῖν
"for I have much to say <u>about you</u>" (Jn. 8:26)

"Surrogate Subject"

An infinitive by definition does not have a subject. The infinitive, though, *can* have a "surrogate subject." This "surrogate subject" is accusative case, not nominative, both in Greek and English. Accusative case is easy to grasp when the "surrogate subject" is an object in its own clause.[2]

English Illustration

Consider this independent clause: "Coach wanted *him*." "Him" is in third position, direct object, and is inflected for objective case accordingly. Now compare the same clause, but with a dependent modifying phrase: "Coach wanted *him* to play shortstop." Notice that "him" is obliquely related to the infinitive "to play," but not actually as subject. (A verbal does not have a subject.) Here, "him" still is direct object in its own clause. At the same time, though, the pronoun "him" is related in a round-a-bout way to the action of the verbal "to play." We have styled this role of the pronoun in our example as the "surrogate subject."

---

[2]See English 5, "Diagramming," p. 504.

♦ *An infinitive's "surrogate subject" is accusative case.*

Greek Example
Thus, an accusative substantive lying around near an infinitive may be its "surrogate subject." For example:

ὁ χρόνος <u>τοῦ τεκεῖν</u> <u>αὐτὴν</u>
"the time for <u>her</u> to give birth" (Lk. 1:57)

Since an infinitive can take its own direct object, you potentially can encounter *two* substantives in accusative case near an infinitive. One will be the "surrogate subject"; the other would be some objective function, such as direct object:

ἐν τῷ εὐλογεῖν <u>αὐτὸν</u> <u>αὐτοὺς</u>
"while <u>he</u> was blessing <u>them</u>" (Lk. 24:51)

The Negative μή

The infinitive takes the negative μή, as do all other non-indicative verb forms. This negative will occur before the infinitive, even if articular: τοῦ μὴ πορεύεσθαι (Lk. 4:42).

Infinitive Functions—Noun & Adjective

Infinitives and infinitive phrases can take on three basic word roles (parts of speech) in a sentence: noun, adjective, and adverb. In this chapter, we look briefly at the first two, the roles of noun and adjective.[3]

---

[3] Our "adjective" role here some call "epexegetic," but this term has little agreed meaning. Such terminological confusion can leave students in a fog about application. Students seem to grasp the concept "adjective" more directly and easily.

Infinitive as Noun

An infinitive can fulfill noun roles within a sentence, that is, can function substantivally. Some basic sentence roles for nouns include subject, object, and apposition. We illustrate these.

Noun Role as Subject

Third Person Singular Copulatives
The infinitive as subject is an infinitive phrase that acts as subject of the main verb. This construction is common when the intransitive verb εἰμί in *third person singular* takes a complement. The infinitive grammatically is the *subject* of εἰμί, and the nominative noun or adjective is the complement. For example:

καλόν ἐστιν ἡμᾶς ὧδε εἶναι
"*to be* here is good for us" (Mt. 17:4)

Unfortunately, English prefers a passive construction for this third person singular grammar; you often will encounter a passive translation style, which requires starting with the impersonal "it" as third person singular, as in "*it is* good for us to be here." Greek, however, does not, in fact, have an "impersonal" form, so this English colloquial penchant for fronting an impersonal passive does not represent the actual grammar of this infinitive construction in Greek.

"Impersonal" Verbs
Another common subject role for the infinitive is its use in conjunction with what are labeled "impersonal verbs" (more an English category than Greek). Two verbs often included in this category are δεῖ ("it is necessary") and ἔξεστι(ν) ("it is lawful"). These constructions are easy to spot, because in English, you want to start the phrase with "it" (neuter, third person singular) as the subject. In Greek, however, the infinitive truly

is functioning as subject of the "impersonal" verb in place of our English passive "it" style.

Use of ἔξεστιν. The impersonal verb ἔξεστιν means, variously according to context, "it is right," "it is necessary," "it is lawful." For example:

<u>οὐκ ἔξεστίν</u> σοι ἔχειν αὐτήν
"*to have* her <u>is not lawful</u> for you" (Mt. 14:4)

In English we are much more inclined toward using a passive construction: "*it is not lawful* for you to have her." Whether to maintain this English passive idiom is a translation issue. Simply be clear that, grammatically in Greek, the infinitive is subject.

Use of δεῖ. Most of the time, the sense of δεῖ is best rendered as "must." The English structure after "must" drops the preposition "to" from the following infinitive, almost creating an imperative sense to the expression. For example:

Ἠλίαν <u>δεῖ</u> <u>ἐλθεῖν</u> πρῶτον
"Elijah <u>must</u> *come* first" (Mt. 17:10)

Noun Role as Object

Direct Object

The infinitive as object is an infinitive phrase that functions as direct object of the main verb. For example:

ὁ Πιλᾶτος ἐζήτει <u>ἀπολῦσαι</u> αὐτόν
"Pilate was seeking *to release* him" (Jn. 19:12)

νυνὶ δὲ καὶ <u>τὸ ποιῆσαι</u> ἐπιτελέσατε
"But now also complete *the doing* (of it)" (2 Cor. 8:11)

Indirect Discourse

Indirect discourse (reported speech) functions as a direct object of the main verb. Greek indicates indirect speech two ways. One way, like English, uses an indicative verb of saying followed by the conjunction ὅτι, "that," as in "said that."

Another Greek method for indirect speech, with no English counterpart, puts the reported speech verb into an infinitive. Translation often has to restore the original indicative form of this idiomatic Greek infinitive. For example, if the original saying were "he is a god," the Greek infinitive would be:

ἔλεγον αὐτὸν <u>εἶναι</u> θεόν.
"They began to say *he was* a god." (Acts 28:6)

Complementary Infinitive

The *complementary infinitive* is an infinitive phrase that functions as a *required* direct object of the main verb and that *completes* its meaning. "Required" means the verbal thought falls apart without the infinitive. Certain verbs "beg" for another verb to finish off the thought as if incomplete without the infinitive. For example, if I were to say "I began" without finishing the thought, you immediately would want to ask me, "'Began' what?" The verb "began" goes begging for a phrase to finish the thought. Verbs taking such a complementary infinitive that we have covered are ἄρχομαι (as aorist ἤρξατο), θέλω, and μέλλω.[4] Note:

ἤρξατο <u>κράζειν</u> καὶ <u>λέγειν</u>
"he began *to cry out* and *to say*" (Mk. 10:47)

Table 22.4—Paradigm of Δύναμαι

δύναμαι	I am able
δύνασαι (δύνῃ)	you are able (sg)
δύναται	he (she, it) is able
δυνάμεθα	we are able
δύνασθε	you are able (pl)
δύνανται	they are able

---

[4]Other verbs are βούλομαι, δέομαι, ὀφείλω, and πειράζω.

A common verb that takes a complementary infinitive is δύναμαι, "I am able," "I can." This verb actually is from the -μι verb conjugation, but, like εἰμί, is common enough in the New Testament and with infinitives to include now. Note:

δύναμαι τοῦτο <u>ποιῆσαι</u>
"I am able *to do* this" (Mt. 9:15)

οὐ δύνασθε <u>σωθῆναι</u>
"you cannot *be saved*" (Acts 15:1)

Object Complement

The *object complement* is a second accusative *essential* to the meaning of the verb's direct object.[5] Without the complementing accusative, the direct object looses sense. Infinitives can function in this way as object complements.

ἠτήσαντο Πιλᾶτον <u>ἀναιρεθῆναι</u> αὐτόν
"they asked Pilate *that he be killed*" (Acts 13:28)

Without the second accusative (the infinitive "to be killed"), the thought is left incomplete: "they asked Pilate," and you in turn yourself are asking immediately, "Asked him what?"

Verbs that *can* have an object complement do not *have* to have one. For example, ποιέω does not have to have an object complement, but when this verb is used with the meaning "I make" (or, "cause to happen"), an object complement infinitive naturally often follows the direct object to complement that direct object ("he makes me to lie down").

♦ *An object complement is essential to the grammatical sense of the direct object.*

---

[5]Omega verbs in vocabulary that can take an object complement are: ἄγω, αἰτέω, ἀπολύω, ἀποστέλλω, γινώσκω, δέχομαι, δοκέω, ἐγείρω, ἐκβάλλω, εὑρίσκω, ἔχω, θέλω, θεωρέω, καλέω, κηρύσσω, κρίνω, λαμβάνω, λέγω, οἶδα, ὁράω, πιστεύω, and ποιέω.

Noun Role as Apposition

The infinitive as apposition is an infinitive phrase that serves to rename a substantive without an intervening verb. Apposition is similar to a predicate noun function, yet no predicative construction is present. The appositive infinitive could substitute for the renamed substantive.

This category is a little difficult of analysis. Efforts to distinguish appositional infinitives from adjectival infinitives (or, as some insist, "epexegetical") render nuances diced so thin as to admit hardly of substance.[6] A clear example of apposition often cited is Paul's declaration in 1 Thess. 4:3:

Τοῦτο γάρ ἐστιν θέλημα τοῦ θεοῦ, ὁ ἁγιασμὸς ὑμῶν, ἀπέχεσθαι ὑμᾶς ἀπὸ τῆς πορνείας, . . .

"For this is God's will, your sanctification, *that you abstain from fornication,* . . ."

The structure is not predicative, and no verb separates grammatical elements that have equivalent meaning.[7]

♦ *An appositive infinitive can substitute entirely for the renamed substantive.*

Infinitive as Adjective

The infinitive can have an adjective role as a modifier. Some call this function "epexegetic," but this terminology is not used consistently in the grammars and can become very confusing to

---

[6]I have yet to get a student successfully to delineate the difference between "explain" and "define." The most succinct one I have gotten was this: "explaining takes more words."

[7]In fact, Paul's statement actually has *two* appositives: the other is the word "sanctification" (ὁ ἁγιασμὸς), which itself renames "God's will," like the infinitive "abstain" renames "sanctification." (Notice the editors have used commas for the appositives.)

the beginning student. What is essential to understand is that an adjectival infinitive is *non-essential* to grammatical sense. One can drop an adjectival infinitive and its clause will still maintain grammatical sense. For example, one could modify a direct object with an infinitive as a second accusative acting as an adjective. In contrast, an object complement to that direct object would be a second accusative that is *essential* to the grammatical sense of the direct object.

- ♦ *An adjectival infinitive is non-essential to the grammatical sense of its clause.*

Modifying A Substantive
Sometimes an infinitive can be used adjectivally to modify the meaning of a substantive. For example:

ἐπλήσθη <u>ὁ χρόνος</u> τοῦ τεκεῖν αὐτὴν.
"<u>The time</u> for her *to give birth* was fulfilled." (Lk. 1:57)

ἰδὼν ὅτι ἔχει <u>πίστιν</u> τοῦ σωθῆναι
"seeing that he had <u>faith</u> *to be saved*" (Acts 14:9)

In the first example, drop the infinitive "to give birth" and the clause still is complete and sensible: "The time was fulfilled." Likewise in the second example, "to be saved" can be dropped and the clause still is complete and sensible: "Seeing that he had faith." Further, neither of these infinitives can substitute for the noun modified and make complete grammatical sense, so they are not in apposition (nor are they the same case).

Modifying A Copulative Complement
The infinitive can modify a copulative complement. In this construction one will encounter a form of εἰμί that has a predicate nominative complement (noun or adjective). The meaning

of the complement itself is modified by an infinitive phrase.[8] Note the following eamples:

οὐκέτι εἰμὶ ἄξιος κληθῆναι υἱός σου
"I am no longer worthy to be called your son" (Lk. 15:19)

ἄξιος εἶ λαβεῖν τὸ βιβλίον
"you are worthy to take the book" (Rev. 5:9)

δυνατός ἐστιν καὶ ποιῆσαι
"He is able also to do" (Rom. 4:21)

ἕτοιμοί ἐσμεν τοῦ ἀνελεῖν αὐτόν
"we are prepared to kill him" (Acts 23:15)

Εἰμί As Infinitive

Εἰμί occurs as an infinitive in the present (εἶναι) and future (ἔσεσθαι) tenses. The future ἔσεσθαι accounts for four out of the five future infinitives in the New Testament.

λιμὸν μεγάλην μέλλειν ἔσεσθαι
"a great famine was going to be" (Acts 11:28)

Infinitive Location

As an infinite verb form, the infinitive does not have person and number (no subject). An infinitive also does not show the verb parameter of mood. Thus, three components of verb location are not needed for the infinitive: mood, person, and number. We are left with just **tense** and **voice**. The location,

---

[8]These instances are *not* the impersonal construction of a subject infinitive; notice how you are not trying to use "it" to begin a passive formulation, because the subject is personal.

then, of the infinitive's verbal components would be: tense, voice, "infinitive," where "infinitive" replaces the mood slot.

An infinitive is a verbal noun and has noun function. An infinitive, however, is not inflected. For this reason, aspects of case, gender, and number cannot be specified in locating an infinitive. Only external indications in a given context reveal an infinitive's nominal aspects (article, prepositions).

After locating tense, voice, "infinitive," you then simply would specify the lexical form and its meaning. For example, βαπτισθῆναι would be located: "aorist passive infinitive, from βαπτίζω, 'I baptize.'"

Diagramming Infinitives

Review pp. 504-7, English 5, "Sentence Diagramming," on diagramming substantival verbals. Then, study the following examples.[9]

Infinitive as Noun

Subject

οὐκ ἔξεστίν σοι ἔχειν αὐτήν
"*to have* her <u>is not lawful</u> for you" (Mt. 14:4)

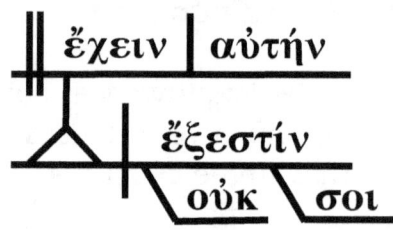

---

[9]We do not provide an example of the noun role of apposition for infinitives. However, for a brief discussion of diagramming apposition, see English 5, "Sentence Diagramming," pp. 510-11.

Object

ἔλεγον αὐτὸν <u>εἶναι</u> θεόν.
"They began to say *he was* a god." (Acts 28:6)

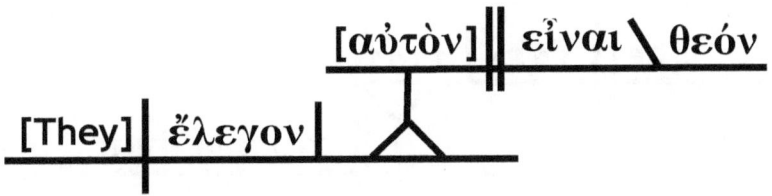

Complementary

δύναμαι τοῦτο <u>ποιῆσαι</u>
"I am able *to do this*" (Mt. 9:15)

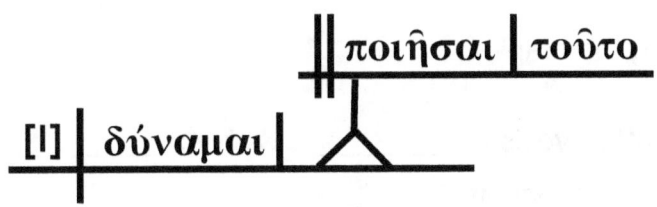

Object Complement

ᾐτήσαντο Πιλᾶτον <u>ἀναιρεθῆναι</u> αὐτόν
"they asked Pilate *that he be killed*" (Acts 13:28)

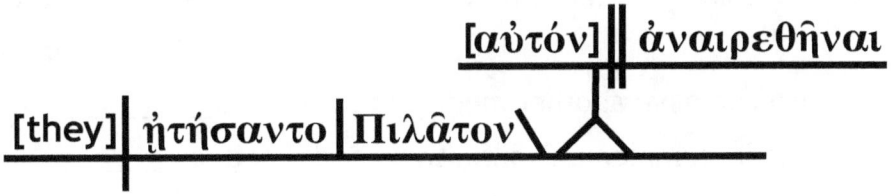

Infinitive as Adjective

ἔχει <u>πίστιν</u> τοῦ σωθῆναι
"he had <u>faith</u> *to be saved*" (Acts 14:9)

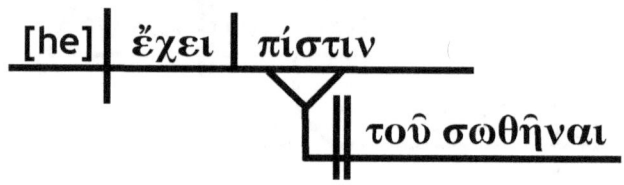

 **Exercise 22**

1. Fill in the blank:

An infinitive is a _____ with no _____ transformed to act as _____, _____, or _____. An infinitive does not need to be inflected to show _____ nor _____ and _____ of a subject. Therefore, an infinitive is part of a non-subject word group classed as a _____. Illustrated in the discussion was the infinitive functioning in a noun role as _____, _____, or _____. The infinitive also can have another modifying role as an _____. An object complement infinitive is defined as _____ (essential/non-essential) to the grammatical sense. An adjectival infinitive is defined as _____ (essential/

non-essential) to the grammatical sense. An appositive infinitive can _____ for the renamed substantive.

2. Infinitive endings:

    2.1 _____ and _____ are always active.

    2.2 _____ is always middle/passive.

    2.3 _____ is either _____ (tense) active or is _____ (tense) passive.

3. True/False:

    3.1 _____ Aorist infinitives have a past time augment.

    3.2 _____ Greek infinitives can take a masculine plural article.

    3.3 _____ Greek infinitives cannot take a preposition.

    3.4 _____ Action kind is always translatable for infinitives.

    3.5 _____ An infinitive can take an object but cannot be modified.

    3.6 _____ An infinitive's "surrogate subject" is in the accusative case.

    3.7 _____ In contrast to the non-indicative moods, the infinitive is negated with οὐ.

    3.8 _____ Indirect discourse functions as the direct object of the verb of saying.

    3.9 _____ The complementary infinitive is not required for the meaning of a verb.

    3.10 _____ The verb δύναμαι requires an infinitive to finish its meaning.

4. Complete the present indicative paradigm for the verb δύναμαι ("I am able"):

   _____ = _____
   _____ = _____
   _____ = _____
   _____ = _____
   _____ = _____
   _____ = _____

5. Translate. Be ready to locate verbs and explain infinitive use.

   5.1 δεῖ σωθῆναι ἡμᾶς. (Acts 4:12)

   5.2 οὐ δύναμαι ἐλθεῖν. (Lk. 14:20)

   5.3 οὐχὶ σὺ εἶ ὁ χριστός; (Lk. 23:39)

   5.4 μέλλει γὰρ Ἡρῴδης ζητεῖν τὸ παιδίον. (Mt. 2:13)

   5.5 ἄφετε (permit) τὰ παιδία ἔρχεσθαι πρός με. (Mk. 10:14)

Chapter 22: Infinitives

5.6 οὐχ ὑμῶν ἐστιν γνῶναι χρόνους ἢ καιρούς. (Acts 1:7)

5.7 εἶχον (ἔχω) ἐξουσίαν ἐκβάλλειν τὰ δαιμόνια. (Mk. 3:15*)

5.8 εὐαγγελίσασθαί με δεῖ τὴν βασιλείαν τοῦ θεοῦ. (Lk. 4:43)

5.9 εἴ τις θέλει πρῶτος εἶναι, ἔσται πάντων ἔσχατος. (Mk. 9:35)

5.10 οὐκ ἔξεστίν σοι ἔχειν τὴν γυναῖκα τοῦ ἀδελφοῦ σου. (Mk. 6:18)

5.11 ἔγραψαν τοῖς μαθηταῖς ἀποδέξασθαι (ἀποδέχομαι) αὐτόν. (Acts 18:27)

5.12 οὐ δυνάμεθα γὰρ ἡμεῖς ἃ εἴδαμεν (εἴδομεν) καὶ ἠκούσαμεν μὴ λαλεῖν. (Acts 4:20)

5.13 παρήγγειλεν (παραγγέλλω) αὐτοῖς (dative d. o.) . . . περιμένειν (περιμένω) τὴν ἐπαγγελίαν τοῦ πατρὸς (Acts 1:4)

5.14 (Scripture says:) ἐπίστευσα, διὸ ἐλάλησα, καὶ ἡμεῖς πιστεύομεν, διὸ καὶ λαλοῦμεν (2 Cor. 4:13)

6. Diagram the following from the exercises above.

   6.1 οὐκ ἔξεστίν σοι ἔχειν τὴν γυναῖκα τοῦ ἀδελφοῦ σου.

   6.2 μέλλει γὰρ Ἡρῴδης ζητεῖν τὸ παιδίον.

6.3 παρήγγειλεν αὐτοῖς περιμένειν τὴν ἐπαγγελίαν τοῦ πατρός.

6.4 εἶχον ἐξουσίαν ἐκβάλλειν τὰ δαιμόνια.

 **Vocabulary 22**

δεῖ, *must, it is necessary*

διό, *therefore, for this reason*

δύναμαι, *I am able, can* (dynamic, aerodynamic, dynasty)

εἶναι, *to be*

ἐλπίς, -ίδος, ἡ, *hope*

ἔξεστιν, *it is right, necessary, lawful*

ἐπαγγελία, ἡ, *promise*

ἔσχατος, -η, -ον, *last, least, end* (eschatology)

εὐαγγελίζω, *I bring good news, announce, preach* (evangelize)

οὐχί, *no, not* (positive answer)

παιδίον, τό, *child, infant* (pediatrics)

χρόνος, ὁ, *time, period, occasion* (chronology, chronicle)

Vocabulary notes:

(1) The verbs δεῖ and ἔξεστιν are so-called "impersonal verbs" (subject: "it") that take an infinitive acting as subject in the place of the English idiom that uses "it."

(2) The verb δύναμαι regularly takes an infinitive to complete its verbal meaning.

(3) The negative οὐχί is used when a positive answer is expected in a rhetorical question, or when the speaker inserts "no" as an interjection ("No, I tell you . . .").

Chapter 23

Adverbial Infinitives

Learning about infinitives involves remembering that, basically, all phrases are used with noun, adjective, or adverb roles in any sentence. A fundamental grammatical concept is that most word group usage in a sentence boils down to these three basic roles, illustrated in the diagram below. Notice that prepositional phrases, infinitives, participles, and dependent clauses *all* can function in similar ways as word groups, with noun, adjective, or adverb roles within independent clauses.

We have discussed noun and adjective roles for infinitives. We now take a look at the adverb role of the infinitive.

Table 23.1—Word Group Functions

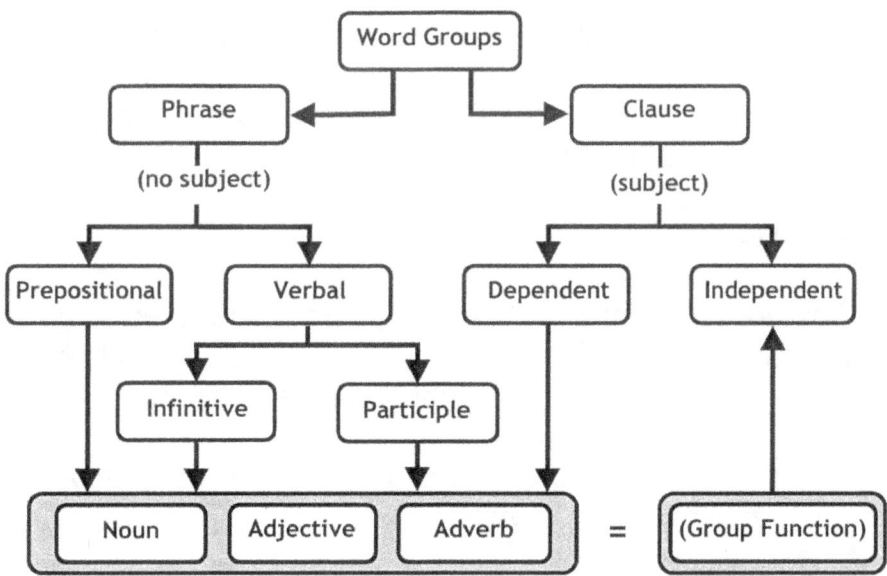

Adverbial Constructions

The main uses of the adverbial infinitive are to express:

- **purpose**—"to," "in order to," "so that"
- **result**—"as a result," "such that"
- **cause**—"because"
- **time**—"before," "while," "after"

To express these adverbial functions, the adverbial infinitive admits to four basic types of constructions. These types are: anarthrous, articular, prepositional, and with conjunctions. We will overview these constructions briefly.

Articular/Anarthrous (Purpose)

In the last chapter we learned that articular and anarthrous infinitives can have noun or adjective roles. Each of these constructions also can have various adverbial uses as well.

Prepositions

The adverbial infinitive can be found constructed with the prepositions διά, εἰς, ἐν, μετά, πρό, and πρός. These prepositions are fronted on the infinitive phrase to express the four adverbial functions of the infinitive.

Conjunctions

The adverbial infinitive can be found constructed with the conjunctions ἕως, πρίν, ὡς, and ὥστε. These conjunctions also are fronted on the infinitive phrase. Note carefully:

♦ *All infinitives constructed with prepositions and conjunctions are adverbial.*

Adverbial Junctions

The adverbial infinitive will express purpose, result, cause, and time. These functions and their various constructions are illustrated briefly. The uses that have an asterisk after them are the primary use of that construction, though these might be used with other adverbial meanings.

Purpose

Anarthrous Infinitive*

προσῆλθον . . . ἐπιδεῖξαι αὐτῷ τὰς οἰκοδομὰς
"they came *to point out* to him the buildings" (Mt. 24:1)

Articular Infinitive (τοῦ)*

εἰσῆλθεν τοῦ μεῖναι σὺν αὐτοῖς.
"He went in *to stay* with them." (Lk. 24:29)

Prepositional Infinitive (εἰς τό; πρὸς τό)*

ἀπήγαγον αὐτὸν εἰς τὸ σταυρῶσαι.
"They led him away *to be crucified.*" (Mt. 27:31)

πάντα δὲ τὰ ἔργα αὐτῶν ποιοῦσιν πρὸς τὸ θεαθῆναι
"they do all their works *to be seen*" (Mt. 23:5)

Conjunction + Infinitive (ὡς)

εἰσῆλθον εἰς κώμην Σαμαριτῶν ὡς ἑτοιμάσαι αὐτῷ
"they entered a Samaritan village *to prepare for him*"
(Lk. 9:52)

Result

Anarthrous Infinitive

οὐ γὰρ ἄδικος ὁ θεὸς <u>ἐπιλαθέσθαι</u> τοῦ ἔργου ὑμῶν
"for God is not unrighteous *such that he overlook* your work"
(Heb. 6:10)

Articular Infinitive (τοῦ)

ἐλευθέρα ἐστὶν ἀπὸ τοῦ νόμου, <u>τοῦ μὴ εἶναι</u> αὐτὴν μοιχαλίδα γενομένην ἀνδρὶ ἑτέρῳ.

"She is free from the law, *as result she is not* an adulteress if she marries another man." (Rom. 7:3)

Prepositional Infinitive (εἰς τό)

<u>εἰς τὸ εἶναι</u> αὐτοὺς ἀναπολογήτους
"*as a result they are* without excuse" (Rom. 1:19)

Conjunction + Infinitive (ὥστε)*

λαλῆσαι οὕτως <u>ὥστε πιστεῦσαι</u> . . . πολὺ πλῆθος
"they spoke in such a manner *that* a great multitude . . . believed" (Acts 14:1)

Cause

Prepositional Infinitive (διὰ τό)*

<u>διὰ τὸ μὴ ἔχειν</u> ῥίζαν ἐξηράνθη
"*because it did not have* root it withered away" (Mk. 4:6)

Time

(1) Antecedent ("before," πρὸ τοῦ, πρίν)

Prepositional Infinitive (πρὸ τοῦ)*

> ἀπ' ἄρτι λέγω ὑμῖν <u>πρὸ τοῦ γενέσθαι</u>
> "I tell you now *before it happens*" (Jn. 13:19)

Conjunction + Infinitive (πρίν, πρὶν ἤ)*

> κύριε, κατάβηθι <u>πρὶν ἀποθανεῖν</u> τὸ παιδίον μου.
> "Sir, please come down *before* my child *dies*" (Jn. 4:49)

(2) Simultaneous ("while," "as," ἐν τῷ)

> ἐφοβήθησαν δὲ <u>ἐν τῷ εἰσελθεῖν</u> αὐτοὺς εἰς τὴν νεφέλην
> "they were terrified *as they entered* into the cloud" (Lk. 9:34)

(3) Subsequent ("after," μετὰ τό)

> <u>μετὰ δὲ τὸ ἐγερθῆναί</u> με προάξω ὑμᾶς εἰς τὴν Γαλιλαίαν.
> "*after I have been raised* I will go before you into Galilee" (Mt. 26:32)

Diagramming

Diagramming adverbial infinitives is simple. The infinitive phrase as an adverb goes underneath the verb modified, but on its own verb line coming from an inverted standard. Two vertical strokes separate the surrogate subject from the infinitive. The surrogate subject is placed in brackets. As in a prepositional phrase, prepositions and conjunctions go on the slanted line coming down from the verb.

Infinitive as Adverbial

μετὰ δὲ τὸ ἐγερθῆναί με προάξω ὑμᾶς εἰς τὴν Γαλιλαίαν.
"*after I have been raised* I will go before you into Galilee" (Mt. 26:32)

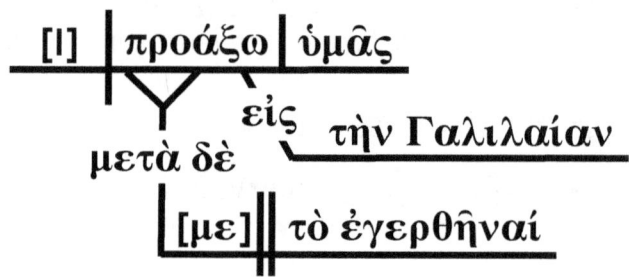

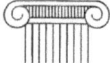 **Exercise 23**

1. Fill in the blank:

    1.1 _____ = Give the correct inflection of the article for an articular *purpose* infinitive.

    1.2 _____ = What prepositions can be used to express a *purpose* infinitive?

    1.3 _____ = What conjunction can be used to express a *result* infinitive?

    1.4 _____ = What preposition is used to express a *cause* infinitive?

    1.5 _____ = What preposition is used to express an *antecedent time* infinitive?

    1.6 _____ = What conjunction can be used to express an *antecedent time* infinitive?

    1.7 _____ = What preposition is used to express a *simultaneous time* infinitive?

Chapter 23: Adverbial Infinitives

1.8 _____ = What preposition is used to express a *subsequent time* infinitive?

2. Translate. Be ready to locate verbs and explain infinitive constructions.

   2.1 πέποιθεν ἐπὶ τὸν θεόν. (Matt. 27:43)

   2.2 πρὶν Ἀβραὰμ γενέσθαι ἐγὼ εἰμί. (John 8:58)

   2.3 οὐδὲν κακὸν εὑρίσκομεν ἐν τῷ ἀνθρώπῳ τούτῳ· (Acts 23:9)

   2.4 μακάριόν ἐστιν μᾶλλον διδόναι (δίδωμι) ἢ λαμβάνειν. (Acts 20:35)

   2.5 μὴ δαιμόνιον δύναται τυφλῶν ὀφθαλμοὺς ἀνοῖξαι; (Jn. 10:21)

   2.6 εἶπεν παραβολὴν διὰ τὸ ἐγγὺς εἶναι Ἰερουσαλὴμ αὐτόν. (Lk. 19:11)

2.7 Ἰωσὴφ υἱὸς Δαυίδ, μὴ φοβηθῇς παραλαβεῖν Μαρίαν τὴν γυναῖκά σου. (Mt. 1:20)

2.8 ἦλθεν (she) ἐκ τῶν περάτων (πέρας) τῆς γῆς ἀκοῦσαι τὴν σοφίαν Σολομῶνος. (Matt. 12:42)

2.9 τότε διήνοιξεν (διανοίγω) αὐτῶν τὸν νοῦν (νοῦς) τοῦ συνιέναι (συνίημι) τὰς γραφάς· (Lk. 24:45)

2.10 ἐρεῖτε (λέγω) ὅτι ὁ κύριος αὐτῶν χρείαν ἔχει· εὐθὺς δὲ ἀποστελεῖ (ἀποστέλλω) αὐτούς. (Mt. 21:3)

2.11 ἰδοὺ ἐξῆλθεν ὁ σπείρων (sower) τοῦ σπείρειν. καὶ ἐν τῷ σπείρειν αὐτὸν ἃ (some) μὲν ἔπεσεν παρὰ τὴν ὁδόν (Mt. 13:3-4)

3. Diagram the following from the exercises above.

εἶπεν παραβολὴν διὰ τὸ ἐγγὺς εἶναι Ἰερουσαλὴμ αὐτόν.

 Vocabulary 23

γλῶσσα, ἡ, *tongue* (glossary, glossalalia, polyglot, etc.)

γραφή, ἡ, *writing, scripture* (graph, graphic, biography, etc.)

εὐθύς, *immediately, next*

κακός, -ή, -όν, *bad, evil, harm* (cacophony)

μακάριος, -α, -ον, *blessed, happy, fortunate*

παραβολή, ἡ, *parable*

παραλαμβάνω, *I take along, accept, receive*

πείθω, *I persuade, trust*

πρίν, *before*

σοφία, ἡ, *wisdom, insight* (philosophy, sophomore)

σπείρω, *I sow*

τυφλός, -ή, -όν, *blind, blind person*

Vocabulary notes:

(1) Distinguish the adverb εὐθύς, "immediately," which is not inflected (and frequent in the New Testament), from the adjective εὐθύς, -εῖα, -ύ, "straight," which is inflected, but occurs only 8 times. The Gospel of Mark has 41 of the 51 occurrences of the adverb εὐθύς in the New Testament! Talk about a habit of style!

(2) The word πρίν is a conjunction, rare in the New Testament, but used with infinitives to express antecedent time.

(3) The verb πείθω is pretty recognizable in most principal parts, though loosing the theta in the second and third principal parts that have sigma suffixes (πείσω, ἔπεισα), and inserting a sigma in fifth and sixth before endings and the aorist passive theta (πεπείσμαι, ἐπείσθην). The one principal part not too recognizable is the fourth, which is *both* a different stem diphthong *and* a *second active* perfect loosing its kappa from the perfect suffix: πέποιθα.

Vocabulary Review 4

The following list summarizes words introduced since Review 3, generally by frequency of occurrence. The number is the chapter.

Vocabularies 19–23

ἀγαπητός 19
ἀρχή 21
ἀσπάζομαι 20
ἄχρι 20
Γαλιλαία 19
γλῶσσα 23
γραφή 23
Δαυίδ 20
δεῖ 22
δεξιός 21
δέχομαι 21
διδάσκαλος 20
διό 22
δοξάζω 19
δύναμαι 22
ἐάν 20

εἶναι 22
ἐλπίς 22
ἔξεστιν 22
ἐπαγγελία 22
ἔσχατος 22
εὐαγγελίζω 22
εὐθύς 23
ἦ 20
ᾔδειν 19
ἤδη 19
θεωρέω 21
θρόνος 19
ἴδε 21
Ἱεροσόλυμα 19
ἱμάτιον 19
ἵνα 20

ἴσθι 21
κακός 23
κἄν 20
κηρύσσω 19
κράζω 21
λίθος 21
λοιπός 21
μακάριος 23
μέσος 21
μηδέ 20
μηδείς 20
μήτε 20
νύξ 19
οἶδα 19
ὅπως 20
ὅταν 20

οὐχί 22
παιδίον 22
παραβολή 23
παραλαμβάνω 23
πείθω 23
Πιλᾶτος 21
πρίν 23
προσκυνέω 20
σοφία 23
σπείρω 23
συνάγω 21
συναγωγή 21
τυφλός 23
χαρά, ἡ 21
χρόνος 22
ὧδε 19

Photo © Gerald L. Stevens

Fig. 18. Hadrian Inscription. Pergamum's acropolis was crowned with the magnificent Temple of Trajan (A.D. 98-117). This acropolis inscription refers to Trajan's successor, Hadrian, as αὐτοκράτωρ ("emperor"). Roman imperial propaganda is background for use of the term παντοκράτωρ for God in the Book of Revelation (1:8; 4:8; 11:17; 15:3; 16:7, 14; 19:6, 15; 21:22). The full inscription reads:

ΑΥΤΟΚΡΑΤΟΡΑΚΑΙΣΑΡΑΘΕΟΥΤΡΑΙΑΝΟΥ
ΠΑΡΘΙΚΟΥΥΙΟΝΘΕΟΥΝΕΡΟΥΑΥΙΩΝΟΝ
ΤΡΑΙΑΝΟΝ ΑΔΡΙΑΝΟΝ ΣΕΒΑΣΤΟΝ
ΑΥΛΟΣΙΟΥΛΙΟΣΚΟΥΑΔΡΑΤΟΣΟΝΕΩ
ΚΟΡΟΣΚΑΙΙΕΡΕΥΣΤΟΥΔΙΟΝΥΣΟΥΜΕΤΑ
ΙΟΥΛΙΑΣΟΥΡΒΑΝΗΣΤΗΣΜΗΤΡΟΣ
ΕΑΥΤΩΝΣΩΤΗΡΑΚΑΙΕΥΕΡΓΕΤΗΝ

αυτοκρατορα καισαρα θεου τραιανου
παρθικου υιον θεου νερου αγιωνον
τραιανον αδριανον σεβαστον
αυλος ιουλιος κουαδρατος ο νεω-
κορος και ιερευς του διονυσου μετα
ιουλιας ουρβανης της μητρος
εαυτων σωτηρα και ευεργετην

The translation is: "When Caesar Trajanus Hardrianus Augustus Parthicus, holy son of the divine Trajan, son of the divine Nerva, was emperor, Aulus Julius Kouadratus, the temple warden and priest of Dionysius along with Julia Ourbanas, [dedicated this for] the protector and benefactor of their own mother." Pergamum is the city that Jesus characterized as "where Satan's throne is" (ὅπου ὁ θρόνος τοῦ σατανᾶ, Rev. 2:13).

Chapter 24

Participles

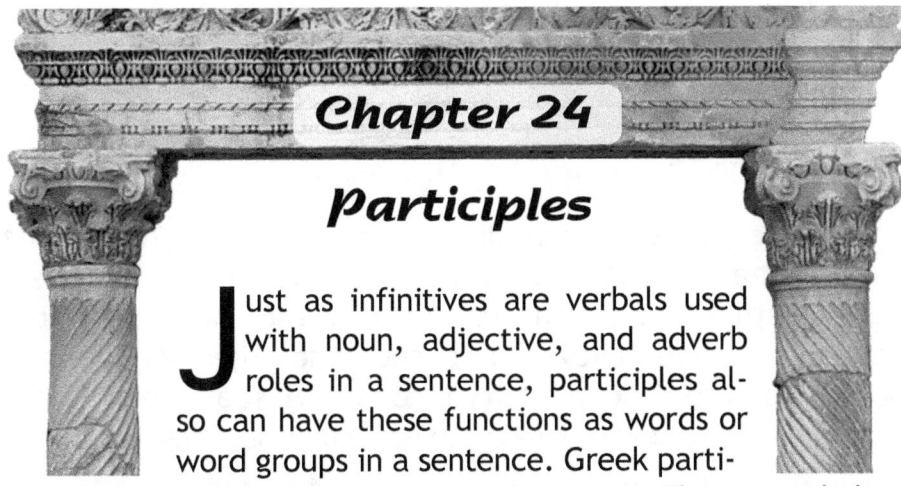

Just as infinitives are verbals used with noun, adjective, and adverb roles in a sentence, participles also can have these functions as words or word groups in a sentence. Greek participles are verbals with adjective functions. Their morphology represents this dual nature of verb and adjective. They show tense and voice as a non-subject verbal; they also show case, gender, and number as an adjective. In this chapter we present the forms of the Greek participle. Paradigms seem many, but nominal inflection patterns are well known and stem suffixes quite similar. Only seven new suffix patterns require attention.

Table 24.1—Word Group Junctions

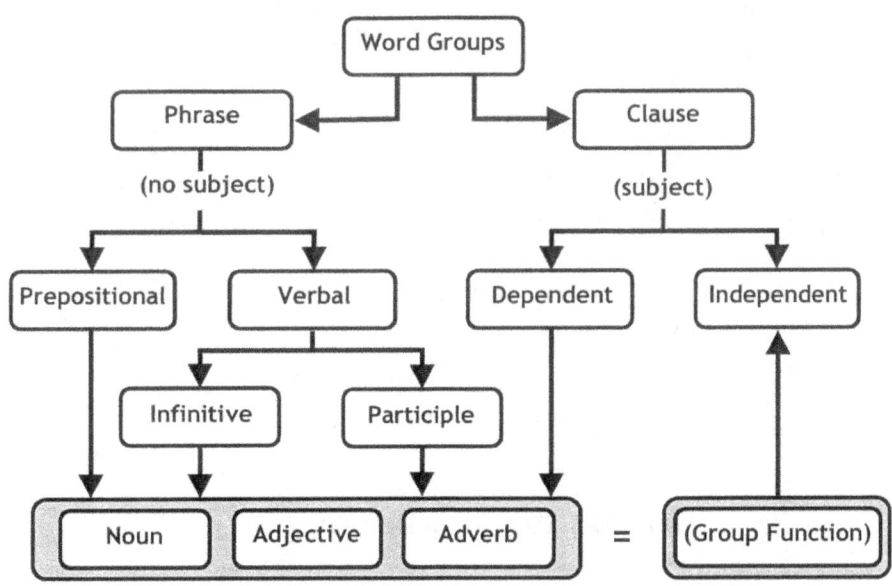

Active Participles

Present Active

The present active participle tense stem has an o thematic vowel and a -ντ participle suffix. Masculine and neuter inflections use third declension, and feminine uses first declension. Participle accents follow typical noun and adjective patterns, not verb patterns. Contract verbs contract just as expected (for example: φιλοῦντες). Note these particular observations:

- **masculine**—repeats the endings of the third declension noun paradigm ἄρχων (Table 7.8, p. 81)
- **neuter**—follows third declension neuter nom./acc. singular with no ending, so the suffix τ drops
- **feminine**—suffix reacts, becoming -ουσ, and follows a first declension "mixed" pattern (Table 5.5, p. 55)

Table 24.2—Present Active Participle

Masculine		Neuter	
Singular	Plural	Singular	Plural
λύων	λύοντες	λῦον	λύοντα
λύοντος	λυόντων	λύοντος	λυόντων
λύοντι	λύουσιν	λύοντι	λύουσιν
λύοντα	λύοντας	λῦον	λύοντα

Feminine	
Singular	Plural
λύουσα	λύουσαι
λυούσης	λυουσῶν
λυούσῃ	λυούσαις
λύουσαν	λυούσας

First Aorist Active

The indicative augment is *not* used. First aorist active has the -σα tense suffix, plus the -ντ participle suffix. Masculine and neuter inflection uses third declension. Feminine uses first declension. (Hint: simply substitute the aorist -σα for the thematic vowel -ο of the present paradigm for most forms.) Typical reactions apply (contracts lengthen: φιλήσας; stops change: πέμψας; liquids loose sigma: κρίνας). Particular observations:

- **masculine**—is like present active participle endings, except nom., sing. reacts, becoming -σας
- **neuter**—follows third declension neuter nom./acc. singular with no ending, so the suffix τ drops
- **feminine**—the suffix reacts, but becomes -σασ; also follows a first declension "mixed" pattern
- **consonants**—review sigma reactions in stops (cf. Table 15.4), such as πέμψας, and liquids, as κρίνας (p. 261)

Table 24.3—First Aorist Active Participle

Masculine		Neuter	
Singular	*Plural*	*Singular*	*Plural*
λύσας	λύσαντες	λῦσαν	λύσαντα
λύσαντος	λυσάντων	λύσαντος	λυσάντων
λύσαντι	λύσασιν	λύσαντι	λύσασιν
λύσαντα	λύσαντας	λῦσαν	λύσαντα

Feminine	
Singular	*Plural*
λύσασα	λύσασαι
λυσάσης	λυσασῶν
λυσάσῃ	λυσάσαις
λύσασαν	λυσάσας

Second Aorist Active

The second aorist active participle is a clone of the present active, except for tense stem and accent. Easy!

Table 24.4—Second Aorist Active Participle

Masculine		Neuter	
Singular	Plural	Singular	Plural
βαλών	βαλόντες	βαλόν	βαλόντα
βαλόντος	βαλόντων	βαλόντος	βαλόντων
βαλόντι	βαλοῦσιν	βαλόντι	βαλοῦσιν
βαλόντα	βαλόντας	βαλόν	βαλόντα

Feminine	
Singular	Plural
βαλοῦσα	βαλοῦσαι
βαλούσης	βαλουσῶν
βαλούσῃ	βαλούσαις
βαλοῦσαν	βαλούσας

Future Active

The future participle is rare, occurring just thirteen times in the New Testament. The active form would be similar to first aorist, but with a -σοντ- thematic vowel pattern, rather than the aorist -σαντ- (λύσοντος rather than λύσαντος). Contracts lengthen (ποιήσων); stops change (ἄξων); liquids drop sigma (κρινῶν).

Perfect First Active

The perfect first active participle uses perfect tense reduplication and a -κ voice suffix. The resultant masculine and neuter active participle suffix is -κοτ; feminine is -κυι. Contracts will lengthen (πεφιληκώς), and stops will change (ἠλπικώς).

Table 24.5—Perfect First Active Participle

Masculine		Neuter	
Singular	Plural	Singular	Plural
λελυκώς	λελυκότες	λελυκός	λελυκότα
λελυκότος	λελυκότων	λελυκότος	λελυκότων
λελυκότι	λελυκόσιν	λελυκότι	λελυκόσιν
λελυκότα	λελυκότας	λελυκός	λελυκότα

Feminine	
Singular	Plural
λελυκυῖα	λελυκυῖαι
λελυκυίας	λελυκυιῶν
λελυκυίᾳ	λελυκυίαις
λελυκυῖαν	λελυκυίας

Perfect Second Active

The perfect second active participle is rare. The old second perfect οἶδα accounts for many of the occurrences (cf. εἰδώς, εἰδότες; εἰδός, εἰδότα; εἰδυῖα, εἰδυῖαι). Remember, however, that this verb has lost its perfect force.

Middle (Passive) Participles

Outside the Sixth Principal Part

Middle/passive participles are a cinch. Nail the following:

♦ *The -μεν suffix always is a middle/passive participle regardless of tense.*

Masculine and neuter is second declension; feminine is first declension ("η pure"). The so-called "deponent" translates as active (as in the indicative). Tense forms are by principal parts:

- **λυόμενος**—present has present tense stem, o thematic vowel, -μεν suffix, and inflection
- **λυσάμενος**—first aorist has first aorist tense stem, -σα aorist suffix, -μεν suffix, and inflection
- **βαλόμενος**—second aorist has second aorist stem, o thematic vowel, -μεν suffix, and inflection
- **λελυμένος**—perfect has reduplicated perfect stem, *no* thematic vowel, -μεν suffix, and inflection

That's all. Just remember, for participles: "-μεν is middle."

The Sixth Principal Part

Table 24.6—Aorist First Passive Participle

Masculine		Neuter	
Singular	*Plural*	*Singular*	*Plural*
λυθείς	λυθέντες	λυθέν	λυθέντα
λυθέντος	λυθέντων	λυθέντος	λυθέντων
λυθέντι	λυθεῖσιν	λυθέντι	λυθεῖσιν
λυθέντα	λυθέντας	λυθέν	λυθέντα

Feminine	
Singular	*Plural*
λυθεῖσα	λυθεῖσαι
λυθείσης	λυθεισῶν
λυθείσῃ	λυθείσαις
λυθεῖσαν	λυθείσας

First Passive Participle

The sixth principal part gives the passive voice for aorist and future tenses. The aorist first passive participle suffix is -θε (instead of indicative -θη). With the -ντ participle suffix, the aorist first passive participle shows a characteristic -θεντ- pattern. Remember consonant interactions with theta (p. 269).

Third declension endings are used in masculine and neuter. The nominative singular and dative plural have sigmas that induce reactions, creating resultant forms. Feminine forms have a characteristic -θεισ- suffix pattern and first declension mixed inflection. Contracts will lengthen (φιληθείς), and stops change (πεμφθείς).

A *future* first passive participle would show a -θησομεν- formation pattern, using a -θη voice suffix rather than -θε, an ο thematic vowel, and the middle voice participle suffix -μεν. The only New Testament occurrence, from λαλέω, is the form λαληθησομένων (Heb. 3:5; note lengthened contract vowel).

Second Passive Participle

The aorist second passive participle drops the θ of the θε passive suffix, leaving just ε. Combined with the -ντ participle suffix, the aorist second passive forms show a characteristic -εντ- pattern (e.g., γραφέντος) in the masculine and neuter (except nom. sg. γραφείς and dat. pl. γραφεῖσιν). Feminine shows up with an -εισ- pattern (e.g., γραφεῖσα).

Εἰμί as a *Participle*

Once you know the present active participle paradigm, you already know the verb εἰμί as a participle! Remove the present active tense stem and add smooth breathing and accent. Voilà!

- *masculine:* ὤν, ὄντος, ὄντι, ὄντα; ὄντες, ὄντων, οὖσιν, ὄντας

- *neuter:* ὄν, ὄντος, ὄντι, ὄν; ὄντα, ὄντων, οὖσιν, ὄντα
- *feminine:* οὖσα, οὔσης, οὔσῃ, οὖσαν; οὖσαι, οὐσῶν, οὔσαις, οὔσας.

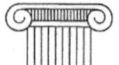
Exercise 24

1. Identify the following present participle components:

   1.1
   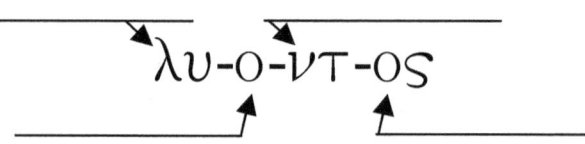

   1.2
   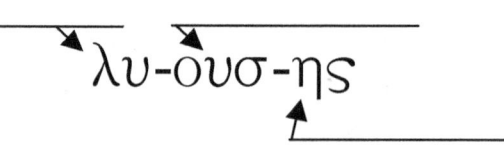

   1.3

2. Locate the following. Specify: tense, voice, "participle" (replacing mood), case, gender, and number. Remember that both mas./neu. *nominative singular* and *dative plural* forms react, hiding the suffix.

   2.0 Example: λύοντος

   Pres., act., part., gen., mas./neu., sing.

2.1 ἀκούοντα

2.2 ἀγαπῶντας

2.3 βλεπομένη

2.4 γραφόμενα

2.5 ἔχουσα

2.6 λέγοντες

2.7 ὄντες

2.8 λέγων

2.9 αἰτοῦσιν

2.10 ἐχούσαις

3. Identify the following aorist participle components:

   3.1 λυ-σα-ντ-ος

   3.2 λυ-σασ-ης

   3.3 βαλ-ο-ντ-ος

   3.4 λυ-σα-μεν-ου

   3.5 λυ-θε-ντ-ος

   3.6 λυ-θεισ-ης

Chapter 24: Participles

4. Locate the following. Remember that mas./neu. *nominative singular* and *dative plural* forms react, hiding the suffix. Stops, liquids react to tense suffix.

   4.1 κηρύξας

   4.2 ἐλθόντων

   4.3 ἐλθοῦσα

   4.4 ἀκούσασα

   4.5 γενομένου

   4.6 δεξάμενος

   4.7 γεννηθέν

   4.8 πορευθέντες

   4.9 βληθείσῃ (βάλλω)

5. Identify the following perfect participle components:

   5.1

   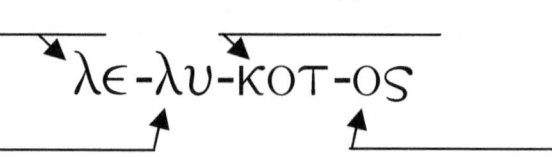

   5.2

   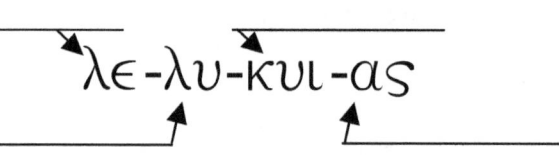

   5.3

   λε-λυ-μεν-ου

6. Locate the following. Remember that mas./neu. *nominative singular* and *dative plural* forms react, hiding the suffix.

   6.1 κεκληκώς (καλέω)

   6.2 πεποιηκότες

   6.3 πεποιηκυία

   6.4 περιβεβλημένοι (περιβάλλω)

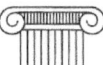 **Participle Morphology Hints**

-οντ-, -ουσ-, -ομεν-, present (+ 2d aor.) suffix patterns

-σαντ-, -σασ-, -σαμεν-, first aorist suffix patterns

-θεντ-, -θεισ-, *passive system suffix patterns*

-κοτ-, -κυι-, -μεν-, *perfect suffix patterns*

Morphology notes:

(1) **Nominative Singular and Dative Plural Forms:** Nominative singular and dative plural forms can hide the suffix patterns in certain masculine and neuter forms, just as the noun stem is hidden in these slots in third declension nouns. Thus, one still has to recognize the following as participle endings without the typical suffix appearance: -ων, -ουσι, -σας, -σασι, -κως, -κοσι, -θεις, -θεισι. Nominative forms are frequent in participles, so be sure to learn to recognize these forms (-ων, -σας, -κως, -θεις). You may have noticed also that the dative plural *participle* ending, -ουσι, is exactly like the present, active, *indicative*, third plural ending. Whether a verb with this ending is a participle or an indicative verb will be clarified by context.

(2) **Neuter Forms:** Neuter nom./acc. singular also reacts and hides the suffix pattern. Thus, one still has to recognize the following as neuter participle endings without the typical suffix appearance: -ον, -σαν, -κος, -θεν.

(3) **Negative:** The negative used with participles is μή, as with all forms outside the indicative (subjunctive, optative, imperative, infinitive).

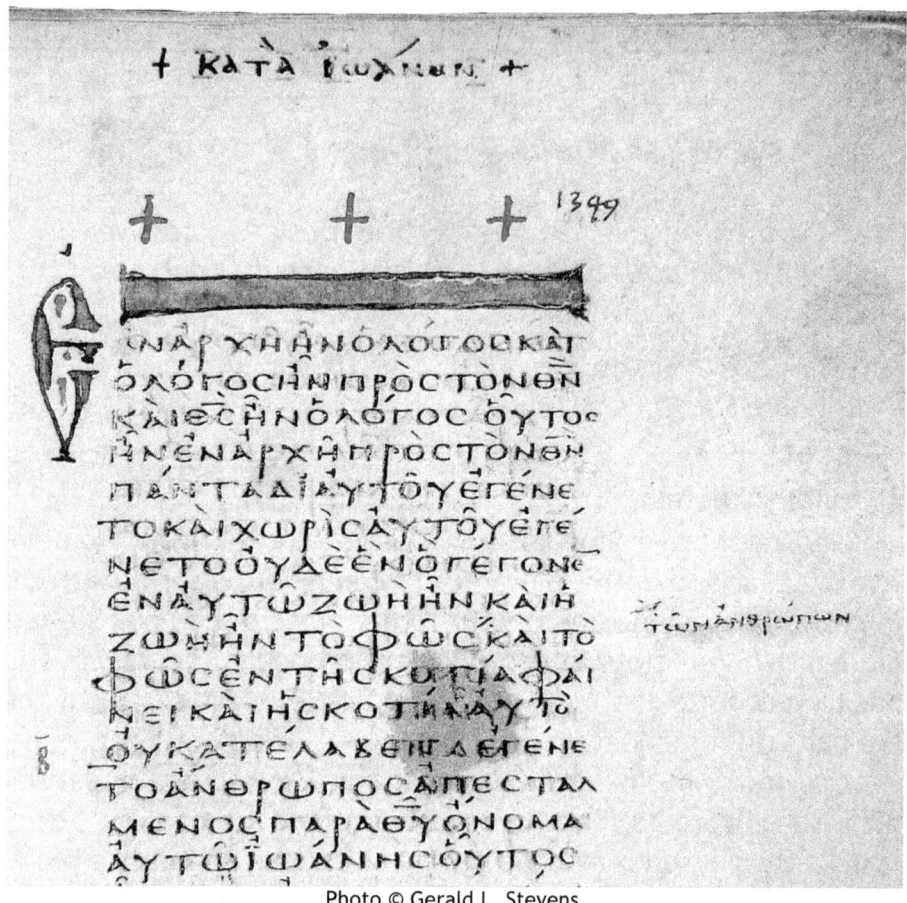

Photo © Gerald L. Stevens

Fig. 19. Codex Vaticanus. In the Vatican library at least since 1475, Codex Vaticanus is one of our most important New Testament manuscripts. Written on parchment, the text has three columns to a page. The right margin here has the scribe's notation of the words "of men" omitted at Jn. 1:4. The script is *uncial*, a form of capital letters (sigma looks like a "C"). The style is called *scripto continua*, or continuous script: no word divisions, no punctuation, and words may continue at the end of one line to the next.

The codex is the book form of today, with leaves folded and bound at the fold, an innovation after scrolls. Parchment, leather worked from animal skins for taking ink, was expensive, so available only at a time when the church had access to greater resources after Constantine (306–337). Before parchment, papyrus had been used, a form of paper made from strips of the papyrus plant grown along the Nile River that were counter-laid and beaten together. One side had vertical strips, the other horizontal.

Chapter 25

Adjectival Participles

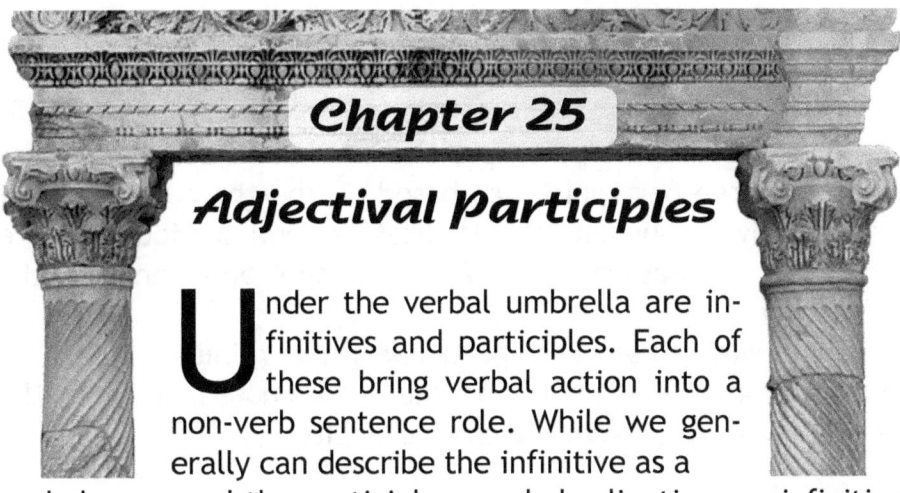

Under the verbal umbrella are infinitives and participles. Each of these bring verbal action into a non-verb sentence role. While we generally can describe the infinitive as a verbal noun and the participle a verbal adjective, an infinitive can function as an adjective and a participle can function as a noun. Our characterizations of verbals, in other words, are not meant to exclude each other but to convey primary function.

In this chapter, we focus on the participle's adjective roles. An adjective has three basic functions: substantive, predicative, and attributive. Reviewing adjectives is advised (Chapter 8).

Table 25.1—Word Group Functions

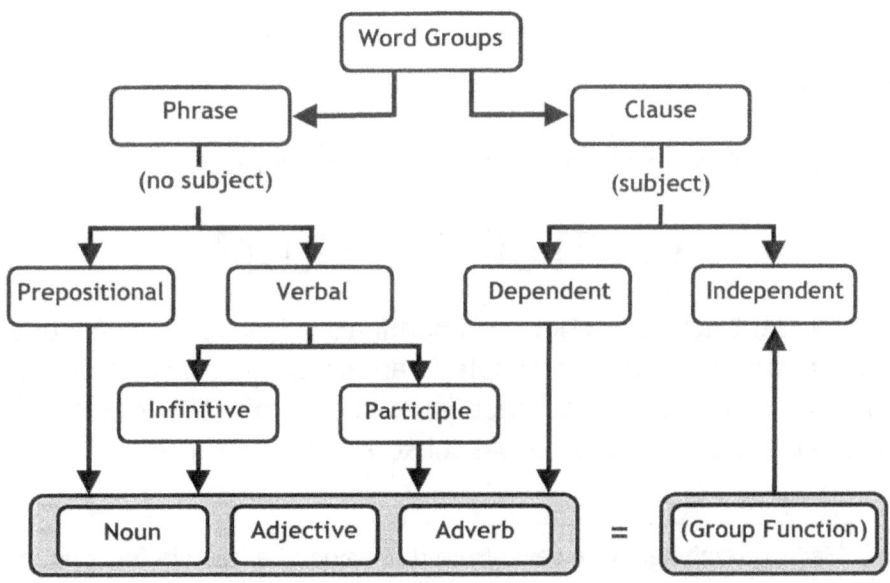

Participles As Substantival

If we describe the participle as a "verbal adjective," we are implying three participle uses based on the three functions of an adjective: substantival, predicative, and attributive.[1] We first cover the easiest participle use to spot and translate, the substantival.

The negative used with participles, like infinitives, is μή. In the following, remember that "articular" does not mean the article always is adjacent to the participle.

Construction

A participle can function substantivally (as a noun), taking on sentence roles such as subject, object, or predicate noun, just as an adjective can. The following dictum will help you recognize substantival participle use quickly:

- *Articular participles always are used substantivally or attributively.*

Translation

Take, for example, this articular construction:

$$\text{ὁ πιστεύων}$$

The present active participle is nominative, masculine, singular. Constructed with the participle is an article in concord. If used substantivally—say, as subject (note the nominative case)—how would we translate this verbal substantive structure?

---

[1] Second reminder. A review of the discussion of adjective function, pp. 91-92, would be most helpful to you at this point. Highly recommended.

One translation technique is to turn the participle into a relative pronoun clause. To do this, first observe the participle's gender and number (masculine, singular) to set up the subject. Then, use a personal pronoun matching the participle's gender and number ("he") with a relative pronoun matching the gender ("who") and follow with the participle's verbal action ("he who believes"). Alternately, you could use a demonstrative pronoun. The resulting expression would be similar to:

- **masculine singular:** *"he who __,"* *"the one who __,"* *"the person who __"*
- **masculine plural:** *"those who __,"* *"the ones who __,"* *"the persons who __"*

The verbal idea of the participle can be expressed as a finite verb, as above. Or, one could use an "-ing" form as well. Note:

- **finite verb:** "he who *believes*," "the one who *believes*," "the person who *believes*"
- **"-ing" form:** "the man *believing*," "the one *believing*," "the person *believing*"

We could change the participle's case, thereby changing its grammatical function. Take, for example, the accusative case:

$$\text{τὸν πιστεύοντα}$$

This verbal substantive structure would translate similarly ("he who believes," "the one who believes," "the one believing"). However, as *accusative* case, this clause would have an *object* function, such as direct object of a verb, or as the object of a preposition requiring accusative case.

Examples

We provide brief examples of the articular participle used as a substantive in noun roles. Notice the attempt to preserve the participle's *action kind* (durative, undefined, perfect) in the example translations.

Participle as Subject

> ὁ πιστεύων εἰς αὐτὸν οὐ κρίνεται.
> "*The one who believes* in him is not judged." (Jn. 3:18)

> ὁ πέμψας με ἀληθής ἐστιν.
> "*The one who sent* me is true." (Jn. 8:26)

> τὸ γεγεννημένον ἐκ τοῦ πνεύματος πνεῦμά ἐστιν.
> "*That which has been born* of the Spirit is spirit." (Jn. 3:6)

Participle as Object

> τί ζητεῖτε τὸν ζῶντα μετὰ τῶν νεκρῶν;
> "Why do you seek *the one who lives* among the dead?" (Jn. 3:18)

> πολλοὶ δὲ τῶν ἀκουσάντων τὸν λόγον ἐπίστευσαν.
> "And many *of those who heard* the word believed." (Acts 4:4)

> εἶπεν τῷ παραλελυμένῳ . . .
> "he said *to the one who was paralyzed* . . ." (Lk. 5:24)

Participle as Predicate Noun

A participle can function substantivally (in the noun role) as the predicate complement of a copulative verb and so is called a predicate noun. The predicate *noun* role is to be distinguished from the predicate *adjective* role. Predicate nouns always are *articular*, but predicate adjectives always are *anarthrous*, by definition (i.e., the "predicative" function discussed below). In the examples of the participle as predicate noun below, notice carefully that each participle is *articular* in construction:

> τὸ πνεῦμά ἐστιν τὸ ζῳοποιοῦν.
> "The Spirit is *the one who makes alive*." (Jn. 6:63)

Ἰησοῦς ἐστιν ὁ ποιήσας αὐτὸν ὑγιῆ.
"Jesus was *the one who made* him well." (Jn. 5:15)

οὗτοί εἰσιν οἱ ἀκούσαντες.
"These are *the ones who heard*." (Lk. 8:14)

ἀλλὰ τοῦτό ἐστιν τὸ εἰρημένον διὰ τοῦ προφήτου Ἰωήλ.
"But this is *that which was spoken* through the prophet Joel." (Lk. 1:45)

Participles As Attributive

Construction

A participle is a verbal adjective. An adjective's main role is to modify—the attributive use. With participles this attributive use can be constructed as articular or anarthrous. The bottom line is that an anarthrous construction is ambiguous, since this construction not only could be a predicate adjective (discussed below) but even an adverbial participle (discussed in the next chapter). Still, you do have this helpful hint:

♦ *Articular participles always are used substantivally or attributively.*

Another way to say this is that the articular participle never will be adverbial. Just remember that any attributive participle as an adjective will exhibit concord with the substantive modified.

Translation

Articular Attributive

μακάριοι οἱ ὀφθαλμοὶ οἱ βλέποντες ἃ βλέπετε.
"Blessed are the eyes *which see* what you see." (Lk. 10:23)

οὐ τιμᾷ τὸν πατέρα <u>τὸν πέμψαντα</u> αὐτόν.
"He does not honor the Father *who sent* him." (Jn. 5:23)

ἡ οἰκονομία τοῦ μυστηρίου <u>τοῦ ἀποκεκρυμμένου</u> ἀπὸ τῶν αἰώνων
"the administration of the mystery *which has been hidden* from the ages" (Eph. 3:9)

ἀλλ᾿ ἐπὶ τῷ θεῷ <u>τῷ ἐγείροντι</u> τοὺς νεκρούς
"but on God *who raises* the dead" (2 Cor. 1:9)

Anarthrous Attributive

ἀδελφοὶ <u>ἠγαπημένοι</u> ὑπὸ κυρίου
"brothers *beloved* by the Lord" (2 Thess. 2:13)

ἤκουσα φωνῆς <u>λεγούσης</u> μοι.
"I heard a voice *speaking* to me." (Acts 22:7)

κληθήσονται υἱοὶ θεοῦ <u>ζῶντος</u>.
"They will be called children *of the living* God." (Rom. 9:26)

ἡμῖν <u>πιστεύσασιν</u> ἐπὶ τὸν κύριον Ἰησοῦν Χριστόν
"to us *who believed* in the Lord Jesus Christ" (Acts 11:17)

ἀγοράσαι παρ᾿ ἐμοῦ χρυσίον <u>πεπυρωμένον</u> ἐκ πυρὸς
"to buy from me gold *which has been refined* by fire" (Rev. 3:18)

Participles As Predicative

Construction

A participle can function predicatively, taking on the role of a predicate adjective used with a copulative verb (such as εἰμί or γίνομαι). Both the subject and the predicate adjective by definition are nominative. The Greek construction can use an explicit form of the copulative verb, as English always requires.

Greek, however, unlike English, also has a special "verbless" predicative construction. Here is the "verbless" dictum again:

♦ *Anarthrous adjectives with articular nouns are predicative if both are nominative.*

Thus, as required by this Greek idiom, the participle functioning as a predicative adjective will be *anarthrous*; the noun that is the subject will be articular.

Translation

Participle as Predicative (Copulative Explicit)

καὶ ἰδοὺ <u>ζῶν</u> εἰμι εἰς τοὺς αἰῶνας τῶν αἰώνων.
"And behold, I am *alive* forever and ever." (Rev. 1:18)

ἡ οἰκία ἦν <u>συνομοροῦσα</u> τῇ συναγωγῇ.
"His house was *next door* to the synagogue." (Acts 18:7)

ἡ γυνὴ ἦν <u>περιβεβλημένη</u> πορφυροῦν καὶ κόκκινον.
"The woman was *clothed* in purple and scarlet." (Rev. 17:4)

Participle as Predicative (Verbless Idiom)

<u>Ζῶν</u> γὰρ ὁ λόγος τοῦ θεοῦ.
"For the Word of God is *living*." (Heb. 4:12)

ὁ λόγος <u>ἐξουθενημένος</u>.
"His speech is *contemptible*." (2 Cor. 10:10)

τί στενὴ ἡ πύλη καὶ <u>τεθλιμμένη</u> ἡ ὁδός.
"Because the gate is narrow and the road is *hard*." (Mt. 7:14)

πυρράζει γὰρ <u>στυγνάζων</u> ὁ οὐρανός
"For the sky is red *and threatening*." (Mt. 16:3)

Grammatical roles can be reversed by the article. Thus, an *articular* participle can function as the *subject* in a predicative construction with an anarthrous adjective. For example:

μακαρία ἡ πιστεύσασα.
"Blessed is *she who believed*." (Lk. 1:45)

Word order here is poetic, emphasizing the predicate adjective by fronting its position in the clause. The English translation correspondingly does the same to reflect this poetic emphasis.

Εἰμί As Participle

ὁ ὢν ἐκ τοῦ θεοῦ τὰ ῥήματα τοῦ θεοῦ ἀκούει.
"*The one who is* from God hears the words of God." (Jn. 8:47)

οἱ μετ' αὐτοῦ ὄντες . . .
"*Those who were* with him . . ." (Jn. 9:40)

οἱ ἀδελφοὶ οἱ ὄντες κατὰ τὴν Ἰουδαίαν . . .
"The brothers *who were* from Judea . . ." (Acts 11:1)

τῆς ἐκκλησίας τῆς οὔσης ἐν Ἰερουσαλὴμ . . .
"of the church *which was* in Jerusalem . . ." (Acts 11:22)

Diagramming

Grammatical Analysis

The adjectival participle diagrams according to its function: (1) substantivally in a subject, object, or predicate nominative slot; (2) predicatively in a complement slot; (3) attributively in a modifying slot underneath the word modified. As a verbal, an

Chapter 25: Adjectival Participles

adjectival participle may require its own verb line lifted on a standard to accommodate its own objects and modifiers.[2]

Examples

Substantival

ὁ πέμψας με ἀληθής ἐστιν.
"*The one who sent* me is true." (Jn. 8:26)

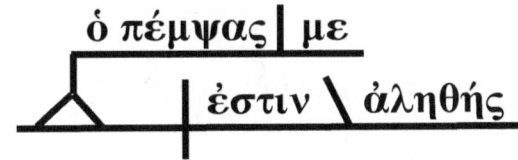

Attributive

οὐ τιμᾷ τὸν πατέρα τὸν πέμψαντα αὐτόν.
"He does not honor the Father *who sent* him." (Jn. 5:23)

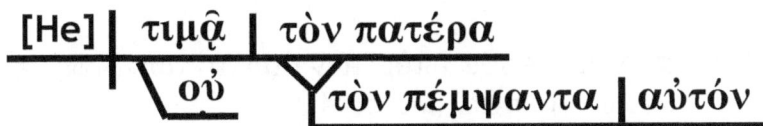

Predicative

καὶ ἰδοὺ ζῶν εἰμι εἰς τοὺς αἰῶνας τῶν αἰώνων.
"And behold, I am *alive* forever and ever." (Rev. 1:18)

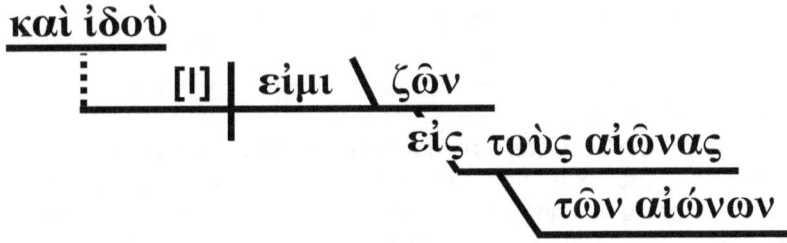

---

[2] Review the diagramming discussion on pp. 504-5.

 **Exercise 25**

1. Translate or, if just a phrase, give a gloss. Be ready to locate participles and explain their construction.

   1.1 τοῖς ἀκουσθεῖσιν³ (Heb. 2:1)

   1.2 τοῖς πεπιστευκόσιν (Acts 18:27)

   1.3 οἱ δὲ κεκλημένοι (καλέω) οὐκ ἦσαν ἄξιοι. (Mt. 22:8)

   1.4 προσεύχεσθε ὑπὲρ τῶν διωκόντων (διώκω, assume masculine) ὑμᾶς. (Mt. 5:44)

   1.5 πολλοὶ δὲ τῶν ἀκουσάντων τὸν λόγον ἐπίστευσαν. (Acts 4:4)

---

³The -θεισ- suffix pattern regularly is a feminine participle. Two lookalike exceptions that will throw you off are: (1) -θεις, a nom., mas., sing. form with *final* sigma, and (2) -θεισιν, a mas./neu., dat., plu. form. (See Table 24.6, p. 382.) The context from which the form ἀκουσθεῖσιν in 1.1 above was taken indicates that the form should be located as *neuter*. As *neuter*, ἀκουσθεῖσιν needs a "what was" style of translation instead of a "those who" formulation.

1.6 τοῖς ἀγαπῶσιν τὸν θεὸν πάντα συνεργεῖ (συνεργέω) εἰς ἀγαθόν. (Rom. 8:28)

1.7 καὶ ἐστὲ ἐν αὐτῷ πεπληρωμένοι, ὅς ἐστιν ἡ κεφαλὴ πάσης ἀρχῆς καὶ ἐξουσίας. (Col. 2:10)

1.8 ἐὰν γὰρ ἀγαπήσητε τοὺς ἀγαπῶντας ὑμᾶς, τίνα μισθὸν (μισθός) ἔχετε; (Mt. 5:46)

1.9 πᾶς[4] γὰρ ὁ αἰτῶν λαμβάνει καὶ ὁ ζητῶν εὑρίσκει καὶ τῷ κρούοντι (κρούω) ἀνοιγήσεται.[5] (Mt. 7:8)

---

[4] The nominative construction πᾶς ὁ with the participle is found often in the New Testament and usually is rendered "Everyone who . . ."

[5] This verb's highly irregular principal parts (see p. 554) illustrates how Koine Greek sometimes developed quite unsystematically. Different forms from different Greek dialects were used (Aeolic, Attic, Doric, Ionic, etc.). The form ἀνοιγήσεται above is future passive, built on the aorist second passive form ἠνοίγην (i.e., the aorist passive suffix θ has been dropped). The *future* second passive built on this aorist second passive form would: not be augmented, have a thematic vowel, and use primary endings.

1.10 οὐ γὰρ ὑμεῖς ἐστε οἱ λαλοῦντες ἀλλὰ τὸ πνεῦμα τοῦ πατρὸς ὑμῶν τὸ λαλοῦν ἐν ὑμῖν. (Mt. 10:20)

1.11 καὶ πάντες οἱ ἀκούσαντες ἐθαύμασαν (θαυμάζω) περὶ τῶν λαληθέντων ὑπὸ τῶν ποιμένων πρὸς αὐτούς. (Lk. 2:18)

2. Diagram the following from the exercises above:

2.1 ἔσεσθε μισούμενοι.

2.2 οἱ δὲ κεκλημένοι οὐκ ἦσαν ἄξιοι.

2.3 πολλοὶ δὲ τῶν ἀκουσάντων τὸν λόγον ἐπίστευσαν.

2.4 ἐὰν γὰρ ἀγαπήσητε τοὺς ἀγαπῶντας ὑμᾶς, τίνα μισθὸν ἔχετε;

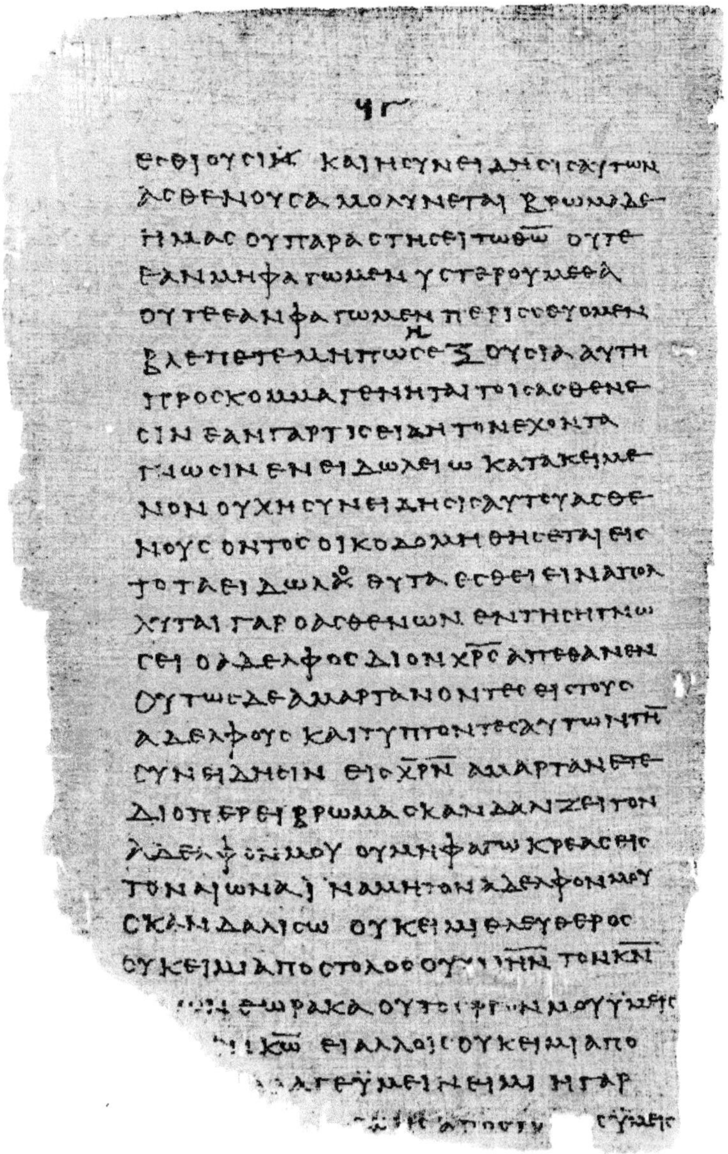

Fig. 20. Manuscript 𝔓46. New Testament Greek manuscripts come in two forms: papyrus and parchment. Older than parchment, papyri manuscripts are judged more valuable for reconstructing the original text. 𝔓46 contains the letters of Paul. The above is folio 47, recto, with 1 Cor. 8:7-9:2. "Recto" is the side of the papyrus sheet that has the horizontal strips; "verso" has the vertical strips. The King James translators did not have the many valuable manuscripts such as 𝔓46 available for their work as we have today.

Chapter 26

Adverbial Participles

Now we present adverbial participles. These participles are used to modify the action of the main verb, that is, the independent clause. This adverbial use has nine categories or ways a main verb's action can be modified. First, we remind you of word groups and their function in the diagram below. Then, we summarize the nine adverbial categories.

Table 26.1—Word Group Functions

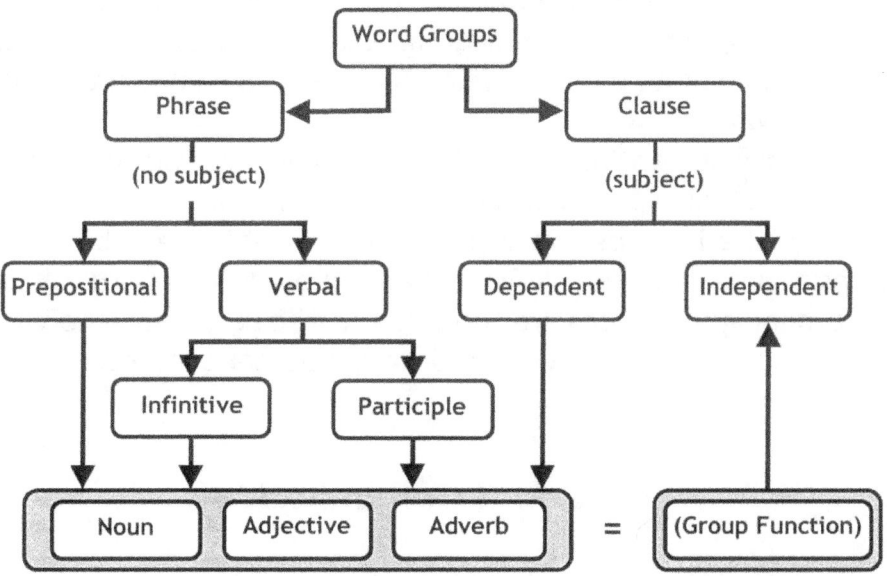

The nine adverbial uses of the participle are summarized briefly below. The adverbial participle is used as:

- **Temporal**—indicating a time sequence tied to the main verb's action: "They came *while he was teaching.*"
- **Purpose**—indicating a purpose for the main verb's action: "He came *seeking fruit.*"
- **Cause**—indicating the reason for the main verb's action: "I give thanks to my God *because I hear* . . . ."
- **Condition**—indicating a contingency on the main verb's action: "*If you keep yourselves,* you do well."
- **Concession**—acknowledging a past or present condition that has had, or still has, an affect on the main verb's action: "*Whereas I was blind,* now I see."
- **Means**—indicating the instrumentality through which the main verb's action is accomplished: "For *by doing this* . . . you will heap . . ."
- **Manner**—indicating the affective emotions or actions accompanying, but not essential to, expressing the main verb's action: "He was going on his way *rejoicing.*"
- **Complementary**—indicating action that is essential to completing the main verb's action: "I do not cease *giving thanks.*"
- **Circumstantial**—indicating additional action incidental to the main verb's action: "He answered *and said.*"

The italicized expressions in the categories itemized above are translations of adverbial Greek participles. What is crucial for determining these uses are the contextual clues, combined with your best estimation as translator of the author's intent.

Adverbial Construction

The adverbial participle is not hard to spot:

- *Most anarthrous participles are adverbial.*

We cannot say "all" because two exceptions apply, which you now know from the previous chapter on adjectival participles:

- **Anarthrous attributive:** sometimes an anarthrous participle will have attributive function modifying a noun. However, *concord with a nearby noun* gives away this exception pretty easily in context.

- **Predicative function:** sometimes an anarthrous participle will have predicative function as the predicate adjective complement to a copulative verb. Again, though, *the presence of εἰμί or γίνομαι* gives away this exception pretty easily in context.

The adverbial participle has a second dictum:

◆ *Adverbial participles often require dependent clauses in translation.*

This means an adverbial participle draws its existence from the main verb and is essentially tied to the main verb. Loosed from the main verb, an adverbial participle looses both its time frame and its reason for existing. *You cannot translate an adverbial participle without identifying the main verb.*

One exception regarding an adverbial participle's relationship to the main verb applies, called the genitive absolute. This idiomatic construction will be analyzed later. The point being made at this time is that, grammatically:

◆ *The genitive absolute, though adverbial in nature, is independent of the main verb.*

We will clarify this genitive absolute exception after presenting adverbial participle examples. We have divided our examples on the basis of the nine categories of use.

Adverbial Junctions

Temporal

Analysis

Participles do not express time. Their tense communicates action kind only. The temporal adverbial participle is indicating only *relative time* in relation to the main verb's action. Relative time is simply sequence, expressed as before, during, or after—or, *antecedent*, *simultaneous*, and *subsequent* time. Although participles as verbals technically do not express action time, we still can give two translation tips about participle tense and *relative* adverbial temporal sequence:

- *Temporal aorist participles normally are understood as antecedent to the main verb.*

- *Temporal present participles normally are understood as simultaneous to the main verb.*

What about the third sequence, subsequent time? In truth, subsequent time participles are rare for our purposes, since this use mainly is tied to future participles, and future participles are rare in the New Testament. Sometimes a present participle has been argued as expressing subsequent time, but again, this circumstance would be quite rare and atypical.

The temporal translation technique is to set up temporal dependent clauses expressing the participle's action. Antecedent clauses (aorist) would begin with "when" or "after." Simultaneous clauses (present) would begin with "while" or "as."

Examples

προσῆλθον αὐτῷ διδάσκοντι
"they came to him *while he was teaching*" (Mt. 21:23)

Observe the following in the example above:

(1) <u>Participle construction</u>: The participle is anarthrous, so is taken as adverbial (most are, so good starting point).

(2) <u>Adverbial function</u>: The translator has decided that a temporal function is intended. Someone could argue another adverbial function was intended, such as causal ("because he was teaching"). Knowledge of the author's style and thought, contextual indications, and general sense of the narrative are the main considerations to weigh. Since a majority of adverbial participles are temporal, numbers are on your side to go with a temporal translation. In fact, *one short cut to dealing with any adverbial participle is to try a temporal translation first*. Then, if temporal does not work, try other adverbial options. Regularly, a temporal idea will work. As the above analysis indicates, understand that:

◆ *Decisions of adverbial participle function are the responsibility of the translator.*

(3) <u>Relative time</u>: The main verb is aorist, so past time. The temporal participle draws its *relative* time from this *past tense* main verb. Thus, the participle, though present tense, is made to reflect the main verb's past time in its own sequence: "was teaching" (that is, not "is teaching"). Noting that this participle is *present* tense, the translator has construed the *relative* time as *simultaneous* to the past tense main verb.

(4) <u>Concord</u>: Grammatical concord reveals the participle's surrogate subject, "he." The participle is dative singular; the participle, then, is constructed to express concord with the dative singular pronoun αὐτῷ to show that this pronoun is the surrogate subject of the participle. Had the subject of the main verb ("they") been surrogate subject of the participle, then the participle would have been inflected as nominative, showing relationship to the main verb subject, and masculine plural, showing concord with the subject's gender (from the context)

and number (from the verb). Had the participle's surrogate subject been the "they" of the main verb, its inflection would have taken a nominative masculine plural form, διδάσκοντες, and the translation changed to "they came to him while *they* were teaching." Thus, we have this dictum:

♦ *Concord is crucial to construing the surrogate subject of an adverbial participle.*

As another temporal participle example:

Καὶ τοῦτο εἰπὼν πάλιν ἐξῆλθεν πρὸς τοὺς Ἰουδαίους
"And *after he had said this*, he went out again to the Jews"
(Jn. 18:38)

Observe the following in the example above:

(1) <u>Participle construction</u>: The participle is anarthrous, so is taken as adverbial (most are, so good starting point).

(2) <u>Adverbial function</u>: The translator has decided that, out of the nine possibilities for adverbial participle use, a temporal function is intended here. Here is a translation tip: *Assume an anarthrous participle is adverbial, then assume the adverbial function is temporal (because many are)*. If temporal does not work, then try other adverbial possibilities. So, first try:

anarthrous → adverbial → temporal

(3) <u>Relative time</u>: The main verb is aorist, so past time. The temporal participle draws its *relative* time from this *past tense* main verb. Thus, the participle, though aorist tense, is made to reflect the main verb's past time in its own sequence: "*had said*" (not "said"). For this aorist participle, *relative* time is construed as *antecedent* (pluperfect) to the main verb (past).

(4) <u>Concord</u>: Grammatical concord reveals the participle's surrogate subject, "he." The nominative singular participle ex-

presses concord with the *subject* of the main verb to show that main verb's subject is the participle's surrogate subject.

Purpose

Analysis

Purpose can be expressed any number of ways as dependent clauses that begin variously: "so that," "in order to," "for the purpose of," or even as an infinitive "to __." If the meaning is result more than purpose, one could use "with the result that."

Example

τοῦτο δὲ ἔλεγεν <u>πειράζων</u> αὐτόν.
"Now he was saying this *in order to test* him." (Jn. 6:6)

The participle is anarthrous, so taken as adverbial, and is nominative masculine singular, so its implied surrogate subject is the subject of the main verb.

Cause

Analysis

Cause often is expressed with dependent clauses that begin with "because," "for," or "since." This form creates a dependent clause structure in English.

Example

καὶ ὁ χιλίαρχος δὲ ἐφοβήθη <u>ἐπιγνοὺς</u> ὅτι Ῥωμαῖός ἐστιν
"And the tribune also was afraid *because he realized* that he [Paul] was a Roman citizen." (Acts 22:29)

The participle is anarthrous, so taken as adverbial, and nominative masculine singular, so its implied surrogate subject is the subject of the main verb. The reason for a tribune to be afraid is given, simply because such fear would be completely out of character and highly unexpected from a professional Roman soldier of this rank without extraordinary circumstances.

Condition

Analysis

Condition is expressed with dependent clauses that begin with "if." This format creates a conditional sentence in English.

Example

<u>ταῦτα</u> γὰρ <u>ποιοῦντες</u> οὐ μὴ πταίσητέ ποτε.
"For *if you do these things*, you will never stumble."
(2 Pet. 1:10)

The participle is anarthrous, so taken as adverbial, and nominative masculine plural, so its implied surrogate subject is the subject of the main verb. One might argue that this use is means: "by doing this." Contingency in the context of 2 Peter's audience and the nature of the actual exhortations seem to point more to a conditional nuance to the participle.

Concession

Analysis

The participle gives expression to a condition or a circumstance that has in the past, or continues in the present, to prevent the action of the main verb from being realized or is in contradistinction to the main verb's thought. The participle is converted into a dependent clause beginning with "though," "although," "even though," or "whereas."

Example

<u>βλέποντες</u> οὐ βλέπουσιν
"*even though seeing*, they do not see" (Mt. 13:13)

Means

Analysis

The participle gives expression to the agency or instrumentality that facilitates the main verb's action. The participle becomes a dependent clause set up by instrumental prepositions such as "by," "with," or "through."

Example

ὃν καὶ ἀνεῖλαν <u>κρεμάσαντες ἐπὶ ξύλου</u>.
"Whom also they killed *by hanging him on a tree*." (Acts 10:39)

Manner

Analysis

The participle gives expression to action associated with, *but not essential to*, the main verb's action in terms of the context surrounding the action. Often, the context involves expressions of emotion. The participle typically can be translated with a simple "-ing" form. Another style makes use of the preposition "with."

Example

ἐπορεύετο γὰρ τὴν ὁδὸν αὐτοῦ <u>χαίρων</u>.
"He went on his way *rejoicing*." (Acts 8:39)

Complementary

Analysis

The participle gives expression to action *essential to completing the thought* of the main verb's action. This function is similar to that of the complementary infinitive. Verbs that commonly require a complement include those of appearing, beginning, being, ceasing, continuing, and showing. The participle typically can be translated with a simple "-ing" form.

Example

οὐ παύομαι εὐχαριστῶν ὑπὲρ ὑμῶν.
"I do not cease *giving thanks* for you." (Eph. 1:16)

Circumstantial

Analysis

The participle gives expression to additional action only incidentally related to the main verb's action. Such a participle typically is converted into an indicative verb coordinated with, and reflecting the mood of, the main verb, joined by the conjunction "and." On some occasions, this participle precedes an imperative command main verb.

One common idiom in the New Testament creating a circumstantial participle is the narrative style of the Synoptic Gospels, "he answered *and said*," which perhaps reflects a common Semitic verbal pattern. The Semitic pattern uses two verbs of saying when just one will do, making the second verb redundant. This two-verb pattern is not the way English reports direct speech, always preferring just one verb of saying. Greek would agree, and handled this Semitic idiom with a circumstantial participle that implied the redundancy of the second verb of saying: ἀπεκρίθη λέγων, "he answered *and said*." Other types of circumstantial participles are given below.

Examples

ταχὺ πορευθεῖσαι εἴπατε τοῖς μαθηταῖς αὐτοῦ
"*Go quickly and* tell his disciples." (Mt. 28:20)

καὶ πάλιν ἀπελθὼν προσηύξατο.
"And again *he went away and* prayed." (Mk. 14:39)

Idiomatic Constructions

Periphrastic

Analysis

A periphrastic construction uses two different verb forms, combining εἰμί and a participle, to create one verbal idea.[1] An indicative verb could do the same more simply. This style was a koine habit, perhaps with emphasis on durative action, but certainly a redundant overemphasis for effect.

In three of the four types of periphrastic constructions, the tense is given by the εἰμί form. Present, imperfect, and future periphrastic tenses are created by respective indicative forms of εἰμί, each with a present participle. A fourth type, the perfect periphrastic, reverses this pattern by getting its tense from the perfect participle with the present indicative of εἰμί.

The participle could be analyzed as a predicate adjective or even as a complementary participle for certain forms of εἰμί. Either way, the translation is simple: just run the two verbs together like you meet them in the text, the indicative form of εἰμί first, followed by the participle in an "-ing" form.

Examples

<u>ἐστὶν καρποφορούμενον</u>
"*it has been bearing fruit*" (Col. 1:6)

<u>ἦν προσδεχόμενος</u> τὴν βασιλείαν τοῦ θεοῦ.
"*He was waiting for* the kingdom of God." (Mk. 15:43)

<u>ἔσεσθε</u> γὰρ εἰς ἀέρα <u>λαλοῦντες</u>.
"For *you will be speaking* into the air." (1 Cor. 14:9)

χάριτι <u>ἐστε σεσῳσμένοι</u>
"by grace *you have been saved*." (Eph. 2:5)

---

[1] Similar to the use of auxiliary verbs in English.

Genitive Absolute

Analysis

The genitive absolute, as the name indicates, is a genitive case participle—thus easy to spot—but without *grammatical* connection to the rest of the sentence. The participle has adverbial force but grammatically is independent (not related directly to the main verb). A key indicator of this grammatical disconnect is the genitive case itself. A genitive noun nearby is constructed with this genitive participle having a surrogate subject relationship. The absolute nature of the grammar is clear, since genitive is not the typical case for subject.

Table 26.2—Genitive Absolute Construction

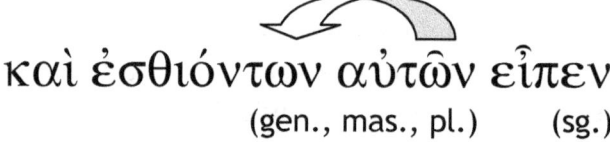

καὶ ἐσθιόντων αὐτῶν εἶπεν
   (gen., mas., pl.)   (sg.)

"and *while they were eating*, he said:"

The genitive structure, as genitive, cannot show relationship to the main verb's subject, which would require the *nominative* case. Thus, the genitive absolute participle is independent of the main verb, even though the participle contributes some verbal action that can be associated with the main verb, usually temporal. The genitive absolute might be mistaken as a special case of the circumstantial participle, but note that the subject changes (a circumstantial subject does not).

In sum: the genitive absolute participle will be anarthrous, genitive, adverbial, usually temporal, and independent of the main verb. Regularly, but not always, the genitive absolute is positioned *before* the main verb.

Chapter 26: Adverbial Participles

Examples

ἀναβάντων αὐτῶν εἰς τὸ πλοῖον ἐκόπασεν ὁ ἄνεμος.
"*After they got into the boat*, the wind stopped." (Mt. 14:32)

ἐξελθόντων αὐτῶν ἀπὸ Βηθανίας ἐπείνασεν.
"*when they came from Bethany*, he grew hungry." (Mk. 11:12)

Diagramming

Diagramming adverbial participles follows the adverbial pattern going under the main verb.[2] A standard may be required to accommodate the participle's own objects and modifiers. Both complementary and periphrastic participles, as essential to the verb action, are put behind the main verb on the same line, but using a standard if having their own clause elements. A genitive absolute, as independent grammatically, is placed in brackets separated from the independent clause.

Participle as Purpose

τοῦτο δὲ ἔλεγεν πειράζων αὐτόν.
"Now he was saying this *in order to test* him." (Mt. 21:23)

---

[2] Expressing temporal, purpose, cause, condition, concession, means, and manner functions related to the verb. English translation often will have a subordinate conjunction with its clause. Review the diagramming discussion, pp. 506–8.

Participle as Complementary

οὐ παύομαι εὐχαριστῶν ὑπὲρ ὑμῶν.
"I do not cease *giving thanks* for you." (Eph. 1:16)

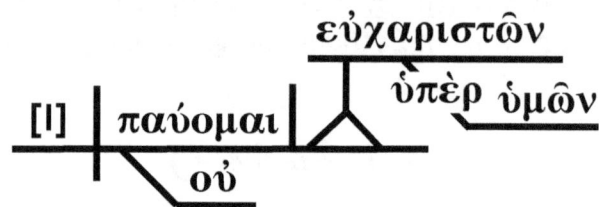

Exercise 26

1. Identify the following adverbial descriptions:

   1.1 _____ = giving a reason for the main verb's action

   1.2 _____ = giving a past or present condition that has had, or still has, an effect on the main verb's action

   1.3 _____ = giving additional action incidental to the main verb's action

   1.4 _____ = giving a time sequence related to the main verb's action

   1.5 _____ = giving a contingency to the main verb's action

   1.6 _____ = giving the affective emotions or actions that accompany the main verb's action (but not essential to)

   1.7 _____ = giving the instrumentality through which the main verb's action is accomplished

Chapter 26: Adverbial Participles   419

1.8 _____ = giving purpose for the main verb's action

1.9 _____ = giving action *essential* to completing the main verb's action

2. Identify the kind of adverbial participle represented in the italicized words in each of the following translations from the New Testament:

2.1 _____ = "I give thanks to my God . . . *because I hear of your love and your faith*." (Phile. 4, 5)

2.2 _____ = "Therefore, *after they had rowed about twenty five or thirty stadia*, they saw Jesus." (Jn. 6:19)

2.3 _____ = "And *if he has committed sins*, they will be forgiven him." (Jms. 5:15)

2.4 _____ = "For *although they knew God*, not as God did they glorify him nor give thanks." (Rom. 1:21)

2.5 _____ = "When he heard this, he was shocked and went away *grieving*, for he had many possessions." (Mk. 10:22)

2.6 _____ = "They did not stop *teaching and proclaiming that Jesus was Messiah*." (Acts 5:42)

2.7 _____ = "And he came *to look for fruit on it*." (Lk. 13:6)

2.8 _____ = "And that one answered *and said* . . . " (Jn. 9:36)

2.9 _____ = "And can any of you *by worrying* add a single hour to your span of life? (Mt. 6:27)

2.10 _____ = "When Jesus had come down from the mountain, great crowds followed him." (Mt. 8:1)

3. Translate. Be ready to identify main verbs, locate participles, and explain their adverbial use.

   3.1 ὀφθαλμοὺς ἔχοντες οὐ βλέπετε; (Mk. 8:18)

   3.2 Ὡς (when) δὲ ἐπαύσατο (παύω) λαλῶν εἶπε· (Lk. 5:4)

   3.3 καὶ τοῦτο πεποιθὼς (πείθω) οἶδα ὅτι μενῶ (don't slip: liquid verb!) (Phil. 1:25)

   3.4 ἴδωμεν (let us see) εἰ ἔρχεται Ἠλίας σώσων αὐτόν. (Mt. 27:49)

   3.5 πάντα ὅσα ἂν αἰτήσητε ἐν τῇ προσευχῇ πιστεύοντες λήμψεσθε (λαμβάνω). (Mt. 21:22)

Chapter 26: Adverbial Participles

3.6 Ἣν ἐνήργησεν (ἐνεργέω, transitive) ἐν τῷ Χριστῷ ἐγείρας αὐτὸν ἐκ νεκρῶν. (Eph. 1:20)

3.7 πορευθέντες ἀπαγγείλατε (ἀπαγγέλλω, aor. imper.) Ἰωάννῃ ἃ ἀκούετε καὶ βλέπετε. (Mt. 11:4)

3.8 ἀκούσας δὲ ὁ νεανίσκος τὸν λόγον ἀπῆλθεν λυπούμενος· (λυπέω) ἦν γὰρ ἔχων κτήματα πολλά. (Mt. 19:22)

3.9 Καὶ ἐλθόντος αὐτοῦ εἰς τὸ ἱερὸν προσῆλθον αὐτῷ διδάσκοντι οἱ ἀρχιερεῖς καὶ οἱ πρεσβύτεροι τοῦ λαοῦ λέγοντες· ἐν ποίᾳ ἐξουσίᾳ ταῦτα ποιεῖς; (Mt. 21:23)

4. Diagram the following from the exercises above:

    4.1 ὀφθαλμοὺς ἔχοντες οὐ βλέπετε;

    4.2 Ὡς δὲ ἐπαύσατο λαλῶν εἶπε·

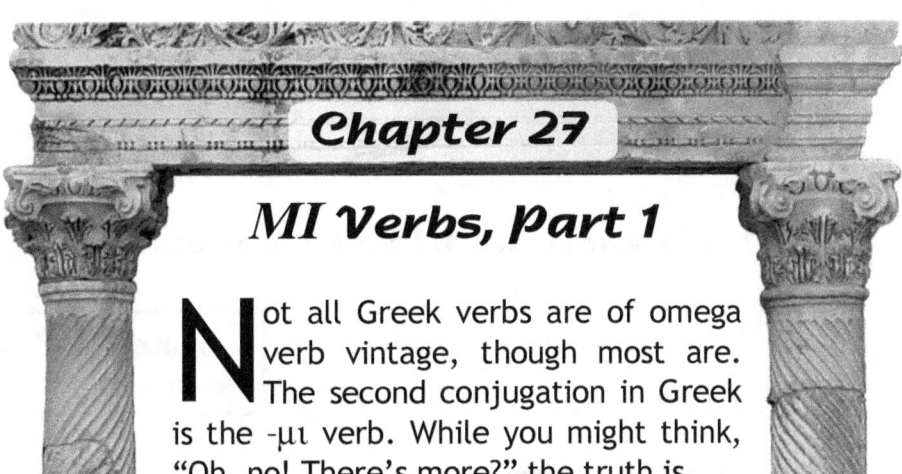

Chapter 27

MI Verbs, Part 1

Not all Greek verbs are of omega verb vintage, though most are. The second conjugation in Greek is the -μι verb. While you might think, "Oh, no! There's more?" the truth is, forms are different only in the first principal part (present, imperfect tenses). All other principal parts have omega verb formation patterns. Once the -μι verb stem is recognized, location falls right into place. In fact, a few little "tricks" of recognition along the way will make short work of locating many -μι verbs. Do not fear. Saving the -μι verb system till now is not dumping on you at the last moment.

New vocabulary is introduced in this chapter, focused on -μι verbs occurring frequently in the New Testament. You already know some -μι verbs. The most frequent is εἰμί, which occurs about 2,462 times! We gave κάθημαι in Vocabulary 3, and the only three New Testament forms of φημί in Vocabulary 18. We gave δύναμαι in the chapter on infinitives, since that verb often requires an infinitive to finish off its verbal expression. So, what do we need to know about these -μι verbs?

First Principal Part

We return to our analysis of the six component parts of any Greek verb. You will notice similarity to the formation of the omega verb perfect tense due to a reduplication process for -μι verbs in the first principal part. In fact, this reduplication feature is what often makes -μι verb location a cinch.

Present Tense

Indicative Mood

Table 27.1—Present Active MI Verb Morphology

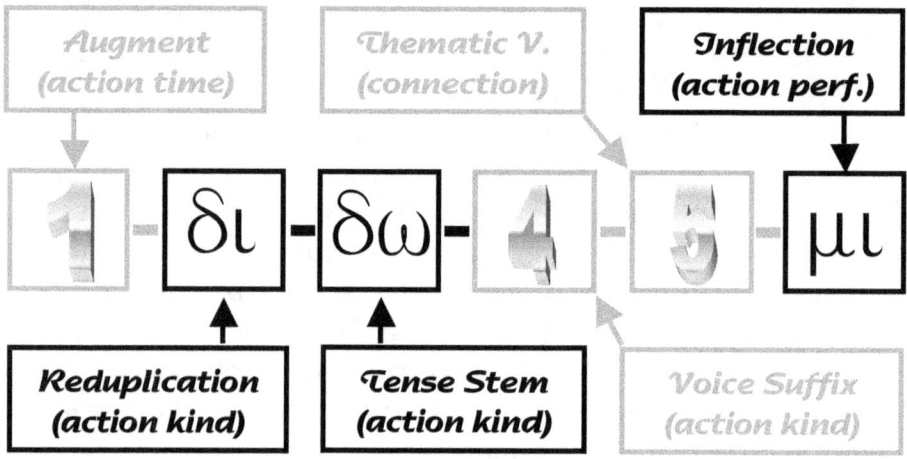

Formation notes:

(1) **Reduplication**—about half of all -μι verbs reduplicate in the first principal part. Some of the most common -μι verbs in the New Testament reduplicate, as does our paradigm verb, δίδωμι. The difference from perfect reduplication is in the vowel: ι instead of ε. This first principal part reduplication means that *four out of six -μι verb tenses have reduplicated stems* for many common -μι verbs (i.e., present, imperfect, perfect, pluperfect). Thus, we have a really nice short cut to a great bulk of -μι verb locations:

♦ *Non-reduplicated -μι verb stems are either aorist or future.*

One quick observation about reduplication and you have narrowed -μι verb tenses down to just two possibilities for location—but wait! There's more! If you order in the next half hour:

- Any ι vowel -μι verb reduplication can be only present or imperfect tense.

- Any ε vowel -μι verb reduplication can be only perfect or pluperfect tense.

You can't beat that with a stick! Order today! ☺

(2) **Lengthening**—the stem vowel is lengthened in three present tense forms (active singular) and in three imperfect forms (active singular). This active singular lengthening is a little tricky, simply because the vocabulary word you memorize is active singular. Thus, the vocabulary form hides the short vowel in the stem you will see in most -μι conjugations. Practically, you may have to remember a -μι verb stem in up to three vowel forms: a short vowel, long vowel present, and alternate long vowel (diphthong) imperfect, as δίδωμι:

$$-\delta o\text{-}, \quad -\delta \omega\text{-}, \quad -\delta o \upsilon\text{-}$$

(3) **Non-thematic**—the -μι verb does not use a theme vowel, which gives the conjugation its other name: non-thematic (or "athematic"). Three exceptions are: (1) future tense, (2) subjunctive mood, and (3) one imperative form (pres., act., 2d, sg.). This formation pattern is similar to the fifth principal part of the omega verb (perfect middle). Good news, though: the non-thematic -μι verb does not involve the consonant reactions that are generated in the fifth principal part formation of the omega verb. ☺

(4) **Distinct endings**—in a *few* forms of the primary *active* the -μι verb has a distinct set of endings: -μι, -σι, -ασι (bold in

the table below) The primary middle forms are exactly like the omega verb.

Table 27.2—Primary MI Endings

Active	Middle
-μι	-μαι
-ς	-σαι
-σι	-ται
-μεν	-μεθα
-τε	-σθε
-ασι	-νται

Non-indicative Moods

Subjunctive

Subjunctive mood, *by definition*, must have a long thematic vowel as its mood sign. Contraction of subjunctive endings with stem vowels all wind up with either an -ῶ- vowel stem, almost always circumflex, or an -ῆ- vowel stem, also almost always circumflex. Easy to spot![1]

Imperative

Imperative mood, *by definition*, takes imperative endings. Thus, you already know these forms from the omega verb.

Optative

Only three conjugated forms of the present optative -μι verb show up in the New Testament: εἴη (3d sg.), from εἰμί, and δυναίμην (1st sg.) and δύναιντο (3d pl.), from the verb δύναμαι.

---

[1]Sometimes an alternate diphthong form is encountered in a few second and third singular forms, -οῖ-, but this too has circumflex accent.

Imperfect Tense

Table 27.3—Imperfect Active MI Verb Morphology

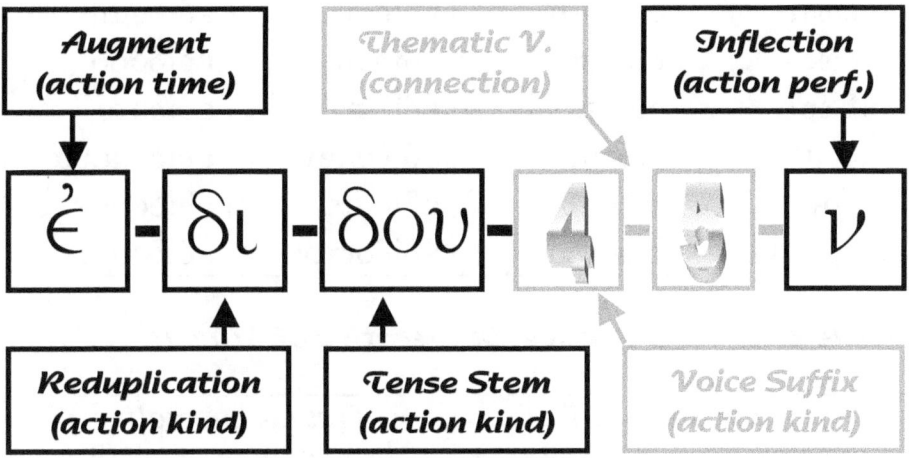

Formation notes:

(1) **Stem**—imperfect stem is built on the present stem exactly as expected in the first principal part. Note active singular long stem vowel variations (present: ω; imperfect: ου).

(2) **Reduplication**—uses the standard iota reduplication of the present tense, again, according to the first principal part.

(3) **Augment**—is used for indicating past time, as usual. You already know consonant and vowel augmentation patterns.

(4) **Non-thematic**—as with present tense.

(5) **Secondary endings**—uses the same secondary endings of the omega verb. Third plural often takes the -σαν option.

Paradigms

Paradigms only need show indicative, subjunctive, and imperative forms. Imperfect, of course, is only indicative.

Table 27.4—Present, Imperfect of Δίδωμι

Present Indicative		Imperfect Indicative	
Active	M/P	Active	M/P
δίδωμι	δίδομαι	ἐδίδουν	ἐδιδόμην
δίδως	δίδοσαι	ἐδίδους	ἐδίδοσο
δίδωσιν	δίδοται	ἐδίδου	ἐδίδοτο
δίδομεν	διδόμεθα	ἐδίδομεν	ἐδιδόμεθα
δίδοτε	δίδοσθε	ἐδίδοτε	ἐδίδοσθε
διδόασιν	δίδονται	ἐδίδοσαν	ἐδίδοντο

Table 27.5—Subjunctive, Imperative of Δίδωμι

Present Subjunctive		Present Imperative	
Active	M/P	Active	M/P
διδῶ	διδῶμαι	-------	-------
διδῷς	διδῷ	δίδου	δίδοσο
διδῷ	διδῷται	διδότω	διδόσθω
διδῶμεν	διδώμεθα	-------	-------
διδῶτε	διδῶσθε	δίδοτε	δίδοσθε
διδῶσιν	διδῶνται	διδότωσαν	διδόσθωσαν

Exercise 27

1. Identify the following -μι verb components:

    1.1

    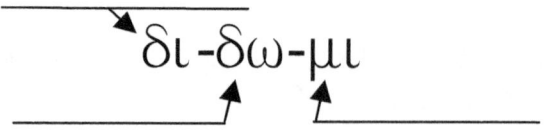

1.2

2. Locate the following forms of the verb δίδωμι.

   2.1 δίδοσαι = _____ _____ _____ _____ _____
   Tense   Voice   Mood   Per/N   Translation

   2.2 διδόασι = _____ _____ _____ _____ _____
   Tense   Voice   Mood   Per/N   Translation

   2.3 ἐδίδους = _____ _____ _____ _____ _____
   Tense   Voice   Mood   Per/N   Translation

   2.4 διδῷται = _____ _____ _____ _____ _____
   Tense   Voice   Mood   Per/N   Translation

   2.5 διδότωσαν = _____ _____ _____ _____ _____
   Tense   Voice   Mood   Per/N   Translation

   2.6 ἐδιδόμην = _____ _____ _____ _____ _____
   Tense   Voice   Mood   Per/N   Translation

   2.7 δίδομεν = _____ _____ _____ _____ _____
   Tense   Voice   Mood   Per/N   Translation

   2.8 διδῶμεν = _____ _____ _____ _____ _____
   Tense   Voice   Mood   Per/N   Translation

   2.9 ἐδίδου = _____ _____ _____ _____ _____
   Tense   Voice   Mood   Per/N   Translation

   2.10 δίδου = _____ _____ _____ _____ _____
   Tense   Voice   Mood   Per/N   Translation

2.11 ἐδίδοντο = _____ _____ _____ _____ _____
                       Tense Voice Mood Per/N Translation

3. Translate. Be ready to locate verbs.

    3.1 νόμον ἱστάνομεν. (Rom. 3:31)

    3.2 παντὶ αἰτοῦντί σε δίδου (Lk. 6:30)

    3.3 ὑπὸ τῶν ὄφεων ἀπώλλυντο. (1 Cor. 10:9)

    3.4 ὁ φιλῶν τὴν ψυχὴν αὐτοῦ ἀπολλύει αὐτήν. (Jn. 12:25)

    3.5 ἐδίδου τοῖς μαθηταῖς, οἱ δὲ μαθηταὶ τοῖς ὄχλοις. (Mt. 15:36)

    3.6 τὴν δύναμιν καὶ ἐξουσίαν αὐτῶν τῷ θηρίῳ διδόασιν. (Rev. 17:13)

3.7 ὁ ποιμὴν ὁ καλὸς τὴν ψυχὴν αὐτοῦ τίθησιν ὑπὲρ τῶν προβάτων. (Jn. 10:11)

_____

_____

3.8 εἰρήνην τὴν ἐμὴν δίδωμι ὑμῖν· οὐ καθὼς ὁ κόσμος δίδωσιν ἐγὼ δίδωμι ὑμῖν. (Jn. 14:27)

_____

_____

 *Vocabulary 27*

ἀπόλλυμι, act.: *I destroy*; mid.: *I perish*

δίδωμι, *I give, grant, allow*

ἵστημι, trans.: *I place, set, cause to stand*; intrans.: *I stand*

τίθημι, *I put, place, lay*

Vocabulary notes:

(1) Notice that ἀπόλλυμι does not reduplicate in the first principal part. All other parts have just one lambda. The omicron is not part of the compound, but rather, the tense stem; therefore, augmentation and reduplication creates an omega. The principal parts are: ἀπόλλυμι, ἀπολέσω (or: ἀπολῶ), ἀπώλεσα, ἀπώλεκα (or: ἀπόλωλα), ἀπολώλεσμαι, and ἀπωλέσθην.

(2) Some verbs occur in *both* the omega verb and -μι verb conjugations. The verb ἀπόλλυμι, for example, also is found as ἀπολλύω. This dual conjugation existence for a few verbs

shows how the New Testament period is a time of transition in Koine Greek. The use of -μι verbs eventually will fall out almost completely.

(2) The verb τίθημι has a stem in -θε-. The subjunctive is either -θῶ- or -θῆ-.

(3) The verb ἵστημι has a stem in -στα-. The subjunctive is either -στῶ- or -στῆ-. The reduplication needs explanation. The reduplicated form would have been στα- → σιστα-. The opening combination σισ-, however, was not acceptable phonetically, so the reduplicated sigma was dropped, and rough breathing substituted in its place. *The rough breathing is the reduplication.* Notice that even in this process *the reduplication vowel iota survives*, continuing to allow identification of the principal part. The perfect would be ἕστηκα. Again, note the rough breathing.

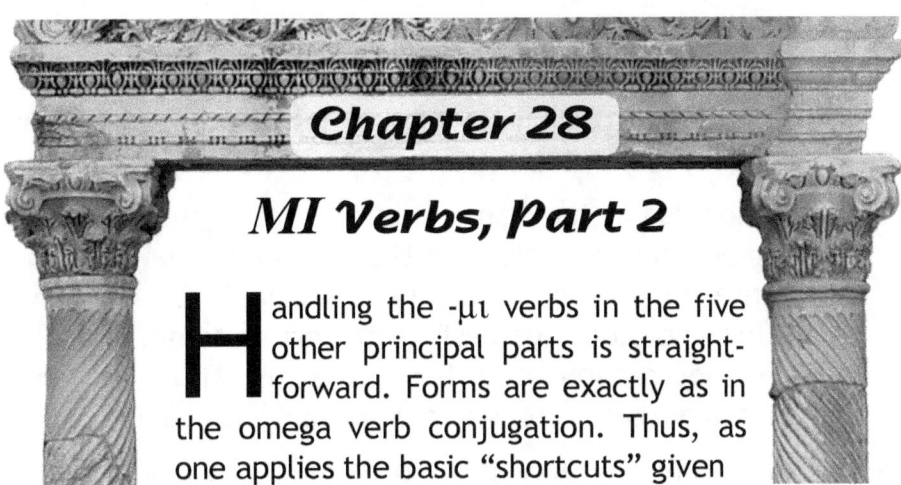

Chapter 28

MI Verbs, Part 2

Handling the -μι verbs in the five other principal parts is straightforward. Forms are exactly as in the omega verb conjugation. Thus, as one applies the basic "shortcuts" given in the previous chapter, location is quick and easy. However, you *do* have to know your principal parts! You just cannot get around that.

Patterns

Here are the basic patterns and a few other notes:

(1) **Reduplication**—that the first principal part -μι verb reduplicates means that *four out of six -μι verb tenses have reduplicated stems* (present, imperfect, perfect, pluperfect) for well-known -μι verbs. Thus, we have these shortcuts:

- Any ι vowel -μι verb reduplication can be only present or imperfect tense.

- Any ε vowel -μι verb reduplication can be only perfect or pluperfect tense.

- Non-reduplicated -μι verb stems are either aorist or future.

433

(2) **Stems**—as we saw in the previous chapter, the verb stem vowel can vary from long to short. Thus, -δω- in some forms will be -δο-; -θη- will be -θε-; -στη- will be -στα-.

(3) **Kappa aorists**—As the name implies, these -μι verbs use a *kappa alpha* pattern instead of sigma alpha for the *aorist active* tense suffix (-κα, -κας, -κεν, -καμεν, -κατε, -καν). Is this form not confused easily with perfect tense? No. Why? *Aorist is not reduplicated,* but perfect is. Three -μι verbs are "kappa aorists": δίδωμι, τίθημι, and ἵημι compounds.

(4) **Moods**—technically, any -μι verb could be any mood. Practically, -μι verbs are a minority, and moods outside of present and aorist tenses are rare. Thus:

♦ *Only present and aorist tense -mi verbs regularly show moods other than the indicative.*

Aorist subjunctive forms *may* include a sigma suffix. These forms are *not* future subjunctive, because, remember:

♦ *There is no future subjunctive!*

(5) **Infinitives**—active forms will be either -ναι or -σαι. The middle/passive is -σθαι.

(6) **Participles**—participles follow principal parts. Aorist has no augment. Nominative, masculine, singular, and dative, masculine, plural react to create resultant forms due to their third declension noun pattern. Review the participle suffix patterns given in the section called "Participle Morphology Hints," p. 389.

One odd pattern is for τίθημι as aorist passive participle. The stem is θε and is not augmented. Coincidentally, the passive suffix also is θε. Greeks, however, did not like the resultant θεθε sound, so changed the stem theta to a tau: τεθείς, τεθέν, τεθεῖσα. This is *not* perfect, because the suffix has a *theta*, not a kappa. Know your principal parts!

Paradigms

Indicative forms comprise the majority of what is seen in the New Testament. We show subjunctive and imperative forms for aorist only. Optative is rare.

Table 28.1—Future Indicative of Δίδωμι

Future Indicative		
Active	Middle	Passive
δώσω	δώσομαι	δοθήσομαι
δώσεις	δώσῃ	δοθήσῃ
δώσει	δώσεται	δοθήσεται
δώσομεν	δωσόμεθα	δοθησόμεθα
δώσετε	δώσεσθε	δοθήσεσθε
δώσουσιν	δώσονται	δοθήσονται

Table 28.2—Aorist Indicative of Δίδωμι

Aorist Indicative		
Active	Middle	Passive
ἔδωκα	ἐδόμην	ἐδόθην
ἔδωκας	ἔδου	ἐδόθης
ἔδωκεν	ἔδοτο	ἐδόθη
ἐδώκαμεν	ἐδόμεθα	ἐδόθημεν
ἐδώκατε	ἔδοσθε	ἐδόθητε
ἔδωκαν	ἔδοντο	ἐδόθησαν

Table 28.3—Aorist Subjunctive of Δίδωμι

Aorist Subjunctive		
Active	Middle	Passive
δῶ (δώσω)	δῶμαι	δοθῶ
δῷς (δώσῃς)	δῷ	δοθῇς
δῷ (δώσῃ)	δῶται	δοθῇ
δῶμεν (-σωμεν)	δώμεθα	δοθῶμεν
δῶτε (δώσητε)	δῶσθε	δοθῆτε
δῶσιν (-σωσι)	δῶνται	δοθῶσι

Table 28.4—Aorist Imperative of Δίδωμι

Aorist Imperative		
Active	Middle	Passive
-------	-------	-------
δός	δοῦ	δόθητι
δότω	δόσθω	δοθήτω
-------	-------	-------
δότε	δόσθε	δόθητε
δότωσαν	δόσθωσαν	δοθήτωσαν

Table 28.5—Perfect Indicative of Δίδωμι

Perfect Indicative	
Active	Midd/Pass
δέδωκα	δέδομαι
δέδωκας	δέδοσαι
δέδωκεν	δέδοται
δεδώκαμεν	δεδόμεθα
δεδώκατε	δέδοσθε
δέδωκαν	δέδονται

Table 28.6—Present Active Participle of Δίδωμι

Masculine		Neuter	
Singular	Plural	Singular	Plural
διδούς	διδόντες	διδόν	διδόντα
διδόντος	διδόντων	διδόντος	διδόντων
διδόντι	διδοῦσιν	διδόντι	διδοῦσιν
διδόντα	διδόντας	διδόν	διδόντα

Feminine	
Singular	Plural
διδοῦσα	διδοῦσαι
διδούσης	διδουσῶν
διδούσῃ	διδούσαις
διδοῦσαν	διδούσας

Table 28.7—Synopsis of Other Participle Forms

		Synopsis	
	Masculine	Neuter	Feminine
Present: m/p	διδόμενος	διδόμενον	διδομένη
Aorist: act.	δούς	δόν	δοῦσα
mid.	δόμενος	δόμενον	δομένη
pas.	δοθείς	δοθέν	δοθεῖσα
Perfect: act.	δεδωκώς	δεδωκός	δεδωκυῖα
m/p	δεδομένος	δεδομένον	δεδομένη

 **Exercise 28**

1. Locate the following forms.

   1.1 ἀποδώσεις = _____ _____ _____ _____ _____
                                 Tense Voice Mood Per/N Translation

   1.2 ἀποδῷ = _____ _____ _____ _____ _____
                       Tense Voice Mood Per/N Translation

   1.3 ἀποδούς = _____ _____ _____ _____ _____ _____
                         Tense Voice Mood Case Gen. Num.

   1.4 ἀπέδωκεν = _____ _____ _____ _____ _____
                         Tense Voice Mood Per/N Translation

   1.5 ἀπέδοντο = _____ _____ _____ _____ _____
                       Tense Voice Mood Per/N Translation

   1.6 ἀποδιδότω = _____ _____ _____ _____ _____
                         Tense Voice Mood Per/N Translation

   1.7 παρεδόθη = _____ _____ _____ _____ _____
                     Tense Voice Mood Per/N Translation

   1.8 παραδῷ = _____ _____ _____ _____ _____
                   Tense Voice Mood Per/N Translation

   1.9 παραδοθήσεται = _____ _____ _____ _____
                           Tense Voice Mood Per/N

   1.10 παρέδωκας = _____ _____ _____ _____
                      Tense Voice Mood Per/N

   1.11 παρεδίδου = _____ _____ _____ _____
                      Tense Voice Mood Per/N

Chapter 28: MI Verbs, Part 2

1.12 ἀφέντες = ____ ____ ____ ____ ____ ____
                    Tense Voice Mood Case Gen. Num.

1.13 ἀφῆτε = ____ ____ ____ ____ _____
                 Tense Voice Mood Per/N Translation

1.14 ἀναστάς = ____ ____ ____ ____ ____ ____
                   Tense Voice Mood Case Gen. Num.

1.15 ἀναστήσονται = ____ ____ ____ ____
                        Tense Voice Mood Per/N

1.16 παρεστηκότων =

____ ____ ____ ____ ____ ____
Tense Voice Mood Case Gen. Num.

1.17 παρέστησαν = ____ ____ ____ ____
                      Tense Voice Mood Per/N

1.18 ἐπιθείς = ____ ____ ____ ____ ____ ____
                   Tense Voice Mood Case Gen. Num.

1.19 ἐπέθηκαν = ____ ____ ____ ____
                    Tense Voice Mood Per/N

1.20 ἐπιθῇς = ____ ____ ____ ____
                  Tense Voice Mood Per/N

1.21 ἐπιθήσεται = ____ ____ ____ ____
                      Tense Voice Mood Per/N

1.22 ἐπιτιθέασιν = ____ ____ ____ ____
                       Tense Voice Mood Per/N

2. Translate. Be ready to locate verbs.

   2.1 ἀποδώσει ἑκάστῳ κατὰ τὴν πρᾶξιν (πρᾶξις) αὐτοῦ. (Mt. 16:27)

   2.2 Πάντα μοι παρεδόθη ὑπὸ τοῦ πατρός μου. (Mt. 11:27)

   2.3 ἄφετε τὰ παιδία ἔρχεσθαι πρός με. (Mk. 10:14)

   2.4 λέγει αὐτῇ ὁ Ἰησοῦς· ἀναστήσεται ὁ ἀδελφός σου. (Jn. 11:23)

   2.5 ἵνα παραστήσωμεν πάντα ἄνθρωπον τέλειον (τέλειος) ἐν Χριστῷ. (Col. 1:28)

   2.6 τότε ἐπετίθεσαν τὰς χεῖρας ἐπ' αὐτοὺς καὶ ἐλάμβανον πνεῦμα ἅγιον. (Acts 8:17)

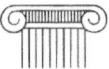 Vocabulary 28

ἀποδίδωμι, act.: *I give back, pay*; mid.: *I sell*

παραδίδωμι, *I hand over, betray*

ἀφίημι, *I permit, forgive*

ἀνίστημι, trans.: *I cause to arise*; intrans.: *I arise*

παρίστημι, trans.: *I present, offer*; intrans.: *I am present, stand by*

ἐπιτίθημι, *I lay upon*

Vocabulary notes:

(1) Notice that all these forms are compounds of the verbs introduced in the previous chapter.

(1) As this vocabulary illustrates, some -μι verbs have been used over time quite flexibly and have developed distinctions of meaning between voices or between their transitive and intransitive applications.

(3) The verb ἵημι in the New Testament occurs only in compound forms, such as ἀφίημι. As Elmer Fudd would say in hot pursuit of Bugs Bunny, this ἵημι is a "wascawy wabbit." This is a one letter verb stem! The stem is the letter epsilon, -ε. In the active singular, this vowel lengthens to -η. Reduplication is a consonant style with rough breathing, ἵη-. Then the ending is added: ἵημι. Compounds are put on the front, but these can react, as prepositions do, as in dropping final vowels, or stop consonants that change in front of the rough breathing due to reduplication: ἀπό + ἵημι → ἀπίημι → ἀφίημι.

Photo © Gerald L. Stevens

Fig. 21. The Temple of Apollo at Corinth. Corinth's Apollo temple was built around 540 B.C., so is one of the more ancient of Greek temples. The Doric peripteral style has more elongated proportions than usual.

The Apostle Paul would have viewed this temple constantly as he came and went along the streets of Corinth during his eighteen month stay. The temple lay east of the shops where he probably plied his trade, along with associates such as Aquila, and northeast of the bema to which Paul was dragged before the proconsul Gallio (Acts 18:1-12).

English Appendix

ΑΩ

English 1

Words

We present English grammar as a foundation for understanding Greek grammar. Our conceptual building blocks are threefold: words, word groups, and sentences. We begin with the concept of "words," even though this starting point has its own built-in problems for lingusts.[1]

Words are the basic units of communication. Words can be classified by function. Words have eight functions—or, job descriptions—what words "do" in a sentence. These job descriptions often are called *parts of speech*. The first four are called *primary* because they are the workhorses; the second four are called *secondary*; that is, they are primary helpers.

Table E1.1—The Eight Parts of Speech

Primary	Secondary
Noun	Pronoun
Verb	Preposition
Adjective	Conjunction
Adverb	Interjection

---

[1] Just as a study of physics will reveal more is involved in the study of elementary particles than the "electrons" and "protons" that comprise an "atom," more also is involved in the study of language than the "words" and "word groups" that comprise a "sentence." We recognize that some linguists find these language categories unsatisfactory. However, when time constraints and other factors hobble our efforts toward scholarship, pragmatics wins: categories such as "words," "word groups," and "sentences" remain useful, because they at least seem immediately familiar.

These eight job descriptions need to be analyzed. We first overview the primary parts of speech: that is, nouns, verbs, adjectives, and adverbs.

Primary Parts of Speech: Nouns, Verbs, Adjectives, Adverbs

Nouns

Nouns name. Name a person, place, or thing and you used a noun. You can name generally: man, residence, document. You can name specifically: Thomas Jefferson, Monticello, Declaration of Independence. *Common nouns* name generally. *Proper nouns* name specifically.[2] The technical word for this job description of naming is *substantive*. Words other than nouns can be used with this naming function; any word used as a noun is called a *substantive*. Such usage is called *substantival*. An adjective used as a noun, for example, is called a substantival adjective, that is, an adjective used substantivally.

Verbs

Verbs act. Describe an action and you used a verb. Verb action can be:
- *durative or imperfective* (on-going): "water *is running*"
- *undefined or perfective* (aoristic[3]): "water *ran*"
- *perfect or combinative* (completed): "water *has run*"

Undefined action is action viewed as a whole from beginning to end. Perfect is not perfective. (Linguists have a strange way of defining terms.) Instead, perfect is a hybrid of the other two.

---

[2]Proper nouns as proper names are capitalized.

[3]"Aorist" often is mispronounced "a-O-rist." In common usage, the first two vowels sound together like "AIR-rist," accenting the first syllable.

English 1: Words

Exercise E1.1

Identify the words in the list below using the following notation:

common noun = Nc   verb, durative = Vd
proper noun = Np   verb, perfect = Vp
                    verb, aoristic = Va

_____ president   _____ has gone
_____ George   _____ village
_____ woman   _____ Bethlehem
_____ Elizabeth   _____ king
_____ computer   _____ Herod
_____ Macintosh   _____ mother
_____ onion   _____ Mary
_____ Vidalia   _____ see
_____ hide   _____ saw
_____ hid   _____ has seen
_____ has hidden   _____ angel
_____ go   _____ Gabriel
_____ went

Adjectives

Adjectives modify nouns. Modify a noun, either by describing or limiting, and you used an adjective. In the phrase, " *tall* tree," the word "tall" is an adjective that describes further the noun "tree." In the phrase, "*that* tree," the word "that" is an adjective that limits the trees you are talking about to just one.

Adverbs

Adverbs modify verbs. Modify a verb, either directly or by asking a question, and you used an adverb. In the phrase "sings *well*," the word "well" is an adverb that directly modifies the verb "sings." (Note that many adverbs end with the suffix "-ly": gent*ly*, wonderful*ly*, bright*ly*.) In the question, "*how* does she sing?" the word "how" is an adverb that asks a question related to the verb.

 **Exercise E1.2**

Identify the words in the list below using the following notation:

    adjective = adj.
    adverb = adv.

____	red	____	diligently
____	beautiful	____	how?
____	small	____	beautifully
____	new	____	what?
____	old	____	when?
____	carefully	____	where?

Before moving to discuss the secondary parts of speech, we want to consolidate the results of the discussion on the primary parts of speech in the exercise below.

English 1: Words

 **Exercise E1.3**

Identify nouns, verbs, adjectives, and adverbs in the following sentences. Specify each verbal action as durative, undefined, or perfect.

1. *The wise farmer quickly cut the ripe corn.*
   (Note: The definite article "the" is a specialized use of the adjective.)

   Nouns: _____
   Verbs: _____
   Adjectives: _____
   Adverbs: _____

2. *How is John studying for that hard test?*
   (Note: The word "for" is a preposition, covered later.)

   Nouns: _____
   Verbs: _____
   Adjectives: _____
   Adverbs: _____

3. *The industrious student already dutifully had taken the long, final exam when he learned he had been exempted.*
   (Note: The word "he" is a pronoun, and "when" is a conjunctive adverb, both covered later.)

   Nouns: _____
   Verbs: _____

Adjectives: _____

Adverbs: _____

4. _____ is another term used with the same meaning as *durative*.
5. _____ is another term used with the same meaning as *undefined*.

Secondary Parts of Speech: Pronouns, Prepositions, Conjunctions, Interjections

We have covered the four primary parts of speech: nouns, verbs, adjectives, and adverbs. The other four parts of speech are *secondary*: pronouns, prepositions, conjunctions, and interjections. These enhance the work of primary parts of speech.

Pronouns

Pronouns substitute for nouns. Substitute "he" for "John" and you used a pronoun. The noun for which the pronoun substitutes technically is called the *antecedent*. English pronouns can be grouped into six major classes: (1) personal, (2) possessive, (3) relative, (4) interrogative, (5) demonstrative, and (6) indefinite.

Prepositions

Prepositions are a small set of words always used as part of a phrase that modifies a noun or verb (see the table below). The preposition always comes first in the phrase (thus, "pre-positioned"). A noun follows the preposition, technically functioning as the *object* of the preposition. Note the prepositional phrase "on the grass" begins with the preposition "on," with the object of the preposition being the noun "grass." These prepositional phrases are used as adjectives or adverbs to modify nouns or verbs. In the phrase, "the man *on the grass*," the prepositional phrase, "on the grass," is used as an adjective modifying the noun "man." In the clause, "the man walking *on the grass*," the prepositional phrase, "on the grass," is used as an adverb modifying the verb "walking."[4]

Table E1.2—Prepositions

aboard	behind	from among	since
about	below	from under	through
above	beneath	in	throughout
across	beside	into	to
after	between	of	under
against	beyond	off	underneath
along	by	on	unto
amid	down	out of	up
among	during	outside	upon
around	except	over	with
at	for	round	within
before	from	round about	

Conjunctions

Conjunctions connect. Connect two or more words (or word groups) and you used a conjunction. So, the phrase "John *and* Jane" uses the conjunction "and" to connect two proper nouns. The phrase "hear *but* do" uses the conjunction "but" to connect two verbs. *Coordinate conjunctions* connect items of equal grammatical rank (e.g., two nouns, both functioning as subject,

---

[4]Here, the entire phrase, "walking on the grass," is used as an adjective modifying the noun "man."

etc.). *Subordinate conjunctions* join clauses of unequal rank, as when connecting a dependent clause to an independent clause. (The matter of clauses will be discussed in the next chapter on "Word Groups.")

Table E1.3—Conjunctions

Coordinate		Subordinate	
and	moreover	as	that
but	then	as if	till
or	therefore	because	unless
nor	yet	before	when
for	still	if	where
however		since	whether

Interjections

Interjections insert feeling. Insert the feeling word "Oh!" and you used an interjection, as in "*Oh*, how I want to make a good grade!" Often, interjections are set off by punctuation with commas. They have no grammatical relationship to the rest of the sentence.

 **Exercise E1.4**

In the following:

circle the (pronouns)

underline the prepositional phrases,

double underline the conjunctions

and box the interjections.

If a sentence has more than one item in a category, number them sequentially for identification.

1. Man, did he ever run around the track with a surge of energy on that last lap!
2. The lady in the first chair on the last row with a smile on her face made an A on this exam.
3. Both Bill and Bob studied and learned the material, but, my, oh my, they did not perform on the test as well as you or I thought they would!
4. The boards left on the grass caused the blades under them to fade from green to brown, yet rain and bright sunlight will revive their color by the end of this week or the next.
5. Since Jean definitely is going, Janice and Taneean will decide today or tomorrow whether they will go with her.

Summary

Almost all word usage will fit into one or more of these eight *parts of speech*, or job descriptions: nouns, verbs, adjectives, adverbs, pronouns, prepositions, conjunctions, and interjections. Naturally, a miscellaneous category still is needed to pick up "particles" and other small tidbits here and there, like a physicist insisting on talking about quarks and gluons after describing the basic idea of an atom's electrons and protons. But with electrons and protons you still have a rudimentary idea of the nature of atoms and how they might combine to form molecules. In grammar, with the eight parts of speech, you have a rudimentary idea of the nature of words and how they might combine to form sentences. The eight parts of speech—know them!

English 2

Word Groups

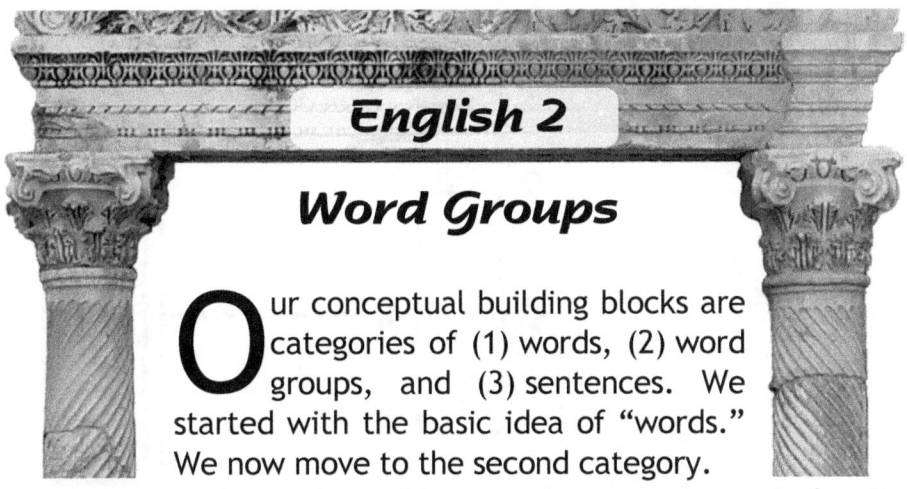

Our conceptual building blocks are categories of (1) words, (2) word groups, and (3) sentences. We started with the basic idea of "words." We now move to the second category. Word groups are words working together as grammatical units. Word groups have two types: phrases and clauses. The logic of phrase and clause operations in a sentence is given in the Table E2.1 on the next page. Refer to this table as we proceed.

Phrase

A *phrase* is a non-subject word group that fulfills a noun, adjective, or adverb job description. Phrases have two types: prepositions and verbals. A phrase may contain a verbal, but a verbal by definition does not have a subject. Thus, a phrase never has a subject. We first look at prepositional phrases.

Prepositional Phrases

In the previous chapter we defined prepositional phrases in discussing parts of speech (see discussion and Table E1.2). We noted that prepositions always work together with other words as part of a grammatical unit, which we called a "prepositional phrase." We can use prepositional phrases to illustrate noun, adjective, and adverb functions of phrases.

Table E2.1—Word Group Functions

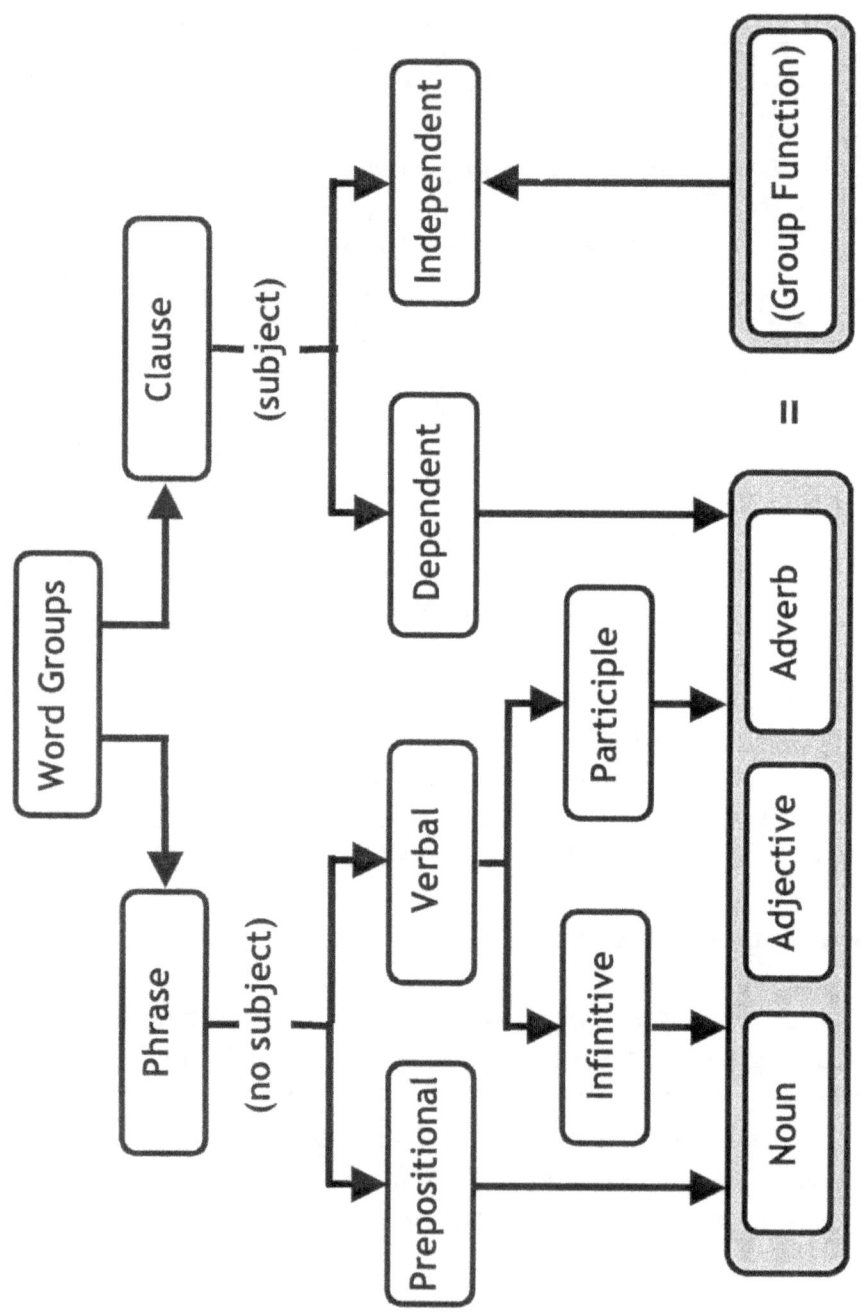

(1) Noun Phrase

A *noun phrase* is a word group functioning as a noun. The statement, "'*To infinity and beyond*' was his motto," has the prepositional phrase, "to infinity and beyond." This phrase is functioning as a noun, and the entire phrase as a unit is functioning as subject of the verb.[1]

(2) Adjectival Phrase

An *adjectival phrase* is a word group functioning as an adjective, that is, modifying a noun. For example, "the bird *on the ground*" uses a prepositional phrase, "on the ground," to modify the noun "bird."

(3) Adverbial Phrase

An *adverbial phrase* functions as an adverb, that is, modifying a verb. For example, "the bird flies *in the air*" uses a prepositional phrase, "in the air," to modify the verb "flies."

Verbal Phrases

The other type of phrase is the verbal. A *verbal* is a verb that is grammatically transformed into other parts of speech but does not have a subject. Verbals themselves are of two types: infinitives and participles.

(1) Infinitive Phrase

An *infinitive* is a verb with no subject transformed to act as a noun, adjective, or adverb. The infinitive often has the preposition "to" in front of the verb: *to run, to say, to do, to go*. Here are examples of infinitive phrase use:
- Noun: "*To pass the class* involves some work."

---

[1] We actually have not defined "subject" yet, which is a sentence level function, but you probably have a general idea that the subject is that part of a sentence that performs the action of the verb.

- Adjective: "The place *to go* was the local cafe."
- Adverb: "He investigated *to learn more*."

(2) Participial Phrase

A *participle* is a verb with no subject transformed to act as an adjective or adverb. This transformation is accomplished by adding the suffix "-ing" to the end of the verb. As an adjective, the participial phrase can:

- Modify a noun: "The candidate *getting the most votes* wins the race."
- Modify a verb: "He spoke freely *forgetting who was there*."
- Be used substantivally (as a noun): "*Taking the test* revealed everything."[2]

Clause

A *clause* is a word group that has a subject and a verb. Remember that a verbal by definition does not have a subject. Having a subject, then, is the main difference between a clause ("*he* is running home") and a verbal phrase ("running home"). Clauses have two types: independent and dependent. First, we look at independent clauses.

Independent Clauses

An *independent clause* is a subject-verb word group that can function independently without further modification as a complete thought expressing a statement or question, a contingency or wish, or a command. Thus, an independent clause tells you both actor and action and is a complete thought.

---

[2] This substantival participle use technically is called a *gerund*.

- <u>Statement or question</u>: John went home. Did John go home?
- <u>Contingency or wish</u>: John should go home. I wish John would go home.
- <u>Command</u>: John, go home! Go home!

By definition, an independent clause is the most basic sentence: "Jesus wept." In print, the word group separated by a period, question, or exclamation mark (and, sometimes, a colon, semicolon, or comma) will have at least one independent clause.

Table E2.2—Clause Connectors

Subordinate Conjunctions	Conjunctive Adverbs	Relative Pronouns
as	after	that
as if	as	which
because	before	what
before	how	who
if	since	whom
since	until	whose
that	when	
till	whenever	
unless	where	
when	wherever	
where	while	
whether	why	

Dependent Clauses

A *dependent* clause is a subject-verb word group that functions as one of three parts of speech—as noun, adjective, or adverb—within any independent clause. Thus, the dependent clause depends on the independent clause for its existence. The dependent clause always begins with either a relative pronoun, a subordinate conjunction, or a conjunctive adverb (an adverb that joins clauses).

(1) Noun Clause

A *noun clause* is a subject-verb word group that functions as a noun within an independent clause. The noun clause is introduced by a relative pronoun. The statement, "*That John make no mistakes* was his goal," has the clause, "That John make no mistakes," which is introduced by the relative pronoun, "that." This clause functions as a noun (subject of the verb) within an independent clause.

(2) Adjective Clause

An *adjective clause* is a subject-verb word group that functions as an adjective, that is, modifying a noun, within an independent clause. The adjective clause is introduced by a relative pronoun, subordinate conjunction, or conjunctive adverb. For example:

- Relative pronoun: "The student *who makes no mistakes* will succeed." The clause, "who makes no mistakes," is introduced by the relative pronoun, "who," acting as subject, and functions as an adjective modifying the noun "student."
- Subordinate conjunction: "He spoke to the crowds *that came to him*." The clause, "that came to him," is introduced by the subordinate conjunction, "that," acting as subject and functions as an adjective modifying the noun "crowds."
- Conjunctive adverb: "Come, see the place *where he lay*." The clause, "where he lay," is introduced by the conjunctive adverb, "where," and functions as an adjective modifying the noun "place."

(3) Adverb Clause

An *adverb clause* is a subject-verb word group that functions as an adverb, that is, modifying a verb within an independent clause. The adverb clause can be introduced either by a subordinate conjunction or a conjunctive adverb. Observe:

- Subordinate conjunction: "Come *before winter arrives.*" The clause, "before winter arrives," is introduced by the subordinate conjunction, "before," and functions as an adverb modifying the verb "come." (Imperatives as independent clauses always have an assumed subject—in this case, "you.")
- Conjunctive adverb: "The lady will try *until she succeeds.*" The clause, "until she succeeds," is introduced by the conjunctive adverb, "until," and functions as an adverb modifying the verb "try."

Exercise E2

1. Identify which is a phrase (P) and which is a clause (C):

   _____ to be confused   _____ as he was eating
   _____ in the library   _____ at the right time
   _____ who were talking   _____ that flew overhead
   _____ studying the book   _____ of the class
   _____ running   _____ because he knew
   _____ to ask that question   _____ knowing the time

2. Compose sentences using for the subject a prepositional noun phrase, infinitive noun phrase, and participle noun phrase:

Prepositional: _____

Infinitive: _____

Participle: _____

3. In the list taken from the paragraph below, identify the following word group functions and part of speech functions for all phrases and dependent clauses. Remember: a "clause" has to have a subject, such as a relative pronoun, performing the action.

Part of Speech:
noun
adjective
adverb

Word Group Function:
Pp = phrase, prepositional
Pvi = phrase, verbal, inf.
Pvp = phrase, verbal, part.
Ci = clause, independent
Cd = clause, dependent

   Pouring rain drenched band members who were lining up on the sidelines to perform their halftime show as the cheerleaders vainly tried to motivate unhappy fans leaving the stands in droves after witnessing their team's dismal first-half performance. The person to save the day was the drummajor of the band, whose spirited and defiant march to midfield inspired fans that just had left to return cheering and clapping.

_____ pouring rain drenched band members
_____ pouring
_____ who were lining up
_____ on the sidelines
_____ to perform their halftime show
_____ as the cheerleaders vainly tried
_____ to motivate unhappy fans

_____ leaving the stands in droves
_____ after witnessing their team's dismal first-half performance
_____ the person to save the day was the drummajor
_____ to save the day
_____ of the band
_____ whose spirited and defiant march to midfield inspired fans
_____ to midfield
_____ that just had left
_____ to return
_____ cheering and clapping

Photo © Gerald L. Stevens

Fig. 22. Herod Atticus Arches. These Arches of Herod Atticus are one of the few surviving remains at Troas, Turkey on the Aegean coastline near the modern village of Dalyan. The Apostle Paul had his famous Macedonian vision at Troas (Acts 16:9-10), which propelled his mission team into Europe. Paul established Christian communities in Philippi, Thessalonica, Berea, and Corinth, and later wrote letters to many of these churches.

Herod Atticus was a key orator and writer of the Second Sophistic movement, a revival of rhetoric in Greece in the second century A.D. He also was a protégé of the emperor Hadrian (117-138), who commissioned Herod to eliminate corruption in the free cities of Asia. Herod was responsible for many building and revitalization projects, especially in Athens. The Odeom of Herod Atticus on the Athens acropolis is still used to this day for both theatrical and musical performances.

English 3

Sentences

We return again to our three conceptual building blocks of words, word groups, and sentences. We started with the basic idea of "words," then moved to the larger category of "word groups." Now, we explore the even broader category of "sentences."

Sentences are independent clauses, with any related dependent clauses, used to express a complete thought. Since the backbone of any sentence is an independent clause, and the backbone of an independent clause is at least one verb with its subject, the crux of any sentence, English or Greek, reduces to the independent verb. This independent verb, also called the main verb, is the axle around which all the grammatical spokes of any sentence wheel turn. Thus, our getting started with sentences basically boils down to understanding the sentence-level functions of the main verb.

The sentence-level functions of the main verb are given by six parameters. Five of these parameters relate to performance of the verb action: (1) performer, (2) receiver, (3) interest, (4) kind, and (5) time. The sixth parameter relates to how much potential the verb action has for taking place, traditionally called: (6) mood. This sixth parameter considers whether the expressed verb action is an actual event, process, or state or only a potential event, process, or state.

First, we will overview the five performance parameters. Then, we discuss the action potential parameter of mood.

Verb Performance Parameters

Subject (action performer)

The *subject* of the verb typically is the action performer: "*Jack* laughed."[1] The *sentence subject* is the verb subject along with all its modifiers: "*Jack, who witnessed the entire episode,* laughed." The entire italicized phrase is subject of the verb.

A *finite verb* is a verb with an expressed or implied subject, because a subject by definition *limits* the verb action to a *particular* action performer, thus making the action finite. Most verbs are finite verbs.

An *infinite verb* has no expressed or implied subject, leaving the verb action unlimited by a subject. The infinite verb, also called a "verbal," has three forms: infinitive, participle, and gerund.[2]

The verb subject itself is governed by three grammatical factors: (1) *person*, (2) *number*, and (3) *voice*. These factors convey the specificity of the finite verb's subject.

(1, 2) Person and Number

Table E3.1—Subject Person Configurations

Person	Singular	Plural
1st	*I*	*we*
2nd	*you*	*you*
3rd	*he, she, it*	*they*

Person and *number* always work together. Subject *person* takes on three forms: (1) *first person* = the person speaking,

---

[1] The passive verb is an exception, of course.
[2] As discussed in the section on verb phrases under word groups.

(2) *second person* = the person spoken to, (3) *third person* = the person spoken about. Subject *number* for each person is *singular* or *plural*. The paired components of person and number yield a total of six possible personal configurations for the verb subject. The table above gives a synopsis of these personal configurations using personal pronouns.

(3) Voice

Voice expresses how the subject participates in the verb action. English verbs have two voices.

Active voice is the subject acting as agent of the verb action: "Sally *trimmed* the rose." The subject "Sally" is acting as agent of the verb action "trimmed."

Passive voice is the subject being acted upon: "Sally *was stung* by a bee."[3] The subject "Sally" is being acted upon by the verb "was stung." Passive voice construction shifts emphasis to the object of the active voice statement. ("The bee stung *Sally*.") In the active voice form of the sentence, note "Sally" is the direct object receiving the verb's action. In the passive voice form, "Sally" is the subject receiving the verb's action.

Exercise E3.1

1. Identify the person (1, 2, 3) and number (s, p) of the subjects in the following sentences:

    _____ *Gail, you are a good friend.*

    _____ *I know that person.*

    _____ *The students worked hard.*

---

[3]Technically, using a form of the auxiliary verb, "to be," with the past participle.

_____ Janice and Johnny, you have a cute dog.

_____ Patricia was late.

_____ We have good times together.

2. Answer the questions below related to the following sentence:

The hungry fish was fooled by the shining lure.

_____ What verb performance parameter is the word *fish*?

_____ What verb performance parameter is the phrase *The hungry fish*?

_____ Is the verb group *was fooled* finite or infinite?

_____ Is the verbal *shining* finite or infinite?

_____ What person and number is the verb group *was fooled*?

_____ What voice is *was fooled*?

Object (action receiver)

(1) Transitive Verbs

A *transitive* verb is a verb that transfers its action onto an object. An *intransitive* verb does not transfer action onto an object.

The *direct object* is the action receiver of a transitive verb: "The class elected *her*." Here, the word "her" is the direct object of the verb "elected."

The *object complement* is a noun or adjective that secondarily fills out (i.e., "completes") the meaning of the direct object: "The class elected her *president*." The noun "president" secondarily fills out the meaning of the direct object, "her."

The *sentence predicate*[4] is the verb, its objects, and all their modifiers: "The class *elected her president because they realized how she had shown great leadership in all areas of school life during the junior year*." In this long sentence, all the italicized words and word groups together comprise the sentence predicate.

(2) Intransitive Verbs

An *intransitive* verb does not transfer action onto an object. Thus, an intransitive verb does not need a direct object to complete its meaning: "I *came*. I *saw*. I *conquered*." Some verbs inherently are transitive or intransitive, while others are determined by customary use. Some verbs by custom are used only transitively: "He *beget* a son." "He *abandoned* the fort." Some verbs by custom are used only intransitively: "I *came*." "I *am*." Many verbs may be used either way: "I *saw*." "I *saw* a kingdom." "I *conquered*." "I *conquered* a kingdom."

The *copulative* verb is an intransitive verb that, while not requiring a direct object to transfer action, may have either a noun or an adjective in the predicate to complete its meaning. Verbs regularly used as copulative in English are *be* and *become*. Verbs that sometimes can be used as copulative include: *seem, appear, prove, look, remain, feel, taste, smell, sound, turn,* and *grow*.

The *predicate noun* is the noun in the predicate of a copulative verb completing its meaning: "John was *captain* of the team." The noun "captain" is used in the predicate to complete the meaning of the copulative verb "was." In effect, the predicate noun renames the subject.[5]

---

[4]Usually identified more simply as just the *predicate*.
[5]Remember that the basic function of the noun is to name.

The *predicate adjective* is the adjective in the predicate of a copulative verb completing its meaning: "She is *capable*." The adjective "capable" is used in the predicate to complete the meaning of the copulative verb "is." In effect, the predicate adjective further describes or limits the subject.[6] Thus, predicate nouns and predicate adjectives simply are two different parts of speech with the same function.

Indirect Object (action interest)

The *indirect object* is that object in the predicate that expresses action interest—the beneficiary or interest of the verb action. The indirect object answers the question "*to* or *for* whom?" or "*to* or *for* what?" The prepositions *to* or *for* are either expressed or implied in the indirect object phrase or clause: "Sally gave the picture *to her*." The prepositional phrase, "to her," functions as the indirect object of the verb "gave." Alternately, this statement could be expressed without a prepositional phrase as: "Sally gave *her* the picture."

Exercise E3.2

1. For the following sentences answer the indicated questions:

    1.1 The manager appointed her coordinator of the project.

    _____ Is the word *appointed* transitive or intransitive?

    _____ What verb performance parameter is the word *her*?

---

[6]Remember that adjectives modify by describing or limiting.

English 3: Sentences

_____ What verb performance parameter is the word *coordinator*?

_____ What verb performance parameter is *appointed her coordinator of the project*?

1.2 I saw, so I helped her. She became my friend, and I was glad.

_____ Is *saw* transitive or intransitive?

_____ Is *helped* transitive or intransitive?

_____ Is *became* transitive or intransitive?

_____ Is *was* transitive or intransitive?

_____ What type of verbs are both *became* and *was*?

_____ What verb performance parameter is *friend*?

_____ What verb performance parameter is *glad*?

2. Circle any indirect objects in the following sentence:

   The receipt was handed to me, so I gave the waitress my charge card.

Tense (action kind, action time)

Tense is a verb parameter that expresses two action components: action kind and action time. English uses additional verbs, called auxiliary verbs, to express these components.

Auxiliary verbs are additional verbs used to create verb phrases for various grammatical purposes. Certain tenses require auxiliary verbs to indicate both kind of action and time of action. For example: "He *will* go tomorrow." The verb "will" is an auxiliary verb used in English to create the future tense. Thus, the verb phrase "will go" is future tense.

Table E3.2—Common Auxiliary Verbs

be	did	may	shall	would
can	do	might	should	
could	have	must	will	

(1) Action Kind

Action kind has three types: (1) durative, (2) perfect, or (3) undefined. The first two represent distinctions in action. The third represents no distinction in action.

Durative action is process. The auxiliary verb for durative action is a form of "to be": "I *am writing.*"[7] Process can be continual (i.e., interrupted: "the faucet *is dripping*") or continuous (i.e., uninterrupted: "the faucet *is running*").

Perfect action is completed.[8] Perfect action is created by combining the past participle with a form of the auxiliary verb "to have." Completed *past* uses *had.* Completed *present* uses *have* or *has.* Completed future uses *will have.*

Undefined action is the whole event beginning to end, but not characterized as either of the other two kinds. Undefined actions presents simply the *what,* but not the *how.* "I *wrote*" envisions no more than an undefined event taken as a whole

---

[7] The construction also uses the present participle (-*ing*).

[8] Technically, linguists call durative action *imperfective* and undefined action *perfective.* The terminology is totally confusing to the beginning student. That "perfect" and "perfective" are not the same animal is a hill too high to climb. So, punting the ball for something like "durative" and "undefined" seems inescapable.

without consideration of how the writing took place. Undefined action often is the default mode for past narration. The focus is more on the "what" than the "how" of the action. So, action kind remains undefined in the action report.

(2) Action Time

Action time has three frames: past, present, and future. *Past tense* is action in the past. *Present tense* is action in the present. *Future tense* is action in the future, and uses the auxiliary verb *will*.

Table E3.3—Tense (Kind, Time)

	Past	Present	Future
Undefined:	*I went.*	*I go.*	*I will go.*
Durative:	*I was going.*	*I am going.*	*I will be going.*
Perfect:	*I had gone.*	*I have gone.*	*I will have gone.*

All three time frames can have all three kinds of actions. Various tenses are used to fulfill these kind of action roles in various time frames.

Kind of action can be exclusive to particular tenses. Past perfect, present perfect, and future perfect always are perfect kind of action, even as their names suggest.

On the other hand, other tenses do double duty for kind of action. That is, a particular tense may be either durative or undefined action. For example, the present tense expression, "I *run*," can be either durative or undefined. Only context will tell. To make clear the durative mode, the construction could use an auxiliary verb: "I *am running*."

However, normally, present tense is assumed durative, and past and future tenses are assumed undefined. Thus, "I *go*," while potentially either durative or undefined, often would be understood as durative. Again, "I *went*" or "I *will go*," while potentially either durative or undefined, often would be understood as undefined. Table E3.3 is a synopsis of tense as action kind and action time for the verb "to go."

Verb Potential Parameter

Mood is a verb parameter indicating the speaker's perspective on the verb action as either actual or only potential. In English, one mood is used for actual action, and two other moods convey decreasing degrees of potential action.[9] Verbs may undergo change to indicate mood. Study the following descriptions.

Indicative Mood (indicated reality)

The *indicative mood* is actual action. More precisely, the indicative mood is indicated reality, either indicated as a statement or indicated as a question. As a statement, the speaker either assumes or asserts the verb action's reality. For example, as assumed reality, one could say, "He cares." As asserted reality, one could say, "You do not care." As asserted falsehood, one could say, "I care." As a question, the speaker seeks to ascertain actuality: "Do you really care?" All of these statements are indicative mood.

Subjunctive Mood (potential reality)

The other two moods indicate only potential reality in decreasing degree. The *subjunctive mood* is potential reality as contingency or logical argument. Subjunctive mood often has auxiliary verbs (creating verb phrases): *could, should, would, may, might*. Contingency involves doubt or wish: "I *might*

---

[9]Greek has four moods by subdividing potential reality into three decreasing degrees, rather than just the two degrees of English.

go"; "I wish he *would go*." Logical argument involves contrary to fact conditions: If I had time, I *would go*."

Imperative Mood (potential reality)

The *imperative mood* is potential reality as command. Imperative mood involves greater contingency than subjunctive. (Any parent working with children knows this.) Imperative mood often uses the verb fronted at the beginning of a clause or uses an auxiliary verb. The command can omit the subject: "*Go!*" has the assumed subject, "You *go!*" Command also can be softened with particular auxiliary verbs into entreaty or permission: "Please, *let us go!*" or "You *may go*."

Exercise E3.3

1. Answer the indicated questions for the following sentences:

    1.1 Not knowing she was coming, we spent all our time as if we had finished our work.

    _____ What action kind and action time is the verb *was coming*?
    _____ What action kind and action time is the verb *spent*?
    _____ What action kind and action time is the verb *had finished*?

    1.2 Though I am laughing hard, he still will tell another joke, which has resulted in uncontrolled fits.

    _____ What action kind and action time is the verb *am laughing*?

_____ What action kind and action time is the verb *will tell*?

_____ What action kind and action time is the verb *has resulted*?

2. Answer the following questions:

    _____ Which mood has the greatest contingency?

    _____ Which mood is used for a contrary to fact condition?

    _____ Which mood is used to ask a question?

    _____ Which mood is used to give a command?

    _____ Which mood is used to make a statement?

3. Specify the mood of the following sentences:

    _____ *In English, one mood is used for actual action, and two other moods convey decreasing degrees of potential action.*

    _____ *Verbs may undergo change to indicate mood.*

    _____ *Study the following descriptions.*

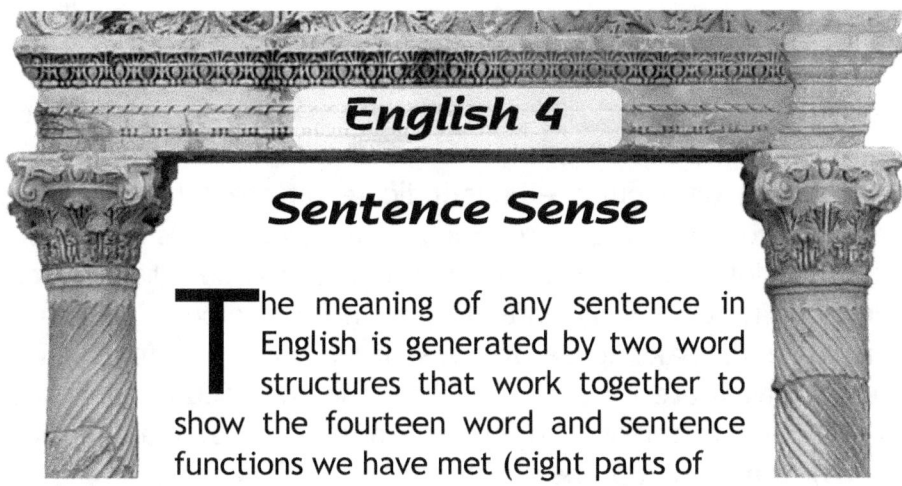

English 4

Sentence Sense

The meaning of any sentence in English is generated by two word structures that work together to show the fourteen word and sentence functions we have met (eight parts of speech, six verb parameters). One word structure is internal, and the other is external. The internal structure is called "inflection." The external structure is word order. These two word structures together help us make sense of the sentence.

Internal Structure—Inflection

Substantive[1] *Inflection*

Why do we spell the pronoun as "*he* can" for subject but not as "*he* book" for the possessive? Because the pronoun's spelling, we learned a long time ago, must be specific to its function.

Inflection is altering the form of a word in some way to indicate word function. Notice in "*he* can" that "he" is the subject of the verb, "can." Thus, the pronoun "he" conveys subject function, a verb parameter, and to do so should be spelled as "he." In contrast, "*he* book" is not a verb clause. Instead, the pronoun here has possessive function. In English, you have to spell "he" differently to convey this possessive function. Thus, correctly, you should have "*his* book." The different spelling, "his," alerts you to the *possessive* function of the pronoun.

---

[1]Reminder: a substantive is any word used as a noun.

Thus, we know "he" and "his" are alternate forms of the *same* word. Though spelled differently, these two forms we long ago learned are the same word.

In short, different spellings indicate different function in a sentence for the same word. Such spelling variations are inflection, and inflection takes on ordered patterns per grammatical function. That is to say, inflection is an *internal* word structure that helps us make sense of the sentence. For example, nouns (substantives) are inflected to show the four noun properties: (1) gender, (2) person, (3) number, and (4) case. We overview each of these noun properties briefly.

(1) Gender

Gender is a noun property that indicates whether a word has male, female, or neuter association. The association is called *masculine*, *feminine*, or *neuter*. Gender is assigned by custom in the native language. For example, "road" is neuter in English but feminine in Greek. To indicate gender in English, a word might be altered (*man*, *woman*), or add a word (*grandfather*, *grandmother*), or might add a suffix, that is, an ending (*host*, *hostess*).

(2, 3) Person and Number

Person and number already have been discussed as verb parameters. Person, evident in personal pronouns, indicates the subject: *I, you, he, she, it*. Notice that the English third person singular pronoun is inflected for gender (*he, she, it*), but the first and second person pronouns are not (*I, you* = masculine or feminine).

Number is singular or plural: *we, you, they*. Notice that first and third person plural are inflected for number (*I, we; he, she, it, they*), but second is not (*you* = singular or plural). For various substantives, English has numerous spelling variations, or inflection, to show plural. Plural inflection includes adding suffixes

(*-en, -ren, -s, -es, -ies, -ves*) or making internal vowel changes (*goose, geese*).

(4) Case

Case is noun (substantive) inflection to indicate any of three fundamental noun (substantive) functions in English sentences: (1) nominative, (2) objective, and (3) possessive. Unfortunately, numerous English words take on various case functions *without* inflection, similar to the first and second person singular pronouns not being inflected for gender (*I, you*), and second personal pronoun not being inflected for number (*you*). English proper nouns, for example, rarely are inflected for case function. English pronouns, on the other hand, regularly show inflection for case. Before we proceed to discuss these case functions, however, two grammar items found in the examples below need brief explanation.

First, *absolute* is a term applied to certain grammatical constructions. Oversimplified, "absolute" means "absolutely not connected." The lack of connection, for example, might be that the subject of a dependent clause is different than the subject of the independent clause. If so, the dependent clause would stand as "absolute" grammatically to the independent clause. In practical terms, you could drop out the absolute (word or word group) and still be left with your essential thought: "*Jane having arrived*, we left for the game." The essential thought is "we left for the game."

Second, *apposition* is an immediately following word that explains the previous word without use of a verb: "our president, *Rick*." Apposition often is easy to spot in English, since the appositive regularly is set off by commas.

With these minor explanations for the terms absolute and apposition, we look at case function below. Remember that not all substantives will use inflection to tip you off to case function, but the other word structuring device in English, word order, often takes over when that is the case. ☺

(a) Nominative Case

Nominative case is that word inflection indicating any substantival function other than object. Non-objective uses of the substantive include:

- **subject** (the most frequent use: "*John* is our leader.")
- **predicate nominative** (a substantive in the predicate of a copulative verb renaming the subject: "John is our *leader*.")
- **vocative** (direct address by the speaker: "*John*, will you lead our group?")
- **exclamation** (a form of interjection: "*Yea*, John is our leader!")
- **nominative absolute** (the nominative noun that is in the absolute clause: "*John* having arrived, we came to order.")
- **nominative of apposition** (a following substantive explaining the previous nominative substantive: "Our leader, *John*, has arrived.")

(b) Objective Case

Objective case is that word inflection indicating any substantival function as object (direct object, indirect object, object of the preposition, etc.). Another term for this case is *accusative*. Objective (accusative) uses of the substantive include:

- **direct object** (a frequent use: "Lancelot called *him*.")
- **object complement** (completes the direct object: "Lancelot called him his *king*.")
- **cognate object** (direct object based on same stem as verb: "Lancelot watched the third *watch* of the night.")
- **object of the preposition** (prepositional phrase object: "Lancelot saw him *on the horse*," in which "horse" is object of the preposition "on")
- **indirect object** (also called the *dative* case: "Lancelot gave *him* his oath.")

- **adverbial noun** (noun, without a prepositional phrase, indicating time, distance, measure, weight, or value: "Lancelot sailed *miles* to reach Camelot.")
- **infinitive objective subject** (infinitive action can be related to a noun using the objective case: "Lancelot asked *him* to give the command.")
- **infinitive object** (the direct object of the infinitive: "Lancelot went to find *him*.")
- **participle object** (the direct object of the participle: "Seeing *him*, Lancelot called out.")
- **objective of apposition** (a following substantive that explains the previous objective substantive: "When he saw Authur, his *king*, Lancelot called out.")

(c) Possessive Case

Possessive case is that word inflection indicating ownership or possession. Another term for this case is *genitive*. We indicate possession three ways in English:

- **apostrophe "s"** (a single, left-curled mark, either followed by the letter "s" or alone: "*John's* group"; all the *students'* grades)
- **preposition "of"** (object of the preposition *of*: "the grades *of the students*")
- **possessive pronouns** (*my, our; your, your, his, her, its, their*: "these are *their* grades")

Exercise E4.1

1. Provide the plural inflection for the following nouns:

   tool = _____   moose = _____

   box = _____   lady = _____

life = _____   foot = _____

child = _____   mouse = _____

2. Fill in the following chart for *I*, the first personal pronoun:

                     Singular   *Plural*

Nominative: _____   _____

Objective: _____   _____

Possessive: _____   _____

3. Fill in the following chart for *you*, the second personal pronoun:

                     Singular   *Plural*

Nominative: _____   _____

Objective: _____   _____

Possessive: _____   _____

4. Fill in the following chart for *she*, the feminine third personal pronoun:

                     Singular   *Plural*

Nominative: _____   _____

Objective: _____   _____

Possessive: _____   _____

5. Identify the case usage in the following using the categories of the discussion above. Has the word been inflected for that usage?

5.1 *He, the tall one, is no longer our coach, but, oh, he was good!*

He = _____

one = _____

coach = _____

oh = _____

good = _____

_____ What case are all these substantives?

5.2 *Jeff having stolen third base, the coach shouted to Bob, our catcher, "Bob, on the next pitch, watch Jeff, the best baserunner of the league!"*

Jeff (1st) = _____

base = _____

Bob (1st) = _____

our = _____

catcher = _____

Bob (2nd) = _____

pitch = _____

Jeff (2nd) = _____

baserunner = _____

league = _____

_____ How many nouns in the previous list would require inflection to show case function?

What does this show about the use of noun inflection in general to generate meaning in English?

Verb Inflection

English verbs actually do not need much inflection to convey action parameters (tense, voice, mood, person, and number) because they mostly use personal pronouns and auxiliary verbs for this purpose. We already have discussed these formation patterns in the previous chapter.

Still, English verbs do show *some* inflection. For example, verbs have singular and plural forms to show subject/verb agreement. Verb inflection also requires understanding the "principal parts" of a verb, and the issue of verb patterns: regular and irregular verbs. First, we look at principal parts.

(1) Principal Parts

Table E4.1—Verb Principal Parts: Examples

Verb	Pres.	Past	Past Part.
hit	hit	hit	hit
come	come	came	come
say	say	said	said
lay	lay	laid	laid
lie	lie	lay	lain
speak	speak	spoke	spoken
eat	eat	ate	eaten
see	see	saw	seen
go	go	went	gone
do	do	did	done

The three key components of an atom are an electron, a proton, and a neutron. Similarly, the three key inflectional components of an English verb are:
  (1) *present tense*, first pers. sing.
  (2) *past tense*, first pers. sing.
  (3) *past participle*

From just these three forms, you can generate the six English tenses for any verb (past, present, future and the corresponding perfect forms). The three *principal parts* of an English verb are the present, past, and past participle of any given verb.

Principal parts simply must be memorized—in any language. Sorry. That's just the deal. The payback is this: memorizing principal parts supercharges language learning. The ability to split an atom is nuclear power; the ability to split a verb is language power.

(2) Formation Patterns
(a) Regular Verbs

Some verbs are called "regular." These verbs follow set patterns for forming past tense (and past participle). That is, to create the past tense form, these verbs either just repeat the present tense form or add a past tense suffix (*-d*, *-ed*, *-t*). For example: *hit, hit, hit*, or *love, loved, loved*.

Third person singular is a minor exception to some verbs with "regular" inflection. The third person singular inflection of some verbs can break an inflection pattern by adding an *-s* or *-es* suffix. For example, all singulars and plurals for any person of the verb "go" use the simple inflected form "go," except third singular: he (she it) *goes*. Again, all singulars and plurals for any person of the verb "have" use the inflected form "have," except third singular: he (she, it) *has*.

(b) Irregular Verbs

Other verbs are called "irregular." These verbs do not use the "regular" suffixes (*-d*, *-ed*, *-t*), but follow "irregular" formation patterns for past tense (and past participle). Usually, this irregularity is an internal spelling change, such as *wind, wound, wound*.

This description of "irregular," however, does not mean inexplicable. Sometimes the history of a verb explains the past tense form. For example, the verb "go" has the principal parts:

go, went, gone. One might understand "gone" is somehow related to "go," but what in the world is this "went"? The past tense, "went," is called "irregular," because "you caint get there from here," as the old town codger told the newly-arrived visitor looking for directions. You simply cannot calculate "went" from "go." This inability is because the verb "go" in its development *borrowed* its past tense form from an already existing Middle English verb that meant to make your way down a path (*wend, went, wenden*), a traveling idea similar to "go."

However, today that word history is forgotten. So, "went" as the past tense of "go" now seems illogical, or "irregular"—meaning, today you just have to memorize the past tense "went" to know the formation of "go." Principal parts of all so-called "irregular" verbs simply have to be memorized. True for English, true for Greek. Fair warning!

Table E4.2—Indicative Verb Formation Patterns

Tense	Active Voice	Passive Voice
Past: reg.	present tense suffixes: *-d, -ed, -t,*	*was (were)* + [pp]
irreg.	various forms, spelling	*was (were)* + [pp]
perf.	*had* + [pp]	*had been* + [pp]
Present:	present tense	*am (is, are)* + [pp]
perf.	*have (has)* + [pp]	*have (has) been* + [pp]
Future:	*will* + [present]	*will be* + [pp]
perf.	*will have* + [pp]	*will have been* + [pp]

(3) Verb Summary

In Table E4.2 we summarize English tense and voice formation for indicative mood verbs by combining the concepts of inflection from this chapter and the use of auxiliary verbs from the last chapter. In the table, the notation "[pp]" stands for "past participle."

Exercise E4.2

1. Provide the three principal parts for the following verbs, and specify whether the formation is regular (i.e., does not change spelling or uses regular suffixes) or irregular (shows internal spelling changes):

Verb	Pres.	Past	Past Part.	Rg.?
cast				
fight				
believe				
get				
sing				

2. Compose sentences using the following verbs in the required tense:

   2.1 *cast*, future passive:

   _____

   2.2 *fight*, past perfect active:

   _____

   2.3 *believe*, past perfect passive:

   _____

   2.4 *get*, future perfect active:

   _____

2.5 *sing*, present perfect active:

External Structure—Word Order

Words can generate meaning by inflection. Many English substantives, however, are not inflected. How do uninflected forms take on meaning in a sentence? Word order.

Word Arrangements

Position of a substantive in English indicates *function*. A native speaker of English perhaps has not thought much about word order, but word order can make all the difference in the world for sentence sense. We can illustrate with an imaginary scene in a busy shopping mall, a card magician at his magic booth trying to get a crowd's attention. Where shall he start? With a verb, of course. The crux of any sentence is the verb. So, our barker begins his smooth little routine by flashing his trick grammar cards.

"Pick a verb, any verb!" he calls out boldly. He finally gets a shopper's attention, who fancies to respond, picking:

hit

The barker, happy to have a hit, pulls out the "hit" verb card, displays it held high, and continues.

"So, to make an independent clause," he says, "we need a subject. Let's take an uninflected proper noun as subject." This time, he makes his own choice. He pulls out a noun card on which is written, "John." He shows the "John" card to the gathering crowd and asks, "Where shall we put the subject?"

"That's easy!" someone in the front quickly volunteers, "at the front!" The barker smiles approvingly and arranges his cards to fit:

John hit.

"Right! In front of the verb. Why?" asks the barker.

"Well," the person calls back impatiently, frustrated he cannot think of what should be an easy answer, "that's just where you're supposed to put it!" The barker brightens into his trademark mischievous smile like a hawk swooping to snag a plump and juicy rabbit supper.

"A better answer is available, though," he responds. "How does the noun 'John' function in this sentence?" The barker this time does not pause for an answer from the crowd. "As a subject, I tell you, as a subject—and, that, my friend," he announces importantly, "is the nominative case function!"

Murmurs sweep through the growing crowd. Energized by this feedback, the barker continues his game.

"Subject function is signaled by word placement *before* the verb. Thus, the position *before* the verb is the *normal* position for the subject of a verb in English."

Loud oohs and ahs attract the attention of other shoppers further down the mall corridor. Knowing exactly how to keep working the crowd, the barker seizes initiative again.

"Let's experiment," he continues. "What if we put our noun card 'John' *after* the verb? Do we still have the same thought?" In a broad sweep before the ever-increasing crowd, he shows the cards switched around:

Hit John.

"No, obviously we do not have the same thought!" someone quickly answers from the crowd.

"Quite different, in fact," someone else volunteers, "and we could suppose John—whoever he is—might be a tad unhappy with this new situation!" Mild laughter ripples along the gathered shoppers, now distracted momentarily from their mall business.

"So what happened?" asks a young boy leaning hard at the front, intent on learning this neat grammar card trick.

"I'll tell you what happened," answers the barker loudly, relieved to seize the crowd's attention again after the humorous ambush. "*Word order changed word function. After* the verb, the noun card 'John' is in *direct object* position, so has objective case function."

"Wow!" exclaims the same child leaning forward in the front row. The crowd laughs again, tickled by the enrapt outburst. The barker, unperturbed, finishes his thought.

"Thus, the position *after* the verb is the *normal* position for the direct object of a verb in English." Heads bob knowingly. A man somewhere in the middle of the crowd seeks to steal the barker's show.

"How about we experiment even more. What if we put your noun card 'John' *after* the verb card as before, but now add one more noun card *after* 'John'? Is that the same thought?" The challenger, obviously pleased with his ploy, is sure that he has so convoluted the grammar cards as to confuse the entertainer hopelessly—but not so this veteran mall barker.

With a laugh, the barker retorts, "That's an easy one!"

Hit John the ball.

"No, this is not the same thought," he replies. "Why, you ask? Position again, my friend, position! If *two* substantives *follow* a verb, the *first* is no longer direct object but the *indirect object*. Why? Because the *normal* position of the *indirect object* in English is *between* the verb and its direct object. So, if two substantives immediately follow a verb, the first one *normally* is taken as the indirect object, and the *second* taken as the direct object."

The crowd, obviously delighted, claps its approval as the embarrassed challenger slips back into anonymity. The barker, sensing crowd approval, seizes the moment's momentum. He raises the ante, proving this is not the first time he's confronted a mall crowd with his grammar cards.

"How about we try another experiment," the barker slyly proposes. "An indirect object can be expressed as a prepositional phrase using 'to' or 'for.' What if we want to make our noun card 'John' the indirect object, but using a prepositional phrase card? Where goes the prepositional phrase card?"

The crowd, too embarrassed to venture a guess, grows awkwardly hushed. Then, a soft voice cautiously speaks up from the obscurity of crowd attendees.

"I think, sir," says the timid but polite, little voice, "that card would go *after* the direct object."

The barker cannot hide his amazement as he searches the crowd for the source of that voice. He discovers, slightly bemused, that his respondent is a little girl. Fixing his gaze on the mother, whom he is sure has fed the correct answer to her child, he quips playfully, "Right you are, my little dearie, right you are! *After* the direct object!" He shuffles the three cards dexterously into the new order the girl has indicated:

Hit the ball to John.

The crowd thunders its applause. The mother, however, has not had any involvement in the affair, and stares down in disbelief, clearly amazed at her own child's correct response.

"Well now. I see your indirect object, and I will raise you one," challenges the barker, clearly not wanting to concede the high ground of mall entertainment to a child. After all, this is *his* crowd. With a quick, nervous glance at the child, he speaks to all, "What if we take out the preposition, and instead put in a comma? What do we have then?" He knows this one always stumps 'em cold. He's playing his ace card. The child, however, is not to be denied.

"*We*," she says with a sparkle in her eye, putting her full emphasis on the plural, "then have the direct address case, a use of the nominative case called the 'vocative.'" Without pause, the child continues, "You will need a comma on your card; still even if you do not have a comma, the card order would say *something besides objective case* was going on." The barker realizes his prized grammar gambit has lost, but his little midget conqueror is not finished.

Raising her short little fingers, the little girl counts as she continues, "We know something besides objective case is going on, because, *first*, we have the absence of the indirect object's proposition 'to', and, *second*, we already have an existing direct object card, 'ball.'" She smiles sweetly as the barker obligingly puts his cards into her indicated order, knowing that he simply cannot deny she is absolutely correct:

Hit the ball, John.

The adults cheer wildly, patting the girl on the shoulder as they disperse, the barker's spell of distraction broken by a little child. The shoppers return to their briefly forgotten commercial chores. The barker knows he is undone, having lost his crowd on the vocative gambit. He slumps back into his chair, shuffling his grammar cards back into the deck to await another opportune mall moment.

The mother, however, continues to stand motionless in her joy, adoringly gazing at her little girl as if captured by a sublime Kodak moment. Then, shaking her head without a word, she turns to move on down the mall, dumbfounded at her child's newfound loquacity. The money she and her husband decided to pour into their child's private tutoring surely was the best investment they had made in a long time. She just cannot wait to tell daddy what happened at the mall today!

"I've got a set of grammar cards I could sell ya, maim!" calls out the barker, but she disappears into Dillards with a dismissive wave of her hand.

Well, we could go on inventing more scenarios with our little card game story. ("You're kidding," you think. No, actually, I'm not.) The parable's point is this: English depends significantly on word order for meaning. English *has* to depend on word order if English is going to be lazy about inflection! The more highly inflected a language is, the less word order is crucial for generating meaning. Greek is highly inflected.

English Sentence Arrangement

The English sentence (independent clause) places words and word groups as follows: (1) subject, (2) verb, (3) direct object,[2] (4) indirect object.[3] Everything else modifies, but modifiers do not change this fundamental structure. Position relative to the modified element is this: (1) adjectives always go before; (2) apposition always goes after; (3) all else varies before or after, but regularly is after. Thus, prepositional phrases, adverbs, and relative clauses vary, but usually come after what they modify. The fundamental order, however, is threefold: subject, verb, object.

(1) Postal Analogy

These three basic sentence positions are like three mailboxes along a postal route into which you can put different grammar packages or even bundles. A package for the subject mailbox might be a single word: a noun or an adjective. An entire bundle could be a word group such as a phrase or clause, along with all modifiers. The subject mailbox could get quite stuffed, in fact, but everything in the box together would function as "subject" of the verb.

So, our grammar truck (sentence) backs up into the postal dock. The first package unloaded would go to the subject box automatically by default. If the first package out, however, had an objective address (with inflection), the postal workers would know to pull that package off the subject line and reroute that

---

[2] For an intransitive verb: predicate nominative, predicate adjective.
[3] As a prepositional phrase; third otherwise, with direct object fourth.

first package to the object line. Then they would continue to expect the next package out to be the subject.

The verb and object mailboxes would be handled similarly. The second package out would be the verb, and the third package out would be the object. Any exceptions to this standard order of subject, verb, object for the arrival of packages off the sentence truck normally would be signaled someway by address (inflection). A mistake in address (wrong inflection) would have to be handled generally by position coming out of the truck. Also the dock workers hopefully would have been around long enough to have accumulated some experience with unloading these sentence trucks. Generally they would know their colors and had learned over time that violet packages almost always are verbs, navy packages almost always nouns, amber packages adjectives, purple prepositions, and so forth.

Any question about connections of packages to each other would be handled generally by assuming those packages closest together go together. Finally, if the receiver of the mail refused shipment, the mail would be sent back via the return address to the sender with a question about sentence sense.

(2) Transitive and Intransitive

This structure (i.e., order of contents inside the sentence truck) is the same regardless the zip code routing of the truck (transitive or intransitive verb): the subject is first; the verb is second. A transitive zip code truck always would have a third package loaded in the truck with objective address for the third mailbox (objective inflection: direct object, indirect object, etc.). An intransitive zip code truck still would have contents with a subject package first and a verb package second, but simply not have any mail for the third mailbox (object). A copulative zip code truck (these are the *be, become* trucks you see a lot on the road these days) also still would have contents with a subject package first and a verb package second; if loaded with a third package, though, even though having a subject type address, the postal worker, seeing the copulative zip code, would leave any third package in third position, but simply on top of the object mailbox, not in the box (your predicate noun, predicate adjective).[4]

 **Exercise E4.3**

Identify what elements in the following sentences are not "normal," or simply are not correct in terms of inflection or word order. Rewrite the sentences in better form for word order and inflection. Specify whether the verb as used is transitive, intransitive, or copulative:

---

[4]How's that for driving a metaphor into the ground?

1. Runs he.

2. Good is her.

3. Dove us the pool into.

4. Hit to him the ball John.

5. A red rose her got from he.

6. To who do this us owe honor?

7. I today turned in homework my.

8. The game won the team that well played.

9. Earned the trip the student whom is going.

10. The man good them gave bus on the he seat.

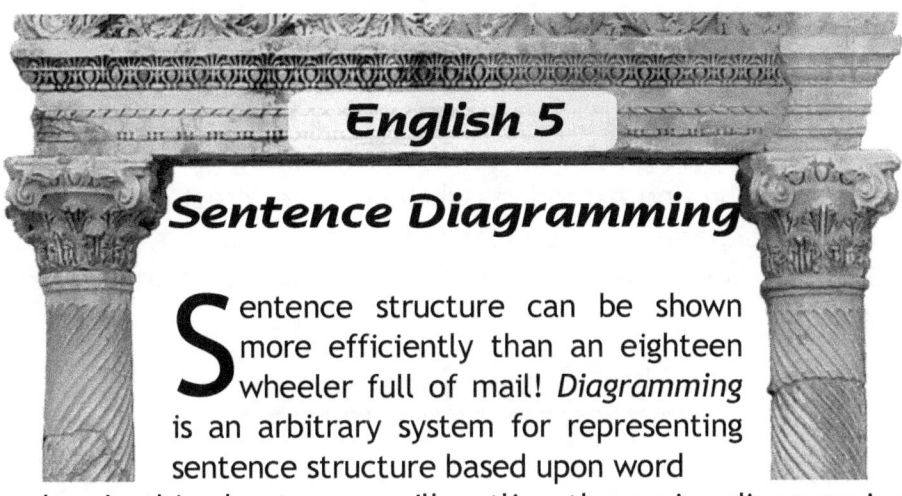

English 5

Sentence Diagramming

Sentence structure can be shown more efficiently than an eighteen wheeler full of mail! *Diagramming* is an arbitrary system for representing sentence structure based upon word order. In this chapter we will outline the major diagramming devices used to cover the bulk of sentence structures, even though some of the grammatical concepts have not been discussed. In the following patterns, notice the centrality of the three basic slots of a sentence from the previous chapter (subject, verb, object).

Transitive Pattern—Object Slots

The crux of any sentence is the verb. Start with the verb (V). Underline this element, and you are on your way to diagramming. All you do is extend the verb line left to hold the subject (S) before the verb and right to hold the direct object (O) after the verb. Auxiliary verbs are considered part of the main verb unit.

Direct Object

$$\underline{\text{S} \mid \text{V} \mid \text{O}}$$

Thus, the main layout of diagramming show English sentence order. That is, the line extended left holds the subject before the verb, separated by a vertical line through the horizontal verb line. The line extended right holds the direct object after the verb, separated by a vertical line that does not break the horizontal verb line. An example would be: "Jim runs marathons."

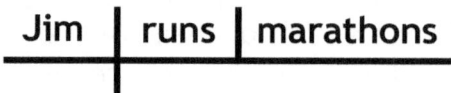

Questions simply invert word order: the auxiliary verb is first. They would diagram as a normal statement: "Does Jim run marathons?" is the same as "Jim does run marathons."

Indirect Object

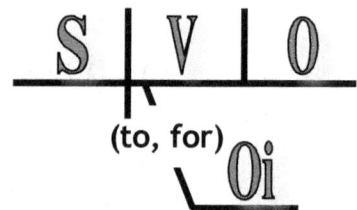

The indirect object uses objective case and goes on a subordinated line underneath the verb, connected by a slanted line running down from the verb line. This indirect object can be a word or a prepositional phrase. If a prepositional phrase, put the preposition *to* or *for* on the slanted line. An example would be: "Jim runs marathons for us."

Jim | runs | marathons
     for
       us

Object Complement

An object complement completes the direct object and is essential to its meaning. In diagramming, this element should follow the direct object, as in its sentence order. Separate the object complement from the direct object by drawing another object divider (does not break the horizontal verb line), but, to distinguish from the direct object, slant this object line back towards the direct object to which this element is related. An example would be: "Jim calls marathons his specialty."

```
Jim | calls | marathons \ specialty
                         \ his
```

Compounds

```
S₁                V₁
   ⟩──┼──⟨         ⟩ O
S₂(and)  (and)V₂
```

Simple means a single grammatical element minus any modifiers. *Compound* means two or more simple elements joined by a conjunction (*and, but,* etc.). Thus:

- A *simple subject* is the single subject minus any modifiers (as is *Judy* in "the talented *Judy*").

- A *compound subject* is the combination of two or more simple subjects ("*Judy* and *Jean*").
- A *simple predicate* is a single verb minus any modifiers (as is *fought* in "*fought* valiantly for hours").
- A *compound predicate* is two or more simple predicates ("*fought* and *won*").
- A *simple sentence* is one independent clause unmodified by any dependent clause. ("*He ran the race.*")
- A *compound sentence* is two or more simple sentences combined. ("*He won the race,* and *his team won the medal.*")

Compound elements simply require dividing the verb line into two lines for that element, then rejoining the two lines back into one. If the two verbs had different direct objects, each split verb line would continue for its own direct object and not rejoin for a common direct object. An example would be: "*Jean* and *Judy laugh* and *sing.*"

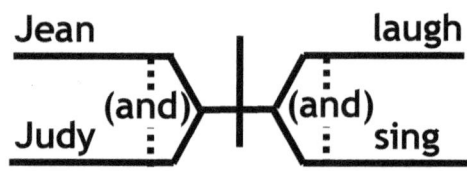

Compound sentences join two independent clause lines at the beginning. An example would be: "Jim reads books, *but* Cindy watches movies."

English 5: Sentence Diagramming

Intransitive Patterns—No Objects

Intransitive Verbs

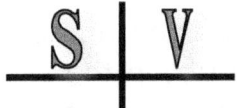

An intransitive verb does not have a direct object. Therefore, the diagram will have only two slots. Whether a verb is used as transitive or intransitive is by custom. Some verbs by custom always are used as intransitive, others always as transitive, and some both ways. Thus, without a direct object in third position, the intransitive diagram is simply a short form of the transitive. An example would be: "Jim runs."

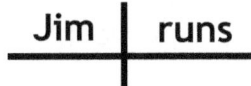

Copulative Verbs

Copulative verbs (*be, become*) distinguish themselves in the intransitive camp because they *always* are used intransitively.[1] They also are distinct because they function as if they could be equated with two kinds of logic statements, one with an "equals" mark (the predicate nominative) or one with a "similar

---

[1] Other verbs sometimes used as copulatives are: *seem, prove, appear, look, remain, feel, taste, smell, sound, turn,* and *grow.*

to" mark (the predicate adjective). This logical connection between a copulative's subject and predicate is even suggested by the term "copulative." That is, the subject and its complement in the predicate are coupled together by the copulative verb in a logical relationship.

The copulative complement (predicate noun, predicate adjective) takes the third slot in the sentence. The complement completes the statement inaugurated by the copulative verb and says something more about the copulative's subject. The complement, however, cannot be considered as direct object, since the copulative verb by definition is intransitive.

In diagramming, then, the copulative complement must be distinguished from a transitive verb's direct object. A vertical object line, as with a transitive direct object, cannot be used to separate the intransitive complement. Instead, a back-slanted line is used, similar to the style for the object complement. An example would be: "Cindy is president."

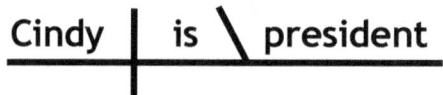

Substantival Patterns

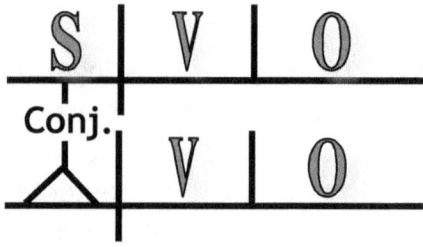

English 5: Sentence Diagramming

Substantival Clauses

Substantival clauses, acting like nouns, fulfill subject or object roles in a sentence; however, as clauses, they need their own verb line for their own subjects and predicates. This substantival verb line is elevated from the independent clause verb line by a symbol called a "standard," which looks like a small music stand arising from the position the clause functions to fulfill in the independent clause. An example would be: *"That he won awards inspired pride."*

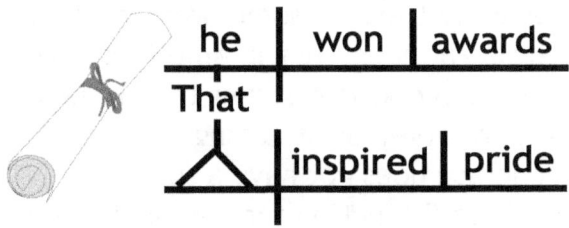

Discourse Clauses

Discourse is speech, that is, what a person says (*direct discourse*) or is reported to have said (*indirect discourse*). Both direct and indirect discourse always are the direct objects of a verb of saying (*ask, note, observe, question, relate, reply, report, respond, say, speak, tell,* etc.). An example would be: "She told me *that Donna was happy.*"

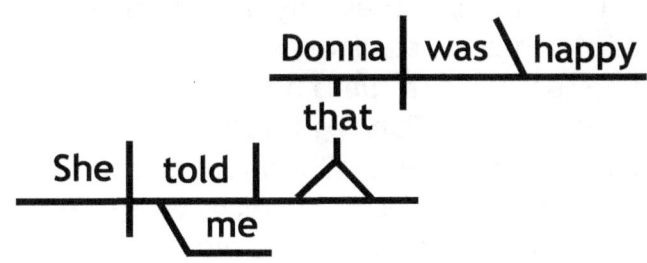

Verbals (Infinitives, Participles)

The main verbals are infinitives and participles. A simple verbal without objects or modifiers can be placed directly in the position of its substantive function (subject, object). Verbals with their own objects and modifiers will need their own verb line, so will need a standard to prop up this line.

(1) Surrogate Subject

Technically, verbal phrases are unlimited by a subject; however, a verbal phrase can have what can be called a "surrogate subject." This surrogate subject is some word that relates to the action of the verbal, although not in an official capacity as a true subject. The word in question seems to act like a subject for an infinitive or participle, as if taking first position in a verbal phrase, but a phrase does not have a subject!

This "surrogate subject" function for verbals is easy to spot for words that are inflected: *the surrogate subject will have objective inflection, not nominative*. This inflection sometimes shows the surrogate's grammatical relationship as *object* in its own clause (*third* position).

(2) Diagramming

In diagramming, this "surrogate subject" is put in brackets in the subject slot to indicate its surrogate role. An infinitive verbal will use a double divider line between this "subject" and the verb, but the participle uses only a single divider line. Various examples of verbal substantive use are:

    (a) Infinitive subject: *"To run* is fun."
    (b) Participle subject: *"Running* is fun."
    (c) Infinitive phrase subject: *"To run races* is fun."
    (d) Participle phrase subject: *"Running races* is fun."
    (e) Infinitive object: "Coach wanted *him to run races.*"
    (f) Participle object: "Coach wanted *him running races.*"

English 5: Sentence Diagramming

Notice that "him" in the last two examples seems to be subject of the infinitive or participle respectively, but actually functions in *third* position as direct object of the verb "wanted" in each sentence. Notice the pronoun's *objective* inflection as a result ("him," not "he").

Modifier Patterns

Words and Phrases

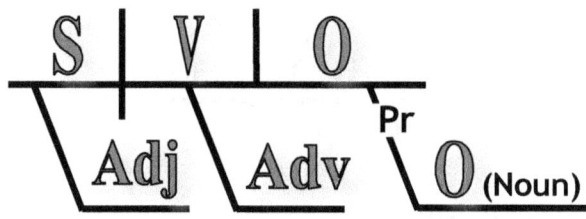

Attributive adjectives, modifying adverbs, and prepositional phrases all use the same form as the indirect object, that is, a slanted line underneath the modified element. In a prepositional phrase, the preposition goes on the slanted line, the noun object on the horizontal. An example would be: *"Talented athletes always break records in each event."*

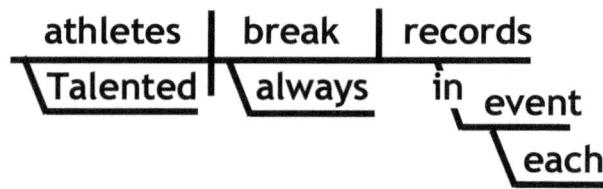

Verbals (Infinitives, Participles)

A simple verbal without any objects or modifiers can be placed directly in the position of its modifying function (adjective, adverb). Verbals with objects and modifiers will need their own verb line, so will use an inverted standard, since modifiers go underneath the element modified. Notice the similarity in diagramming both infinitives and participles. Examples include:
   (a) Infinitive adjective: "The athlete *to beat* holds records."
   (b) Participle adjective: "The athlete *running* holds records."
   (c) Infinitive adverb: "She came *to run*."

English 5: Sentence Diagramming   **507**

(d) Participle adverb: "She came *running*."
(e) Infinitive adverb phrase: "She came *to run her best race*."
(f) Participle adverb phrase: "She came *running her best race*."

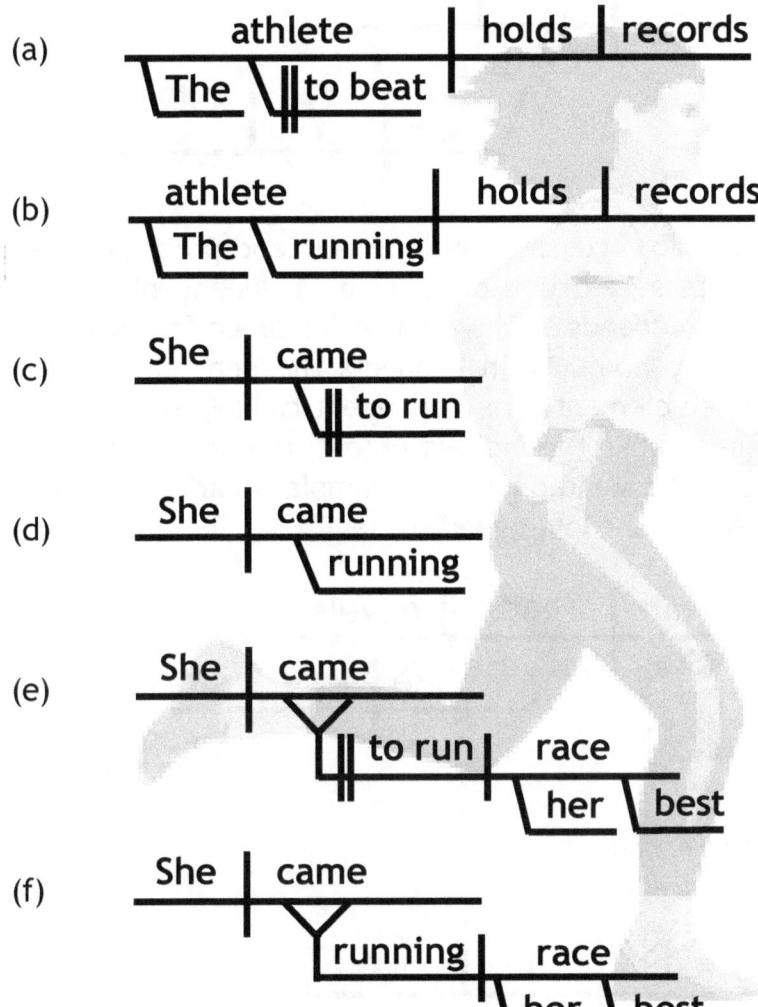

Dependent Clauses

(1) Subordinate Conjunctions

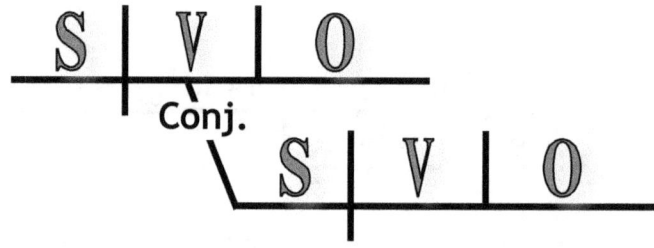

By definition, clauses have subjects and predicates, so any clause needs a verb line of its own. A dependent clause is a modifier, so depends on the element modified for its existence. A subordinate conjunction connects the dependent clause to the modified element. The dependent clause, as all modifiers, is diagrammed like the indirect object; the related conjunction is placed on the slanted line. An example would be: "Jean reads novels because she loves good stories."

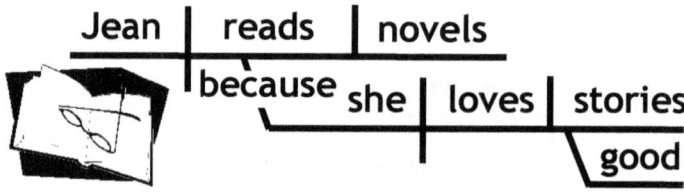

(2) Relative Pronouns

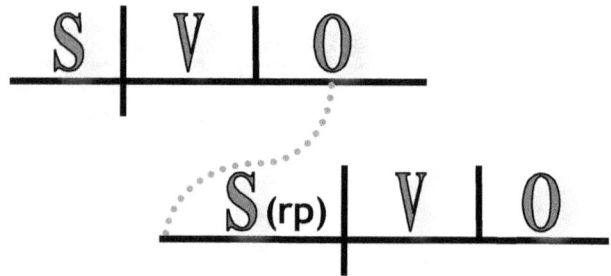

English 5: Sentence Diagramming

A *complex sentence* is an independent clause with at least one dependent clause. The presence of a dependent clause by definition creates a complex sentence. Any sentence that has a subordinate conjunction is a complex sentence, because subordinate conjunctions always lead to dependent clauses.

Relative pronouns are subordinate conjunctions that have five distinctive features:

(1) They are a special, restricted class of conjunctions (*who, whom, whose, which, that, what*).
(2) They introduce a dependent clause.
(3) Their clause acts as an adjective to modify an antecedent substantive.
(4) They have either a subject or object function within their own clause.
(5) They can be compounded with the suffix *-ever* to relativize the antecedent (*whoever, whomever, whichever, whatever*).

Examples would include: (1) as the subject in their clause: "John found volunteers *who* gave donations." (2) as the object: "John found volunteers *whom* you knew." (In each example the antecedent modified is "volunteers.")

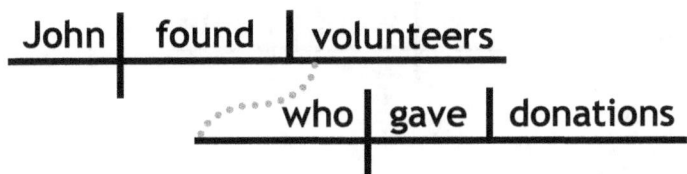

Independent Patterns

Absolute Constructions

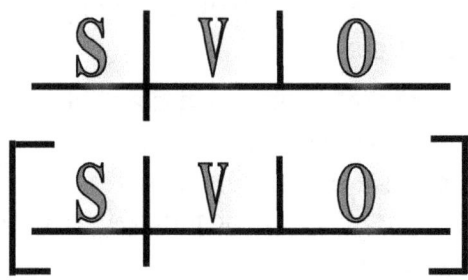

Absolute constructions grammatically are independent elements. They are not integral to another clause. Brackets around the entire independent construction are meant to indicate this independence from other clauses (cf. "surrogate subjects"). For example: *"Rain having begun,* we went home."

```
  ┌ Rain │ having begun ┐
  └──────┼──────────────┘
         │
    we   │ went │ home
         │
```

Appositive Constructions

$$\underline{\text{S}\mid\text{V}\mid\text{O}} = \underline{\text{S}\mid\text{V}\mid\text{O}}$$

English 5: Sentence Diagramming

An appositive is a word, phrase, or clause explaining a substantive that immediately follows the substantive without an intervening verb. As an independent item grammatically, the appositive is set off by commas. In diagramming, the appositive is set on a separate line with an equals mark toward the substantive explained. An example is: "Tilly, *our crumb scout*, constantly patrols the kitchen floor."

Exercise E5

Diagram the following sentences. Be prepared to analyze and describe the individual sentence components in terms of words, word groups, and sentence functions:

1. Jack sings.
2. Jack sings songs.
3. Jack sings songs for us.
4. Jack sings us songs, his compositions.
5. Jack writes and sings his own songs.
6. Jack is a songwriter.
7. Jack became famous.
8. That Jack sings songs surprises no one.
9. He said that Jack had a future in songwriting.
10. Jack's goal was writing a hit.
11. To write that hit song was always possible.
12. The publisher came to hear Jack's winning song.
13. After they heard his song, they wrote Jack a contract.

14. When they left, Jack celebrated with his friends, who were happy for him.
15. We call Jack, who now is famous, our own local hero.

Answer Key and Indexes

ΑΩ

Answer Key

:onfirmation that you are learning the assigned material. At the same time, be aware that overdependence upon this tool could jeopardize your ability to become competent in dealing with the Greek of the New Testament. One signal of a problem is any significant discrepancy between performance in these exercises and performance on sectional exams. Another signal would be constantly being totally "stumped" whenever you attempt to translate a New Testament passage.

---

1. Learn the alphabet.
2. (2) synezōopoiēsen hymas syn autōi,
(4) paraptōmata. exaleipsas to kath'
3.2 3 smooth, 4 rough, 2 iota subscript
3.4 line 1
3.6 no; the pairs γγ, γκ, γξ, and γχ are not present
3.8b lambda (λ), line 4
3.9b yes
4.2 αὐ-τῷ
4.4 συν-ε-ζω-ο-ποι-η-σεν
5.2 circumflex is restricted to ultima if ultima is long
5.4 long, because circumflex may stand over long syllables only

5.6 short, because acute may stand over antepenult only if ultima is short

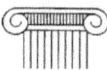 **Exercise 2**

2. λέγ-ω = *I say, am saying*
    λέγ-εις = *you say, are saying (sg.)*
    λέγ-ει = *he (she, it) says, is saying*
    λέγ-ομεν = *we say, are saying*
    λέγ-ετε = *you say, are saying (pl.)*
    λέγ-ουσι(ν) = *they say, are saying*
3.2 *we are receiving*; pres., act., ind., 1st pl.
3.4 *you are wishing*; pres., act., ind., 2nd pl.
3.6 *you are knowing*; pres., act., ind., 2nd pl.
3.8 *we are finding*; pres., act., ind., 1st pl.
3.10 *they are hearing*; pres., act., ind., 3rd pl.
4.2
     [they] | ἀκούουσιν

 **Exercise 3**

2. λέγ-ομαι = *I am called, am being calling*
    λέγ-ῃ = *you are called, are being called (sg.)*
    λέγ-εται = *he (she, it) is called, is being called*
    λεγ-όμεθα = *we are called, are being called*
    λέγ-εσθε = *you are called, are being called (pl.)*
    λέγ-ονται = *they are called, are being called*
4.2 *we are, become*; pres., mid. deponent, ind., 1st pl.
4.4 *he (she, it) is known*; pres., pass., ind., 3rd sg.
4.6 *they go into*; pres., mid. deponent, ind., 3rd pl.
4.8 *he (she, it) sits down*; pres., mid. deponent, ind., 3rd sg.

4.10 *you are proceeding*; pres., mid. deponent, ind., 2nd pl.
4.12 *I am saying (for myself)*; pres., mid., ind., 1st sg.
5.2   [they] | ἀκούονται

Exercise 4

2. θε-ός = *God* (nominative: subject)
    θε-οῦ = *of God* (genitive)
    θε-ῷ = *to God* (dative)
    θε-όν = *God* (accusative: direct object)
4. εὐαγγέλι-ον = *good news* (nominative: subject)
    εὐαγγελί-ου = *of the good news* (genitive)
    εὐαγγελί-ῳ = *to the good news* (dative)
    εὐαγγέλι-ον = *good news* (accusative: direct object)
6.2 *Christ* (dir. obj.); acc., mas., sg.
6.4 *of sons*; gen., mas., pl.
6.6 *children* (sub./dir. obj.); nom./acc., neu., pl.
6.8 *to signs*; dat., neu., pl.
6.10 *heavens* (sub.); nom., mas., pl.
6.12 *to a world*; dat., mas., sg.
7.2 We do not believe in a sign.
7.4 The messenger from heaven is speaking words to men.
8.

ὁ ἄγγελος | λέγει | λόγους
ἐκ οὐράνου \ ἀνθρώποις

Exercise 5

2. ἡμέρ-α = *day* (nominative: subject)
    ἡμέρ-ας = *of a day* (genitive)

ἡμέρ-ᾳ = *to a day* (dative)
ἡμέρ-αν = *day* (accusative: direct object)
4. θάλλασ-α = *sea* (nominative: subject)
θαλλάσ-ης = *of a sea* (genitive)
θαλλάσ-ῃ = *to a sea* (dative)
θάλλασ-αν = *sea* (accusative: direct object)
6. ἁμαρτί-αι = *sins* (nominative: subject)
ἁμαρτι-ῶν = *of sins* (genitive)
ἁμαρτί-αις = *to sins* (dative)
ἁμαρτί-ας = *sins* (accusative: direct object)
7.2 *voices* (dir. obj.); acc., fem., pl.
7.4 *love*; (dir. obj.) acc., fem., sg.
7.6 *glory* (dir. obj.); acc., fem., sg.
7.8 *to disciples*; dat., mas., pl.
8.2 *He is sitting down and we are proceeding.*
8.4 *I have a kingdom of glory (a glorious kingdom).*
8.6 *Disciples of John are hearing Jesus, and they are writing words of life.*
9.

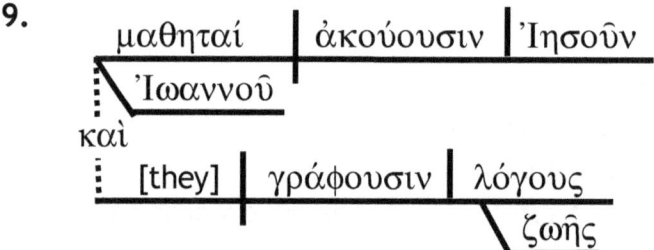

 **Exercise 6**

1.2 *You are going in peace.* (Acts 16:36)
1.4 *He goes into a wilderness place.* (Lk. 4:42*)[1]
1.6 *And he goes into the Pharisee's house.* (Lk. 7:36*)

---

[1]The asterisk indicates the text has been adapted.

1.8 *But why do you see (look at) the splinter in your brother's eye? (Mt. 7:3)*

2. δὲ

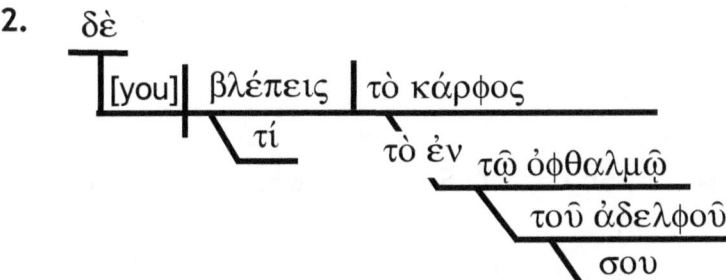

 **Exercise 7**

2.2 -ες
2.4 -ν
2.6 -εις
4.2 nominative
5.2 *Or were you baptized in the name of Paul? (1 Cor. 1:13)*
5.4 *grace, mercy, peace from God the Father (1 Tim. 1:2)*
5.6 *Therefore Peter is going from city to city.*
5.8 *For a man is not from woman but woman from man (1 Cor. 11:8)*
5.10 *And he receives the scroll from the hand of the angel (Rev. 10:10*)*

 **Exercise 8**

1.2 First Declension

	Feminine			Mas.	
	α-Sng.	η-Sng.	Mix S.	-ης Nom.	Plurals
	-α	-η	-α	-ης	-αι
	-ας	-ης	-ης	-ου	-ων
	-ᾳ	-ῃ	-ῃ	-ῃ	-αις
	-αν	-ην	-αν	-ην	-ας

2.2 Substantival: adjective taking the function of a noun
3.2 *poor*; substantival as direct object
3.4b *helpless*; substantival as predicate nominative
4.2 attributive
4.4 articular, nominative
6. Copulative verb: an intransitive verb that may take a complement that completes its meaning
7.2 proper name vs. noun, proper name
7.4b (Ἰησοῦς) ἐστιν ὁ χριστὸς. Proper name precedence.
8.2 *Salt is good.* (Mk. 9:50)
8.4 *eighteen years* (Lk. 13:16)
8.6 *and of the whole church* (Rm. 16:23)
8.8 *Then the devil takes him to the holy city.* (Mt. 4:5)
8.10 *And after a long time, the master of those slaves comes.* (Mt. 25:19)
8.12 *And he says to him: "Every man first serves the good wine."* (Jn. 2:10)

9.2

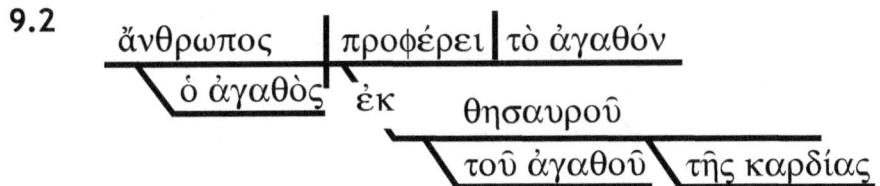

 Exercise 9

- **2.** 2ⁿᵈ
- **4.** Neuter nominative and accusative have only the vowel omicron (-ο) instead of -ον.
- **5.2b** ἡμεῖς γινόμεθα = <u>we</u> become
- **5.2d** αὐτοὶ πιστεύουσιν = <u>they</u> are believing
- **6.** 3ʳᵈ; anarthrous
- **8.2** <u>We</u> have a law. (Jn. 19:7)
- **8.4** <u>They</u> do not believe in me. (Jn. 16:9)
- **8.6** Therefore the disciples say to one another. (Jn. 4:33)
- **8.8** Then the mother of the sons of Zebedee with her sons goes to him. (Mt. 20:20*)

Exercise 10

- **1.2** rough stop
- **1.4** elision (dropping) of final vowel before a beginning vowel
- **1.6** same as 1.4
- **1.8** same as 1.4
- **1.10** same as 1.4
- **2.2** Behold, <u>I</u> am sending my messenger. (Mk. 11:10)
- **2.4** Truly I tell you, they have their reward. (Mk. 6:5)
- **2.6** <u>We</u> have a law and according to the law, he ought to die. (Jn. 19:7)

2.8   Glory in the highest to God (or: to God in the highest) and upon earth peace among men of good will. (Lk. 2:14)[2]
2.10 We have peace with God through our Lord Jesus Christ. (Rom. 5:1)
2.12 But from the days of John the Baptist until now the kingdom of heaven is suffering violence. (Mt. 11:12)

 **Exercise 11**

1.2b genitive, ablative, *than*
2.   genitive
3.2   πρῶτος, δεύτερος, τρίτος
4.2   *But now you say that we see.* (Jn. 9:41)
4.4   *He says, "I am not the Messiah."* (Jn. 1:20*)
4.6   *He is stronger than I (am); of whom I am not worthy.* (Mt. 3:11)
4.8   *But I have the witness greater than John's.* (Jn. 5:36)
4.10 *But you do not believe, because you are not from my sheep.* (Jn. 10:26)
4.12 *I hear about your faith in Christ Jesus and the love that you have for all the saints.* (Col. 1:4*)
5.2

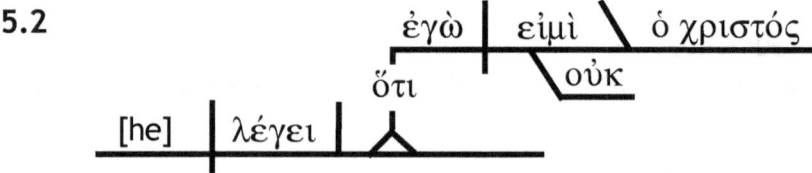

---

[2]Ask your instructor about the different readings in manuscript copies and their significance; some have the genitive εὐδοκίας; others have the nominative εὐδοκία. Also, whose good will? Human or divine? Cf. Phil. 2:13.

5.4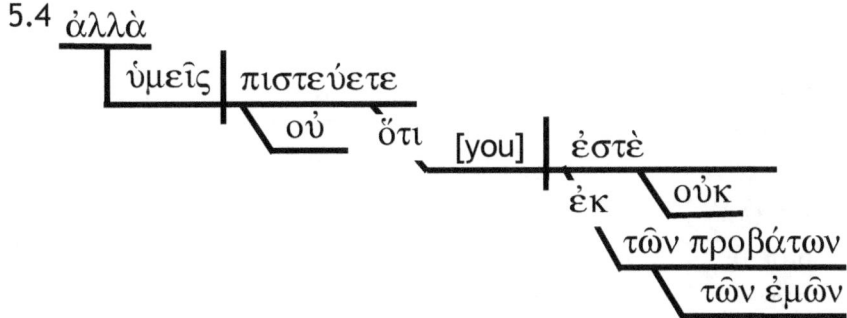

 **Exercise 12**

1.2 Do you fear God? (Lk. 23:40*)
1.4 All are seeking you. (Mk. 1:37)
1.6 How much do you owe? (Lk. 16:7)
1.8 You do not walk according to love. (Rom. 14:15*)
1.10 We ourselves are comforted by God. (2 Cor. 1:4)
1.12 And Jesus says (said) a certain man has (had) two sons. (Lk. 15:11*)
1.14 Do you believe, O King Agrippa, in the prophets? (Acts 26:27)
1.16 From whom do the kings of the earth take toll or tribute? (Mt. 17:25)
1.18 Then he said to his disciples, "The harvest is plentiful, but the workers (are) few. (Mt. 9:37)
λέγει is <u>present</u> tense. If this is narrative, λέγει needs to be <u>past</u> time. Thus, λέγει should be translated <u>said</u>. This use is called the "<u>historical</u> present."

 **Exercise 13**

1.2 present

1.4 first
1.6 deponent
1.8 past time
1.10 customary
1.12 conative
2.2 ἐβαλλ-
2.4 ὡδευ-
2.6 ἠνε-
2.8 ἰσχυ-
4. ἀνέβλεπον = I was looking up
ἀνέβλεπες = you were looking up (sg.)
ἀνέβλεπεν = he (she, it) was looking up
ἀνεβλέπομεν = we were looking up
ἀνεβλέπετε = you were looking up (pl.)
ἀνέβλεπον = they were looking up
6.2 They were asking for peace (reconciliation). (Acts 12:20)
6.4 And she was dying. (Lk. 8:42)
6.6 Just as you are walking in the truth. (3 Jn. 1:3)
6.8 And he was not staying in a house but among the tombs. (Lk. 8:27)
6.10 And he was saying this signifying what kind of death he was about to die. (Jn. 12:33)
6.12 "Men, brothers! I am a Pharisee, a son of the Pharisees. I am being judged concerning the hope and resurrection of the dead." (Acts 23:6)

 **Exercise 14**

2. ἤμην = I was
ἦς = you were (sg.)
ἦν = he (she, it) was
ἦμεν (ἤμεθα) = we were

ἦτε = *you were (pl.)*
ἦσαν = *they were*

3.2 *He still had (was having)³ one beloved son. (Mk. 12:6)*

3.4 *He was falling upon the ground and was praying. (Mk. 14:35)*

3.6 *If David, therefore, calls him Lord, how is he his son? (Mk. 22:45)*
   καλεῖ Identify the "if" verb.
   indicative Identify the mood of the "if" verb.
   determined Logic is determined or undetermined?
   fulfilled What is the assumption about the "if"?
   first What class conditional sentence?

3.8 *Therefore the one who teaches another, do you not teach yourself? (Rom. 2:21)*

3.10 *Jesus was saying to them, "If you were children of Abraham, you would do the works of Abraham. (Jn. 8:39)*
   ἐστε Identify the "if" verb.
   indicative Identify the mood of the "if" verb.
   determined Logic is determined or undetermined?
   unfulfilled What is the assumption about the "if"?
   second What class conditional sentence?

3.12 *The one who eats my flesh and drinks my blood abides in me and I abide in him. (Jn. 6:56)*

 **Exercise 15**

2. π, β, φ + σ = ψ
    κ, γ, χ + σ = ξ
    τ, δ, θ + σ = σ

---

³The verb ἔχω in the imperfect is augmented as εἰχ-.

- 3.2 γραψ-
- 3.4 ἀξ-
- 4.2 διδαξ-
- 5.2 γεννη-
- 6.

$$\underbrace{\gamma\nu\omega}_{\text{future stem}}\text{-}\underbrace{\sigma}_{\text{tense suffix}}\text{-}\underbrace{o}_{\text{them. vowel}}\text{-}\underbrace{\mu\varepsilon\nu}_{\text{ending}}$$

- 8. αἰτήσομαι = *I will ask*
  αἰτήσῃ = *you will ask (sg.)*
  αἰτήσεται = *he (she, it) will ask*
  αἰτησόμεθα = *we will ask*
  αἰτήσεσθε = *you will ask (pl.)*
  αἰτήσονται = *they will ask*
- 9.2 *I am going away and you will seek me.* (Jn. 8:21)
- 9.4 *And why are they being baptized for them?* (1 Cor. 15:29)
- 9.6 *But the righteous out of faith will live.* (Rom. 1:17)
- 9.8 *And the two will be one flesh.* (Mt. 19:5)
- 9.10 *That the Lord himself will descend from heaven.* (1 Thess. 4:16)
- 9.12 *Now the Jerusalem above is free, which is our mother.* (Gal. 4:26)

 **Exercise 16**

- 2.2 **Augment**   **Aorist Suffix**
  ἐγεννα-   ἐγεννη-
- 2.4 ἐπηρωτα-   ἐπηρωτη-
- 4. ἔπεμψα = *I sent*
  ἔπεμψας = *you sent (sg.)*
  ἔπεμψεν = *he (she, it) sent*

ἐπέμψαμεν = *we sent*
ἐπέμψατε = *you sent (pl.)*
ἔπεμψαν = *they sent*

6.2 The cup that I drink you will drink. (Mk. 10:39)
6.4 And your fathers killed them. (Lk. 11:47)
6.6 For many times he falls into the fire, and many times into the water. (Mt. 17:15)
6.8 People loved more the darkness than the light; for their deeds were evil. (Jn. 3:19)

 Exercise 17

1.2 False
1.4 True
1.6 False
1.8 True
1.10 True

2.

$$\underset{\underset{\text{2}^{\text{nd}} \text{ aor. stem}}{\uparrow}}{\overset{\overset{\text{augment}}{\searrow}}{\overset{}{\grave{\epsilon}}}}\text{-}\beta\alpha\lambda\underset{\underset{\text{ending}}{\uparrow}}{\overset{\overset{\text{them. vowel}}{\searrow}}{\text{-o-}}}\nu$$

4. κρινῶ = *I will judge*
κρινεῖς = *you will judge (sg.)*
κρινεῖ = *he (she, it) will judge*
κρινοῦμεν = *we will judge*
κρινεῖτε = *you will judge (pl.)*
κρινοῦσιν = *they will judge*

6.2 Now you are releasing your servant. (Lk. 2:29)
6.4 By their fruits you will know them. (Mt. 7:16)
6.6 For whom God sent speaks the words of God. (Jn. 3:34)
6.8 And it came about after three days that they found him in the temple. (Lk. 2:46)

528   *New Testament Greek Primer*

6.10   *They reported what the chief priests and the elders told them.* (Acts 4:23)

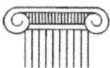 **Exercise 18**

- **1.2**   False
- **1.4**   False
- **1.6**   False
- **2.2**   **Augment**   **Aorist Suffix**
  ἐγεννα-   ἐγεννηθη-
- **2.4**   ἐπηρωτα-   ἐπηρωτηθη-
- **4.**   ἐπέμφθην = *I was sent*
  ἐπέμφθης = *you were sent (sg.)*
  ἐπέμφθη = *he (she, it) was sent*
  ἐπέμφθημεν = *we were sent*
  ἐπέμφθητε = *you were sent (pl.)*
  ἐπέμφθησαν = *they were sent*
- **6.2**   *And mountains were not found.* (Rev. 16:20)
- **6.4**   *Through your will they were and they were created.* (Rev. 4:11)
- **6.6**   *Now the ruler of this world will be cast outside.* (Jn. 12:31)
- **6.8**   *Therefore whether you eat or drink or do anything, do all things unto the glory of God.* (1 Cor. 10:31)

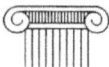 **Exercise 19**

- **1.2**   Fifth
- **1.4**   Reduplication
- **1.6**   Alpha
- **1.8**   Kappa

1.10	Voice Suffix	
2.2	**Reduplication**	**Voice Suffix**
	βεβαπτιζ-	βεβαπτικα-
2.4	ἠτε-	ἠτηκα-
4.	ἠτήκα = *I have asked*	
	ἠτήκας = *you have asked (sg.)*	
	ἠτήκεν = *he (she, it) has asked*	
	ἠτήκαμεν = *we have asked*	
	ἠτήκατε = *you have asked (pl.)*	
	ἠτήκαν = *they were sent*	
6.	ἐκεκρίκειν = *I had decided*	
	ἐκεκρίκεις = *you had decided (sg.)*	
	ἐκεκρίκει = *he (she, it) had decided*	
	ἐκεκρίκειμεν = *we had decided*	
	ἐκεκρίκειτε = *you had decided (pl.)*	
	ἐκεκρίκεισαν = *they had decided*	
7.2	*He is not here, but he has been raised. (Lk. 24:6)*	
7.4	*Your garments are moth-eaten. (Jas. 5:2)*	
7.6	*Beloved, now we are children of God. (1 Jn. 3:2)*	
7.8	*This gospel of the kingdom will be preached. (Mt. 24:14)*	
7.10	*I know where you dwell, where Satan's throne is. (Rev. 2:13)*	
7.12	*This one came to him by night and said to him, "Rabbi, we know that you are a teacher who has come from God." (Jn. 3:2)*	

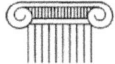 **Exercise 20**

1.2	False
1.4	False
1.6	True
1.8	False

1.10 True

2.

$$\underbrace{\lambda\upsilon}_{\text{future stem}} \text{-} \underbrace{\sigma}_{\text{tense suffix}} \text{-} \underbrace{\omega}_{\text{lengthened them. vowel}} \text{-} \underbrace{\mu\epsilon\nu}_{\text{ending}}$$

4. πέμψω = I send, might send
πέμψῃς = you send, might send (sg.)
πέμψῃ = he (she, it) sends, might send
πέμψωμεν = we send, might send
πέμψητε = you send, might send (pl.)
πέμψωσιν = they send, might send

6.2 They greeted him. (Mk. 9:15)
6.4 She greeted Elizabeth. (Lk. 1:40)
6.6 Joseph, son of David, stop fearing. (Mt. 1:20)
6.8 Do not greet anyone along the way. (Lk. 10:4)
6.10 And if you greet your brothers only, what more are you doing? (Mt. 5:47)
6.12 And if I told you earthly things and you do not believe, how will you believe if I tell you heavenly things? (Jn. 3:12)

 **Exercise 21**

1.2 d. -ουσιν
1.4 a. -σθωσαν
1.6 c. aorist
2.2 I am in their midst. (Mt. 18:20)
2.4 Tell this stone that it become bread. (Lk. 4:3)
2.6 Enter into the joy of your Lord. (Mt. 25:21)
2.8 Let what you heard from the beginning abide in you. (1 Jn. 2:24)

2.10 If anyone should keep my word, he will not see death forever. (Jn. 8:51)

2.12 He said, "Father, the hour has come; glorify your Son, in order that the Son might glorify you." (Jn. 17:1)

 **Exercise 22**

2.2 -σθαι

3.2 False

3.4 False

3.6 True

3.8 True

3.10 True

4. δύναμαι = *I am able*
δύνασαι (δύνῃ) = *you are able (sg.)*
δύναται = *he (she, it) is able*
δυνάμεθα = *we are able*
δύνασθε = *you are able (pl.)*
δύνανται = *they are able*

5.2 *I am not able to come.* (Lk. 14:20)

5.4 *Herod is going to seek the child.* (Mt. 2:13)

5.6 *It is not for you to know the times or the seasons.* (Acts 1:7)

5.8 *It is necessary that I proclaim (I must proclaim) the kingdom of God.* (Lk. 4:43)

5.10 *To have your brother's wife is not lawful.* (Mk. 6:18)

5.12 *For the things which we saw and heard we are not able not to speak.* (Acts 4:20)

5.14 *Scripture says, "I believed, therefore I spoke."* <u>We believe, therefore we also speak.</u> (2 Cor. 4:13)

6.2

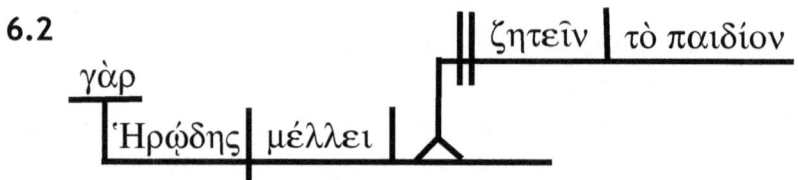

6.4

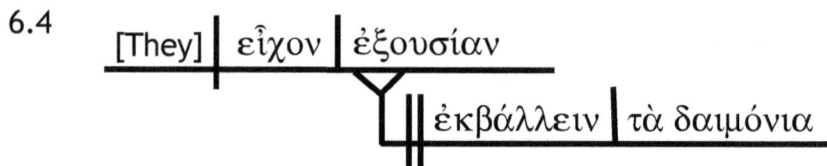

 **Exercise 23**

- **1.2** εἰς, πρός
- **1.4** διά
- **1.6** πρίν
- **1.8** μετά
- **2.2** Before Abraham was, *I* am. (Jn. 8:58)
- **2.4** To give is more blessed than to receive. (Acts 20:35)
- **2.6** He told a parable because he was near to Jerusalem. (Lk. 19:11)
- **2.8** She came from the ends of the earth to hear the wisdom of Solomon. (Mt. 12:42)
- **2.10** You will say that their master has need; and immediately he will send them. (Mt. 21:3)
- **3.**

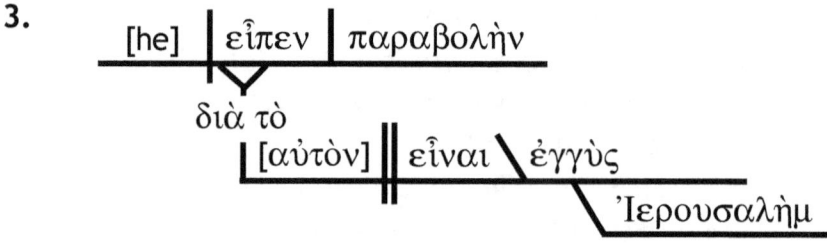

 **Exercise 24**

1.2

present stem → λυ-ουσ-ης ← pres. part. fem. suffix
fem. inflection ↑

2.2 ἀγαπῶντας: pres., act., part., acc., mas., pl.
2.4 γραφόμενα: pres., mid., part., nom./acc., neu., pl.
2.6 λέγοντες: pres., act., part., nom., mas., pl.
2.8 λέγων: pres., act., part., nom., mas., sg.
2.10 ἐχούσαις: pres., act., part., dat., fem., pl.

3.2

aorist stem → λυ-σασ-ης ← aor. part. fem. suffix
fem. inflection ↑

3.4

aorist stem → λυ-σα-μεν-ου ← aor. suffix
mid. part. suffix ↑   ↑ mas. ending

3.6

aorist stem → λυ-θεισ-ης ← aor. pass. fem. suffix
fem. ending ↑

4.2 ἐλθόντων: 2nd aor., act., part., gen., mas./neu., pl.
4.4 ἀκούσασα: aor., act., part., nom., fem., sg.
4.6 δεξάμενος: aor., mid., part., nom., mas., sg.

534 **New Testament Greek Primer**

4.8   πορευθέντες: aor., pass., part., nom., mas., pl.

5.2
```
      perf. redup.   perf. stem
         ↘             ↘
         λε-λυ-κυι-ας
      act. fem. suffix ↑   ↑ fem. ending
```

6.2   πεποιηκότες: perf., act., part., nom., mas., pl.
6.4   περιβεβλημένοι: perf., mid., part., nom., mas., pl.

 **Exercise 25**

1.2   *to those who have believed* (Acts 18:27)
1.4   *Pray for those who persecute you.* (Mt. 5:44)
1.6   *To those who love God, he works all things unto the good.* (Rom. 8:28)
1.8   *For if you love those who love you, what reward do you have?* (Mt. 5:46)
1.10 *For you are not the ones speaking but the Spirit of your Father (is) the one who speaks in you.* (Mt. 10:20)

2.2

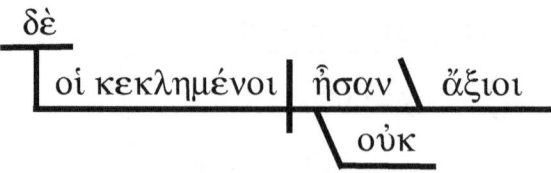

2.4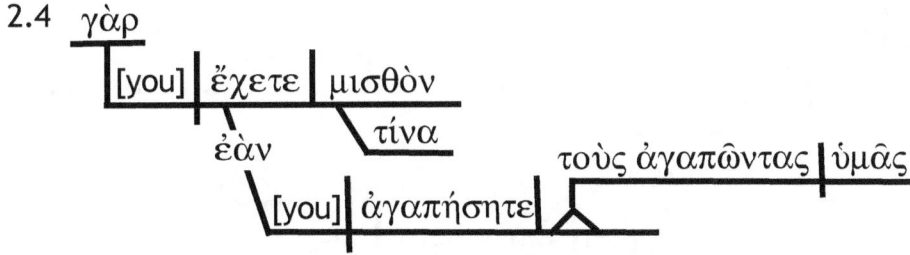

 **Exercise 26**

1.2 concession
1.4 temporal
1.6 manner
1.8 purpose
2.2 temporal
2.4 concession
2.6 complementary
2.8 circumstantial
2.10 temporal
3.2 *And when he stopped speaking, he said, . . .* (Lk. 5:4)
       speaking: complementary participle
3.4 *Let us see if Elijah comes to save him.* (Mt. 27:49)
       to save: purpose participle expressed as infinitive
3.6 *Which (power) worked in Christ when he raised him from the dead.* (Eph. 1:20)
       when he raised: temporal antecedent participle
3.8 *When the young man heard this statement, he went away grieving, for he had many possessions.* (Mt. 19:22)
       When . . . heard: temporal antecedent participle
       grieving: manner participle
       had: periphrastic participle, using imperfect of εἰμί (ἦν) and present active participle of ἔχω (ἔχων)

4.2

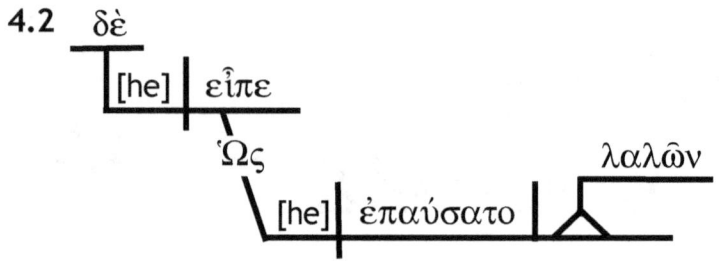

Exercise 27

1.2

$$\overset{\text{augment}}{\underset{\text{reduplication}\uparrow}{\overset{\downarrow}{\acute{\epsilon}}\text{-}\delta\iota\text{-}}}\overset{\overset{\text{pres. stem}}{\downarrow}}{\delta\text{o}\upsilon}\text{-}\underset{\uparrow\text{ secondary ending}}{\nu}$$

2.2 διδόασι: pres., act., ind., 3rd pl., δίδωμι
2.4 διδῶται: pres., mid./pass., subj., 3rd sg., δίδωμι
2.6 ἐδιδόμην: impf., mid./pass., ind., 1st sg., δίδωμι
2.8 διδῶμεν: pres., act., subj., 1st pl., δίδωμι
2.10 δίδου: pres., act., impr., 2nd sg., δίδωμι
3.2 *Give to every one who asks you. (Lk. 6:30)*
3.4 *The one who loves his life destroys it. (Jn. 12:25)*
3.6 *They give their power and authority to the beast. (Rev. 17:13)*
3.8 *My peace I give to you; not as the word gives do I give to you. (Jn. 14:27)*

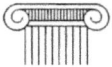 **Exercise 28**

1.2 ἀποδῷ: aor. subj.: act. 3rd sg. or mid. 2nd sg., ἀποδίδωμι
1.4 ἀπέδωκεν: aor., act., ind., 3rd sg., ἀποδίδωμι
1.6 ἀποδιδότω: pres., act., impr., 3rd sg., ἀποδίδωμι
1.8 παραδῷ: aor. subj.: act. 3rd sg. or mid. 2nd sg., παραδίδωμι
1.10 παρέδωκας: aor., act., ind., 2nd sg., παραδίδωμι
1.12 ἀφέντες: aor., act., part., nom., mas., pl., ἀφίημι
1.14 ἀναστάς: aor., act., part., nom., mas., sg., ἀνίστημι
1.16 παρεστηκότων: perf., act., part., gen., mas., pl., παρίστημι
1.18 ἐπιθείς: aor., act., part., nom., mas., sg., ἐπιτίθημι
1.20 ἐπιθῇς: aor., act., subj., 2nd sg., ἐπιτίθημι
1.22 ἐπιτιθέασιν: pres., act., ind., 3rd pl., ἐπιτίθημι
2.2 *All things have been given to me by my Father.* (Mt. 11:27)
2.4 *Jesus said to her, "Your brother will arise."* (Jn. 11:23)
2.6 *Then they placed their hands upon them and they were receiving the Holy Spirit.* (Acts 8:17)

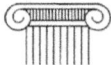 **Exercise E1.1**

Nc	president	Vp	has gone
Np	George	Nc	village
Nc	woman	Np	Bethlehem
Np	Elizabeth	Nc	king
Nc	computer	Np	Herod
Np	Macintosh	Nc	mother
Nc	onion	Np	Mary

Np	Vidalia	Vd	see
Vd	hide	Va	saw
Va	hid	Vp	has seen
Vp	has hidden	Nc	angel
Vd	go	Np	Gabriel
Va	went		

Exercise E1.2

adj.	red	adv.	diligently
adj.	beautiful	adv.	how?
adj.	small	adv.	beautifully
adj.	new	adv.	what?
adj.	old	adv.	when?
adv.	carefully	adv.	where?

Exercise E1.3

1. Nouns: *farmer, corn*
   Verbs: *cut*
   Adjectives: *The, wise, the, ripe*   Adverbs: *quickly*
2. Nouns: *John, test*
   Verbs: *is, studying*
   Adjectives: *that, hard*
   Adverbs: *How*
3. Nouns: *student, exam*
   Verbs: *had taken, learned, had been exempted*
   Adjectives: *The, industrious, the, long, final*
   Adverbs: *already, dutifully, when*
4. Imperfective

5. Aorist

 **Exercise E1.4**

1. [Man,] did (he) ever run ¹around the track ²with a surge ³of energy ⁴on that last lap!

2. The lady ¹in the first chair ²on the last row ³with a smile ⁴on (her) ⁵face made an A on this exam.

3. Both Bill ¹and Bob studied ²and learned the material, ³but, [my, oh my,] ¹(they) did not perform on the test as well as ²(you) ⁴or ³(I) ⁴thought (they) would!

4. The boards left ¹on the grass caused the blades ²under ³(them) to fade ⁴from green ¹to brown, ²yet rain ²and bright sunlight will revive (their) ⁵color ⁶by the end ³of (this) week ³or the next.

5. ¹Since Jean definitely is going, Janice ²and Taneean will decide today ³or tomorrow ⁴whether ¹(they) will go with ²(her.)

 **Exercise E2**

1.
    P to be confused   C as he was eating
    P in the library   P at the right time

540 New Testament Greek Primer

    C who were talking   C that flew overhead
    P studying the book   P of the class
    P running   C because he knew
    P to ask that question   P knowing the time

3.
- Ci pouring rain drenched band members
- Pvp pouring
- Cd who were lining up
- Pp on the sidelines
- Pvi to perform their halftime show
- Cd as the cheerleaders vainly tried
- Pvi to motivate unhappy fans
- Pvp leaving the stands in droves
- Cd after witnessing their team's dismal first-half performance
- Ci the person to save the day was the drummajor
- Pvi to save the day
- Pp of the band
- Cd whose spirited and defiant march to midfield inspired fans
- Pp to midfield
- Cd that just had left
- Pvi to return
- Pvp cheering and clapping

 **Exercise E3.1**

1.
- 2s *Gail, you are a good friend.*
- 1s *I know that person.*
- 3p *The students worked hard.*

2p *Janice and Johnny, you have a cute dog.*
3s *Patricia was late.*
1p *We have good times together.*

2.
subject What verb performance parameter is *fish*?
complete subject What verb performance parameter is *The hungry fish*?
finite Is *was fooled* finite or infinite?
infinite Is *shining* finite or infinite?
3s What person and number is *was fooled*?
passive What voice is *was fooled*?

 **Exercise E3.2**

1.1
Transitive: Is *appointed* transitive or intransitive?
Direct object: What verb performance parameter is *her*?
Object complement: What verb performance parameter is *coordinator*?
Complete predicate: What verb performance parameter is *appointed her coordinator of the project*?

1.2
Intransitive: Is *saw* transitive or intransitive?
Transitive: Is *helped* transitive or intransitive?
Intransitive: Is *became* transitive or intransitive?
Intransitive: Is *was* transitive or intransitive?
Copulative: What type verbs are both *became* and *was*?
Predicate nominative: What verb performance parameter is *friend*?
Predicate adjective: What verb performance parameter is *glad*?

2.

The receipt was handed (to me,) so I gave (the waitress my) charge card.

 **Exercise E3.3**

1.1

<u>durative, past</u>: What action kind and time is *was coming*?
<u>undefined, past</u>: What action kind and time is *spent*?
<u>perfect, past</u>: What action kind and time is *had finished*?

1.2

<u>durative, present</u>: What action kind and time is *am laughing*?
<u>undefined, future</u>: What action kind and time is *will tell*?
<u>perfect, present</u>: What action kind and time is *has resulted*?

2.

<u>Imperative</u>: Which mood has the greatest contingency?
<u>Subjunctive</u>: Which mood is used for a contrary to fact condition?
<u>Indicative</u>: Which mood is used to ask a question?
<u>Imperative</u>: Which mood is used to give a command?
<u>Indicative</u>: Which mood is used to make a statement?

3.

<u>Indicative</u>: *In English, one mood is used for actual action, and two other moods convey decreasing degrees of potential action.*
<u>Subjunctive</u>: *Verbs may undergo change to indicate mood.*
<u>Imperative</u>: *Study the following descriptions.*

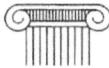 **Exercise E4.1**

1.

tool =	tools	moose =	moose
box =	boxes	lady =	ladies
life =	lives	foot =	feet
child =	children	mouse =	mice

2.

	Sg.	Pl.
Nominative:	I	we
Objective:	me	us
Possessive:	my	our

3.

	Sg.	Pl.
Nominative:	you	you
Objective:	you	you
Possessive:	your	your

4.

	Sg.	Pl.
Nominative:	she	they
Objective:	her	them
Possessive:	her	their

5.1

He = nominative (subject)
one = nominative (apposition)
coach = nominative (predicate)
oh = nominative (exclamation)
good = nominative (predicate)
nominative: What case are all these substantives?

5.2

Jeff (1st) =	nominative (absolute)
base =	objective (direct obj.)
Bob (1st) =	objective (preposition)
our =	possessive
catcher =	objective (apposition)
Bob (2nd) =	nominative (vocative)
pitch =	objective (preposition)
Jeff (2nd) =	objective (direct obj.)
baserunner =	nominative (apposition)
league =	objective (preposition)
1 (our)	How many nouns in the previous list required inflection to show case function?

Exercise E4.2

Verb	Pres.	Past	Past Part.	Rg.?
cast	cast	cast	cast	yes
fight	fight	fought	fought	no
believe	believe	believed	believed	yes
get	get	got	gotten	no
sing	sing	sang	sung	no

1. He runs. (intransitive)
2. She is good. (copulative)
3. We dove into the pool. (transitive)
4. John hit the ball to him. (transitive)
5. She got a red rose from him. (transitive)
6. To whom do we owe this honor? (transitive)

Answer Key

7. I turned in my homework today. (transitive)
8. The team that played well won the game. (transitive)
9. The student who is going earned the trip. ("is going": intransitive; "earned": transitive)
10. The good man gave them his seat on the bus. (transitive)

Photo © Gerald L. Stevens

Fig. 23. Sardis Bathhouse. Of the beautiful remains at the ancient site of Sardis in Turkey is the "Bathhouse." The detailed scrollwork and carving of the original have been reconstructed by supplementing surviving material from the second century A.D. The Sardis bathhouse actually was a complex that afforded a gymnasium for sporting events and public baths. Since the floor was completely covered in white marble, the structure also has been called the "Marble Hall." Public baths were places of important social activity in the Roman world. The buildings included statues to gods and goddesses, various works of art, and displays of Roman imperial propaganda. The ancient bathhouse perhaps is the institution that best shows the amalgamation of Greek and Roman worlds in architecture, function, and social interaction. This thorough blending of two worlds is why this ancient society often is labeled the "Greco-Roman world."

In the Book of Revelation, Christ wrote a letter to the church at Sardis. In his assessment of the church he charged that members had "defiled their garments" (Rev. 3:4). This image usually is taken as a metaphor for how they lived their lives in the context of Sardis and its pagan culture. Such issues of Christ and culture always have been part of the ongoing struggle to define faith and practice.

Vocabulary Summary

he following list summarizes the words introduced in this grammar arranged alphabetically. The number is the chapter. The frequency is 50 or more times.

Ἀβραάμ, *Abraham* 16
ἀγαθός, *good* 8
ἀγαπάω, *I love* 12
ἀγάπη, *love* 5
ἀγαπητός, *beloved* 19
ἄγγελος, *angel* 4
ἅγιος, *holy* 8
ἄγω, *I lead* 17
ἀδελφός, *brother* 4
αἷμα, *blood* 14
αἴρω, *I take up* 13
αἰτέω, *I ask* 13
αἰών, *eternity* 11
αἰώνιος, *eternal* 8
ἀκολουθέω, *I follow* 12
ἀκούω, *I hear* 2
ἀλήθεια, *truth* 13
ἀλλά, *but* 7
ἀλλήλοις, *to one another* 9
ἀλλήλους, *one another* 9
ἀλλήλων, *of one another* 9
ἄλλος, *other* 8
ἁμαρτία, *sin* 5
ἀμήν, *truly* 10
ἄν, *(particle)* 14
ἀνά, *up* 3
ἀναβαίνω, *I go up* 15
ἀνήρ, *man, husband* 7
ἄνθρωπος, *man* 4
ἀνίστημι, *I cause to arise; I arise* 28
ἀνοίγω, *I open* 15
ἀντί, *against* 6
ἅπαξ, *once* 11
ἀπέθανον, *I died* 17
ἀπέρχομαι, *I go away* 3
ἀπό, *away from* 3
ἀποδίδωμι, *I give back, pay; I sell* 28
ἀποθνῄσκω, *I die* 13
ἀποκρίνομαι, *I answer* 3
ἀποκτείνω, *I kill* 16
ἀπόλλυμι, *I destroy, perish* 27
ἀπολύω, *I release* 17
ἀποστέλλω, *I send* 10
ἀπόστολος, *apostle* 15
ἄρα, *then, therefore* 14
ἄρτος, *bread* 6
ἀρχή, *beginning* 21
ἀρχιερεύς, *high priest* 11
ἄρχω, *I rule; mid.: I begin* 14
ἀσπάζομαι, *I greet* 20
αὕτη, *this, these* (fem.) 10
αὐτοί, *they* 9
αὐτός, *he (she, it, self, same)* 9
ἀφίημι, *I permit, forgive* 28

ἄχρι, *up to* 20
βάλλω, *I throw* 11
βαπτίζω, *I baptize* 15
βασιλεία, *kingdom* 5
βασιλεύς, *king* 12
βλέπω, *I see* 6
Γαλιλαία, *Galilee* 19
γάρ, *for* 7
γεννάω, *I beget* 12
γῆ, *earth, land* 5
γίνομαι, *I am, become* 3
γινώσκω, *I know* 2
γλῶσσα, *tongue* 23
γραμματεύς, *scribe* 18
γραφή, *writing, scripture* 23
γράφω, *I write* 2
γυνή, *woman, wife* 7
δαιμόνιον, *demon* 18
Δαυίδ, *David* 20
δέ, *and, but, now, so* 1
δεῖ, *must, it is necessary* 22
δέκα, *ten* 10
δεξιός, *right* 21
δεύτερος, *second* 11
δέχομαι, *I receive* 21
διά, *through* 1
διδάσκαλος, *teacher* 20
διδάσκω, *I teach* 14
δίδωμι, *I give, grant, allow* 27
δίκαιος, *righteous* 15
δικαιοσύνη, *justice, righteousness* 6
διό, *therefore* 22

δίς, *twice* 11
δοκέω, *I think, seem* 18
δόξα, *glory* 5
δοξάζω, *I glorify* 19
δοῦλος, *slave* 10
δύναμαι, *I am able* 22
δύναμις, *power* 11
δύο, *two* 2
δώδεκα, *twelve* 16
ἐάν, *if, when* 20
ἑαυτοῦ, *him-(her, it)-self* 9
ἑαυτῶν, *our-(your, them)-selves* 9
ἔβαλον, *I threw* 17
ἔβην, *I went* 17
ἐγείρω, *I raise* 10
ἐγώ, *I* 9
ἐγενόμην, *I became* 17
ἔγνων, *I knew* 17
ἔθνος, *Gentile, nation* 7
εἰ, *if* 14
εἶδον, *I saw* 17
εἴκοσι, *twenty* 11
εἰμί, *I am* 8
εἶναι, *to be* 22
εἶπον, *I said* 17
εἰρήνη, *peace* 6
εἷς, *one* 1
εἰς, *into* 2
εἰσέρχομαι, *I go into* 3
εἴτε, *if, whether* 18
ἐκ, *from, out of* 2
ἕκαστος, *each, every* 15

ἑκατόν, *one hundred* 11
ἐκβάλλω, *I throw out, drive out* 15
ἐκεῖ, *there* 11
ἐκεῖνος, *that, those* 10
ἐκκλησία, *church* 13
ἔλαβον, *I took, received* 17
ἐλπίς, *hope* 22
ἐμαυτοῦ, *myself* 9
ἐμός, *my* 9
ἐν, *in* 1
ἕν, *one* (neuter) 11
ἐννέα, *nine* 9
ἐντολή, *commandment* 17
ἐνώπιον, *before* 14
ἕξ, *six* 6
ἐξέρχομαι, *I go out* 3
ἔξεστιν, *it is lawful, right* 22
ἐξουσία, *authority* 6
ἔξω, *outside* 18
ἐπαγγελία, *promise* 22
ἐπερωτάω, *I ask* 18
ἔπεσον, *I fell* 17
ἐπί, *on, upon* 2
ἔπιον, *I drank* 17
ἐπιτίθημι, *I lay upon* 28
ἑπτά, *seven* 7
ἔργον, *work* 4
ἔρχομαι, *I come, go* 3
ἐρωτάω, *I ask* 18
ἐσθίω, *I eat* 2
ἔσομαι, *I shall be* 15
ἔσχατος, *last* 22

Vocabulary Summary

ἔσχον, *I had* 17
ἕτερος, *another* 14
ἔτι, *still, yet* 14
εὐαγγελίζω, *I bring good news* 22
εὐαγγέλιον, *good news, gospel* 4
εὐθύς, *immediately* 23
εὑρίσκω, *I find* 2
εὗρον, *I found* 17
ἔφαγον, *I ate* 17
ἔφη, *he (she) was saying* 18
ἔχω, *I have* 2
ἕως, *until* 10
ζάω, ζήω, *I live* 12
ζητέω, *I seek* 12
ζωή, *life* 5
ἡ, *the* (fem.) 6
ἤ, *or, than* 7
ἥ, *who, whom, whose* (fem.) 11
ᾖ, *he might be* 20
ἤγαγον, *I led, brought* 17
ᾔδειν, *I was knowing* 19
ἤδη, *now, already* 19
ἦλθον, *I went, came* 17
ἡμεῖς, *we* 9
ἡμέρα, *day* 5
ἡμέτερος, *our* 9
ἤμην, *I was* 13
ἤνεγκα, *I brought* 17
θάλασσα, *sea* 5
θάνατος, *death* 11
θέλημα, *will* 18
θέλω, *I wish, want* 2
θεός, *God* 1

θεωρέω, *I observe* 21
θρόνος, *throne* 19
ἴδε, *Behold!* 21
ἴδιος, *his, its, her* 9
ἰδού, *Behold!* 7
ἱερόν, *temple* 16
Ἱεροσόλυμα, *Jerusalem* 19
Ἱερουσαλήμ, *Jerusalem* 15
Ἰησοῦς, *Jesus* 4
ἱμάτιον, *garment* 19
ἵνα, *in order that, so that* 20
Ἰουδαῖος, *Jew* 8
ἴσθι, *You be!* 21
Ἰσραήλ, *Israel* 16
ἵστημι, *I place, set, stand* 27
Ἰωάννης, *John* 5
κἀγώ, *and I* 14
κάθημαι, *I sit down* 3
καθώς, *as, just as* 7
καί, *and* 1
καιρός, *season, time* 6
κακός, *bad, evil* 23
καλέω, *I call* 12
καλός, *good, beautiful* 8
κἄν, *even though* (= καὶ ἄν) 20
καρδία, *heart* 5
καρπός, *fruit* 17
κατά, *down* 3
καταβαίνω, *I go down* 15
κεφαλή, *head* 16
κηρύσσω, *I preach* 19

κόσμος, *world* 4
κράζω, *I cry out* 21
κρείττων, *better* 11
κρίνω, *I judge* 13
κύριος, *lord, master* 4
λαλέω, *I speak* 12
λαμβάνω, *I take, receive* 2
λαός, *people* 10
λέγω, *I say* 2
λίθος, *stone* 21
λόγος, *word* 4
λοιπός, *remaining, rest* 21
λύω, *I loose* 2
μαθητής, *disciple* 5
μακάριος, *happy* 23
μάλιστα, *most* 11
μᾶλλον, *more* 11
μαρτυρέω, *I witness, testify* 14
μέγας, *great* 8
μείζων, *greater* 11
μέλλω, *I am about to, am going to* 13
μέν, *indeed, on the one hand* 7
μένω, *I remain, abide, stay* 13
μέσος, *middle* 21
μετά, *with, after* 4
μή, *no, not* 12
μηδέ, *but not, nor* 20
μηδείς, *no one* 20
μήτε, *and not, neither* 20
μήτηρ, *mother* 15
μία, *one* (fem.) 11

μόνος, alone, only 8
μυριάδες, myriads 11
μύριοι, ten thousand 11
Μωϋσῆς, Moses 15
νεκρός, dead 8
νόμος, law 10
νῦν, now 11
νύξ, night 19
ὁ, ἡ, τό, the 6
ὅ, what, which, that 11
ὁδός, way, road 6
οἶδα, I know 19
οἰκία, house 6
οἶκος, house, building 13
οἷος, as 10
ὀκτώ, eight 8
ὅλος, whole 8
ὄνομα, name 7
ὅπου, where 11
ὅπως, that, in order that 20
ὁράω, I see 12
ὄρος, mountain 18
ὅς, who, whose, whom 11
ὅσος, as much as 10
ὅστις, who, whoever, which 12
ὅταν, when, whenever 20
ὅτε, when 11
ὅτι, that, because 11
οὐ, no, not 1
οὐδέ, and not, neither, nor 10
οὐδείς, no one, nothing 8
οὖν, therefore 7
οὐρανός, heaven 4
οὔτε, and not 14
οὗτος, this, these 10
οὕτως, thus, so 11
οὐχί, no, not 22
ὀφθαλμός, eye, sight 6
ὄχλος, crowd 7
παιδίον, child 22
πάλιν, again 10
παρά, beside 5
παραβολή, parable 23
παραδίδωμι, I hand over, betray 28
παρακαλέω, I comfort 12
παραλαμβάνω, I take, receive 23
παρίστημι, I present, offer; I am present, stand by 28
πᾶς, every, all 8
πατήρ, father 7
Παῦλος, Paul 7
πείθω, I persuade, trust 23
πέμπω, I send 15
πέντε, five 5
περί, around 5
περιπατέω, I walk 12
Πέτρος, Peter 7
Πιλᾶτος, Pilate 21
πίνω, I drink 16
πίπτω, I fall 14
πιστεύω, I believe 2
πίστις, faith 7
πιστός, faithful 17
πλείων, more than 11
πληρόω, I fulfill 12
πλοῖον, boat, ship 16
πνεῦμα, wind, spirit 7
ποιέω, I do, make, produce 12
ποῖος, which? what? what type? 12
πόλις, city 7
πολύς, much, many 8
πονηρός, evil 15
πορεύομαι, I go, proceed 3
πόσος, how much? 12
πούς, foot 14
πρεσβύτερος, elder, older person 17
πρίν, before 23
πρό, before 4
πρός, to, toward 3
προσέρχομαι, I go, come to, approach 3
προσεύχομαι, I pray 14
προσκυνέω, I worship, reverence 20
πρόσωπον, face 16
προφήτης, prophet 5
πρῶτος, first 8
πῦρ, fire 16
πῶς, how? 11
ῥῆμα, word 17
σάββατον, Sabbath 17
σάρξ, flesh 7
σεαυτοῦ, yourself 9
σημεῖον, sign, wonder, miracle 4

Σίμων, Simon 16
σός, your (sg.) 9
σοφία, wisdom 23
σπείρω, I sow 23
στόμα, mouth 15
σύ, you (sg.) 9
σύν, with 6
συνάγω, I gather, bring together 21
συναγωγή, synagogue, assembly 21
σῴζω, I heal, save 13
σῶμα, body 7
τέ, and, and so 7
τέκνον, child 4
τέσσαρες, four 4
τηρέω, I keep, observe 14
τίθημι, I put, place, lay 27
τίς, who? which? what? 12
τις, someone, something 12

τό, the (neu.) 6
τοιοῦτος, such 10
τόπος, place 6
τοσοῦτος, so much 10
τότε, then 7
τοῦτο, this, these (neu.) 10
τρεῖς, three 3
τρίς, three times 11
τρίτος, third 11
τυφλός, blind, blind person 23
ὕδωρ, water 16
υἱός, son 4
ὑμεῖς, you (pl.) 9
ὑμέτερος, your (pl.) 9
ὑπάγω, I go, go away 15
ὑπάρχω, I am, exist 12
ὑπέρ, over, above 4
ὑπό, under 4
φασίν, they say 18
Φαρισαῖος, Pharisee 6

φέρω, I bring, carry 17
φημί, I say 18
φησίν, he (she) says 18
φοβέομαι, I am afraid 12
φωνή, sound, voice 5
φῶς, light, fire 16
χαίρω, I rejoice 16
χαρά, joy 21
χάρις, grace, favor 7
χείρ, hand 7
χίλιοι, one thousand 11
Χριστός, messiah, Christ, Anointed 4
χρόνος, time 22
ψυχή, life, soul 5
ὧδε, here 19
ὥρα, hour 13
ὡς, as, that, how, about, while 11
ὥστε, so that, therefore 15

Photo © Gerald L. Stevens

Fig. 24. Curetes Street. This is the famous white marble of Curetes Street in Ephesus, Turkey, leading from the upper city's governmental buildings, public baths, monuments, temples, and terrace homes of the aristocratic wealthy to the lower city's Library of Celsus and Mazeus-Mithridates Gate into the lower agora marketplace and the famous Ephesian theater.

In opening his letter to the Ephesians, Paul alluded to the notable wealth of the Ephesian elite by way of reminding the Ephesians of an even richer hope in Christ. Thus, Paul prayed that "the eyes of your heart might be enlightened, in order that you may know what is the hope of His calling, what are the riches of the glory of His inheritance in the saints" (Eph. 1:18).

principal parts

The following list beginning on the next page summarizes principal parts for verbs occurring fifty or more times in the New Testament. A dash line indicates a part that does not appear in the New Testament. Second aorist forms are indicated with an asterisk. An alternate spelling variation of the same verb is given in parentheses.

Principal Parts

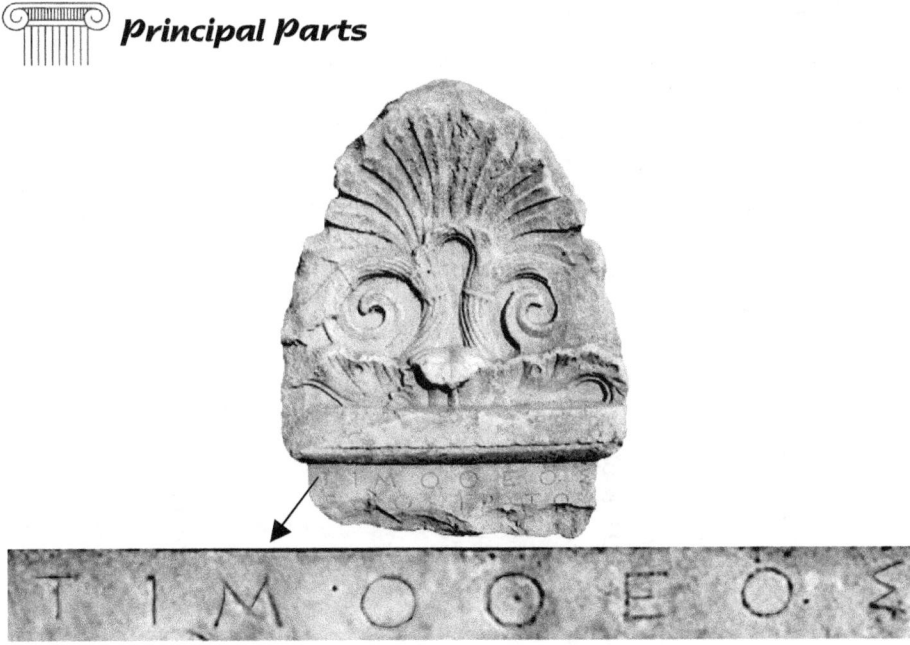

Photo © Gerald L. Stevens

Fig. 25. Timotheos Inscription. In the Roman Agora of Athens, a new area built by the Romans to compete with the ancient Greek agora, is this inscription on a tombstone: ΤΙΜΟΘΕΟΣ (Τιμόθεος, "Timothy").

Principal Parts

First	Second	Third	Fourth	Fifth	Sixth
ἀγαπάω	ἀγαπήσω	ἠγάπησα	ἠγάπηκα	ἠγάπημαι	ἠγαπήθην
ἄγω	ἄξω	ἤγαγον*	ἦχα	ἦγμαι	ἤχθην
αἴρω	ἀρῶ	ἦρα	ἦρκα	ἦρμαι	ἤρθην
αἰτέω	αἰτήσω	ᾔτησα	ᾔτηκα	ᾔτημαι	ᾐτήθην
ἀκολουθέω	ἀκολουθήσω	ἠκολούθησα	ἠκολούθηκα	ἠκολούθημαι	ἠκολουθήθην
ἀκούω	ἀκούσω	ἤκουσα	ἀκήκοα	ἤκουσμαι	ἠκούσθην
ἀναβαίνω	ἀναβήσομαι	ἀνέβην*	ἀναβέβηκα	------	------
ἀνίστημι	ἀναστήσω	ἀνέστησα	ἀνέστηκα	ἀνέστημαι	ἀνεστάθην
ἀνοίγω	ἀνοίξω	ἀνέῳξα (ἠνέῳξα, ἤνοιξα)	ἀνέῳγα	ἀνέῳγμαι (ἠνέῳγμαι)	ἀνεῴχθην ἠνεῴχθην, ἠνοίχθην, ἠνοίγην)
ἀπέρχομαι	ἀπελεύσομαι	ἀπῆλθον*	ἀπελήλυθα	------	------
ἀποθνῄσκω	ἀποθανοῦμαι	ἀπέθανον*	------	------	------
ἀποκρίνομαι	------	ἀπεκρινάμην	------	------	ἀπεκρίθην
ἀποκτείνω	ἀποκτενῶ	ἀπέκτεινα	------	------	ἀπεκτάνθην

Principal Parts

First	Second	Third	Fourth	Fifth	Sixth
ἀπόλλυμι	ἀπολέσω (ἀπολῶ)	ἀπώλεσα	ἀπόλεκα (ἀπόλωλα)	ἀπολώλεσμαι	ἀπωλέσθην
ἀπολύω	ἀπολύσω	ἀπέλυσα	------	ἀπολέλυμαι	ἀπελύθην
ἀποστέλλω	ἀποστελῶ	ἀπέστειλα	ἀπέσταλκα	ἀπέσταλμαι	ἀπεστάλην
ἄρχω	ἄρξω	ἦρξα	------	------	------
ἀσπάζομαι	------	ἠσπασάμην	------	------	------
ἀφίημι (ἀφίω, ἀφέω)	ἀφήσω	ἀφῆκα	------	ἀφέομαι	ἀφέθην
βάλλω	βαλῶ	ἔβαλον*	βέβληκα	βέβλημαι	ἐβλήθην
βαπτίζω	βαπτίσω	ἐβάπτισα	------	βεβάπτισμαι	ἐβαπτίσθην
βλέπω	βλέψω	ἔβλεψα	------	------	------
γεννάω	γεννήσω	ἐγέννησα	γεγέννηκα	γεγέννημαι	ἐγεννήθην
γίνομαι	γενήσομαι	ἐγενόμην*	γέγονα	γεγένημαι	ἐγενήθην
γινώσκω	γνώσομαι	ἔγνων*	ἔγνωκα	ἔγνοσμαι	ἐγνώσθην
γράφω	γράψω	ἔγραψα	γέγραφα	γέγραμμαι	ἐγράφην
δεῖ [impersonal, third singular form; imperfect, ἔδει]					
δέχομαι	δέξομαι	ἐδεξάμην	------	δέδεγμαι	ἐδέχθην

Principal Parts

First	Second	Third	Fourth	Fifth	Sixth
διδάσκω	διδάξω	ἐδίδαξα	------	------	ἐδιδάχθην
δίδωμι	δώσω	ἔδωκα	δέδωκα	δέδομαι	ἐδόθην
δοκέω	------	ἔδοξα	------	------	------
δοξάζω	δοξάσω	ἐδόξασα	------	δεδόξασμαι	ἐδοξάσθην
δύναμαι	δυνήσομαι	------	------	------	ἠδυνήθην
ἐγείρω	ἐγερῶ	ἤγειρα	------	ἐγήγερμαι	ἠγέρθην
εἰμί (impf. ἤμην)	ἔσομαι	------	------	------	------
εἰσέρχομαι	εἰσελεύσομαι	εἰσῆλθον*	εἰσελήλυθα	------	------
ἐκβάλλω	ἐκβαλῶ	ἐξέβαλον*	------	------	ἐξεβλήθην
ἐξέρχομαι	ἐξελεύσομαι	ἐξῆλθον*	ἐξελήλυθα	------	------
ἔξεστιν [thirty-one times; three times as the participle form ἐξόν]					
ἐπερωτάω	ἐπερωτήσω	ἐπηρώτησα	------	------	------
ἔρχομαι	ἐλεύσομαι	ἦλθον*	ἐλήλυθα	------	------
ἐρωτάω	ἐρωτήσω	ἠρώτησα	------	------	------
ἐσθίω	φάγομαι	ἔφαγον*	------	------	------
εὐαγγελίζω	------	εὐηγγέλισα	------	εὐηγγέλισμαι	εὐηγγελίσθην

Principal Parts

First	Second	Third	Fourth	Fifth	Sixth
εὑρίσκω	εὑρήσω	εὗρησα (εὗρον)*	εὕρηκα	-----	εὑρέθην
ἔχω (impf. εἶχον)	ἕξω	ἔσχον*	ἔσχηκα	-----	-----
ζάω	ζήσω	ἔζησα	-----	-----	-----
ζητέω	ζητήσω	ἐζήτησα	-----	-----	ἐζητήθην
θέλω (impf. ἤθελον)	-----	ἠθέλησα	-----	-----	-----
θεωρέω	θεωρήσω	ἐθεώρησα	-----	-----	-----
ἵστημι	στήσω	ἔστησα (ἔστην)	ἕστηκα	-----	ἐστάθην
κάθημαι	καθήσομαι	-----	-----	-----	-----
καλέω	καλέσω	ἐκάλεσα	κέκληκα	κέκλημαι	ἐκλήθην
καταβαίνω	καταβήσομαι	κατέβην*	καταβέβηκα	-----	-----
κηρύσσω	-----	ἐκήρυξα	-----	-----	ἐκηρύχθην
κράζω	κράξω	ἔκραξα	κέκραγα	-----	-----
κρίνω	κρινῶ	ἔκρινα	κέκρικα	κέκριμαι	ἐκρίθην

Principal Parts

First	Second	Third	Fourth	Fifth	Sixth
λαλέω	λαλήσω	ἐλάλησα	λελάληκα	λελάλημαι	ἐλαλήθην
λαμβάνω	λήμψομαι	ἔλαβον*	εἴληφα	------	------
λέγω	ἐρῶ	εἶπον*	εἴρηκα	εἴρημαι	ἐρρέθην
μαρτυρέω	μαρτυρήσω	ἐμαρτύρησα	μεμαρτύρηκα	μεμαρτύρημαι	ἐμαρτυρήθην
μέλλω	μελλήσω	------	------	------	------
μέλω (impers. 3rd sg., μέλει; imperfect, ἔμελεν; pres. imperative, μελέτω)					
μένω	μενῶ	ἔμεινα	μεμένηκα	------	------
οἶδα	εἰδήσω	------	οἶδα (εἰδῆτε, εἰδῆς = subjunctive forms)	------	------
ὁράω	ὄψομαι	εἶδον*	ἑόρακα (ἑώρακα)	------	ὤφθην
παραδίδωμι	παραδώσω	παρέδωκα	παραδέδωκα	παραδέδομαι	παρεδόθην
παρακαλέω	------	παρεκάλεσα	------	παρακέκλημαι	παρεκλήθην
πείθω	πείσω	ἔπεισα	πέποιθα	πέπεισμαι	ἐπείσθην
πέμπω	πέμψω	ἔπεμψα	------	------	ἐπέμφθην
περιπατέω	περιπατήσω	περιεπάτησα	------	------	------
πίνω	πίομαι	ἔπιον*	πέπωκα	------	------

Principal Parts

First	Second	Third	Fourth	Fifth	Sixth
πίπτω	πεσοῦμαι	ἔπεσον* (ἔπεσα)	πέπτωκα	-----	-----
πιστεύω	πιστεύσω	ἐπίστευσα	πεπίστευκα	πεπίστευμαι	ἐπιστεύθην
πληρόω	πληρώσω	ἐπλήρωσα	-----	πεπλήρωμαι	ἐπληρώθην
ποιέω	ποιήσω	ἐποίησα	πεποίηκα	πεποίημαι	-----
πορεύομαι	πορεύσομαι	-----	-----	πεπόρευμαι	ἐπορεύθην
προσέρχομαι	-----	προσῆλθον*	προσελήλυθα	-----	-----
προσεύχομαι	προσεύξομαι	προσηυξάμην	-----	-----	-----
προσκυνέω	προσκυνήσω	προσεκύνησα	-----	-----	-----
σπείρω	-----	ἔσπειρα	-----	ἔσπαρμαι	ἐσπάρην
συνάγω	συνάξω	συνήγαγον*	-----	συνῆγμαι	συνήχθην
σῴζω (σώζω)	σώσω	ἔσωσα	σέσωκα	σέσωσμαι	ἐσώθην
τηρέω	τηρήσω	ἐτήρησα	τετήρηκα	τετήρημαι	ἐτηρήθην
τίθημι	θήσω	ἔθηκα	τέθεικα	τέθειμαι	ἐτέθην
ὑπάγω	-----	-----	-----	-----	-----
ὑπάρχω	-----	-----	-----	-----	-----
φέρω	οἴσω	ἤνεγκα*	ἐνήνοχα	-----	ἠνέχθην

Principal Parts

First	Second	Third	Fourth	Fifth	Sixth
φημί [three other forms in the New Testament: ἔφη (impf., act.), φησί (pre., act.), φασί (pre., act.)]					
φοβέω	-------	-------		-------	ἐφοβήθην
χαίρω	χαρήσομαι	ἐχάρην (ἐχαίρησα)	-------	-------	ἐχάρην

paradigms

The following tables summarize basic paradigms used in this grammar. Nominal patterns, as in nouns, adjectives, comparisons, and numerals, often show basic first, second, and third declension inflections. Pronouns follow these patterns too, though some distinctions do apply. Proper names are a breed to themselves; sometimes they follow a recognizable pattern, but sometimes do not. Some have no inflection, similar to English proper names.

Minor changes in morphology result from various letter reactions when endings are added. Certain vowels contract. Others, such as stem vowels, can lengthen into long vowels or diphthongs. Consonants change due to reactions with stops, liquids, and sibilants.

 **Declensions, Article, Nouns, Etc.**

Second Declension			
Mas./Fem.		Neuter	
Sing.	Plu.	Sing.	Plu.
-ος	-οι	-ον	-α
-ου	-ων	-ου	-ων
-ῳ	-οις	-ῳ	-οις
-ον	-ους	-ον	-α

First Declension						
Singular						Plu.
Feminine			Masculine		All
-α	-η	-α	-ης	-ας	-αι
-ας	-ης	-ης	-ου	-ου	-ων
-ᾳ	-ῃ	-ῃ	-ῃ	-ᾳ	-αις
-αν	-ην	-αν	-ην	-αν	-ας

Third Declension[1]					
Mas/Fem		Neuter[2]			
Sng.	Plu.	Sng.	Plu.	Sng.	Plu.
-ς/--	-ες	--	-α	-ος	-η
-ος	-ων	ος	-ων	-ους	-ων
-ι	-σι(ν)	-ι	-σι(ν)	-ει	-σι(ν)
-α/-ν	-ας	--	-α	-ος	-η

The Article

Masculine		Neuter		Feminine	
ὁ	οἱ	τό	τά	ἡ	αἱ
τοῦ	τῶν	τοῦ	τῶν	τῆς	τῶν
τῷ	τοῖς	τῷ	τοῖς	τῇ	ταῖς
τόν	τούς	τό	τά	τήν	τάς

[1] Letter reactions obscure the ending in: (1) nom. sg., (2) dat. pl.
[2] A second set is ἔθνος. Table 7.11, p. 83.

Noun Paradigms

4.2 (2D Mas.)		4.4 (2D Neu.)	
λόγος	λόγοι	δῶρον	δῶρα
λόγου	λόγων	δώρου	δώρων
λόγῳ	λόγοις	δώρῳ	δώροις
λόγον	λόγους	δῶρον	δῶρα
5.2 (1D "α pure")		5.4 (1D "η pure")	
καρδία	καρδίαι	ἀγάπη	ἀγάπαι
καρδίας	καρδιῶν	ἀγάπης	ἀγαπῶν
καρδίᾳ	καρδίαις	ἀγάπῃ	ἀγάπαις
καρδίαν	καρδίας	ἀγάπην	ἀγάπας
5.6 (1D Mixed)		5.8 (1D Mas., -ης nom.)	
δόξα	δόξαι	μαθητής	μαθηταί
δόξης	δοξῶν	μαθητοῦ	μαθητῶν
δόξῃ	δόξαις	μαθητῇ	μαθηταῖς
δόξαν	δόξας	μαθητήν	μαθητάς
5.9 (1D "α pure" cntr.)		(1D Proper Name)	
γῆ	-------	Ἰωάννης	-------
γῆς	-------	Ἰωάννου	-------
γῇ	-------	Ἰωάννῃ	-------
γῆν	-------	Ἰωάννην	-------
(Irreg. Prop. Name)		7.7 (3D Typical)	
Ἰησοῦς	-------	σάρξ	σάρκες
Ἰησοῦ	-------	σαρκός	σαρκῶν
Ἰησοῦ	-------	σαρκί	σαρξί(ν)
Ἰησοῦν	-------	σάρκα	σάρκας

7.8 (3D Significant)		7.9 (3D Neuter)	
ἄρχων	ἄρχοντες	σῶμα	σώματα
ἄρχοντος	ἀρχόντων	σώματος	σωμάτων
ἄρχοντι	ἄρχουσιν	σώματι	σώμασιν
ἄρχοντα	ἄρχοντας	σῶμα	σώματα
7.10 (3D Distinctive)		7.11 (3D Odd)	
πίστις	πίστεις	ἔθνος	ἔθνη
πίστεως	πίστεων	ἔθνους	ἐθνῶν
πίστει	πίστεσιν	ἔθνει	ἔθνεσιν
πίστιν	πίστεις	ἔθνος	ἔθνη

Pronoun and Number Paradigms

9.2 (1ˢᵗ Per.: I, we)		9.3 (2ⁿᵈ Per.: you, you)	
ἐγώ	ἡμεῖς	σύ	ὑμεῖς
ἐμοῦ	ἡμῶν	σοῦ	ὑμῶν
ἐμοί	ἡμῖν	σοί	ὑμῖν
ἐμέ	ἡμᾶς	σέ	ὑμᾶς
9.4 (3ʳᵈ Per.: he, they)		9.5 (3ʳᵈ Per.: it, they)	
αὐτός	αὐτοί	αὐτό	αὐτά
αὐτοῦ	αὐτῶν	αὐτοῦ	αὐτῶν
αὐτῷ	αὐτοῖς	αὐτῷ	αὐτοῖς
αὐτόν	αὐτούς	αὐτό	αὐτά
9.6 (3ʳᵈ Pers.: she, they)		9.7 (Possessive: my = m)	
αὐτή	αὐταί	ἐμός	ἐμοί
αὐτῆς	αὐτῶν	ἐμοῦ	ἐμῶν
αὐτῇ	αὐταῖς	ἐμῷ	ἐμοῖς
αὐτήν	αὐτάς	ἐμόν	ἐμούς

Paradigms

9.7 (Possessive: my = n)		9.7 (Possessive: my = f)	
ἐμόν	ἐμά	ἐμή	ἐμαί
ἐμοῦ	ἐμῶν	ἐμῆς	ἐμῶν
ἐμῷ	ἐμοῖς	ἐμῇ	ἐμαῖς
ἐμόν	ἐμά	ἐμήν	ἐμάς
9.7 (Possessive: our = m)		9.7 (Possessive: our = n)	
ἡμέτερος	ἡμέτεροι	ἡμέτερον	ἡμέτερα
ἡμετέρου	ἡμετέρων	ἡμετέρου	ἡμετέρων
ἡμετέρῳ	ἡμετέροις	ἡμετέρῳ	ἡμετέροις
ἡμέτερον	ἡμετέρους	ἡμέτερον	ἡμέτερα
9.7 (Possessive: our = f)		9.7 (Posses.: your = m)	
ἡμετέρα	ἡμέτεραι	σός	σοί
ἡμετέρας	ἡμετέρων	σοῦ	σῶν
ἡμετέρᾳ	ἡμετέραις	σῷ	σοῖς
ἡμετέραν	ἡμετέρας	σόν	σούς
9.7 (Possessive: your = n)		9.7 (Possessive: your = f)	
σόν	σά	σή	σαί
σοῦ	σῶν	σῆς	σῶν
σῷ	σοῖς	σῇ	σαῖς
σόν	σά	σήν	σάς
9.7 (Posses.: your = m)		9.7 (Possessive: your = n)	
ὑμέτερος	ὑμέτεροι	ὑμέτερον	ὑμέτερα
ὑμετέρου	ὑμετέρων	ὑμετέρου	ὑμετέρων
ὑμετέρῳ	ὑμετέροις	ὑμετέρῳ	ὑμετέροις
ὑμέτερον	ὑμετέρους	ὑμέτερον	ὑμέτερα

9.7 (Possessive: your = f)		9.7 (Pos.: his, their = m)	
ὑμετέρα	ὑμέτεραι	ἴδιος	ἴδιοι
ὑμετέρας	ὑμετέρων	ἰδίου	ἰδίων
ὑμετέρᾳ	ὑμετέραις	ἰδίῳ	ἰδίοις
ὑμετέραν	ὑμετέρας	ἴδιον	ἰδίους
9.7 (Po.: own, their = n)		9.7 (Pos.: her, their = f)	
ἴδιον	ἴδια	ἰδία	ἴδιαι
ἰδίου	ἰδίων	ἰδίας	ἰδίων
ἰδίῳ	ἰδίοις	ἰδίᾳ	ἰδίαις
ἴδιον	ἴδια	ἰδίαν	ἰδίας
9.9 (Ref.: my/ourselves = m)		9.9 (Ref.: my/ourselves = f)	
---------	---------	---------	---------
ἐμαυτοῦ	ἑαυτῶν	ἐμαυτῆς	ἑαυτῶν
ἐμαυτῷ	ἑαυτοῖς	ἐμαυτῇ	ἑαυταῖς
ἐμαυτόν	ἑαυτούς	ἐμαυτήν	ἑαυτάς
9.9 (R.: your/yourselves = m)		9.9 (R.: your/yourselves = f)	
---------	---------	---------	---------
σεαυτοῦ	ἑαυτῶν	σεαυτῆς	ἑαυτῶν
σεαυτῷ	ἑαυτοῖς	σεαυτῇ	ἑαυταῖς
σεαυτόν	ἑαυτούς	σεαυτήν	ἑαυτάς
9.9 (him/themselves = m)		9.9 (it/themselves = n)	
---------	---------	---------	---------
ἑαυτοῦ	ἑαυτῶν	ἑαυτοῦ	ἑαυτῶν
ἑαυτῷ	ἑαυτοῖς	ἑαυτῷ	ἑαυτοῖς
ἑαυτόν	ἑαυτούς	ἑαυτό	ἑαυτά

9.9 (R.: her/themselves = f)		9.10 (Indef.: someone)	
---------	---------	τις	τινές
ἑαυτῆς	ἑαυτῶν	τινός	τινῶν
ἑαυτῇ	ἑαυταῖς	τινί	τισί(ν)
ἑαυτήν	ἑαυτάς	τινά	τινάς
9.10 (Indef.: something)		9.11 (Neg.: no one = m)	
τι	τινά	οὐδείς	-------
τινός	τινῶν	οὐδενός	-------
τινί	τισί(ν)	οὐδενί	-------
τι	τινά	οὐδένα	-------
9.11 (Neg.: anything = n)		9.11 (Neg.: no one = f)	
οὐδέν	-------	οὐδεμία	-------
οὐδενός	-------	οὐδεμιᾶς	-------
οὐδενί	-------	οὐδεμιᾷ	-------
οὐδέν	-------	οὐδεμίαν	-------
9.12 (Dem.: this, these = m)		9.12 (Dem.: this, these = n)	
οὗτος	οὗτοι	τοῦτο	ταῦτα
τούτου	τούτων	τούτου	τούτων
τούτῳ	τούτοις	τούτῳ	τούτοις
τοῦτον	τούτους	τοῦτο	ταῦτα
9.12 (Dem.: this, these = f)		9.12 (Dem.: that, those = m)	
αὕτη	αὗται	ἐκεῖνος	ἐκεῖνοι
ταύτης	τούτων	ἐκείνου	ἐκείνων
ταύτῃ	ταύταις	ἐκείνῳ	ἐκείνοις
ταύτην	ταύτας	ἐκεῖνον	ἐκείνους

9.12 (Dem.: that, those = n)		9.12 (Dem.: that, those = f)	
ἐκεῖνο	ἐκεῖνα	ἐκείνη	ἐκεῖναι
ἐκείνου	ἐκείνων	ἐκείνης	ἐκείνων
ἐκείνῳ	ἐκείνοις	ἐκείνῃ	ἐκείναις
ἐκεῖνο	ἐκεῖνα	ἐκείνην	ἐκείνας
9.13 (Rel.: who = m)		9.13 (Rel.: who = n)	
ὅς	οἵ	ὅ	ἅ
οὗ	ὧν	οὗ	ὧν
ᾧ	οἷς	ᾧ	οἷς
ὅν	οὕς	ὅ	ἅ
9.13 (Rel.: who = f)		9.14 (Ind. Rel.: whoever)	
ἥ	αἵ	(Only nominative in NT)	
ἧς	ὧν	m = ὅστις	οἵτινες
ᾗ	αἷς	f = ἥτις	αἵτινες
ἥν	ἅς	n = ὅτι	ἅτινα
9.15 (Cor.: such = m)		9.15 (Cor.: such = n)	
τοιοῦτος	τοιοῦτοι	τοιοῦτο	τοιοαῦτα
τοιούτου	τοιούτων	τοιούτου	τοιούτων
τοιούτῳ	τοιούτοις	τοιούτῳ	τοιούτοις
τοιοῦτον	τοιούτους	τοιοῦτο	τοιαῦτα
9.15 (Cor.: such = f)		9.16 (Int.: who? = m/f)	
τοιαύτη	τοιαῦται	τίς	τίνες
τοιαύτης	τοιαύτων	τίνος	τίνων
τοιαύτῃ	τοιαύταις	τίνι	τίσι(ν)
τοιαύτην	τοιαύτας	τίνα	τίνας

9.16 (Int.: what? = n)		9.16 (Int.: how many? = m)	
τί	τίνα	πόσος	πόσοι
τίνος	τίνων	πόσου	πόσων
τίνι	τίσι(ν)	πόσῳ	πόσοις
τί	τίνα	πόσον	πόσους
11.2 (Car.: 1 = m)		11.2 (Car.: 1 = n)	
εἷς	-------	ἕν	-------
ἑνός	-------	ἑνός	-------
ἑνί	-------	ἑνί	-------
ἕνα	-------	ἕν	-------
11.2 (Car.: 1 = f)		11.2 (Car.: 2 = m/n/f)	
μία	-------	-------	δύο
μιᾶς	-------	-------	δύο
μιᾷ	-------	-------	δυσί
μίαν	-------	-------	δύο
11.2 (Car.: 3 = m/f)		11.2 (Car.: 3 = n)	
-------	τρεῖς	-------	τρία
-------	τριῶν	-------	τριῶν
-------	τρισί	-------	τρισί
-------	τρεῖς	-------	τρία
11.2 (Car.: 4 = m/f)		11.2 (Car.: 4 = n)	
-------	τέσσαρες	-------	τέσσαρα
-------	τεσσάρων	-------	τεσσάρων
-------	τέσσαρσι	-------	τέσσαρσι
-------	τέσσαρας	-------	τέσσαρα

 **Omega Verbs**

Present & Imperfect (First Principal Part)

Present—1PP		Imperfect—1PP	
Active	*Mid./Pass*	*Active*	*Mid./Pass*
Indicative		**Indicative**	
λύω	λύομαι	ἔλυον	ἐλυόμην
λύεις	λύῃ	ἔλυες	ἐλύου
λύει	λύεται	ἔλυε	ἐλύετο
λύομεν	λυόμεθα	ἐλύομεν	ἐλυόμεθα
λύετε	λύεσθε	ἐλύετε	ἐλύεσθε
λύουσι	λύονται	ἔλυον	ἐλύοντο
Subjunctive			
λύω	λύωμαι		
λύῃς	λύῃ		
λύῃ	λύηται		
λύωμεν	λυώμεθα		
λύητε	λύησθε		
λύωσι	λύωνται		
Imperative			
-------	-------		
λῦε	λύου		
λυέτω	λυέσθω		
-------	-------		
λύετε	λύεσθε		
λυέτωσαν	λυέσθωσαν		

Future (Second & Sixth Principal Parts)

| FUTURE—2PP | | FUTURE—6PP | |
Active	Middle	1st Passive	2nd Passive
Indicative		**Indicative**	
λύσω	λύσομαι	λυθήσομαι	γραφήσομαι
λύσεις	λύσῃ	λυθήσῃ	γραφήσῃ
λύσει	λύσεται	λυθήσεται	γραφήσεται
λύσομεν	λυσόμεθα	λυθησόμεθα	γραφησόμεθα
λύσετε	λύσεσθε	λυθήσεσθε	γραφήσεσθε
λύσουσι	λύσονται	λυθήσονται	γραφήσονται

Contract Verb Endings (ε, ο, α)

Present
    Ind. Act.: -ῶ, -εῖς, -εῖ, -οῦμεν, -εῖτε, -οῦσι
              -ῶ, -οῖς, -οῖ, -οῦμεν, -οῦτε, -οῦσι
              -ῶ, -ᾷς, -ᾷ, -ῶμεν, -ᾶτε, -ῶσι
    Mid.: -οῦμαι, -ῇ, -εῖται, -ούμεθα, -εῖσθε, -οῦνται
        -οῦμαι, -οῦ, -οῦται, -ούμεθα, -οῦσθε, -οῦνται
        -ῶμαι, -ᾷ, -ᾶται, -ώμεθα, -ᾶσθε, -ῶνται
    Subj. Act.: -ῶ, -ῇς, -ῇ, -ῶμεν, -ῆτε, -ῶσι
               -ῶ, -οῖς, -οῖ, -ῶμεν, -ῶτε, -ῶσι
               -ῶ, -ᾷς, -ᾷ, -ῶμεν, -ᾶτε, -ῶσι
    Mid.: -ῶμαι, -ῇ, -ῆται, -ώμεθα, -ῆσθε, -ῶνται
        -ῶμαι, -οῖ, -ῶται, -ώμεθα, -ῶσθε, -ῶνται
        -ῶμαι, -ᾷ, -ᾶται, -ώμεθα, -ᾶσθε, -ῶνται

Imperfect
    Ind. Act.: -ουν, -εις, -ει, -οῦμεν, -εῖτε, -ουν
              -ουν, -ους, -ου, -οῦμεν, -οῦτε, -ουν
              -ων, -ας, -α, -ῶμεν, -ᾶτε, -ων
    Mid.: -ούμην, -οῦ, -εῖτο, -ούμεθα, -εῖσθε, -οῦντο
        -ούμην, -οῦ, -οῦτο, -ούμεθα, -οῦσθε, -οῦντο
        -ώμην, -ῶ, -ᾶτο, -ώμεθα, -ᾶσθε, -ῶντο

First Aorist—Regular (Third & Sixth Principal Parts)

First Aorist—3PP		First Aorist—6PP
Active	Middle	Passive
Indicative		**Indicative**
ἔλυσα	ἐλυσάμην	ἐλύθην
ἔλυσας	ἐλύσω	ἐλύθης
ἔλυσε	ἐλύσατο	ἐλύθη
ἐλύσαμεν	ἐλυσάμεθα	ἐλύθημεν
ἐλύσατε	ἐλύσασθε	ἐλύθητε
ἔλυσαν	ἐλύσαντο	ἐλύθησαν
Subjunctive		**Subjunctive**
λύσω	λύσωμαι	λυθῶ
λύσῃς	λύσῃ	λυθῇς
λύσῃ	λύσηται	λυθῇ
λύσωμεν	λυσώμεθα	λυθῶμεν
λύσητε	λύσησθε	λυθῆτε
λύσωσι	λύσωνται	λυθῶσι
Imperative		**Imperative**
-------	-------	-------
λῦσον	λῦσαι	λύθητι
λυσάτω	λυσάσθω	λυθήτω
-------	-------	-------
λύσατε	λύσασθε	λύθητε
λυσάτωσαν	λυσάσθωσαν	λυθήτωσαν

Second Aorist—Irregular (Third & Sixth Principal Parts)

Second Aorist—3PP Active	Middle	Second Aorist—6PP Passive	
Indicative		**Indicative**	
ἔλιπον	ἐλιπόμην		ἐγράφην
ἔλιπες	ἐλίπου		ἐγράφης
ἔλιπε	ἐλίπετο		ἐγράφη
ἐλίπομεν	ἐλιπόμεθα		ἐγράφημεν
ἐλίπετε	ἐλίπεσθε		ἐγράφητε
ἔλιπον	ἐλίποντο		ἐγράφησαν
Subjunctive		**Subjunctive**	
λίπω	λίπωμαι		γραφῶ
λίπῃς	λίπῃ		γραφῇς
λίπῃ	λίπηται		γραφῇ
λίπωμεν	λιπώμεθα		γραφῶμεν
λίπητε	λίπησθε		γραφῆτε
λίπωσι	λίπωνται		γραφῶσι
Imperative		**Imperative**	
-------	-------		-------
λίπε	λιποῦ		γράφηθι
λιπέτω	λιπέσθω		γραφήτω
-------	-------		-------
λίπετε	λίπεσθε		γράφητε
λιπέτωσαν	λιπέσθωσαν		γραφήτωσαν

Perfect (Fourth & Fifth Principal Parts)

PERFECT—4PP		PERFECT—5PP
1st Active	*2nd* Active	Mid./Pass.
Indicative		**Indicative**
λέλυκα	γέγραφα	λέλυμαι
λέλυκας	γέγραφας	λέλυσαι
λέλυκε	γέγραφε	λέλυται
λελύκαμεν	γεγράφαμεν	λελύμεθα
λελύκατε	γεγράφατε	λέλυσθε
λελύκασι	γεγράφασι	λέλυνται
Subjunctive[3]		**Subjunctive**
ὦ λελυκώς		ὦ λελυμένος
ᾖς λελυκώς		ᾖς λελυμένος
ᾖ λελυκώς		ᾖ λελυμένος
ὦμεν λελυκότες		ὦμεν λελυμένοι
ἦτε λελυκότες		ἦτε λελυμένοι
ὦσι λελυκοτες		ὦσι λελυμένοι
Imperative		**Imperative**
-------		-------
λέλυκε		λέλυσο
λελυκέτω		λελύσθω
-------		-------
λελύκετε		λέλυσθε
λελυκέτωσαν		λελύσθωσαν

---

[3] Usually formed periphrastically in the New Testament, except forms of the verb οἶδα (εἰδῶ, etc.).

Pluperfect (Fourth & Fifth Principal Parts)

| PLUPERFECT—4PP | | PLUPERFECT—5PP | |
1ˢᵗ Active	2ⁿᵈ Active	Mid./Pass.	
Indicative		**Indicative**	
ἐλελύκειν	ἐληλύθειν[4]	ἐλελύμην	
ἐλελύκεις	ἐληλύθεις	ἐλέλυσο	
ἐλελύκει	ἐληλύθει	ἐλέλυτο	
ἐλελύκειμεν	ἐληλύθειμεν	ἐλελύμεθα	
ἐλελύκειτε	ἐληλύθειτε	ἐλέλυσθε	
ἐλελύκεισαν	ἐληλύθεισαν	ἐλέλυντο	

Liquid Verbs (Future and Aorist)

| FUTURE—2PP | | AORIST—3PP | |
Active	Middle	Active	Middle
Indicative		**Indicative**	
μενῶ	μενοῦμαι	ἔμεινα	ἐμεινάμην
μενεῖς	μενῇ	ἔμεινας	ἐμείνω
μενεῖ	μενεῖται	ἔμεινε	ἐμείνατο
μενοῦμεν	μενούμεθα	ἐμείναμεν	ἐμεινάμεθα
μενεῖτε	μενεῖσθε	ἐμείνατε	ἐμείνασθε
μενοῦσι	μενοῦνται	ἔμειναν	ἐμείναντο

---

[4]From ἔρχομαι.

 ## ΜΙ Verbs

δίδωμι—Present & Imperfect

Present—1PP		Imperfect—1PP	
Active	*Mid./Pass*	*Active*	*Mid./Pass*
Indicative		**Indicative**	
δίδωμι	δίδομαι	ἐδίδουν	ἐδιδόμην
δίδως	δίδοσαι	ἐδίδους	ἐδίδοσο
δίδωσι	δίδοται	ἐδίδου	ἐδίδοτο
δίδομεν	διδόμεθα	ἐδίδομεν	ἐδιδόμεθα
δίδοτε	δίδοσθε	ἐδίδοτε	ἐδίδοσθε
διδόασι	δίδονται	ἐδίδοσαν*	ἐδίδοντο
Subjunctive		*(or ἐδίδουν)	
διδῶ	διδῶμαι		
διδῷς	διδῷ		
διδῷ	διδῷται		
διδῶμεν	διδώμεθα		
διδῶτε	διδῶσθε		
διδῶσι	διδῶνται		
Imperative			
-------	-------		
δίδου	δίδοσο		
διδότω	διδόσθω		
-------	-------		
δίδοτε	δίδοσθε		
διδότωσαν	διδόσθωσαν		

δίδωμι—Future

Future—2PP		Future—6PP
Active	Middle	Passive
Indicative		Indicative
δώσω	δώσομαι	δοθήσομαι
δώσεις	δώσῃ	δοθήσῃ
δώσει	δώσεται	δοθήσεται
δώσομεν	δωσόμεθα	δοθησόμεθα
δώσετε	δώσεσθε	δοθήσεσθε
δώσουσιν	δώσονται	δοθήσονται

δίδωμι—First Aorist (Regular)[5]

First Aorist—3PP		First Aorist—6PP
Active	*Middle*	*Passive*
Indicative		**Indicative**
ἔδωκα		ἐδόθην
ἔδωκας		ἐδόθης
ἔδωκεν		ἐδόθη
ἐδώκαμεν		ἐδόθημεν
ἐδώκατε		ἐδόθητε
ἔδωκαν		ἐδόθησαν
Subjunctive		**Subjunctive**
δώσω		δοθῶ
δώσῃς		δοθῇς
δώσῃ		δοθῇ
δωσώμεν		δοθῶμεν
δώσητε		δοθῆτε
δωσώσι		δοθῶσι
Imperative		**Imperative**

		δόθητι
		δοθήτω

		δόθητε
		δοθήτωσαν

[5]*Non-thematic first aorist* -μι verbs occur in the *active indicative* only (δίδωμι also has an active subjunctive variation). All other non-thematic -μι verb active and middle forms are *second* aorist. Labeling a theta sixth principal part as "first aorist" passive is inaccurate. Using the *same* terminology—"first aorist," "second aorist"—for *two different phenomena* in third and sixth principal parts is confusing since the third is about the aorist *stem* formation and the sixth is about the aorist *voice* formation.

δίδωμι—Second Aorist (Irregular)[6]

Second Aorist—3PP		Second Aorist—6PP
Active	*Middle*	*Passive*
Indicative		**Indicative**
	ἐδόμην	
	ἔδου	
	ἔδοτο	
	ἐδόμεθα	
	ἔδοσθε	
	ἔδοντο	
Subjunctive		**Subjunctive**
δῶ	δῶμαι	
δῷς	δῷ	
δῷ	δῷται	
δῶμεν	δώμεθα	
δῶτε	δῶσθε	
δῶσιν	δῶνται	
Imperative		**Imperative**
-------	-------	
δός	δοῦ	
δότω	δόσθω	
-------	-------	
δότε	δόσθε	
δότωσαν	δόσθωσαν	

---

[6]See the previous note on "first aorist" and "second aorist" terminological confusion between third and sixth principal parts.

δίδωμι—Perfect & Pluperfect

| PERFECT—4/5PP || PLUPERFECT—4PP |
Active	Mid./Pass.	Active
Indicative		**Indicative**
δέδωκα	δέδομαι	ἐδεδώκειν
δέδωκας	δέδοσαι	ἐδεδώκεις
δέδωκεν	δέδοται	ἐδεδώκει
δεδώκαμεν	δεδόμεθα	εδεδώκειμεν
δεδώκατε	δέδοσθε	ἐδεδώκειτε
δέδωκαν	δέδονται	ἐδεδώκεισαν

The Verb Εἰμί

	Present	Imperfect	Future
Indicative			
	εἰμί	ἤμην	ἔσομαι
	εἶ	ἦς[7]	ἔσῃ
	ἐστί	ἦν	ἔσται
	ἐσμέν	ἦμεν[8]	ἐσόμεθα
	ἐστέ	ἦτε	ἔσεσθε
	εἰσί	ἦσαν	ἔσονται
Subjunctive			
	ὦ		
	ᾖς		
	ᾖ		
	ὦμεν		
	ἦτε		
	ὦσι		
Imperative			

	ἴσθι		
	ἔστω[9]		

	ἔστε		
	ἔστωσαν		

[7] An alternate form is ἦσθα (Mt. 26:69; Mk. 14:67).
[8] An alternate form is ἤμεθα (Mt. 23:30; Acts 27:37; Gal. 4:3; Eph. 2:3).
[9] An alternate form is ἤτω (1 Cor. 16:22; Jms. 5:12).

Photo © Gerald L. Stevens

Fig. 26. The Temple of Hephaestus. The structure is situated in a commanding position overlooking the Ancient Agora of Athens, Greece. This temple is the most well preserved in Athens and is one of the best examples of the Doric peripteral style.

Subject Index

This subject index is provided for the student to be able to cross-reference topics across different chap-ters, as well as to integrate the material on English grammar into the discussions on Greek grammar. Sometimes page numbers infer the discussion that follows on subsequent pages. A slight redundancy in the index is intentional.

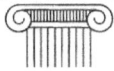 **Subject Index**

Ablative Function 135, 139
Absolute 479, 480, 510
Acadian Way 174
Accents
　contract verbs 175
　contraction 57
　diphthongs 7
　enclitics 110, 95, 198
　general rules 10
　infinitives 344
　liquid verbs 260
　oxytone 57 n. 1
　participles 378
　proclitics 110 n. 1
Accusative
　adverbial 481
　cognate accusative 480
　defined 480
　direct object 480

Action Kind 312-13, 334
Action Time 227, 312-13
Active Voice 467
Acute Accent 4
Adjective
　always attributive forms 99
　anarthrous 93-94
　articular 92
　attributive 91
　comparisons 154
　concord 90
　construction 92-93
　declensions 89
　defined 447
　diagramming 99
　predicate adj. 92
　predicate nom. 92
　predicative 92

　pronoun pattern 111
　substantival 91, 154
　two termination 90
Adriatic Sea 284
Adverb
　comparisons 155
　conjunctive 162-63
　defined 153
　diagramming 164
　formation 153
Adverbials 457
Adversatives 160
Aegean Sea 282, 284
Agency 139
Agora 174, 553, 560, 582
Agreement
　concord 64-65, 89, 392, 397, 409-10
　neuter plural 51
　subject/verb 51, 484

Akiba 342
Alexander IV 254
Alexander the Great x, 20, 254
Alphabet
  capital letters 4
  consonants 6-7
  formation 11-13
  gamma combina. 7
  liquids 8
  sibilants 8
  stops 8
  vowels 5-6
Anabaton 74
Anarthrous 64
Antecedent 109
Antepenult 9-10
Aorist Tense
  asigmatic 261
  first aorist act. 247
    compensatory lengthening 261
    contract lengthening 245
    defined 247, 446
    formation 243-45
    liquid 261
    suffix 245
  first aorist mid. 247
  first aorist pass. 271
  imperative 335
  infinitive 344
  kappa aorist 434
  kind of action 243
  μι verb 435
  middle deponent 246
  optative 321-22
  participles 437
  passive stem 268
  passive system
    aorist first pass. 271
    aorist second pass. 274, 275-76

contract lengthening 270
  future first pass. 272
  future second pass. 276
  passive deponent 271
  passive suffix 268
  theta interactions 269
  translation 247-49
second aorist active
  defined 256
  formation 257
  stems 256
second aorist mid. 258
second passive 275
subjunctive 317
translation 322-25
Apposition 353, 356 n. 9
Aquila 442
Artemis 174
Article
  anaphoric 69 n. 1
  anarthrous 64
  antecedent ref. 68
  articular 64
  concord 64-65
  diagramming 51, 71
  formation 63
  grouping 67
  inherent articular 67
  position 65-66
  specificity 66
  substitution
    demonstrative pronoun 69
    personal pronoun 69
Asia 464
Asigmatic Aorist 261

Asklepion 310
Asklepios 310
Athematic 425
Athena x, 20
Athenian Warrior 42
Athens 464, 582
Attic
  dialect 82 n. 8
  genitive 82 n. 8
  reduplication 288
Attributive 91
Augment
  compound verbs 244, 268
  past time 192-94, 244, 257, 268, 297
Augustus xx
Bathhouse 546
Bema 442
Benedictions 326
Berea 464
Breathing Marks 4, 5, 7, 432, 441
Calyx Krater 42
Cases 43-44
  accusative 480
  dative 44
  genitive 44, 481
  interior 44
  nominative 44, 480
  vocative 44
Cassander 254
Causal Clause
  διὰ τό + infin. 368
  participles 411
  with γάρ 161
  with ὅτι 163
Chariot 74
Circumflex Accent 4, 175
Circumstantial Participle 414
Clauses
  coordinate 160-61

Subject Index

dependent 161-63
independent 160
relative 119, 162, 509
subordinate 161
Codex 390
Cognate 480
Colossae 190
Comparisons
  ablative of 156
  accusative of 156
  adjective 154
  adverb 155
  conjunction ἤ 156
  degrees 153
  diagramming 164
  irregular 155
  positive for superlative 155
Compensatory Lengthening 261
Complementary Infinitive 351
Complementary Participle 413
Complex
  sentence 509
  sibilant 287
Compound
  predicate 500
  sentence 500
  subject 500
  verbs 37, 135, 187, 289, 441
Conative Imperfect 199
Concord 64-65, 89, 392, 397, 409-10
Conditional Sentences
  classes
    1st 211-12
    2nd 212-13, 327
    3rd 213, 327
    4th 214, 328
  diagramming 215-16

flow diagram 210, 326
grammar
  contingency 209
  indicative 209
  "if"/"then" 207
logic
  determined 207-8
  undeterm. 208-9
mood as key 211
participle use 406, 412
particle of contingency 211, 222
Conjugation 23, 423
Conjunctions
  coordinate
    adversative 160
    causal 161
    copulative 160
    inferential 161
  subordinate 161-63
Consonants 8
Constantine 390
Constantinople 3
Contract Verbs
  defined 175
  imperative 334
  imperfect act. 194, 197
  imperfect mid. 198
  indicative vs. subjunctive 319
  lengthening 232, 245, 270, 273, 290, 294, 298, 300
  lexical form 176
  present tense 176
Contraction 57, 260
Copulative Verb 179
Copulatives 160
Corinth 442, 464
Coronis 4
Cuirass 342

Culminative Aorist 248
Curetes Street 560
Customary Imperfect 199
Dative
  defined 44
  direct object 178, 332
  indirect object 44
  instrumental function 132
  locative function 132
  personal interest 135
  prepositions 132-34
Deaspiration 287 n.1
Declension 44
Degradation Vowel 276
Deliberative Future 236
Demetrius 174
Dental
  defined 8
  drops before κα 289-90
"*Deponent Future*" 233, 236
"*Deponent*" *Verbs* 31, 32, 200, 236, 246, 249, 271, 316, 326, 334, 345, 382
Diaeresis 4
Diagramming
  absolutes 510
  adjectives 99, 506
  adverbs 164
  apposition 510-11
  article 51, 71
  comparisons 164
  complex sentences 508-9
  conditional sentences 215-16
  conjunctions 164
  depend. clause 164

direct object 47
discourse 165, 503
indirect object 498
infinitives 356-58,
  369-70, 506-7
numerals 165
participles 504-5,
  506-7
predicate adjective
  501-2
predicate noun 501-2
prepositional phrase
  148, 506
prepositions
pronouns 137
questions 498
relative pronouns 164
simple sentence 25,
  497
subjects and verbs 47
substantives 497-99
Dialect 82 n. 8
Dictionary Format 79-
  80
Diphthongs 5
Direct Object
  cases for 177, 332
Discourse
  diagramming 165,
    503
  direct 162
  indirect 162
Doric 442, 582
Double Consonants 6
Dramatic Aorist 248
Dramatic Perfect 303
Durative 23, 24, 191,
  446
Durative Imperfect 192
Durative Present 23-24
Δύναμαι 351
Dyrrhachium 284
Ἥδειν not pluperfect
  309

Edited Greek Text 104
  n. 8
Εἰμί
  copulative verb 95
  enclitic 95, 198
  future 235
  imperative 336
  imperfect 198
  infinitive 355
  levels of precedence
    96
  linking verb 96
  no voice 95
  optative 326
  participle 383-84
  present 95
  subjunctive 320
  verbless predicative
    98
  voice 95, 198
Elision 4 n. 1
Emphasis (subject) 112
Enclitics 110, 110 n.1,
  95
English Grammar
  Clause 458
    connectors 459
    dependent 459
      adjective 460
      adverb 461
      noun 460
    independent 458
  Definitions
    absolute 479
    accusative 480
    action kind 472
    action time 473
    active voice 467
    adjectival phrase
      457
    adjective 447
    adjective clause
      460
    adverb 448

adverb clause 461
adverbial noun 481
adverbial phrase
  457
antecedent 509
aoristic action 446
apposition 479
appositive 511
auxiliary verb 472
case 479
clause 458
cognate object 480
completed action
  446
compound ele-
  ments 499
conjunction 451
conjunctive adverb
  459
copulative verb 469
dependent clause
  459
direct discourse
  503
direct object 468,
  480
discourse 503
durative act. 446,
  472
exclamation 480
finite verb 466
future tense 473
gender 478
imperative mood
  475
imperfective ac-
  tion 446
ind. clause 458
ind. object 470
indicative mood
  474
indirect discourse
  503
indirect object 481

Subject Index

infinite verb 466
infinitive object 481
infinitive objective subject 481
infinitive phrase 457
inflection 477
interjection 452
intransitive verb 469
irregular verb 485
mood 474
nom. absolute 480
nominative case 480
nominative of apposition 480
noun 446
noun clause 460
noun phrase 457
number 466
object 468
object complement 468, 480
obj. of prep. 480
objective case 480
objective of apposition 481
part of speech 445
participal object 481
participial phrase 458
passive voice 467
past tense 473
perfective act. 446, 472
person 466
phrase 455
possessive case 481
predicate adjective 470
predicate nomina-
tive 480
predicate noun 469
prepositions 450
present tense 473
pronouns 450
regular verb 485
relative pronoun 459, 509
sentence 465
sentence predicate 469
simple element 499
subject 466
subjun. mood 474
subord. conj. 459
surrogate sub. 504
tense 471
transitive verb 468
undefined act. 446, 472
verb 446
vocative 480
voice 467
Diagramming
independent
absolute 510
appositive 510-11
intransitive
basic 501
copulative 501-2
modifier
dependent
clauses 508-9
verbals 506-7
words and phrases 506
substantival
clauses 503
discourse 503
verbals 504-5
transitive 497
compounds 499-500
dir. obj. 497
ind. obj. 498
obj. com. 499
Parts of Speech 445
primary
adjective 447
adverb 448
noun 446
verb 446
secondary
conjunction 451
interjection 452
preposition 450
pronoun 450
Phrase 455
prepositional 455
verbal 457
Sentence Sense
internal structure
substantive 477-81
case 479
gender 478
per./num. 478
verb 484-87
formation 485
prin. parts 484
summary 486
external structure 488-95
Sentences
defined 465
verb action
indirect object 470
object 468
subject 466
tense 471
verb potential 474
imperative 475
indicative 474
subjunctive 474
Epaphras 190
Epexegetic 348 n. 3
Ephesians (inhabitants)

560
Ephesus 174, 190, 560
Epistolary Aorist 248
Etruscan 108
Europe 310, 464
Exekias 42
Expected Answers 180-81
Final Sigma 12
First Declension
  alpha declension 53
  contract 57
  singular patterns
    "α pure" 53
    "η pure" 54
    "ης nominative" (= masculine) 56
  mixed 56
  stem types 62
Future Perfect 301
Future Tense
  active
    contract 232, 234
    defined 228
    deponent 233
    formation 228-32
    liquid 259-60
    liquid suffixes 260
    tense suffix 229, 260
  consonant reactions 230-32
  deponent 236
  irregular 230
  μι verbs 433, 435
  middle 234
  passive 274, 276
  periphrastic 415
  translation 235-36
Galen the Physician 310
Gamma Combinations 7
Γάρ 87
Gender

article 65
  defined 478
definite article
  feminine sec. dec. 46
  masculine first dec. 56
  table sequence 107
Genitive
  absolute 407
  defined 481
  direct object 178
  of possession 112
  of relationship 157
  subjective/objective 181-82
Gallic 108
Gallio 442
Gethsemene 108
Γίνομαι 37, 179
Gladiator 88, 108
Gnomic Aorist 248
Gold Stater x
Gradation Vowel 276
Grave Accent 4
Greco-Roman 108, 546
Greece 464
Greek Key 20
Greek New Testament 104 n. 8
Hadrian 342, 376, 464
Hebrews, Letter of 104 n. 8
Herod Atticus 464
Herod the Great 88
Hidden Stems 231-32, 244
Hierapolis 190
Historical Present 69 n. 2
Hoplite Soldier 74
Ἴδε 338, 341
Ἰδού 338, 341
Ignatius 88
Imperative Future 236

Imperative Mood
  analysis 333
  command 333
  "deponent" 334
  distinct endings 333
  εἰμί 336
  formation 334
  μι verbs 435-36
  negative 336
  prohibition 337
  tense signif. 336
  third person problem 333
  timeless 334
  translation 336-38
Imperfect Tense
  defined 191
  formation
    active 192
    contracts 194
    μι verbs 427
    mid./pass. 197
  translation 198, 200
Impersonal Verbs 363
Inceptive Imperfect 198
Ingressive Aorist 248

Indicative Mood
  defined 474
  time element 191
Indicative Verb System 312
Indirect Discourse 350-51
Indirect Object 44, 470, 498
Infinitives
  action kind 346
  being modified 347
  constructions 345, 366
  defined 457
  "deponent" 345

Subject Index

diagramming
  adjectival 356-58
  adverbial 369-70
εἰμί 355
epexegetic 353
formation 344
functions
  adjectival
    modifying 354
    substantival 349-51
  adverbial
    cause 368
    purpose 367
    result 368
    time 369
impersonal verbs 349, 364
inflection 345
location 355-56
μι verbs 434
negative 348
preposition construction 346
"surrogate subject" 347-48
taking objects 346
verb character 343
verbals 343
Inflection
  English 477-81
  Greek 21, 43, 53, 75
Ingressive Aorist 248
Inherent Articular 67
Instrumental Function 139
Intensive Perfect 303
Interior Cases 44
Intransitive 37, 95, 179, 441, 495, 497
Iota Insert 288
Iota Subscript 6
Irregular Verbs 255, 485-86

Ἴστημι 432
Jesus x, xxii, 108, 206, 310, 376
Josephus 88
Julius Caesar 108
Καί 160
Kappa Aorists 434
Kind of Action
  durative 23, 24, 191, 322-23, 336, 346, 446
  perfect 302-3, 285, 296, 346, 446
  undefined 228, 243, 322-23, 336, 346, 446
King James Version 104 n. 8, 404
Koine 3, 155, 432
Krinides 284
Labials 8
Laodicea 190, 206
Lemnos 282
Lengthening
  contracts 232, 245, 270, 273, 300
  thematic vowel 316
  verb stem vowel 261
  vowels 193, 288, 297
Letter Insert, Added
  iota 288
  epsilon 288
  eta 276, 289, 295
  omega 289
  sigma 295
Lexical 25
Library of Celsus viii, 560
Liquid Aorist 261
Liquid Future 259-60
Liquid Verb 258-59, 345, 379, 380, 381, 383
Liquids 8, 258-59

Location 25
Locative Function 139
Luke 108, 310
Lycus River 190
LXX 310
Macedonia 254, 284
Macedonian Vision 464
Main Verb 21, 465, 497
Manuscripts
  𝔓46 104 n. 8, 404
  Vaticanus 390
Marble Hall 546
Marble Way 174
Marcus Aurelius 310
Marks
  accents 4
  breathing 4, 5, 7
  coronis 4
  diaeresis 4
  elision 4 n. 1
  punctuation 4-5
Mazeus-Mithridates Gate 560
Μὴ Γένοιτο 320
MI Verbs
  aorist 435
  compounds 431
  dual conjugations 431
  endings
    primary 426
    secondary 427
  future 433, 435
  imperative 426
  imperfect 427
  infinitive 434
  kappa aorists 434
  lengthening 425, 434
  non-thematic 425, 427
  optative 426
  paradigms 435-37
  participles 434-35
  perfect 436

present tense 424-26
reduplication
  imperfect 427
  perfect 425, 433
  present 424, 433
  non-redup. 433
  rough breathing 432
  subjunctive 426
"Middle Deponent" 246, 249
Middle Voice
  lexical distinctions 32-33
  primary 33
  secondary 196
  translation 32
Mirmillones 108
Mood
  contingency 313-14
  defined 474
  imperative 333, 428, 434, 436
  indicative 23, 191, 428
  infinitives 355-56
  optative 320
  participles 384
  subjunctive 315
Mount Athos 282
Mount Cadmus 190
Moveable ν 24 n. 1, 78 n. 4
Neapolis 284
Negative
  defined 319, 336
  emphatic 181, 319
  imperative 336
  infinitives 348
  μή 180, 319
  optative 319
  οὐ 16
  participles 389
  subjunctive 319

Neuter Pattern 111
Neuter Plural 51
Nile River 390
Nominative
  defined 480
  predicate 92, 480
  uses 480
Non-thematic Verb 425
Nouns
  components 478-79
  contraction 57
  defined 446
  dictionary format 79-80
  gender 46, 56, 65, 82, 478
  location 45
  of action 182
Number
  concord 64-65, 89, 392, 397, 409-10
  neuter plural 51
  subject/verb 51, 484
Numerals
  adverbials 159
  cardinal 157
  multiple units 158
  ordinal 158
Object Clause (ὅτι) 162, 163
Object Complement 352, 480
Objective Case 480
Οἶδα 309
Ὅλος 99
Omega Verb 95 n. 7, 423
Omicron Declension 75
Optative Mood
  alternate mood sign 321
  background 320
  benedictions 326

conditional sentence 214, 328
"deponent" 326
εἰμί 326
formation 320-21
iota mood sign 321
μι verbs 435
tense signif. 322
thematic vowel 321
timeless 322
translation 325-26
Oxytone 57 n.1
𝔓46 104 n. 8
Palatals 8
Papyrus 390
Paradigm 23
Parchment 390, 404
Participle
  accents 378
  adjective character 391
  adjectival use
    attributive 397
    predicative 395
    substantival 392
  adverbial use
    cause 411
    circumstantial 414
    complementary 413-14
    concession 412
    condition 412
    manner 413
    means 413
    purpose 411
    summarized 406
    temporal 408-10
  anarthrous but attributive 398
  articular translation 392-93
  attributive
    constructions 395
    translation 395-96

Subject Index

concord 397, 409-10
contracts 378
defined 458
"deponent" 382
diagramming
  adjectival 398-99
  adverbial 417-18
εἰμί 383-84, 398
formation
  aor. act. 379-80
  aor. mid. 382
  aor. pass. 382-83
  future act. 380
  future pass. 383
  perf. act. 380-81
  perf. mid. 382
  pres. act. 378
  pres. mid. 382
  sec. aor. act. 380
  sec. aor. mid. 382
idiomatic
  genitive abs. 416
  periphrastic 415
kind of action 408
liquids 379
location 384
μι verbs 437
negative 392
predicative
  construct. 396-97
  translation 397-98
relative time 408-10
substantival
  construction 392
  examples 394-95
  translation 392-93
  "surrogate subject" 409-10
translation procedure 392-93, 396, 409-10
verbal 391
Particle of Contingency 211, 222

Πᾶς 99
"Passive Deponent" 271-72
Passive Voice 29
  agency 31
  defined 29, 467
  translation 29
Paul the Apostle 88, 174, 190, 284, 310, 404, 442, 464
Penult 9-10
Perfect Tense
  defined 285, 446
  formation
    first active 285, 289, 292
    mid./pass. formation 293
    reactions 295
    second active 291, 292
  kind of action 302
  οἶδα not perfect 309
  translation 302-3
Perfective 302, 446
Pergamum 310, 376
Periphrasis 415
Peripteral 442, 582
Person and Number 23, 478-79
Philippi 284, 464
Pluperfect Tense
  augment drops 297
  defined 296
  ᾔδειν not pluperfect 309
  first active 297
  formation 296-301
  kind of action 285, 296
  mid./pass. 299
  second active 298
  translation 299, 301, 302

Position 22, 488-95
Postpositives 87
Precedence 96-98
Predicate Adjective 37
Predicate Complement 37
Predicate Nominative 96
Predicate Noun 37, 96
Predicative 92
Predictive Future 235
Prepositions
  case 132-34
  compounds 187
  contextualization 131
  defined 131
  diagramming 148
  directional 37-38
  function 135
  prepositional phrase 47, 455-57
  spelling variations 136
  translation 132, 96-105
Present Tense
  defined 23
  formation
    active 23
    mid./pass. 29-30
  kind of action 23
  translation 24, 30-31
Primary Endings 33, 233, 274, 295, 316
Primary Tenses 33
Principal Parts 22, 23, 228
  1st 23
  2nd 228
  3rd 244
  4th 286
  5th 293
  6th 267
Proclitics 64, 110 n. 1

Proconsul 442
Prohibition
  imperative 337
  subjunctive 323
Pronouns
  categories 109
    correlative 121
    demonstrative 118
    indefinite 117
    indef. relative 120
    intensive 113
    interrogative 122
    negative 117
    personal 110
    possessive 114
    reciprocal 116
    reflexive 116
    relative 119, 162
  concord 115
  diagramming 166, 508
  subject emphasis 112
  summary 123
  use 109, 125, 450
Pronunciation 5-7
Proper Nouns 52
Prophetic Aorist 248
Punctiliar 248
Punctuation 4-5
Purpose Clause
  ἵνα with subjunctive 325
  infinitive 367
  ὅπως with subjunctive 325
  participle 411
Questions
  deliberative 323
  diagramming 498
  expected answers 180-81
  punctuation 4-5
Quotations 162, 305-51, 503

Recto 404
Reduplication
  consonants 286-87, 297
  vowels 288-89, 297
Reformation 3
Relative Pronoun 119, 172, 324
Renaissance 310
Result Clause 368
Revelation, Book of 376, 546
Rhetoric 464
Rhetorical Questions 180
Roman Agora 553
Root 224
Root Fallacy 225-26
Rough Breathing 4, 5, 7, 432, 441
Rough Stop 286
Roxana 254
Sardis 546
Satan 376
Scribe 390
Scripto Continua 390
Scroll 390
Second Aorist 256
Second Declension 44
  comparisons 154
  concord 46
  formation
    feminine 46
    nouns 44
    oxytone 57 n.1
    two-termination adj. 90
  stem types 75
  vowel declension 44, 75
Second Sophistic 464
Secondary Endings 196, 257, 271, 290, 298, 301, 321

Secondary Tenses 195, 246
Sibilants 287
Sigma Stop Reactions 76, 230-32, 245, 345, 379, 380, 381, 383
Simon bar Kockba 342
Smooth Breathing 4, 5, 7
Smooth Stop 287
Square of Stops 8
Stop Consonants 8
Subject
  agreement with verb 51, 484
  compound 499
  diagramming 25, 497
  genitive absolute 416
  infinitive as 349
  neuter plural 51
  participle as 394
  relative pronoun as 164
  versus predicate nom. 96-97
Subjunctive Mood
  conditional sentences 213, 327-28
  contracts 319
  defined 315
  "deponent" 316
  εἰμί 320, 332
  formation 316, 318-19
  lengthening 316
  μι verb 426, 428, 434, 436
  negative 319
  tense signif. 322
  timeless 316
  translation 323-25
  translation summary 323
Subordinate Conjunc-

tion 162
Substantival Clause
  (ὅτι) 162
Substantive 91-92, 93,
  94, 98, 349-53, 392-
  95, 446
Superlative
  defined 154
  growing disuse 155
Syllabification
  divisions 9
  positions 9-10
  quantity 10
Syncopation 87
Temple
  Apollo 442
  Hephaestus 582
  Trajan 376
Tense Prefix 286, 288,
  294
Tense Stem 223-25
Tense Suffix 229, 245,
  273, 288
Terracotta 282
Thematic Verb 23, 423
Thematic Vowel 30,
  194, 232, 257, 273,
  276
Thessalonians (inhabi-
  tants) 310
Thessalonica x, 254,
  464
Thessaloniki x, 254
Theta Reactions 269-
  70, 345, 383
Third Declension 75
  comparisons 154
  concord 65
  consonant decl. 75
  dictionary format 79
  endings 75
  formation
    adjectives 89
    noun 75-78

sigma reactions 80-81
Tiberius xxii
Time of Action 23, 191,
  227, 243, 285, 315-
  16, 336, 346, 408-10,
  473
Timothy 553
Timothy, Letters of
  104 n.8
Τίθημι 431
Titus 104 n.8
Token 282
Tombstone 553
Trajan 108
Transitive Verb 441,
  468-69, 495, 497
Translation
  interpretation 39-41
  tenses
    aorist 247-49
    future 235-36
    imperative 336-38
    imperfect 198, 200
    optative 325-26
    participles 392-93,
      396, 397, 409-10
    perfect 302-3
    pluperfect 299,
      301, 302
    present 24
    subjunctive 323
Transliteration 13
Troas 464
Ultima 9-10
Uncial 390
Undefined Action Kind
  228, 243, 322-23,
  336, 346, 446
Ὑπάρχω 179
Vatican 390
Vaticanus 390
Verbal Adjective 391
Verbal Noun 343
"Verbless Predicative"

98
Verbs
  agreement with
    subject 51, 484
  augment 192-94,
    244, 257, 268, 297
  compounds 187
  contraction 175
  defined 446
  diagramming 501-10
  hidden stem 231-32,
    244
  intransitive 466-69,
    495, 497
  irregular 225
  letter insert 289
  liquid 258-59
  middle voice suffix
    382
  morphology slots
    187-89
  parameters
    mood 23, 191, 313-
      14, 315, 320,
      333, 355-56, 384,
      428, 434, 436,
      474-75
    person 23, 478-79
    tense 312, 471
    voice 467
  participial suffix 378
  passive suffix 271
  reduplication 285
  root 224
  root fallacy 225-26
  subject verb agree-
    ment 51, 484
  substantive inflec-
    tion 378, 382
  tense stem 223-25
  tense suffix 229, 245,
    260, 271, 289
  thematic vowel 30
  transitive 495, 497

verb stem 225
Verso 404
Via Egnatia 284
Vocabulary Cards 226
Vocative 44
Voice 29, 95, 467
Voice Suffix
  aorist passive 268
  future passive 272
  perfect active 289
  perfect middle 294
  pluperfect active 297
Votive Offering 310
Vowels
  augmentation 193
  compensatory
    lengthening 261

contraction 57, 176, 194, 318-19, 334, 345, 378
contract verbs
  contraction 176, 194, 318-19, 334, 345, 378
  definition 175
  imperative 334
  infinitives 345
  lengthening 232, 245-46, 270-71, 290, 294, 298, 300, 345, 379, 380, 381, 383
  liquid aorist 260
  participles 378, 379, 380, 381, 383
  subjunctive 318-19
  synopsis 571
  gradation 276
  perf. mid. insert 295
  quantity 5
  reduplication 288
  syllable quantity 10
  syllable rules 9
  tense stem add. 276
  tense suffix reaction 261, 269, 289, 298, 345, 379, 381
  ultima quantity 10
Word Order 22, 488-95
Zeta (voiced) 6

www.ingramcontent.com/pod-product-compliance
Lightning Source LLC
Chambersburg PA
CBHW060301010526
44108CB00042B/2599